Asian Reader

3rd edition

Edited by

Professor Ed Frame
&
Jennifer Talyor Ph.D.
Valencia Community College

THOMSON

SOUTH-WESTERN

Asian Reader
Trimmer/Duiker/Spielvogel/Nelson/Gochberg/Frame

Executive Editors:
Michele Baird, Maureen Staudt & Michael Stranz

Project Development Manager:
Linda de Stefano

Marketing Coordinators:
Lindsay Annett and Sara Mercurio

Production/Manufacturing Supervisor:
Donna M. Brown

Pre-Media Services Supervisor:
Dan Plofchan

Rights and Permissions Specialists:
Kalina Hintz and Bahman Naraghi

Cover Image
Getty Images*

The Adaptable Courseware Program consists of products and additions to existing Thomson products that are reproduced from camera-ready copy. Peer review, class testing, and accuracy are primarily the responsibility of the author(s).

Asian Reader / Trimmer / Duiker / Spielvogel / Nelson / Gochberg / Frame
p. 280
ISBN 0-324-37367-8

International Divisions List

Asia (Including India):
Thomson Learning
(a division of Thomson Asia Pte Ltd)
5 Shenton Way #01-01
UIC Building
Singapore 068808
Tel: (65) 6410-1200
Fax: (65) 6410-1208

Australia/New Zealand:
Thomson Learning Australia
102 Dodds Street
Southbank, Victoria 3006
Australia

Latin America:
Thomson Learning
Seneca 53
Colonia Polano
11560 Mexico, D.F., Mexico
Tel (525) 281-2906
Fax (525) 281-2656

Canada:
Thomson Nelson
1120 Birchmount Road
Toronto, Ontario
Canada M1K 5G4
Tel (416) 752-9100
Fax (416) 752-8102

UK/Europe/Middle East/Africa:
Thomson Learning
High Holborn House
50-51 Bedford Row
London, WC1R 4LS
United Kingdom
Tel 44 (020) 7067-2500
Fax 44 (020) 7067-2600

Spain (Includes Portugal):
Thomson Paraninfo
Calle Magallanes 25
28015 Madrid
España
Tel 34 (0) 91446-3350
Fax 34 (0) 91445-6218

Acknowledgements

The content of this text has been adapted from the following product(s):

The Hymns of the Rig-Veda

R.K. Narayan - A Horse and Two Goats (0-15-506205-0)

World History (with InfoTrac) Duiker/Spielvogel (0-534-60363-7)

*ACP-World Culture Resource Series, TextChoice Edition Nelson (0-324-27566-8)

PREFACE

One of the most important aspects of teaching is having accessible a textbook, in one volume, reflecting the subject matter being taught. In an attempt to provide such a work this volume is an anthology of writings that are appropriate to the needs of a course in Asian humanities. Within the volume a brief historical survey of each area is offered and, in addition, readings are including that reflect each particular culture's rich, philosophical, religious and literary contributions. The main cultures examined are India, China, and Japan with the Japanese section also including information concerning Korea and Vietnam. In the context of Asian religious contributions there are included several of the most important texts from Hinduism, Buddhism, Confucianism and through the Chinese poetry, Daoism.

It is an almost impossible task to attempt a single anthology covering such a vast range of ideas as are found in the three major cultures of India, China and Japan. Therefore, the text represents a starting point from which the teacher can add more current readings and information as the need arises. It would be of particular importance to find short stories from contemporary Asian writers since they are among some of the best being written in today's world.

Ed Frame
Professor of Humanities
Valencia Community College May, 2003

BIOGRAPHICAL INFORMATION

Ed Frame has been a professor of humanities at Valencia Community College for eight years. His experiences in Asia and South East Asia are long and extensive. He served in the Peace Corps for two years in Malaysia and, after graduate work, returned there on a Fulbright research scholarship where he did research on the music and culture of the Dusan, Murut and Bajau peoples on the island of Borneo. He was a professor at the University of Wisconsin / Green Bay, where he taught Western and non-Western music. For several years he taught performing arts / ethnomusicology at Universiti Sains in West Malaysia as a professor in the school of humanities. Mr. Frame, his wife and four children have returned to Asia numerous times and most recently spent the summer of 2001 traveling in India, China and Malaysia. Reflecting his experience and background Mr. Frame now teaches Asian humanities and world mythology on Valencia's West Campus.

Jennifer Taylor has been a professor at Valencia Community College for ten years. Her love of Asian culture was inspired by her doctoral work in Mythological Studies and her dissertation includes a chapter on the story of Sita and Rama from India. She has taught special topics courses on the Epic Traditions of Greece and India as well as Classical Mythology and Arthurian Traditions. Her first Masters degree was from Florida State University in Classics. Her BA was in Humanities from the University of Central Florida. Dr. Taylor has a deep and abiding interest in comparative studies and has traveled extensively in Europe and the United States. Reflecting these interests, Dr. Taylor currently teaches Asian Humanities, Greek and Roman Humanities, and Mythology on Valencia's East Campus.

Table of Contents

PART I:

India

Land of the spirit,
you remain while others fade.
Truth is powerful.

–Edward M. Frame

India

Holy City of Shiva, Varanasi (Banaras) View 1

Holy City of Shiva, Varanasi (Banaras) View 2

Holy City of Shiva, Varanasi (Banaras) View 3

Sitar Guru

Historical Perspective of India

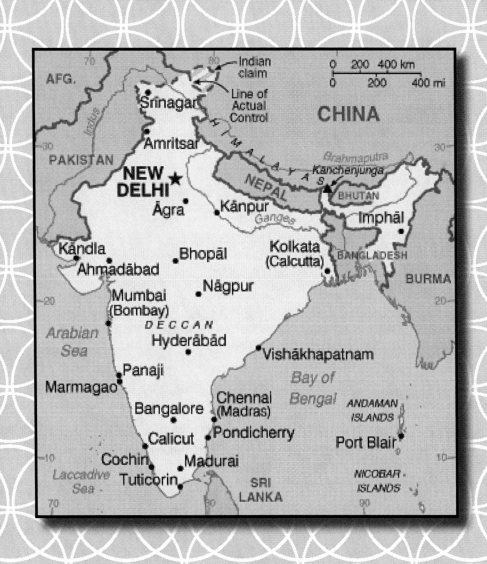

Ancient India

© Freer Gallery of Art, Smithsonian Institution, Washington, D.C.

ANCIENT
INDIA

FOCUS QUESTIONS

- What were the chief features of Harappan civilization, and in what ways was it similar to the civilizations that arose in Egypt and Mesopotamia?
- What roles did the caste system and the family play in Indian society?
- What are the main tenets of Hinduism and Buddhism, and how did each religion influence Indian civilization?
- Why was India unable to maintain a unified empire in the first millennium B.C.E., and how was the Mauryan Empire temporarily able to overcome the tendencies toward disunity?
- ➤ What effects did the Aryans have on Indian civilization?

*A*rjuna was despondent as he prepared for battle. In the opposing army were many of his friends and colleagues, some of whom he had known since childhood. In despair, he turned for advice to Krishna, his chariot driver, who, unknown to Arjuna, was in actuality an incarnation of the Indian deity Vishnu. "Do not despair of your duty," Krishna advised his friend.

> *To be born is certain death,*
> *to the dead, birth is certain.*
> *It is not right that you should sorrow*
> *for what cannot be avoided. . . .*

If you do not fight this just battle
you will fail in your own law
and in your honor,
and you will incur sin.

Krishna's advice to Arjuna is contained in the Bhagavadgita, one of India's most sacred classical writings, and reflects one of the key tenets in Indian philosophy—the belief in reincarnation, or rebirth of the soul. It also points up the importance of doing one's duty without regard for the consequences. Arjuna was a warrior, and according to Aryan tribal tradition, he was obliged to follow the code of his class. "There is more joy in doing one's own duty badly," advised Krishna, "than in doing another man's duty well."

In advising Arjuna to fulfill his obligation as a warrior, the author of the Bhagavadgita, writing around the second century B.C.E. about a battle that took place almost a thousand years earlier, was by implication urging all readers to adhere to their own responsibility as members of one of India's major classes. Henceforth, this hierarchical vision of a society divided into groups, each with clearly distinct roles, would become a defining characteristic of Indian history.

The Bhagavadgita is part of a larger work that deals with the early history of the Aryan peoples who entered India from beyond the mountains north of the Khyber Pass between 1500 and 1000 B.C.E. When the Aryans arrived, India had already had a thriving civilization for almost two thousand years. The Indus valley civilization, although not as well known today as the civilizations of Mesopotamia and Egypt, was just as old; and its political, social, and cultural achievements were equally impressive. That civilization, known to historians by the names of its two major cities, Harappa and Mohenjo-Daro, emerged in the late fourth millennium B.C.E., flourished for over one thousand years, and then came to an abrupt end about 1500 B.C.E. It was soon replaced by a new society dominated by the Aryan peoples. The new civilization that emerged represented a rich mixture of the two cultures—Harappan and Aryan—and evolved over the next three thousand years into what we know today as India.

Thus India was and still is a land of diversity. This diversity is evident in its languages and cultures as well as in its physical characteristics. India possesses a bewildering array of languages, few of which are mutually intelligible. It has a deserved reputation, along with the Middle East, as a cradle of religion. Two of the world's major religions, Hinduism and Buddhism, originated in India; and a number of others, including Sikhism and Islam (the latter of which entered the South Asian subcontinent in the ninth or tenth century C.E.), continue to flourish there.

Although today this beautiful mosaic of peoples and cultures has been broken up into a number of separate independent states, the region still possesses a coherent history that despite its internal diversity is recognizably Indian. It is to the origins and early development of that culture that we now turn. ●

BACKGROUND TO THE EMERGENCE OF CIVILIZATION IN INDIA

In its size and diversity, India seems more like a continent than a single country. That diversity begins with the geographical environment. The Indian subcontinent, shaped like a spade hanging from the southern ridge of Asia, is composed of a number of core regions. In the far north are the Himalayan and Karakoram mountain ranges, home to the highest mountains in the world. Directly to the south of the Himalayas and the Karakoram range is the rich valley of the Ganges, India's "holy river" and one of the core regions of Indian culture. To the west is the Indus River valley. Today the latter is a relatively arid plateau that forms the backbone of the modern state of Pakistan, but in ancient times it enjoyed a more balanced climate and served as the cradle of Indian civilization.

South of India's two major river valleys lies the Deccan, a region of hills and an upland plateau that extends from the Ganges valley to the southern tip of the Indian subcontinent. The interior of the plateau is relatively hilly and dry, but the eastern and western coasts are occupied by lush plains, which are historically among the most densely populated regions of India. Off the southeastern coast is the island known today as Sri Lanka. Although Sri Lanka is now a separate country quite distinct politically and culturally from India, the island's history is intimately linked with that of its larger neighbor.

In this vast region live a rich mixture of peoples: Dravidians, probably descended from the Indus River culture that flourished at the dawn of Indian civilization, over four thousand years ago; Aryans, descended from the pastoral peoples who flooded southward from Central Asia in the second millennium B.C.E.; and hill peoples, who may have lived in the region prior to the rise of organized societies and thus may have been the earliest inhabitants of all.

HARAPPAN CIVILIZATION: A FASCINATING ENIGMA

In the 1920s, archaeologists discovered the existence of agricultural settlements dating back well over six thousand years in the lower reaches of the Indus River valley in modern Pakistan. Those small mudbrick villages eventually gave rise to the sophisticated human communities that historians call Harappan civilization. Although today the area is relatively arid, during the third and fourth millennia B.C.E., it evidently received much more abundant rainfall, and the valleys of the Indus River and its tributaries supported a thriving civilization that may have covered a total area of over 600,000 square miles, from the Himalayas to the coast of the Indian Ocean. More than seventy sites have been unearthed since the area was first discovered in the 1850s, but the main sites are at the two major cities, Harappa, in the Punjab, and Mohenjo-Daro, nearly 400 miles to the south near the mouth of the Indus River (see Map 2.1).

The origin of the Harappans is still debated, but some scholars have suggested on the basis of ethnographic and linguistic analysis that the language and physical characteristics of the Harappans were similar to those of the Dravidian peoples who live in the Deccan Plateau today. If that is so, Harappa is not simply a dead civilization, whose culture and peoples have disappeared into the sands of history, but a part of the living culture of the Indian subcontinent.

Political and Social Structures

In several respects, Harappan civilization closely resembled the cultures of Mesopotamia and the Nile valley. Like them, it probably began in tiny farming villages scattered throughout the river valley, some dating back to as early as 6500 or 7000 B.C.E. These villages thrived and grew until by the middle of the third millennium B.C.E. they could support a privileged ruling elite living in walled cities of considerable magnitude and affluence. The center of

MAP 2.1 Ancient Harappan Civilization. This map shows the location of the first civilization that arose in the Indus River valley, which today is located in the contemporary state of Pakistan. ➤ *What were the names of the two largest urban centers that have so far been excavated?*

CHINA

AFGHANISTAN

PAKISTAN

IRAN

■ Harappa

Mohenjo-Daro ■

Indus River

INDIA

Arabian Sea

0   200   400   600 Kilometers

0   200   400 Miles

power was the city of Harappa, which was surrounded by a brick wall over 40 feet thick at its base and more than $3\frac{1}{2}$ miles in circumference. The city was laid out on an essentially rectangular grid, with some streets as wide as 30 feet. Most buildings were constructed of kiln-dried mudbricks and were square in shape, reflecting the grid pattern. At its height, the city may have had as many as 80,000 inhabitants, as large as some of the most populous urban centers in Sumerian civilization.

Both Harappa and Mohenjo-Daro were divided into large walled neighborhoods, with narrow lanes separating the rows of houses. Houses varied in size,

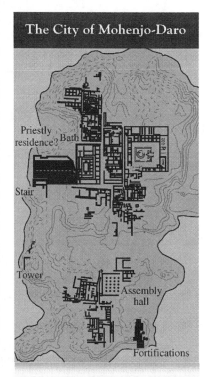

The City of Mohenjo-Daro

Priestly residence?   Bath

Stair

Tower

Assembly hall

Fortifications

THE CITY OF THE DEAD. Mohenjo-Daro was one of the two major cities of the ancient Indus River civilization. In addition to rows on rows of residential housing, it had a ceremonial center, with a royal palace and a sacred bath that was probably used by the priests as a means of achieving ritual purity. The bath, reminiscent of water tanks in modern Hindu temples, is shown in the center of the photograph here, with the remnants of a Buddhist stupa, constructed centuries later, on the right.

with some as high as three stories, but all followed the same general plan based on a square courtyard surrounded by rooms. Bathrooms featured an advanced drainage system, which carried wastewater out to drains located under the streets and thence to sewage pits beyond the city walls. But the cities also had the equivalent of the modern slum. At Harappa, tiny dwellings for workers have been found near metal furnaces and the open areas used for pounding grain.

Unfortunately, Harappan writing has not yet been deciphered, so historians know relatively little about the organization of the Harappan state. However, recent archaeological evidence suggests that unlike its contemporaries in Egypt and Sumer, Harappa was not a centralized monarchy with a theocratic base but a collection of over fifteen hundred towns and cities loosely connected by ties of trade and alliance and ruled by a coalition of landlords and rich merchants. There were no royal precincts or imposing burial monuments, and there are few surviving stone or terra-cotta images that might represent kings, priests, or military commanders. There are clear signs, however, that religion had advanced beyond the stage of spirit worship to belief in a single god or goddess of fertility. Presumably, priests at court prayed to this deity to maintain the fertility of the soil and guarantee the annual harvest.

As in Mesopotamia and Egypt, the Harappan economy was based primarily on agriculture. Wheat, barley, rice, and peas were apparently the primary crops. The presence of cotton seeds at various sites suggests that the Harappan peoples may have been the first to master the cultivation of this useful crop and possibly introduced it, along with rice, to other societies in the region. But Harappa also developed an extensive trading network that extended to Sumer and other civilizations to the west. Textiles and foodstuffs were apparently imported from Sumer in exchange for metals such as copper, lumber, precious stones, and various types of luxury goods. Much of this trade was conducted by ship via the Persian Gulf, although some undoubtedly went by land.

Harappan Culture

Archaeological remains indicate that the Indus valley peoples possessed a culture as sophisticated as that of the Sumerians to the west. Although Harappan architecture was purely functional and shows little artistic sensitivity, the aesthetic quality of some of the pottery and sculpture is superb. Harappan painted pottery, wheel-turned and kiln-fired, rivals equivalent work produced elsewhere. Sculpture, however, was the Harappans' highest artistic achievement. Some artifacts possess a wonderful vitality of expression. Fired clay seals show a deft touch in carving animals such as elephants, tigers, rhinoceros, and antelope, and figures made of copper or terra-cotta show a lively sensitivity and a sense of grace and movement that is almost modern.

Unfortunately, the only surviving examples of Harappan writing are the pictographic symbols inscribed on the clay seals. The script contained more than four hundred characters, but most are too stylized to be identified by their shape, and scholars have thus far been unable to decipher them. There are no apparent links with Mesopotamian scripts. Until the script is deciphered, much about the Harappan civilization must remain, as one historian termed it, a fascinating enigma.

© Borromeo/Art Resource, NY

© Scala/Art Resource, NY

HARAPPAN SEALS. The Harappan peoples, like their contemporaries in Mesopotamia, developed a writing system to record their spoken language. Unfortunately, it has not yet been deciphered. Most extant examples of Harappan writing are found on fired clay seals depicting human figures and animals. These seals have been found in houses and were probably used to identify the owners of goods for sale. Other seals may have been used as amulets or have had other religious significance. Several depict religious figures or ritualistic scenes of sacrifice.

A Lost Civilization?

Until recently, the area north of the Indus River was presumed to be isolated from the emerging river valley civilizations to the south. But archaeologists have now discovered the remnants of a lost culture there that dates back at least to the late third millennium B.C.E. Bronze Age mudbrick settlements surrounded by irrigated fields have been found along a series of oases that stretch several hundred miles from the Caspian Sea into modern-day Afghanistan. There are also clear indications of the domestication of sheep and goats and of widespread trade with other societies in the region, along with tantalizing hints—in the form of an engraved stone seal found at one site—that the inhabitants of the region were in the process of developing their own form of writing. Although the founders of this mysterious civilization remain unknown, it is now clear that the rudiments of civilization in ancient times were not limited to the great river valleys located on the edges of the African and Asian continents.

THE ARRIVAL OF THE ARYANS

One of the great mysteries of Harappan civilization is how it came to an end. Archaeologists working at Mohenjo-Daro have discovered signs of first a gradual decay and then a sudden destruction of the city and its inhabitants around 1500 B.C.E. Many of the surviving skeletons have been found in postures of running or hiding, reminiscent of the ruins of the Roman city of Pompeii, destroyed by the eruption of Mount Vesuvius in 79 C.E.

These tantalizing signs of flight before a sudden catastrophe have led some scholars to surmise that the city of Mohenjo-Daro (the name was applied by archaeologists and means "city of the dead") and perhaps the remnants of Harappan civilization were destroyed by the Aryans, nomads from the north, who arrived in the subcontinent around the middle of the second millennium B.C.E. Although the Aryans were almost certainly not as sophisticated culturally as the Harappans, like many nomadic peoples, they excelled at the art of war. As in Mesopotamia and the Nile valley, most contacts between pastoral and agricultural peoples proved unstable and ended in armed conflict. Nevertheless, it is doubtful that the Aryan invaders were directly responsible for the final destruction of Mohenjo-Daro. More likely, Harappan civilization had already fallen on hard times, perhaps as a result of climatic change in the Indus valley. Archaeologists have found clear signs of social decay, including evidence of trash in the streets, neglect of public services, and overcrowding in urban neighborhoods. Mohenjo-Daro itself may have been destroyed by an epidemic or by natural phenomena such as floods, an earthquake, or a shift in the course of the Indus River. If that was the case, the Aryans conquered a people whose moment of greatness had already passed.

The Early Aryans

Historians know relatively little about the origins and culture of the Aryans before they entered India, although they were part of the extensive group of Indo-European-speaking peoples who inhabited vast areas in what is now Siberia and the steppes of Central Asia. Whereas other Indo-European-speaking peoples moved westward and eventually settled in Europe, the Aryans moved south across the Hindu Kush into the plains of northern India. Between 1500 and 1000 B.C.E., they gradually advanced eastward from the Indus valley, across the fertile plain of the Ganges, and later southward into the Deccan Plateau until they had eventually extended their political mastery over the entire subcontinent and its Dravidian inhabitants, although Dravidian culture survived to remain a prominent element in the evolution of traditional Indian civilization.

After they settled in India, the Aryans gradually adapted to the geographical realities of their new homeland and abandoned the pastoral life for agricultural pursuits. They were assisted by the introduction of iron, which probably came from the Middle East, where it had first been introduced by the Hittites (see Chapter 1) about 1500 B.C.E. The invention of the iron plow, along with the development of irrigation, allowed the Aryans and their indigenous subjects to clear the dense jungle growth along the Ganges River and transform the Ganges valley into one of the richest agricultural regions in all of South Asia. The Aryans also developed their first writing system and were thus able to transcribe the legends that previously

THE DUTIES OF A KING

Kautilya, India's earliest known political philosopher, was an adviser to the Mauryan rulers. The Arthasastra, *though written down at a later date, very likely reflects his ideas. This passage sets forth some of the necessary characteristics of a king, including efficiency, diligence, energy, compassion, and concern for the security and welfare of the state. In emphasizing the importance of winning popular support as the means of becoming an effective ruler, the author echoes the view of the Chinese philosopher Mencius, who declared that the best way to win the empire is to win the people (see Chapter 3).*

THE ARTHASASTRA

Only if a king is himself energetically active do his officers follow him energetically. If he is sluggish, they too remain sluggish. And, besides, they eat up his works. He is thereby easily overpowered by his enemies. Therefore, he should ever dedicate himself energetically to activity. . . .

A king should attend to all urgent business; he should not put it off. For what has been thus put off becomes either difficult or altogether impossible to accomplish.

The vow of the king is energetic activity; his sacrifice is constituted of the discharge of his own administrative duties; his sacrificial fee [to the officiating priests] is his impartiality of attitude toward all; his sacrificial consecration is his anointment as king.

In the happiness of the subjects lies the happiness of the king; in their welfare, his own welfare. The welfare of the king does not lie in the fulfillment of what is dear to him; whatever is dear to the subjects constitutes his welfare.

Therefore, ever energetic, a king should act up to the precepts of the science of material gain. Energetic activity is the source of material gain; its opposite, of downfall.

In the absence of energetic activity, the loss of what has already been obtained and of what still remains to be obtained is certain. The fruit of one's works is achieved through energetic activity—one obtains abundance of material prosperity.

---

had been passed down from generation to generation by memory. Most of what is known about the early Aryans is based on oral traditions passed on in the Rigveda, an ancient work that was written down after the Aryans arrived in India (the Rigveda is one of several Vedas, or collections of sacred instructions and rituals).

As in other Indo-European societies, each of the various Aryan tribes was led by a chieftain, called a *raja* ("prince"), who was assisted by a council of elders composed of other leading members of the tribe; like them, he was normally a member of the warrior class, called the *kshatriya*. The chief derived his power from his ability to protect his tribe from rival groups, an ability that was crucial in the warring kingdoms and shifting alliances that were typical of early Aryan society. Though the *rajas* claimed to be representatives of the gods, they were not gods themselves.

As Aryan society grew in size and complexity, the chieftains began to be transformed into kings, usually called *maharajas* ("great princes"). Nevertheless, the tradition that the ruler did not possess absolute authority remained strong. Like all human beings, the ruler was required to follow the *dharma*, a set of laws that set behavioral standards for all individuals and classes in Indian society (see the box above).

While competing groups squabbled for precedence in India, powerful new empires were rising to the west. First came the Persian Empire of Cyrus and Darius. Then came the Greeks. After two centuries of sporadic rivalry and warfare, the Greeks achieved a brief period of regional dominance in the late fourth century B.C.E. with the rise of Macedonia under Alexander the Great. Alexander had

heard of the riches of India, and in 330 B.C.E., after conquering Persia, he launched an invasion of the east (see Chapter 4). In 326, his armies arrived in the plains of northwestern India. They departed almost as suddenly as they had come, leaving in their wake Greek administrators and a veneer of cultural influence that would affect the area for generations to come.

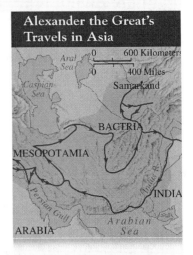

Alexander the Great's Travels in Asia

The Mauryan Empire

The Alexandrian conquest was only a brief interlude in the history of the Indian subcontinent, but it played a formative role, for on the heels of Alexander's departure came the rise of the first dynasty to control much of the region. The founder of the new state, who took the royal title Chandragupta Maurya (324–301 B.C.E.), drove out the Greek occupation forces after the departure of Alexander and solidified his control over the northern Indian plain. He established the capital of his new Mauryan Empire at Pataliputra (modern Patna) in the Ganges valley (see the map on p. 53). Little is known of his origins, although some sources say he had originally fought on the side of the invading Greek forces but then angered Alexander with his outspoken advice.

Little, too, is known of Chandragupta Maurya's empire. Most accounts of his reign rely on a lost work written by Megasthenes, a Greek ambassador to the Mauryan court, in about 302 B.C.E. Chandragupta Maurya was apparently advised by a brilliant court official named Kautilya, whose name has been attached to a treatise on politics called the *Arthasastra*. The work actually dates from a later time, but it may well reflect Kautilya's ideas.

Although the author of the *Arthasastra* follows Aryan tradition in stating that the happiness of the king lies in the happiness of his subjects, the treatise also asserts that when the sacred law of the *dharma* and practical politics collide, the latter must take precedence: "Whenever there is disagreement between history and sacred law or between evidence and sacred law, then the matter should be settled in accordance with sacred law. But whenever sacred law is in conflict with rational law, then reason shall be held authoritative.[1]" The *Arthasastra* also emphasizes ends rather than means, achieved results rather than the methods employed. For this reason, it has often been compared to Machiavelli's

famous political treatise of the Italian Renaissance, *The Prince*, written more than a thousand years later.

As described in the *Arthasastra*, Chandragupta Maurya's government was highly centralized and even despotic: "It is power and power alone which, only when exercised by the king with impartiality, and in proportion to guilt, over his son or his enemy, maintains both this world and the next."[2] The king possessed a large army and a secret police responsible to his orders (according to the Greek ambassador Megasthenes, Chandragupta Maurya was chronically fearful of assassination, a not unrealistic concern for someone who had allegedly come to power by violence). Reportedly, all food was tasted in his presence, and he made a practice of never sleeping twice in the same bed in his sumptuous palace. To guard against corruption, a board of censors was empowered to investigate cases of possible malfeasance and incompetence within the bureaucracy.

The ruler's authority beyond the confines of the capital may often have been limited, however. The empire was divided into provinces that were ruled by governors. At first, most of these governors were appointed by and reported to the ruler, but later the position became hereditary. The provinces themselves were divided into districts, each under a chief magistrate appointed by the governor. At the base of the government pyramid was the village, where the vast majority of the Indian people lived. The village was governed by a council of elders; membership in the council was normally hereditary and was shared by the wealthiest families in the village.

⟡ **A HARAPPAN BUST.** This 4,000-year-old bust found at Mohenjo-Daro displays an elaborate beard, a pair of eyes originally inlaid with shell, and a toga decorated with a trefoil design. Although the trefoil had been used in Egypt and Mesopotamia as a sacred symbol representing stars and deities, little is known about the identity of this Harappan figure or whether the creative execution reflects the influence of other nearby civilizations.

Caste and Class: Social Structures in Ancient India

When the Aryans arrived in India, they already possessed a strong class system based on a ruling warrior class. They apparently held the indigenous peoples in some contempt and assigned them to a lower position in society. The result was a set of social institutions and class divisions that have persisted with only minor changes down to the present day.

THE CASTE SYSTEM

At the base of the social system that emerged from the clash of cultures was the concept of the superiority of the invading peoples over their conquered subjects. In a sense, it became an issue of color, because the Aryan invaders, a primarily light-skinned people, were contemptuous of their subjects, who were dark. Light skin came to imply high status, whereas dark skin suggested the opposite.

The concept of color, however, was only the physical manifestation of a division that took place in Indian society on the basis of economic functions. Indian classes (called *varna*, literally, "color," and commonly known as "castes" in English) did not simply reflect an informal division of labor. Instead, they were a set of rigid social classifications that

SOCIAL CLASSES IN ANCIENT INDIA

The Law of Manu is a set of behavioral norms allegedly prescribed by India's mythical founding ruler, Manu. The treatise was probably written in the first or second century B.C.E. *The following excerpt describes the various social classes in India and their prescribed duties.*

THE *LAW OF MANU*

For the sake of the preservation of this entire creation, the Exceedingly Resplendent One [the Creator of the Universe] assigned separate duties to the classes which had sprung from his mouth, arms, thighs, and feet.

Teaching, studying, performing sacrificial rites, so too making others perform sacrificial rites, and giving away and receiving gifts—these he assigned to the [brahmins].

Protection of the people, giving away of wealth, performance of sacrificial rites, study, and nonattachment to sensual pleasures—these are, in short, the duties of a kshatriya.

Tending of cattle, giving away of wealth, performance of sacrificial rites, study, trade and commerce, usury, and agriculture—these are the occupations of a vaisya.

The Lord has prescribed only one occupation [karma] for a sudra, namely, service without malice of even these other three classes.

Of created beings, those which are animate are the best; of the animate, those which subsist by means of their intellect; of the intelligent, men are the best; and of men, the [brahmins] are traditionally declared to be the best.

The code of conduct—prescribed by scriptures and ordained by sacred tradition—constitutes the highest dharma; hence a twice-born person, conscious of his own Self [seeking spiritual salvation], should be always scrupulous in respect of it.

---

determined not only one's occupation but also one's status in society and one's hope for ultimate salvation (see "Escaping the Wheel of Life" later in this chapter). There were five major castes in Indian society in ancient times. At the top were two castes, collectively viewed as the aristocracy, which clearly represented the ruling elites in Aryan society prior to their arrival in India: the priests and the warriors.

The priestly caste, known as the *brahmins*, was usually considered to be at the top of the social scale. Descended from seers who had advised the ruler on religious matters in Aryan tribal society (*brahmin* meant "one possessed of *Brahman*," a term for the supreme god in the Hindu religion), they were eventually transformed into an official class after their religious role declined in importance. Megasthenes described this caste as follows:

> From the time of their conception in the womb they are under the care and guardianship of learned men who go to the mother and . . . give her prudent hints and counsels, and the women who listen to them most willingly are thought to be the most fortunate in their offspring. After their birth the children are in the care of one person after another, and as they advance in years their masters are men of superior accomplishments. The philosophers reside in a grove in front of the city within a moderate-sized enclosure. They live in a simple style and lie on pallets of straw and [deer] skins. They abstain from animal food and sexual pleasures, and occupy their time in listening to serious discourse and in imparting knowledge to willing ears.[3]

The second caste was the *kshatriya*, the warriors. Although often listed below the *brahmins* in social status, many *kshatriyas* were probably descended from the ruling warrior class in Aryan society prior to the conquest of India and thus may have originally ranked socially above the *brahmins*, although they were ranked lower in religious terms. Like the *brahmins*, the *kshatriyas* were originally iden-

tified with a single occupation—fighting—but as the character of Aryan society changed, they often switched to other forms of employment. At the same time, new conquering families from other castes were sometimes tacitly accepted into the ranks of the warriors.

The third-ranked caste in Indian society was the *vaisya* (literally, "commoner"). The *vaisyas* were usually viewed in economic terms as the merchant caste. Some historians have speculated that the *vaisyas* were originally guardians of the tribal herds but that after settling in India, many moved into commercial pursuits. Megasthenes noted that members of this caste "alone are permitted to hunt and keep cattle and to sell beasts of burden or to let them out on hire. In return for clearing the land of wild beasts and birds which infest sown fields, they receive an allowance of corn from the king. They lead a wandering life and dwell in tents."[4] Although this caste was ranked below the first two in social status, it shared with them the privilege of being considered "twice-born," a term referring to a ceremony at puberty whereby young males were initiated into adulthood and introduced into Indian society. After the ceremony, male members of the top three castes were allowed to wear the "sacred thread" for the remainder of their lives.

Below the three "twice-born" castes were the *sudras*, who represented the great bulk of the Indian population. The *sudras* were not considered fully Aryan, and the term probably originally referred to the conquered Dravidian population. Most *sudras* were peasants or artisans or worked at other forms of manual labor. They had only limited rights in society (see the box above). In recent years, DNA samples have revealed that most upper-caste South Indians share more genetic characteristics with Europeans than their lower-caste counterparts do, thus tending to confirm the hypothesis that the Aryans established their political and social dominance over the indigenous Dravidian population.

At the lowest level of Indian society, and in fact not even considered a legitimate part of the caste system itself, were the untouchables (also known as outcastes, or *pariahs*). The untouchables probably originated as a slave class consisting of prisoners of war, criminals, ethnic minorities, and other groups considered outside Indian society. Even after slavery was outlawed, the untouchables were given menial and degrading tasks that other Indians would not accept, such as collecting trash, handling dead bodies, or serving as butchers or tanners (handling dead meat). According to the estimate of one historian, they may have accounted for a little more than 5 percent of the total population of India in antiquity.

The life of the untouchables was extremely demeaning. They were not considered human, and their very presence was considered polluting to members of the other *varna*. No Indian would touch or eat food handled or prepared by an untouchable. Untouchables lived in special ghettos and were required to tap two sticks together to announce their presence when they traveled outside their quarters so that others could avoid them.

Technically, the caste divisions were absolute. Individuals supposedly were born, lived, and died in the same caste. In practice, some upward or downward mobility probably took place, and there was undoubtedly some flexibility in economic functions. But throughout most of Indian history, caste taboos remained strict. Members were generally not permitted to marry outside their caste (although in practice, men were occasionally allowed to marry below their caste but not above it). At first, attitudes toward the handling of food were relatively loose, but eventually that taboo grew stronger, and social mores dictated that sharing meals and marrying outside one's caste were unacceptable.

The people of ancient India did not belong to a particular caste as individuals but as part of a larger kin group commonly referred to as the *jati*, a system of extended families that originated in ancient India and still exists in somewhat changed form today. Although the origins of the *jati* system are unknown (there are no indications of strict class distinctions in Harappan society), the *jati* eventually became identified with a specific caste living in a specific area and carrying out a specific function in society. Each caste was divided into thousands of separate *jatis*, each with its own separate economic function.

Caste was thus the basic social organization into which traditional Indian society was divided. Each *jati* was itself composed of hundreds or thousands of individual nuclear families and was governed by its own council of elders. Membership in this ruling council was usually hereditary and was based on the wealth or social status of particular families within the community.

In theory, each *jati* was assigned a particular form of economic activity. Obviously, though, not all families in a given caste could take part in the same vocation, and as time went on, members of a single *jati* commonly engaged in several different lines of work. Sometimes an entire *jati* would have to move its location in order to continue a particular form of activity. In other cases, a *jati* would adopt an entirely new occupation in order to remain in a certain area. Such changes in habitat or occupation introduced the possibility of movement up or down the social scale. In this way, an entire *jati* could sometimes engage in upward mobility, even though it was not possible for individuals, who were tied to their caste identity for life.

The caste system may sound highly constricting, but there were persuasive social and economic reasons why it survived for so many centuries. In the first place, it provided an identity for individuals in a highly hierarchical society. Although an individual might rank lower on the social scale than members of other castes, it was always possible to find others ranked even lower. Caste was also a means for new groups, such as mountain tribal people, to achieve a recognizable place in the broader community. Perhaps equally important, caste was a primitive form of welfare system. Each *jati* was obliged to provide for any of its members who were poor or destitute. Caste also provided an element of stability in a society that all too often was in a state of political anarchy.

DAILY LIFE IN ANCIENT INDIA

Beyond these rigid social stratifications was the Indian family. Not only was life centered around the family, but the family, not the individual, was the most basic unit in society. The ideal was an extended family, with three generations living under the same roof. It was essentially patriarchal, except along the Malabar coast, near the southwestern tip of the subcontinent, where a matriarchal form of social organization prevailed down to modern times. In the rest of India, the oldest male traditionally possessed legal authority over the entire family unit.

The family was linked together in a religious sense by a series of commemorative rites to ancestral members. This ritual originated in the Vedic era and consisted of family ceremonies to honor the departed and to link the living and the dead. The male family head was responsible for leading the ritual. At his death, his eldest son had the duty of conducting the funeral rites.

The importance of the father and the son in family ritual underlined the importance of males in Indian society. Male superiority was expressed in a variety of ways. Women could not serve as priests (although in practice, some were accepted as seers), nor were they normally permitted to study the Vedas. In general, males had a monopoly on education, since the primary goal of learning to read was to carry on family rituals. In high-class families, young men, after having been initiated into the sacred thread, began Vedic studies with a *guru* (teacher). Some then went on to higher studies in one of the major cities. The goal of such an education might be either professional or religious. Such young men were not supposed to marry until after twelve years of study.

In general, only males could inherit property, except in a few cases where there were no sons. According to law, a woman was always considered a minor. Divorce was prohibited, although it sometimes took place. According to the *Arthasastra*, a wife who had been deserted by her husband could seek a divorce. Polygamy was fairly rare and apparently occurred mainly among the higher classes, but husbands were permitted to take a second wife if the first was barren. Producing children was an important aspect of marriage, both because children provided security for their parents in old age and because they were a physical proof of male potency. Child marriage was common for young girls, whether because of the desire for children or because daughters represented an economic liability to their parents. But perhaps the most graphic symbol of women's subjection to men was the ritual of *sati* (often written *suttee*), which required the wife to throw herself on her dead husband's funeral pyre. The Greek visitor Megasthenes reported "that he had heard from some persons of wives burning themselves along with their deceased husbands and doing so gladly; and that those women who refused to burn themselves were held in disgrace."[4] All in all, it was undoubtedly a difficult existence. According to the *Law of Manu*, an early treatise on social organization and behavior in ancient India, probably written in the first or second century B.C.E., women were subordinated to men—first to their father, then to their husband, and finally to their sons:

> She should do nothing independently
>   even in her own house.
> In childhood subject to her father,
>   in youth to her husband,
> and when her husband is dead to her sons,
>   she should never enjoy independence. . . .
>
> She should always be cheerful,
>   and skillful in her domestic duties,
> with her household vessels well cleansed,
>   and her hand tight on the purse strings. . . .
>
> Though he be uncouth and prone to pleasure,
>   though he have no good points at all,
> the virtuous wife should ever
>   worship her lord as a god.[5]

At the root of female subordination to the male was the practical fact that as in most agricultural societies, men did most of the work in the fields. Females were viewed as having little utility outside the home and indeed were considered an economic burden, since parents were obliged to provide a dowry to acquire a husband for a daughter. Female children also appeared to offer little advantage in maintaining the family unit, since they joined the families of their husbands after the wedding ceremony.

Despite all of these indications of female subjection to the male, there are numerous signs that in some ways women often played an influential role in Indian society, and the Hindu code of behavior stressed that they should be treated with respect. Indians appeared to be fascinated by female sexuality, and tradition held that women often used their sexual powers to achieve domination over men. The author of the Mahabharata, a vast epic of early Indian society, complained that "the fire has never too many logs, the ocean never too many rivers, death never too many living souls, and fair-eyed woman never too many men." Despite the legal and social constraints, women often played an important role within the family unit, and many were admired and honored for their talents. It is probably significant that paintings and sculpture from ancient and medieval India frequently show women in a role equal to that of men, and the tradition of the henpecked husband is as prevalent in India as in many Western societies (see the box on p. 46).

Homosexuality was not unknown in India. It was condemned in the law books, however, and generally ignored by literature, which devoted its attention entirely to erotic heterosexuality. The *Kamasutra*, a textbook on sexual practices and techniques dating from the second century C.E. or slightly thereafter, mentions homosexuality briefly and with no apparent enthusiasm.

The Economy

The Aryan conquest did not drastically change the economic character of Indian society. Not only did most Aryans take up farming, but it is likely that agriculture expanded rapidly under Aryan rule with the invention of the iron plow and the spread of northern Indian culture into the Deccan Plateau. One consequence of this process was to shift the focus of Indian culture from the Indus valley farther eastward to the Ganges River valley, which even today is one of the most densely populated regions on earth. The flatter areas in the Deccan Plateau and in the coastal plains were also turned into cropland.

For most Indian farmers, life was harsh. Among the most fortunate were those who owned their own land, although they were required to pay taxes to the state. Many others were sharecroppers or landless laborers. They were subject to the vicissitudes of the market and often paid exorbitant rents to their landlord. Concentration of land in large holdings was limited by the tradition of dividing property among all the sons, but large estates worked by hired laborers or rented out to sharecroppers were not uncommon, particularly in areas where local *rajas* derived much of their wealth from their property.

Another problem for Indian farmers was the unpredictability of the climate. India is in the monsoon zone.

THE HENPECKED MONK

W omen were often portrayed in traditional Indian literature as seductresses, luring innocent males from following their higher spiritual nature. This passage is from the Sutrakrtanga, one of the sacred books of the Jain religion. While the object of concern is technically not that familiar figure of ridicule, the henpecked husband, the passage indicates the concern that many men in ancient India felt when exposed to the wiles of their female contemporaries.

THE SUTRAKRTANGA

A celibate monk shouldn't fall in love,
and though he hankers after pleasure he should hold
himself in check,
for these are the pleasures
which some monks enjoy.

If a monk breaks his vows,
and falls for a woman,
she upbraids him and raises her foot to him,
and kicks him on the head.

"Monk, if you won't live with me
as husband and wife,
I'll pull out my hair and become a nun,
for you shall not live without me!"

But when she has him in her clutches
it's all housework and errands!

"Fetch a knife to cut this gourd!"
"Get me some fresh fruit!"

"We want wood to boil the greens,
and for a fire in the evening!"
"Now paint my feet!"
"Come and massage my back!" ...

"Bring me the chair with the twine seat,
and my wooden-soled slippers to go out walking!"
So pregnant women boss their husbands,
just as though they were household slaves.

When a child is born, the reward of their labors,
she makes the father hold the baby.
And sometimes the fathers of sons
stagger under their burdens like camels.

They get up at night, as though they were nurses,
to lull the howling child to sleep,
and, though they are shamefaced about it,
scrub dirty garments, just like washermen. ...

So, monks, resist the wiles of women;
avoid their friendship and company.
The little pleasure you get from them
will only lead you into trouble!

The monsoon is a seasonal wind pattern in southern Asia that blows from the southwest during the summer months and from the northeast during the winter. The southwest monsoon is commonly marked by heavy rains. When the rains were late, thousands starved, particularly in the drier areas, which were especially dependent on rainfall. Strong governments attempted to deal with such problems by building state-operated granaries and maintaining the irrigation works, but strong governments were rare, and famine was probably all too common. The staple crops in the north were wheat, barley, and millet, with wet rice common in the fertile river valleys. In the south, grain and vegetables were supplemented by various tropical products, cotton, and spices such as pepper, ginger, cinnamon, and saffron.

By no means were all Indians farmers. As time passed, India became one of the most advanced trading and manufacturing civilizations in the ancient world. After the rise of the Mauryas, India's role in regional trade began to expand, and the subcontinent became a major transit point in a vast commercial network that extended from the rim of the Pacific to the Middle East and the Mediterranean Sea. This regional trade went both by sea and by camel caravan. Maritime trade across the Indian Ocean may have begun as early as the fifth century B.C.E. It extended eastward as far as Southeast Asia and China and southward as far as the straits between Africa and the island of Madagascar. Westward went spices, perfumes, jewels, textiles, precious stones and ivory, and wild animals. In return, India received gold, tin, lead, and wine.

India's expanding role as a manufacturing and commercial hub of the ancient world was undoubtedly a spur to the growth of the state. Under Chandragupta Maurya, the central government became actively involved in commercial and manufacturing activities. It owned mines and vast crown lands and undoubtedly earned massive profits from its role in regional commerce. Separate government departments were established for trade, agriculture, mining, and the manufacture of weapons, and the movement of private goods was vigorously taxed. Nevertheless, a significant private sector also flourished; it was dominated by great caste guilds, which monopolized key sectors of the economy. A money economy probably came into operation during the second century B.C.E., when copper and gold coins

IN THE BEGINNING

As Indians began to speculate about the nature of the cosmic order, they came to believe in the existence of a single monistic force in the universe, a form of ultimate reality called Brahman. Today the early form of Hinduism is sometimes called Brahmanism. In the Upanishads, the concept began to emerge as an important element of Indian religious belief. It was the duty of the individual self—called the Atman—to achieve an understanding of this ultimate reality so that after death the self would merge in spiritual form with Brahman. Sometimes Brahman was described in more concrete terms as a creator god—eventually known as Vishnu—but more often in terms of a shadowy ultimate reality. In the following passage from the Upanishads, the author speculates on the nature of ultimate reality.

THE UPANISHADS

In the beginning . . . , this world was just being, one only, without a second. Some people, no doubt, say: "In the beginning . . . , this world was just nonbeing, one only, without a second; from that nonbeing, being was produced." But how indeed . . . could it be so? How could being be produced from nonbeing? . . .

In the beginning this world was being alone, one only, without a second. Being thought to itself: "May I be many, may I procreate." It produced fire. That fire thought to itself: "May I be many, may I procreate." It produced water. Therefore, whenever a person grieves or perspires, then it is from fire [heat] alone that water is produced. That water thought to itself: "May I be many, may I procreate." It produced food; it is from water alone that food for eating is produced. . . . That divinity (Being) thought to itself: "Well, having entered into these three divinities [fire, water, and food] by means of this living self, let me develop names and forms.

---

were introduced from the Middle East. This in turn led to the development of banking. But village trade continued to be conducted by means of cowry shells (highly polished shells used as a medium of exchange throughout much of Africa and Asia) or barter throughout the ancient period.

ESCAPING THE WHEEL OF LIFE: THE RELIGIOUS WORLD OF ANCIENT INDIA

Like Indian politics and society, Indian religion is a blend of Aryan and Dravidian culture. The intermingling of those two civilizations gave rise to an extraordinarily complex set of religious beliefs and practices, filled with diversity and contrast. Out of this cultural mix came two of the world's great religions, Buddhism and Hinduism, and several smaller ones, including Jainism and Sikhism.

Hinduism

Evidence about the earliest religious beliefs of the Aryan peoples comes primarily from sacred texts such as the Vedas, a set of four collections of hymns and religious ceremonies transmitted by memory through the centuries by Aryan priests. Many of these religious ideas were probably common to all of the Indo-European peoples before their separation into different groups at least four thousand years ago. Early Aryan beliefs were based on the common concept of a pantheon of gods and goddesses representing great forces of nature similar to the immortals of Greek mythology. The Aryan ancestor of the Greek father-god Zeus, for example, may have been the deity known in early Aryan tradition as Dyaus (see Chapter 4).

The parent god Dyaus was a somewhat distant figure, however, who was eventually overshadowed by other, more functional gods possessing more familiar human traits. For a while, the primary Aryan god was the great warrior god Indra. Indra summoned the Aryan tribal peoples to war and was represented in nature by thunder. Later, Indra declined in importance and was replaced by Varuna, lord of justice, who eventually evolved into the modern deity Vishnu. Other gods and goddesses represented various forces of nature or the needs of human beings, such as fire, fertility, and wealth (see the box above).

The concept of sacrifice was a key element in Aryan religious belief in Vedic times. As in many other ancient cultures, the practice may have begun as human sacrifice, but later animals were used as substitutes, although human sacrifice was practiced in some isolated communities down to modern times. The priestly class, the *brahmins*, played a key role in these ceremonies.

Another element of Aryan religious belief in ancient times was the ideal of asceticism. By the sixth century B.C.E., self-sacrifice or even self-mutilation had begun to replace sacrifice as a means of placating or communicating with the gods. Apparently, the original motive for asceticism was to achieve magical powers, but later, in the Upanishads (a set of commentaries on the Vedas compiled in the sixth century B.C.E.), it was seen as a means of spiritual meditation that would enable the practitioner to reach beyond material reality to a world of truth and bliss beyond earthly joy and sorrow: "Those who practice penance and faith in the forest, the tranquil ones, the knowers of truth, living the life of wandering mendicancy—they depart, freed from passion, through the door of the sun, to where dwells, verily . . . the imperishable Soul."[6] It is possible that another motive was to permit those with strong religious convictions to communicate directly with metaphysical reality without having to rely on the priestly class at court.

Asceticism, of course, has been practiced in other religions, including Christianity and Islam, but it seems particularly identified with Hinduism, the religion that emerged from early Indian religious tradition. Eventually, asceticism evolved into the modern practice of body training that we know as *yoga* (union), which is accepted today as a meaningful element of Hindu religious practice.

REINCARNATION

Another new concept also probably began to appear around the time the Upanishads were written—the idea of reincarnation. This is the idea that the individual soul is reborn in a different form after death and progresses through several existences on the wheel of life until it reaches its final destination in a union with the Great World Soul, *Brahman*. Because life is harsh, this final release is the objective of all living souls.

A key element in this process is the idea of *karma*—that one's rebirth in a next life is determined by one's *karma* (actions) in this life. Hinduism places all living species on a vast scale of existence, including the four classes and the untouchables in human society. The current status of an individual soul, then, is not simply a cosmic accident but the inevitable result of actions that that soul has committed in a past existence.

At the top of the scale are the *brahmins*, who by definition are closest to ultimate release from the law of reincarnation. The *brahmins* are followed in descending order by the other castes in human society and the world of the beasts. Within the animal kingdom, an especially high position is reserved for the cow, which even today is revered by Hindus as a sacred beast. Some have speculated that the unique role played by the cow in Hinduism derives from the value of cattle in Aryan pastoral society. But others have pointed out that cattle were a source of both money and food and suggest that the cow's sacred position may have descended from the concept of the sacred bull in Dravidian culture.

The concept of *karma* is governed by the *dharma*, or the law. A law regulating human behavior, the *dharma* imposes different requirements on different individuals depending on their status in society. Those high on the social scale, such as *brahmins* and *kshatriyas*, are held to a more strict form of behavior than are *sudras*. The *brahmin*, for example, is expected to abstain from eating meat, because that would entail the killing of another living being, thus interrupting its *karma*.

How the concept of reincarnation originated is not known, although it was apparently not unusual for early peoples to believe that the individual soul would be reborn in a different form in a later life. In any case, in India the concept may have had practical causes as well as consequences. In the first place, it tended to provide religious sanction for the rigid class divisions that had begun to emerge in Indian society after the Aryan conquest, and it provided moral and political justification for the privileges of those on the higher end of the scale.

At the same time, the concept of reincarnation provided certain compensations for those lower on the ladder of life. For example, it gave hope to the poor that if they behaved properly in this life, they might improve their condition in the next. It also provided a means for unassimilated groups such as ethnic minorities to find a place in Indian society while at the same time permitting them to maintain their distinctive way of life.

The ultimate goal of achieving "good" *karma*, as we have seen, was to escape the cycle of existence. To the sophisticated, the nature of that release was a spiritual union of the individual soul with the Great World Soul, *Brahman*, described in the Upanishads as a form of dreamless sleep, free from earthly desires. Such a

© Scala/Art Resource, NY

TRIPLE-HEADED SIVA In the first centuries of the first millennium C.E., Hindus began to adopt Buddhist rock art. One of the most outstanding examples is at the Elephanta Caves, near the modern city of Mumbai (Bombay). Dominating the cave is this 18-foot-high triple-headed statue of Siva, representing the Hindu deity in all his various aspects. The central figure presents him in total serenity, enveloped in absolute knowledge. The angry profile on the left portrays him as the destroyer, struggling against time, death, and other negative forces. The right-hand profile shows his loving and feminine side in the guise of his beautiful wife Parvati.

The rich variety and earthy character of many Hindu deities are repugnant to many Christians and Muslims, to whom God is an all-seeing and transcendent deity. Many Hindus, however, regard the multitude of gods as simply different manifestations of one ultimate reality. The various deities also provide a useful means for ordinary Indians to personify their religious feelings. Even though some individuals among the early Aryans attempted to communicate with the gods through sacrifice or asceticism, most Indians undoubtedly sought to satisfy their own individual religious needs through devotion, which they expressed through ritual ceremonies and offerings at a Hindu temple. Such offerings were not only a way to seek salvation, but also a means of satisfying all the aspirations of daily life.

Over the centuries, then, Hinduism changed radically from its origins in Aryan tribal society and became a religion of the vast majority of the Indian people. Concern with a transcendental union between the individual soul and the Great World Soul contrasted with practical desires for material wealth and happiness; ascetic self-denial contrasted with an earthy emphasis on the pleasures and values of sexual union between marriage partners. All of these became aspects of Hinduism, the religion of 70 percent of the Indian people.

Buddhism: The Middle Path

In the sixth century B.C.E., a new doctrine appeared in northern India that soon began to rival Hinduism's popularity throughout the subcontinent. This new doctrine was called Buddhism. The historical founder of Buddhism, Siddhartha Gautama, was a native of a small principality in the foothills of the Himalaya Mountains in what is today southern Nepal. He was born in the mid-sixth century B.C.E., the son of a ruling *kshatriya* family. According to tradition, the young Siddhartha was raised in affluent surroundings and trained, like many other members of his class, in the martial arts. On reaching maturity, he married and began to raise a family. However, at the age of twenty-nine he suddenly discovered the pain of illness, the sorrow of death, and the degradation caused by old age in the lives of ordinary people and exclaimed: "Would that sickness, age, and death might be forever bound!" From that time on, he decided to dedicate his life to determining the cause and seeking the cure for human suffering.

To find the answers to these questions, Siddhartha abandoned his home and family and traveled widely. At first he tried to follow the model of the ascetics, but he eventually decided that self-mortification did not lead to a greater understanding of life and abandoned the practice. Then one day after a lengthy period of meditation under a tree, he finally achieved enlightenment as to the meaning of life and spent the remainder of his life preaching it. His conclusions, as embodied in his teachings,

© Royal Smeets Offset, Weert

➤ DANCING SIVA The Hindu deity Siva is often presented in the form of a bronze statue, performing a cosmic dance in which he simultaneously creates and destroys the universe. While his upper right hand creates the cosmos, his upper left hand reduces it in flames, and the lower two hands offer eternal blessing. Siva's dancing statues present to his followers the visual message of his power and compassion.

concept, however, was undoubtedly too ethereal for the average Indian, who needed a more concrete form of heavenly salvation, a place of beauty and bliss after a life of disease and privation.

It was probably for this reason that the Hindu religion—in some ways so otherworldly and ascetic—came to be peopled with a multitude of very human gods and goddesses. It has been estimated that the Hindu pantheon contains more than 33,000 deities. Only a small number are primary ones, however, notably the so-called trinity of gods: Brahman the Creator, Vishnu the Preserver, and Siva (originally the Vedic god Rudra) the Destroyer. Although Brahman (sometimes in his concrete form called Brahma) is considered to be the highest god, Vishnu and Siva take precedence in the devotional exercises of many Hindus, who can be roughly divided into Vishnuites and Saivites. In addition to the trinity of gods, all of whom have wives with readily identifiable roles and personalities, there are countless minor deities, each again with his or her own specific function, such as bringing good fortune, arranging a good marriage, or guaranteeing a son in childbirth.

became the philosophy (or as some would have it, the religion) of Buddhism. According to legend, the Devil (the Indian term is *Mara*) attempted desperately to tempt him with political power and the company of beautiful girls. But Siddhartha Gautama resisted:

Pleasure is brief as a flash of lightning
Or like an autumn shower, only for a moment. . . .
Why should I then covet the pleasures you speak of?
I see your bodies are full of all impurity:
Birth and death, sickness and age are yours.
I seek the highest prize, hard to attain by men—
The true and constant wisdom of the wise.[7]

How much the modern doctrine of Buddhism resembles the original teachings of Siddhartha Gautama is open to debate, since much time has elapsed since his death and original texts relating his ideas are lacking. Nor is it certain that Siddhartha even intended to found a new religion or doctrine. In some respects, his ideas could be viewed as a reformist form of Hinduism, much as Martin Luther saw Protestantism as a reformation of Christianity. Siddhartha accepted much of the belief system of Hinduism, if not all of its practices. For example, he accepted the concept of reincarnation and the role of *karma* as a means of influencing the movement of individual souls up and down in the scale of life. He followed Hinduism in praising nonviolence and borrowed the idea of living a life of simplicity and chastity from the ascetics. Moreover, his vision of metaphysical reality—commonly known as Nirvana—is closer to the Hindu concept of *Brahman* than it is to the Christian concept of heavenly salvation. Nirvana, which involves an extinction of selfhood and a final reunion with the Great World Soul, is sometimes likened to a dreamless sleep or to a kind of "blowing out" (as of a candle). Buddhists occasionally remark that someone who asks for a description does not understand the concept.

At the same time, the new doctrine differed from existing Hindu practices in a number of key ways. In the first place, Siddhartha denied the existence of an individual soul. To him, the Hindu concept of *Atman*—the individual soul—meant that the soul was subject to rebirth and thus did not achieve a complete liberation from the cares of this world. In fact, Siddhartha denied the ultimate reality of the material world in its entirety and taught that it was an illusion to be transcended. Siddhartha's idea of achieving Nirvana was based on his conviction that the pain, poverty, and sorrow that afflict human beings are caused essentially by their attachment to the things of this world. Once worldly cares are abandoned, pain and sorrow can be overcome. With this knowledge comes *bodhi*, or wisdom (source of the term *Buddhism* and the familiar name for Gautama the Wise: Gautama Buddha).

Achieving this understanding is a key step on the road to Nirvana, which, as in Hinduism, is a form of release

Chronology

ANCIENT INDIA

Harappan civilization	c. 2600–1900 B.C.E.
Arrival of the Aryans	c. 1500 B.C.E.
Life of Gautama Buddha	c. 560–480 B.C.E.
Invasion of India by Alexander the Great	326 B.C.E.
Mauryan dynasty founded	324 B.C.E.
Reign of Chandragupta Maurya	324–301 B.C.E.
Reign of Asoka	269–232 B.C.E.
Collapse of Mauryan dynasty	183 B.C.E.
Rise of Kushan Kingdom	c. first century C.E.

from the wheel of life. According to tradition, Siddhartha transmitted this message in a sermon to his disciples in a deer park at Sarnath, not far from the modern city of Benares (also known as Varanasi). Like so many messages, it is deceptively simple and is enclosed in four noble truths: life is suffering; suffering is caused by desire; the way to end suffering is to end desire; and the way to end desire is to avoid the extremes of a life of vulgar materialism and a life of self-torture and to follow the "Middle Path." This Middle Path, which is also known as the Eightfold Way, calls for right knowledge, right purpose, right speech, right conduct, right occupation, right effort, right awareness, and right meditation (see the box on p. 51).

Buddhism also differed from Hinduism in its relative egalitarianism. Although Siddhartha accepted the idea of reincarnation (and hence the idea that human beings differ as a result of *karma* accumulated in a previous existence), he rejected the Hindu division of humanity into rigidly defined castes based on previous reincarnations and taught that all human beings could aspire to Nirvana as a result of their behavior in this life—a message that likely helped Buddhism win support among people at the lower end of the social scale.

In addition, Buddhism was much simpler than Hinduism. Siddhartha rejected the panoply of gods that had become identified with Hinduism and forbade his followers to worship his person or his image after his death. In fact, many Buddhists view Buddhism as a philosophy rather than a religion.

After Siddhartha Gautama's death in 480 B.C.E., dedicated disciples carried his message the length and breadth of India. Buddhist monasteries were established throughout the subcontinent, and temples and stupas (stone towers housing relics of the Buddha) sprang up throughout the countryside.

HOW TO ACHIEVE ENLIGHTENMENT

One of the most famous passages in Buddhist literature is the sermon at Sarnath, which Siddhartha Gautama delivered to his followers in a deer park outside the holy city of Varanasi (Benares), in the Ganges River valley. Here he set forth the key ideas that would define Buddhist beliefs for centuries to come.

THE SERMON AT BENARES

Thus have I heard: at one time the Lord dwelt at Benares at Isipatana in the Deer Park. There the Lord addressed the five monks:—

"These two extremes, monks, are not to be practiced by one who has gone forth from the world. What are the two? That conjoined with the passions and luxury, low, vulgar, common, ignoble, and useless; and that conjoined with self-torture, painful, ignoble, and useless. Avoiding these two extremes the Tathagata has gained the enlightenment of the Middle Path, which produces insight and knowledge and tends to calm, to higher knowledge, enlightenment, Nirvana.

"And what, monks, is the Middle Path, of which the Tathagata has gained enlightenment, which produces insight and knowledge, and tends to calm, to higher knowledge, enlightenment, Nirvana? This is the noble Eightfold Way: namely, right view, right intention, right speech, right action, right livelihood, right effort, right mindfulness, right concentration. This, monks, is the Middle Path, of which the Tathagata has gained enlightenment, which produces insight and knowledge, and tends to calm, to higher knowledge, enlightenment, Nirvana.

1. Now this, monks, is the noble truth of pain: birth is painful, old age is painful, sickness is painful, death is painful, sorrow, lamentation, dejection, and despair are painful. Contact with unpleasant things is painful, not getting what one wishes is painful. In short the five groups of graspings are painful.
2. Now this, monks, is the noble truth of the cause of pain: the craving, which tends to rebirth, combined with pleasure and lust, finding pleasure here and there; namely, the craving for passion, the craving for existence, the craving for nonexistence.
3. Now this, monks, is the noble truth of the cessation of pain, the cessation without a remainder of craving, the abandonment, forsaking, release, nonattachment.
4. Now this, monks, is the noble truth of the way that leads to the cessation of pain: this is the noble Eightfold Way; namely, right view, right intention, right speech, right action, right livelihood, right effort, right mindfulness, right concentration.

"And when, monks, in these four noble truths my due knowledge and insight with its three sections and twelve divisions was well purified, then, monks, . . . I had attained the highest complete enlightenment. This I recognized. Knowledge arose in me, insight arose that the release of my mind is unshakable; this is my last existence; now there is no rebirth."

Women were permitted to join the monastic order but only in an inferior position. As Siddhartha had explained, women are "soon angered," "full of passion," and "stupid": "That is the reason . . . why women have no place in public assemblies . . . and do not earn their living by any profession." Still, the position of women tended to be better in Buddhist societies than it was elsewhere in ancient India (see the box on p. 52).

During the next centuries, Buddhism began to compete actively with Hindu beliefs, as well as with another new faith known as Jainism. Jainism was founded by Mahavira, a contemporary of Siddhartha Gautama. Resembling Buddhism in its rejection of the reality of the material world, Jainism was more extreme in practice. Where Siddhartha Gautama called for the "middle way" between passion and luxury and pain and self-torture, Mahavira preached a doctrine of extreme simplicity to his followers, who kept no possessions and relied on begging for a living. Some even rejected clothing and wandered through the world naked. Perhaps because of its insistence on a life of poverty, Jainism failed to attract enough adherents to become a major doctrine and never received official support. According to tradition, however, Chandragupta Maurya accepted Mahavira's doctrine after abdicating the throne and fasted to death in a Jain monastery.

ASOKA, A BUDDHIST MONARCH

Buddhism received an important boost when Asoka, the grandson of Chandragupta Maurya, converted to Buddhism in the third century B.C.E. Asoka (269–232 B.C.E.) is widely considered the greatest ruler in the history of India. Reportedly, Asoka began his reign conquering, pillaging, and killing, but after his conversion to Buddhism, he began to regret his bloodthirsty past and attempted to rule benevolently.

Asoka directed that banyan trees and shelters be placed along the road to provide shade and rest for weary travelers. He sent Buddhist missionaries throughout India and ordered the erection of stone pillars with official edicts and Buddhist inscriptions to instruct people in the proper way (see Map 2.2). According to tradition, his son converted the island of Sri Lanka to Buddhism, and the peoples there accepted a tributary relationship with the Mauryan Empire.

THE VOICES OF SILENCE

M ost of what is known about the lives of women in ancient India comes from the Vedas or other texts written by men. Classical Sanskrit was the exclusive property of upper-caste males for use in religious and court functions. There are a few examples of women's writings that date from this period. In the first poem quoted here, a Buddhist nun living in the sixth century B.C.E. reflects on her sense of spiritual salvation and physical release from the drudgery of daily life. The other two poems were produced several hundred years later in southern India by anonymous female authors at a time when strict Hindu traditions had not yet been established in the area. Poetry and song were an essential part of daily life, as women sang while working in the fields, drawing water at the well, or reflecting on the hardships of their daily lives. The second poem quoted here breathes the sensuous joy of sex, while the third expresses the simultaneous grief and pride of a mother as she sends her only son off to war.

"A WOMAN WELL SET FREE! HOW FREE I AM"

A woman well set free! How free I am,
How wonderfully free, from kitchen drudgery.
Free from the harsh grip of hunger,
And from empty cooking pots,
Free too of that unscrupulous man,
The weaver of sunshades.
Calm now, and serene I am,
All lust and hatred purged.
To the shade of the spreading trees I go
And contemplate my happiness.

Translated by Uma Chakravarti and Kumkum Roy

"WHAT SHE SAID TO HER GIRLFRIEND"

What she said to her girlfriend:
On beaches washed by seas
older than the earth,
in the groves filled with bird-cries,
on the banks shaded by a punnai
clustered with flowers,
    when we made love
my eyes saw him
and my ears heard him;

my arms grow beautiful
in the coupling
and grow lean
as they come away.
    What shall I make of this?

Translated by A. K. Ramanujan

"HER PURPOSE IS FRIGHTENING, HER SPIRIT CRUEL"

Her purpose is frightening, her spirit cruel.
That she comes from an ancient house is fitting, surely.
In the battle the day before yesterday,
her father attacked an elephant and died there on the field.
In the battle yesterday,
her husband faced a row of troops and fell.
And today,
she hears the battle drum,
and, eager beyond reason, gives him a spear in his hand,
wraps a white garment around him,
smears his dry tuft with oil,
and, having nothing but her one son,
"Go!" she says, sending him to battle.

Translated by George L. Hart III

THE RULE OF THE FISHES: INDIA AFTER THE MAURYAS

After Asoka's death in 232 B.C.E., the Mauryan Empire began to decline. In 183 B.C.E., the last Mauryan ruler was overthrown by one of his military commanders, and India slipped back into disunity. A number of new kingdoms, some of them perhaps influenced by the memory of the Alexandrian conquests, arose along the fringes of the subcontinent in Bactria, known today as Afghanistan. In the first century C.E., Indo-European-speaking peoples fleeing from the nomadic Xiongnu warriors in Central Asia seized power in the area and proclaimed the new Kushan Kingdom (see Chapter 9). For the next two centuries, the Kushanas extended their political sway over northern India as far as the central Ganges valley, while other kingdoms scuffled for predominance elsewhere on the subcontinent. India would not see unity again for another five hundred years.

Several reasons for India's failure to maintain a unified empire have been proposed. Some historians suggest that a decline in regional trade during the first millennium C.E. may have contributed to the growth of small land-based kingdoms, which drew their primary income from agriculture. The tenacity of the Aryan tradition with its emphasis on tribal rivalries may also have contributed. Although the Mauryan rulers tried to impose a more centralized organization, clan loyalties once again came to the fore after the collapse of the Mauryan dynasty. Furthermore, the behavior of the ruling class was characterized by what Indians call the "rule of the fishes," which glorified warfare as the natural activity of the king and the aristocracy. The *Arthasastra*, which set forth a model of a centralized Indian state, assumed that war was the "sport of kings."

THE EXUBERANT WORLD OF INDIAN CULTURE

Few cultures in the world are as rich and varied as that of India. Most societies excel in some forms of artistic and literary achievement and not in others, but India has produced great works in almost all fields of cultural endeavor—art and sculpture, science, architecture, literature, and music.

Literature

The earliest known Indian literature consists of the four Vedas, which were passed down orally from generation to generation until they were finally written down after the Aryan conquest of India. The Rigveda dates from the second millennium B.C.E. and consists of over a thousand hymns that were used at religious ceremonies. The other three Vedas were written considerably later and contain instructions for performing ritual sacrifices and other ceremonies. The Brahmanas and the Upanishads served as commentaries on the Vedas.

The language of the Vedas was Sanskrit, one of the Indo-European family of languages. After the Aryan conquest of India, Sanskrit gradually declined as a spoken language and was replaced in northern India by a simpler tongue known as Prakrit. Nevertheless, Sanskrit continued to be used as the language of the bureaucracy and literary expression for many centuries after that and, like Latin in medieval Europe, served as a common language of communication (*lingua franca*) between various regions of India. In the south, a variety of Dravidian languages continued to be spoken.

As early as the fifth century B.C.E., Indian grammarians had already codified Sanskrit in order to preserve the authenticity of the Vedas for the spiritual edification of future generations. A famous grammar written by the scholar Panini in the fourth century B.C.E. set forth four thousand grammatical rules prescribing the correct usage of the spoken and written language. This achievement is particularly impressive in that Europe did not have a science of linguistics until the nineteenth century, when it was developed partly as a result of the discovery of the works of Panini and later Indian linguists.

After the development of a writing system sometime in the first millennium B.C.E., India's holy literature was probably inscribed on palm leaves stitched together into a book somewhat similar to the bamboo strips used during the

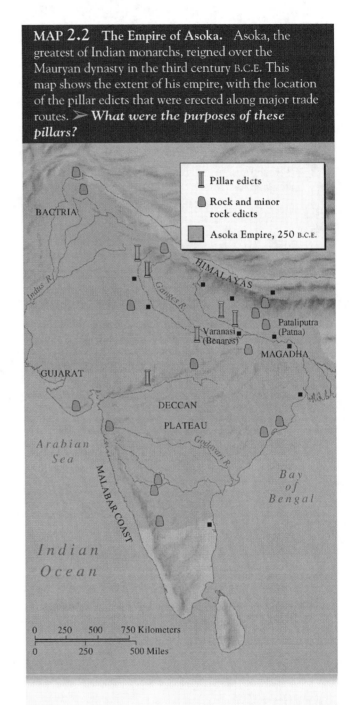

MAP 2.2 **The Empire of Asoka.** Asoka, the greatest of Indian monarchs, reigned over the Mauryan dynasty in the third century B.C.E. This map shows the extent of his empire, with the location of the pillar edicts that were erected along major trade routes. ➤ *What were the purposes of these pillars?*

Pillar edicts

Rock and minor rock edicts

Asoka Empire, 250 B.C.E.

BACTRIA

Indus R.

Ganges R.

HIMALAYAS

Varanasi (Benares)

Pataliputra (Patna)

MAGADHA

GUJARAT

DECCAN PLATEAU

Arabian Sea

Godavari R.

MALABAR COAST

Bay of Bengal

Indian Ocean

0   250   500   750 Kilometers

0   250   500 Miles

same period in China. Also written for the first time were India's great historical epics, the Mahabharata and the Ramayana. Both of these epics may have originally been recited at religious ceremonies, but they are essentially historical writings that recount the martial exploits of great Aryan rulers and warriors.

The Mahabharata, consisting of more than 90,000 stanzas, was probably written about 100 B.C.E. and describes in great detail a war between cousins for control of the kingdom about 1000 B.C.E. Interwoven in the narrative are many fantastic legends of the Hindu gods. Above all, the Mahabharata is a tale of moral confrontations and an elucidation of the ethical precepts of the *dharma* (see the box

DRAUPADI'S HUMILIATION

In the Mahabharata, the great Indian epic, Draupadi, wife of the five Pandava brothers, is humiliated by both her husbands and their enemies. One of her husbands insults her by betting and losing her in a dice game to their rival cousins, who in turn demand that Draupadi be summoned immediately to be disrobed in public. Furious, she arrives with her hair unbraided, a sign that she is undergoing her monthly cycle. During such periods women were segregated from men to safeguard the latter from menstrual pollution.

Humiliated, Draupadi implores Lord Krishna for assistance in reinstating her honor. As one of the cousins attempts to unravel her sari, all are amazed at the never-ending folds of her garment. Although the disrobing is foiled, Draupadi's humiliation is complete. She vows revenge, refusing to rebraid her hair until it is bathed in the blood of the cousin. The famous scene has remained a favorite and occurs at a pivotal climax of the epic.

THE MAHABHARATA

Then how was it that a woman like me, wife to the Parthas, friend to you, Lord Krishna, sister of Dhristadyumna, came to be dragged into the hall? Subjected to the law of women, stained with blood, shuddering in my sole piece of clothing, I was grievously dragged into the assembly of the Kurus. In the midst of the kings, inside the hall, overrun by my menses, they watched me, the Dhartarastras [the sons of Dhrtarashtra], and burst out laughing, the foul-minded! ... Am I not ... [Draupadi], by Law the daughter-in-law of Bhisma and Dhrtarashtra? And I was forcibly reduced to a slave!

---

above). The most famous section of the book is the so-called Bhagavadgita, a sermon by the legendary Indian figure Krishna on the eve of a major battle. In this sermon, mentioned at the beginning of this chapter, Krishna sets forth one of the key ethical maxims of Indian society: in taking action, one must be indifferent to success or failure and consider only the moral rightness of the act itself.

The Ramayana, written at about the same time, is much shorter than the Mahabharata. It is an account of a semi-legendary ruler named Rama who, as the result of a palace intrigue, is banished from the kingdom and forced to live as a hermit in the forest. Later, he fights the demon-king of Sri Lanka (Ceylon), who has kidnapped his beloved wife, Sita. Like the Mahabharata, the Ramayana is strongly imbued with religious and moral significance. Rama himself is portrayed as the ideal Aryan hero, a perfect ruler and an ideal son, while Sita projects the supreme duty of female chastity and wifely loyalty to her husband. The Ramayana is a story of the triumph of good over evil, duty over self-indulgence, and generosity over selfishness. It combines filial and erotic love, conflicts of human passion, character analysis, and poetic descriptions of nature (see the box on p. 55).

The Ramayana also has all the ingredients of an enthralling adventure: giants, wondrous flying chariots, invincible arrows and swords, and magic potions and mantras. One of the real heroes of the story is the monkey-king Hanuman, who flies from India to Sri Lanka to set the great battle in motion. It is no wonder that for millennia the Ramayana has remained a favorite among Indians of all age groups, including a hugely popular TV version produced in recent years.

Architecture and Sculpture

After literature, the greatest achievements of early Indian civilization were in architecture and sculpture. Some of the earliest examples of Indian architecture stem from the time of Emperor Asoka, when Buddhism became the religion of the state. Until the time of the Mauryas, Aryan buildings had been constructed of wood. With the rise of the empire, stone began to be used as artisans arrived in India seeking employment after the destruction of the Per-

ASOKA'S PILLAR. Stone pillars like this polished sandstone column, which is 32 feet high, were erected during the reign of Emperor Asoka in the third century B.C.E. Commemorating events in the life of the Buddha, announcing official edicts, or marking routes to the holy sites, they were placed on major trunk roads throughout the Indian subcontinent. The massive size of these pillars, some of which weighed up to 50 tons, underscores the engineering skills of the peoples of ancient India.

RAMA AND SITA

*O*ver the ages, the conclusion of the Indian epic, the Ramayana, has been the focus of considerable debate. After a long period of captivity at the hands of the demon Ravana, Sita is finally liberated by her husband, King Rama. Although the two enjoy a joyful reunion, the people of Rama's kingdom continue to voice suspicions that she has been defiled by her captor, and he is forced to banish her to a forest, where she gives birth to twin sons. The account reflects the tradition, expressed in the Arthasastra, that a king must place the needs of his subjects over his personal desires. Here we read of Rama's anguished decision as he consults with his brother, Lakshmana.

By accepting banishment, Sita bows to the authority of her husband and the established moral order. Subservient and long-suffering, she has been lauded as the ideal heroine and feminine role model, imitated by generations of Indian women. At the close of the Ramayana, Rama decides to take Sita back "before all my people." She continues to feel humiliated, however, and begs Mother Earth to open up and swallow her.

THE RAMAYANA

"A king must be blameless."

"Such words pierce my heart," said Lakshmana. "Fire himself proved her innocent. She is fired gold, poured into golden fire!"

Rama said, "Lakshmana, consider what is a king. Kings cannot afford blame. Ill fame is evil to kings; they above all men must be beyond reproach. . . . See into what a chasm of sorrow a King may fall. . . ."

Lakshmana said, "Gradually everything seems to change again, and even an Emperor must pay his way through life."

Rama faced his brother. "It must be! It's all the same, can't you see? Where there is growth there is decay; where there is prosperity there is ruin; and where there is birth there is death."

Lakshmana sighed hopelessly. "Well, what will you do?"

"Sita expects to go to the forests tomorrow. Let Sumantra the Charioteer drive you both there, and when you arrive by the river Ganga abandon her."

"She will die. Your child will die!"

"No," said Rama. "I command you! Not a word to anyone."

Lakshmana said, "Surely a king is remote and lonely, and very far from reason. We cannot speak to you. . . ."

Rama said, "Each person can be told what he will understand of the nature of the world, and no more than that—for the rest, take my word." . . .

Sita was forever beautiful. Wearing her ornaments she turned slowly around and looked at every person there. "Rama, let me prove my innocence, here before everyone."

"I give my permission," said Rama.

Then Sita stepped a little away from him and said, "Mother Earth, if I have been faithful to Rama take me home, hide me!"

Earth rolled and moved beneath our feet. With a great rumbling noise the ground broke apart near Sita and a deep chasm opened, lighted from below with bright lights like lightning flashes, from the castles of the Naga serpent kings. . . .

On that throne sat Mother Earth. Earth was not old, she was fair to look on, she was not sad but smiling. She wore flowers and a girdle of seas. Earth supports all life, but she feels no burden in all that. She is patient. She was patient then, under the Sun and Moon and through the rainfalls of countless years. She was patient with seasons and with kings and farmers; she endured all things and bore no line of care from it.

But this was the end of her long patience with Rama. Earth looked at her husband Janaka and smiled. Then she stretched out her arms and took her only child Sita on her lap. She folded her beautiful arms around her daughter and laid Sita's head softly against her shoulder as a mother would. Earth stroked her hair with her fair hands, and Sita closed her eyes like a little girl.

The throne sank back underground and they all were gone; the Nagas dove beneath the ground and the crevice closed gently over them, forever.

---

sian Empire by Alexander. Many of these stone carvers accepted the patronage of Emperor Asoka, who used them to spread Buddhist ideas throughout the subcontinent.

There were three main types of religious structure: the pillar, the stupa, and the rock chamber. During Asoka's reign, many stone columns were erected alongside roads to commemorate the events in the Buddha's life and mark pilgrim routes to holy places. Weighing up to 50 tons each and rising as high as 32 feet, these polished sandstone pillars were topped with a carved capital, usually depicting lions uttering the Buddha's message. Ten remain standing today.

A stupa was originally meant to house a relic of the Buddha, such as a lock of his hair or a branch of the famous Bodhi tree, and was constructed in the form of a burial mound (the pyramids in Egypt also derived from burial mounds). Eventually, the stupa became a place for devotion and the most familiar form of Buddhist architecture. It rose to considerable heights and was surmounted with a spire, possibly representing the stages of existence en route to Nirvana. According to legend, Asoka ordered the construction of 84,000 stupas throughout India to promote the Buddha's message. A few survive today, including the famous stupa at Sanchi, begun under Asoka and completed two centuries later.

The final form of early Indian architecture is the rock chamber carved out of a cliff on the side of a mountain.

THE BIRTH OF THE BUDDHA.   As Buddhism evolved, transforming Gautama Buddha from mortal to god, so did Buddhist art change as well. The representation of the Buddha in statuary and in relief panels began to illustrate the story of his life. Reflecting the multicultural influences on the Kushan dynasty, local artists blended Indian with Hellenistic and Central Asian traditions in what is known as the Gandharan style. Here the infant Siddhartha Gautama is seen emerging from his mother's hip, welcomed by the Hindu gods Indra and Brahma. Notice that his mother, Queen Maya, dressed in Greek-style draperies and with wreathed hair, appears in the form of a traditional earth spirit standing under a tree. At this time, both Buddhism and Christianity adopted the halo from earlier traditions as a sign of divinity.

Asoka began the construction of these chambers to provide rooms to house monks or wandering ascetics and to serve as halls for religious ceremonies. The chambers were rectangular in form, with pillars, an altar, and a vault, reminiscent of Roman basilicas in the West. The three most famous chambers of this period are at Bhaja, Karli, and Ajanta; this last one contains twenty-nine rooms.

All three forms of architecture were embellished with decorations. Consisting of detailed reliefs and freestanding statues of deities, other human figures, and animals, these decorations are permeated with a sense of nature and the vitality of life. Many reflect an amalgamation of popular and sacred themes, of Buddhist, Vedic, and pre-Aryan religious motifs, such as male and female earth spirits. Until the second century C.E., Siddhartha Gautama was represented only through symbols, such as the wheel of life, the Bodhi tree, and the footprint, perhaps because artists felt that it was impossible to render a visual impression of the Buddha in the state of Nirvana. After the spread of Mahayana Buddhism in the second century, when the Buddha was portrayed as a god, his image began to appear in stone.

By this time, India had established its own unique religious art. The art is permeated by sensuousness and exuberance and is often overtly sexual. These scenes are meant to express otherworldly delights, not the pleasures of this world. The sensuous paradise that adorned the religious art of ancient India represented salvation and fulfillment for the ordinary Indian.

Science

Our knowledge of Indian science is limited by the paucity of written sources, but it is evident that ancient Indians had amassed an impressive amount of scientific knowledge in a number of areas. Especially notable was their work in astronomy, where they charted the movements of the heavenly bodies and recognized the spherical nature of the earth at an early date. Their ideas of physics were similar to those of the Greeks; matter was divided into the five

© Robert Harding Picture Library

⇜ SANCHI GATE AND STUPA.   First constructed during the reign of Emperor Asoka in the third century B.C.E., the stupa at Sanchi was enlarged over time, eventually becoming the greatest Buddhist monument in the entire Indian subcontinent. Originally intended to house a relic of the Buddha, the stupa became a holy place for devotion and a familiar form of Buddhist architecture. Sanchi's four elaborately carved stone gates, each over 40 feet high, display exciting statues of Buddhist symbolism, including both animals and human figures.

Courtesy William J. Duiker

⇜ A BUDDHIST CHAPEL.   Carved out of solid rock cliffs during the Mauryan dynasty, these rock chambers served as small meditation halls for traveling Buddhist monks. Initially, they resembled freestanding shrines of wood and thatch from the Vedic period. Subsequently, chapels such as this fifth-century one at Ajanta evolved into elaborate structures reminiscent of Roman basilicas in the West. Witness the ornate columns, the ribbed vault, and the statue of the Buddha incorporated into the stupa.

elements of earth, air, fire, water, and ether. Many of their technological achievements are impressive, notably the quality of their textiles and the massive stone pillars erected during the reign of Asoka. The pillars weighed up to 50 tons each and were transported many miles to their final destination.

CONCLUSION

While the peoples of North Africa and the Middle East were actively building the first civilizations, a similar process was getting under way in the Indus River valley. Much has been learned about the nature of the Indus valley civilization in recent years, but without written records there are inherent limits to our understanding. How did the Harappan people deal with the fundamental human problems mentioned at the close of Chapter 1? The answers remain tantalizingly elusive.

As often happened elsewhere, however, the collapse of Harappan civilization did not lead to the total disappearance of its culture. The new society that eventually emerged throughout the subcontinent after the coming of the Aryans was clearly an amalgam of two highly distinctive cultures, Aryan and Dravidian, each of which made a significant contribution to the politics, the social institutions, and the creative impulse of ancient Indian civilization.

With the rise of the Mauryan dynasty in the fourth century B.C.E., the distinctive features of a great civilization begin to be clearly visible. It was extensive in its scope, embracing the entire Indian subcontinent and

© Royal Smeets Offset, Weert

⋙ THE IDEAL BUDDHIST COUPLE.   Although originally the Aryans, a pastoral people, espoused a patriarchal religion peopled with male deities preoccupied with conquest and war, after their arrival in India they gradually incorporated female fertility spirits inherited from the local agrarian societies into their pantheon. This stylized couple, who welcome the faithful to the Buddhist rock temple at Karli, symbolize the essence of human life, at harmony with both the temporal and spiritual worlds. This sculpture dates from the first century C.E.

eventually, in the form of Buddhism and Hinduism, spreading to China and Southeast Asia. But the underlying ethnic, linguistic, and cultural diversity of the Indian people posed a constant challenge to the unity of the state. After the collapse of the Mauryas, the subcontinent would not come under a single authority again for several hundred years.

In the meantime, another great experiment was taking place far to the northeast, across the Himalaya Mountains. Like many other civilizations of antiquity, the first Chinese state was concentrated on a major river system. And like them, too, its political and cultural achievements eventually spread far beyond their original habitat. In the next chapter, we turn to the civilization of ancient China.

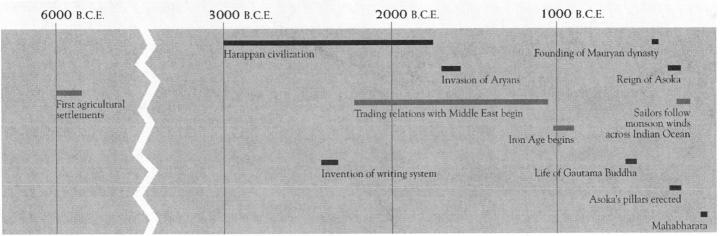

6000 B.C.E.	3000 B.C.E.	2000 B.C.E.	1000 B.C.E.

Harappan civilization

Invasion of Aryans

Founding of Mauryan dynasty

Reign of Asoka

First agricultural settlements

Trading relations with Middle East begin

Sailors follow monsoon winds across Indian Ocean

Iron Age begins

Invention of writing system

Life of Gautama Buddha

Asoka's pillars erected

Mahabharata

CHAPTER NOTES

1. Quoted in Richard Lannoy, *The Speaking Tree: A Study of Indian Culture and Society* (London, 1971), p. 318.
2. The quotation is from ibid., p. 319. Note also that the *Law of Manu* says that "punishment alone governs all created beings. . . . The whole world is kept in order by punishment, for a guiltless man is hard to find."
3. Strabo's *Geography*, book 15, quoted in Michael Edwardes, *A History of India: From the Earliest Times to the Present Day* (London, 1961), p. 55.
4. Ibid., p. 54.
5. From the *Law of Manu,* quoted in A. L. Basham, *The Wonder That Was India* (London, 1961), pp. 180–181.
6. Mundaka Upanishad 1:2, quoted in William Theodore de Bary et al., eds., *Sources of Indian Tradition* (New York, 1966), pp. 28–29.
7. Quoted in Ananda K. Coomaraswamy, *Buddha and the Gospel of Buddhism* (New York, 1964), p. 34.

SUGGESTED READING

Several standard histories of India provide a good overview of the ancient period. One of the most readable and reliable is S. Wolpert, *New History of India*, 3d ed. (New York, 1989). V. A. Smith's edition of *The Oxford History of India*, 4th ed. (Oxford, 1981), although somewhat out of date, contains a wealth of information on various aspects of early Indian history. Also of note is H. H. Dodwell, ed., *The Cambridge History of India*, 6 vols. (Cambridge, 1922–1953).

By far the most informative and readable narrative on the history of India in premodern times is still A. L. Basham, *The Wonder That Was India* (London, 1961), which contains informative sections on prehistory, economy, language, art and literature, society, and everyday life. Also useful is A. L. Basham, ed., *A Cultural History of India* (Oxford, 1975). For a stimulating analysis of Indian culture and society in general, consult R. Lannoy, *The Speaking Tree: A Study of Indian Culture and Society* (London, 1971). R. Thapar, *Interpreting Early India* (Delhi, 1992), provides a recent view by an Indian historian.

Because of the relative paucity of archaeological exploration in South Asia, evidence for the Harappan period is not as voluminous as for areas such as Mesopotamia and the Nile valley. Some of the best work has been written by scholars who actually worked at the sites. For a recent account, see J. M. Kenoyer, *Ancient Cities of the Indus Valley Civilization* (Karachi, 1998). A somewhat more extensive study is B. Allchin and R. Allchin, *The Birth of Indian Civilization, India and Pakistan Before 500 B.C.* (New York, 1968). For a detailed and well-illustrated analysis, see G. L. Possehl, ed., *The Harappan Civilization: A Contemporary Perspective* (Amherst, N.Y., 1983). Commercial relations between Harappa and its neighbors are treated in S. Ratnagar, *Encounters: The Westerly Trade of the Harappan Civilization* (Oxford, 1981). On the Mauryan period, see D. D. Kosambi, *The Culture and Civilization of Ancient India* (London, 1965), and R. Thapar, *Asoka and the Decline of the Mauryas* (Oxford, 1961).

There are a number of good books on the introduction of Buddhism into Indian society. Buddha's ideals are presented in A. K. Coomaraswamy, *Buddha and the Gospel of Buddhism* (London, 1916; rev. ed., New York, 1964), and E. Conze, *Buddhism: Its Essence and Development* (Oxford, 1951). Also see H. Nakamura and M. B. Dasgupta, *Indian Buddhism: A Survey with Bibliographical Notes* (New Delhi, 1987). H. Akira, *A History of Indian Buddhism: From Sakyamuni to Early Mahayana* (Honolulu, 1990), provides a detailed analysis of early activities by Siddhartha Gautama and his followers. The intimate relationship between Buddhism and commerce is discussed in Liu Hsin-ju, *Ancient India and Ancient China: Trades and Religious Exchanges* (Oxford, 1988).

Hinduism, its origins and development, is the subject of B. Walker, *Hindu World*, 2 vols. (London, 1969). For a more general treatment, see S. N. Dasgupta, *A History of Indian Philosophy*, 5 vols. (Cambridge, 1922–1955), and S. Radhakrishnan, *Indian Philosophy*, rev. ed., 2 vols. (London, 1958).

There are a number of excellent surveys of Indian art, including the comprehensive S. L. Huntington, *The Art of Ancient India: Buddhist, Hindu, Jain* (New York, 1985), and the concise *Indian Art* (London, 1976) by R. Craven. See also V. Dehejia's *Devi: The Great Goddess* (Washington, D.C., 1999) and *Indian Art* (London, 1997).

Few general surveys of Indian literature exist, perhaps because of the magnitude and diversity of India's literature. A good textbook for college students is E. C. Dimock, *The Literatures of India: An Introduction* (Chicago, 1974), which traces Indian literary achievement from the epics to the modern Hindi film.

Many editions of Sanskrit literature are available in English translation. Many are available in the multivolume *Harvard Oriental Series*. For a shorter annotated anthology of selections from the Indian classics, consult S. N. Hay, ed., *Sources of Indian Tradition*, 2 vols. (New York, 1988), or J. B. Alphonso-Karkala, *An Anthology of Indian Literature*, 2d rev. ed. (New Delhi, 1987), put out by the Indian Council for Cultural Relations.

The Mahabharata and Ramayana have been rewritten for 2,500 years. Fortunately, the vibrant versions, retold by William Buck and condensed to 400 pages each, reproduce the spirit of the originals and enthrall today's imagination. See W. Buck, *Mahabharata* (Berkeley, Calif., 1973) and *Ramayana* (Berkeley, Calif., 1976). On the role played by women writers in ancient India, see S. Tharu and K. Lalita, eds., *Women Writing in India: 600 B.C. to the Present*, vol. 1 (New York, 1991).

 # INFOTRAC COLLEGE EDITION

For additional reading, go to InfoTrac College Edition, your online research library at http://web1.infotrac-college.com

Enter the search term "Vedas" using Keywords.

Enter the search term "Hinduism" using the Subject Guide.

Enter the search term "Buddhism" using the Subject Guide.

Enter the search terms "India history" using Keywords.

Enter the search terms "Upanishad or Rigveda or Mahabharata" using Keywords.

WRITINGS ON HINDUISM

1
......

THE HYMNS OF THE RIG-VEDA

The hymns of the Rig-Veda are the first known works of literature of the Indian I subcontinent. They are the oldest part of the sacred literature of the Aryans, an Indo-European people who invaded and conquered northwestern India between 2000 and 1500 B.C. In the subsequent centuries, they penetrated farther into the interior of the subcontinent, reaching its eastern edge by 500 B.C. Their religious literature evolved into a vast body of literary compositions collectively known as the Veda. With changing conditions and the mingling of Aryans with indigenous people, the Aryan religion itself changed, and by the centuries just before the beginning of the Christian era, it had developed into Hinduism, which has since remained the majority religion of India.

Aryans believed that the Veda was holy literature. Hindus, too, consider it to be their most sacred scripture. In Sanskrit, the language of the Veda, the word veda means "knowledge." Hindus believe, as did the Aryans, that the Veda is eternal and contains divine knowledge revealed to ancient seer-poets who delivered it through their inspired utterances. These utterances were preserved in memory and transmitted orally from generation to generation for centuries, with close attention to accuracy of content and pronunciation, before they came to be written down. The Veda actually consists of four individual collections, each also called a Veda. These are the Rig-Veda, the Yajur-Veda, the Sam-Veda, and the Atharva-Veda. Each of these four Vedas has two distinct parts: the first, from an earlier time, is a collection of hymns called the Samhita, and the second is a series of texts on ritual and metaphysics. The Samhita of the Rig-Veda is the oldest of the four Samhitas. It is a product of the Aryan experience, from the time when they were still in their original home in West Central Asia until the early centuries of their settlement in India. Amidst predominantly Indian material it still contains strong memories of a primitive Indo-European past. While the later Vedic literature reflects considerable mixing of the Aryan and the non-Aryan cultures, the hymns of the Rig-Veda are almost entirely Aryan. They are also the most mytho-poetic part of the Veda. It is these qualities, the poetry as well as the antiq-

uity of the Rig-Vedic hymns, that endow the Rig-Veda, and indeed the Veda as a whole, with their profound significance. As observed by Max Muller, the famous nineteenth-century translator of ancient Indian literature: "The Veda has a twofold interest: it belongs to the history of the world and to the history of India. . . . As long as man continues to take an interest in the history of his race, and as long as we collect in libraries and museums the relics of former ages, the first place in that long row of books which contains the records of the Aryan branch of mankind will belong forever to the Rig-Veda" One should add that, within the Rig-Veda, that first place belongs to its hymns.

As we see them in the Rig-Vedic hymns, the Aryans were cow-herding nomads. Perhaps the main reason for their movement away from their original home and the eventual invasion of India was a search for new pastures. As cattle-herders, they had little use for the towns and cities of the pre AryanIndus Valley civilization. Instead, the Aryans lived in the open country in make-

shift dwellings, moving from place to place according to their needs for good grazing grounds. Not much advanced in the arts of civilization, the Aryans were, however, strongly equipped for fighting. They were physically large and stalwart and aggressive in character. They knew how to make bronze and fashion weaponsftom it. They also built fast light-wheeled chariots pulled by horses. The Aryans probably introduced the horse to India.

Sociologically, the Aryans were a tribal people held together by ties of blood and kinship, their loyalty, during their early career in India, limited to their respective tribes and to their race. They distinguished themselves from the non-Aryan Indians as people ofa superior varna ("color'). In fact, they called themselves arya, a Sanskrit word meaning "noble." Their social and political organization was rudimentary. Although there was division of function among its members as needed on occasion, all members of a tribe were fundamentally equal and there were no strict class distinctions. By and large, all men were cattle-herders in times of peace, and all were soldiers in times of war. Priestly functions were entrusted to those who were considered able to perform them best, rather than because ofa permanent class distinction. We learn about all these and other features of Aryan life from the Rig-Vedic hymns.

Naturally, the hymns tell more about the religion of the Aryans than about any other aspect of their culture. The Aryan religion centered on their belief in numerous gods whom they worshiped with a rite called the yajna ("sacrifice'), which involved offering of food and drink to the gods, with recitations of selected hymns, often in the presence of fire. The more important yajnas included on-site ritual slaughter and cooking of animals offered to the gods along with libations of soma, an exhilarating drink made from the freshly pressed juice ofa plant whose name is not known. After the ritual oblations, the worshipers themselves consumed the food and drink, believing that the gods had descended among them to partake of their offerings and rejoice with them in the blessings of life.

As would be the case with any culture, the gods of the Aryans are personifications of important facets of their experience. Since the Aryans lived amidst nature and depended for their survival on uncontrolled nature, their gods represented these natural forces. Nature also combined with significant and memorable activities in their lives, such as war, in shaping the attributes of their gods.

The Rig-Veda contains more than a thousand hymns. They are arranged in ten mandalas ("circles" or "books"), each of these books, according to tradition, ascribed to one seer-poet or a family, or school, of seer-poets. Within each book, the hymns generally are arranged according to the deities to whom they are addressed. Hymns to Agni, the god of fire, generally come first; those to Indra, the god of rain and war, come next; and after them, the hymns to other gods and deified objects follow. One book, the ninth, is almost entirely devoted to the god Soma. The following selection provides a small sampling of hymns about four major deities—Indra, Agni, Soma, and Varuna—and a minor one, Ushas.

Since Indra is the most popular god in the Rig-Veda, we shall read the hymns dedicated to him first. The Rig-Veda has more hymns about him than about any other god. The Aryans found him to be a most convivial and congenial deity. He epitomizes their interests and character perfectly. He is, above all, a warrior god heroically defeating his enemies as Aryans wanted to defeat the non Aryans. He loves to drink and goes into battle drunk with soma and followed by his army of celestial soldiers, maruts, also drunk. In a very large number of hymns, he fights against and cuts down into pieces a dragon named Vritra. This dragon represents the leadership of the native Indians against whom the Aryans had to fight to conquer India. Indra's weapon is vajra, the thunderbolt, which shows his Indo-European connection with the Greek god Zeus.

The thunderbolt is also an essential part of Indra's identity as a nature god, the god of rain. By dismembering the dragon in his battle against Vritra, he brings out the sun (which symbolizes freeing of nature) and, more importantly, he frees the waters, which means that Indra brings rain. The dragon stands for the thick, black clouds blocking the sun and holding the rain as a prisoner. Furthermore, Indra's battle against the dragon also depicts—in the form of myth—a collision between two diametrically opposed cultures: the nomadic culture of the Aryans and the pre Aryanagrarian and settled culture of India. In some of the Rig-Vedic hymns, the dragon is shown lying on a mountain slope, blocking the river waters. The dragon seems to personify the low clams that the pre-Aryans built on mountain slopes to flood the plains on either side of the rivers in order to irrigate their fields and to fertilize them with the silt from the rivers. Such use of water, however, did not suit the Aryans; creating large expanses of wetland destroyed pastures and impeded the mobility so essential to their military and political expansion. The destruction of the dragon means the destruction of the very economic basis of the pre-Aryan culture.

Second to Indra in the number of hymns devoted to him, Agni (etymologically from the same root as "ignite), the god of fire, is actually the most important Aryan god. He is considered the priest of gods and the god of priests. As the god of

fire, he especially personifies the sacrificial fire. All important sacrifices are made in his presence or, rather, through him. He is the carrier of sacrifices to the gods and a messenger between mortals and immortals. The hymns often describe Agni as one who goes in front. This shows his high place among the gods. It also has a literal meaning, because in their eastward expansion, the Aryans burned forests before them in order to advance. As fire was considered the purest and the most purifying element, Agni was the very embodiment of purity. He had three forms: earthly as fire, atmospheric as lightning, and heavenly as the sun. For every sacrificial ritual, he had to be brought out anew by friction, with a wooden drill. He is, therefore, called the child of sticks. But he also can be born of stone, by the striking of one stone against another. Agni is, in fact, energy that resides not only in wood and forests, and in stones, rocks, and mountains, but in everything. This concept of Agni as dwelling in all things is of great significance in the evolution of Indian religious philosophy.

The god Soma is deified soma juice. His role in the pantheon parallels that of Agni in some ways. Along with Agni, he is present at important sacrifices in the form of libations of soma. He also acts as a mediator between humans and gods, bringing them even closer together than does Agni. For not only do gods come down to quaff soma with the mortals, the latter—partaking of the drink themselves—become godlike during the ritual. They believe that, in the drink they imbibe, it is Soma who enters their being and transforms mere humans into himself It is easy to see that this belief in communion with divinity, has a basis in the actual consciousness-altering property of the substance that is soma. As a concept, Soma, like Agni, has important implications for the future evolution of Indian religious thought, where the human self is seen as essentially divine in nature and capable of uniting with the eternal and divine reality underlying all existence. In firm, Soma remains closer to the liquid he personifies and is, on the whole, less of a personal being than the other main gods of the Aryans.

Older in name—because his name is connected with the Greek god of the sky, Uranus—Varuna appears in the history of Aryan religion later than Agni and Indra. His emergence reflects the stage in Indian history when the Aryans had begun to mingle with the non Aryans, and the social and moral values based on the natural ties of blood and kinship no longer sufficed for individual and social well-being. A diversifying society needed more deliberatively formulated rules of conduct and morality for its maintenance and stability. Varuna is the guardian of right conduct and moral law. He particularly watches over the keeping of contracts, the foundation of social order. He severely punishes those guilty of breach of promise and other kinds of ethical wrongdoing. Instead of material offerings, he expects his worshipers to offer good conduct. So the worshipers approach him trembling with fear. Varuna is also the guardian of rita, an etherlike entity that is supposed to permeate the cosmos and sustain its regular functioning, as the proper circulation of blood sustains the health of a living organism. Varuna thus applies himself to the protection of both the cosmic and the moral order—the two are inseparable from each other. Breach of the moral laws can have a disruptive effect on the cosmic order.

The Aryan gods are mainly male and associated with phenomena in the sky. Prominent among the few female deities is Ushas, goddess of the dawn. Thus, she too is a sky god. In form, she is closer to the phenomenon she represents than to being a personalized deity. Hymns addressed to her give beautiful descriptions of the rising dawn. The Aryans' love of nature and the poetic quality of the verses, both characteristic features of the Rig-Vedic compositions, are here at their best.

Besides the hymns to gods, the following selection also includes a hymn addressed to the sacrificial horse and two hymns about the myths of creation. The hymns of creation provide an interesting contrast to the biblical account of creation found in Genesis (Selection 6). The Rig-Vedic creation myth states that the birth of the world came from the dismemberment of a primeval being, Purusha. The creation hymns, as well as the hymn to the sacrificial horse, exemplify the symbolic power of sacrifice.

INDRA

HYMN 111.31

Wise, teaching, following the thought of order,[1] the sonless gained a grandson from his daughter.[2]

Fain, as a sire, to see his child prolific, he sped to meet her with an eager spirit.

The son left not his portion to the brother, he made a home to hold him who should gain it.

What time his parents[3] gave the priest[4] his being, of the good pair one acted, one promoted.

Agni was born trembling with tongue that flickered, so that the Red's great children[5] should be honored.

1 The cosmic order.

2 The meaning is obscure. Perhaps it is a metaphorical reference to the priest whose function it is to generate the sacrificial fire with a wooden drill, the lower stick of which is considered female (hence daughter) and is producer of fire.

3 The drill made of two sticks (parents) to produce fire by friction.

4 Agni, the god of fire, is considered to be the priest of gods.

5 Rays of the sun.

From *Hymns of the Rig-Veda,* trans. Ralph T. H. Griffith. London, 1889. Reprinted Varanasi (India): Chowkhamba Sanskrit Series Office, 1963. [Hymns 111.31, 32, I.32;1.1, IV.5, 6, X.5, 51; IX.1, 3, 4; 11.28, V.85, VII.87, 89; 1.113; 1.163; X.129; X.90].

Great is their germ, that born of them is mighty, great the bays' lord's approach through sacrifices.[6]

Conquering bands upon the warrior waited: they recognized great light from out the darkness.

The conscious dawns went forth to meet his coming, and the sole master of the kine[7] was Indra.

The sages freed them from their firm-built prison: the seven priests drove them forward with their spirit.

All holy order's pathway they discovered: he,[8] full of knowledge, shared these deeds through worship.

When Sarama[9] had found the mountain's fissure, that vast and ancient place she plundered thoroughly,

In the floods' van she led them forth, light-footed: she who well knew came first unto their lowing.

Longing for friendship came the noblest singer:[10] the hill poured forth its treasure for the pious.

The hero[11] with young followers fought and conquered, and straightway Angiras[12] was singing praises.

Peer of each noble thing, yea, all-excelling, all creatures doth he know, he slayeth Sushna.[13]

Our leader, fain for war, singing from heaven, as friend he saved his lovers from dishonor.

They sat them down with spirit fain for booty, making with hymns a way to life eternal.

And this is still their place of frequent session, whereby they sought to gain the months[14] through order.

Drawing the milk of ancient seed prolific, they joyed as they beheld their own possession.

Their shout of triumph heated earth and heaven. When the kine showed, they bade the heroes rouse them.

Indra drove forth the kine, that Vritra-slayer,[15] while hymns of praise rose up and gifts were offered.

For him the cow, noble and far-extending, poured pleasant juices, bringing oil and sweetness.

---

6 Indra, the horse-driving (bays' lord) warrior and rain god is born of the sun's rays and the kindling of the sacrificial fire.

7 Literally "cows"; or, figuratively, the sun's rays.

8 The priests performing worship.

9 Indra's hound (female). She goes in front of the released cows or waters.

10 The "noblest singer" stands for a group, a famous family of priests, the Angirases.

11 Indra.

12 See footnote 10.

13 The name of an enemy.

14 Monthly festivals.

15 An enemy slain by Indra. Vritra figures frequently, as a demon, dragon, or snake, in the hymns to Indra.

They made a mansion for their father,[16] deftly provided him a great and glorious dwelling;

With firm support parted and stayed the parents,[17] and, sitting, fixed him there erected, mighty.

What time the ample chalice[18] had impelled him, swift waxing, vast, to pierce the earth and heaven,

Him in whom blameless songs are all united: all powers invincible belong to Indra.

I crave thy powers, I crave thy mighty friendship: full many a team[19] goes to the Vritra-slayer.

Great is the land, we seek the prince's favor. Be thou, O Maghavan,[20] our guard and keeper.

He, having found great, splendid, rich dominion, sent life and motion to his friends and lovers.

Indra, who shone together with the heroes, begat the song, the fire, and sun and morning.

Vast, the house-friend, he set the waters flowing, all-lucid, widely spread, that move together.

By the wise cleansings of the meath[21] made holy, through days and nights they speed the swift streams onward.

To thee proceed the dark, the treasure-holders, both of them sanctified by Surya's[22] bounty.

The while thy lovely storming friends, O Indra, fail to attain the measure of thy greatness.

Be lord of joyous songs, O Vritra-slayer, bull dear to all, who gives the power of living.

Come unto us with thine auspicious friendship, hastening, mighty one, with mighty succours.

Like Angiras I honor him with worship; and renovate old song for him the ancient.

Chase thou the many godless evil creatures; and give us, Maghavan, heaven's light to help us.

Far forth are spread the purifying waters: convey thou us across them unto safety.

Save us, our charioteer, from harm, O Indra, soon, very soon, make us win spoil of cattle.

His kine their lord hath shown, even Vritra's slayer: through the black hosts he passed with red attendants.

16 Indra.

17 Heaven and earth.

18 The bowl of soma juice.

19 Hymns, sent forth like teams of horses.

20 Another name for Indra.

21 Soma, the holy drink.

22 Surya is the sun as a god.

Teaching us pleasant things by holy order, to us hath he thrown open all his portals.

Call we on Maghavan, auspicious Indra, best hero in this fight where spoil is gathered.

The strong who listens, who gives aid in battles, who slays the Vritras, wins and gathers riches.

HYMN 111.32

Drink thou this soma, Indra, lord of soma; drink thou the draught of noon-day which thou lovest.

Puffing thy cheeks, impetuous, liberal giver, here loose thy two bay horses and rejoice thee.

Quaff it pure, meal-blent, mixed with milk, O Indra; we have poured forth the soma for thy rapture.

Knit with the prayer-fulfilling band of Maruts,[23] yea, with the Rudras,[24] drink till thou art sated;

Those who gave increase to thy strength and vigor, the Maruts singing forth thy might, O Indra.

Drink thou, O fair of cheek, whose hand wields thunder, with Rudras band-ed, at our noon libation.

They, even the Maruts who were there, excited with song the meathcreated strength of Indra.

By them impelled to act he reached the vitals of Vritra, though he deemed that none might wound him.

Pleased, like a man, with our libation, Indra, drink, for enduring hero might, the soma.

Lord of bays, moved by sacrifice come hither: thou with the swift ones stir-rest floods and waters.

When thou didst loose the streams to run like racers in the swift contest, having smitten Vritra

With flying weapon where he lay, O Indra, and, godless, kept the goddesses encompassed.

With reverence let us worship mighty Indra, great and sublime, eternal, ever-youthful,

Whose greatness the dear world-halves have not measured, no, nor con-ceived the might of him the holy.

Many are Indra's nobly wrought achievements, and none of all the gods transgress his statutes.

He beareth up this earth and heaven, and, doer of marvels, he begat the sun and morning.

HYMN 1.32

23 Indra's celestial soldiers.

24 Gods of the storm.

I will declare the manly deeds of Indra, the first that he achieved, the thunder-wielder.

He slew the dragon, then disclosed the waters, and cleft the channels of the mountain torrents.

He slew the dragon lying on the mountain: his heavenly bolt of thunder Tvashtar[25] fashioned.

Like lowing kine in rapid flow descending the waters glided downward to the ocean.

Impetuous as a bull, he chose the soma, and in three sacred beakers drank the juices.

Maghavan grasped the thunder for his weapon, and smote to death this first-born of the dragons.

When, Indra, thou hadst slain the dragons' first-born, and overcome the charms of the enchanters,[26]

Then, giving life to sun and dawn and heaven, thou foundest not one foe to stand against thee.

Indra, with his own great and deadly thunder smote into pieces Vritra, worst of Vritras.

As trunks of trees, what time the axe hath felled them, low on the earth so lies the prostrate dragon.

He, like a mad weak warrior, challenged Indra, the great impetuous many-slaying hero.

He, brooking not the clashing of the weapons, crushed—Indra's foe—the shattered forts in falling.

Footless and handless still he challenged Indra, who smote him with his bolt between the shoulders.

Emasculate yet claiming manly vigor, thus Vritra lay with scattered limbs dissevered.

There as he lies like a bank-bursting river, the waters taking courage flow above him.

The dragon lies beneath the feet of torrents which Vritra with his greatness had encompassed.

Then humbled was the strength of Vritra's mother: Indra hath cast his deadly bolt against her.

The mother was above, the son was under, and like a cow beside her calf lay Danu.[27]

Rolled in the midst of never-ceasing currents flowing without a rest forever onward,

The waters bear off Vritra's nameless body: the foe of Indra sank to during darkness.

25 The god of the forge and crafts.

26 The enemies of the Aryans, and of Indra, were believed to possess the powers of magic.

27 This reference to Vritra's mother suggests the matriarchal orientation of a pre-Aryan Indian civilization.

Guarded by Ahi[28] stood the thralls of Dasas,[29] the waters stayed like kine
    held by the robber.

But he, when he had smitten Vritra, opened the cave wherein the floods had
    been imprisoned.

A horse's tail[30] wart thou when he, O Indra, smote on thy bolt; thou, God
    without a second,

Thou hast won back the kine, hast won the soma; thou hast let loose to flow
    the seven rivers.

Nothing availed him lightning, nothing thunder, hailstorm or mist which he
    had spread around him:

When Indra and the dragon strove in battle, Maghavan gained the victory
    forever.

Whom rawest thou to avenge the dragon, Indra, that fear possessed thy heart
    when thou hadst slain him;

That, like a hawk affrighted through the regions, thou crossed nine-and-
    ninety flowing rivers?

Indra is king of all that moves and moves not, of creatures tame and horned,
    the thunder-wielder.

Over all living men he rules as sovereign, containing all as spokes within the
    felly.

AGNI

HYMN I.1

I praise Agni, the chosen priest, god, minister of sacrifice, The hotar,[31] lav-
    isher of wealth.

Worthy is Agni to be praised by living as by ancient seers. He shall bring
    hitherward the gods.

Through Agni man obtains wealth, yea, plenty waxing day by day, Most rich
    in heroes, glorious.

Agni, the perfect sacrifice which thou encompassest about Verily goeth to
    the gods.

May Agni, sapient-minded priest, truthful, most gloriously great, The god,
    come hither with the gods.

Whatever blessing, Agni, thou wilt grant unto thy worshiper, That, Angiras,
    is indeed thy truth.

To thee, dispeller of the night, O Agni, day by day with prayer Bringing thee
    reverence, we come;

Ruler of sacrifices, guard of law eternal, radiant one, Increasing in thine own
    abode.

---

28 The cloud-serpent holding water in.

29 A non-Aryan people against whom the Aryans were fighting.

30 To become a "horse's tail" means to disappear fast.

31 The invoking priest, one who calls the gods to enjoy the offerings.

Be to us easy of approach, even as a father to his son: Agni, be with us for our weal.

Hymn W.5

How shall we give with one accord oblation to Agni, to Vaisvanara[32] the bounteous?

Great light, with full high growth hath he uplifted, and, as a pillar bears the roof, sustains it.

Reproach not him who, God and self-reliant, vouchsafed this bounty unto me a mortal,

Deathless, discerner, wise, to me the simple, Vaisvanara most manly, youthful Agni.

Sharp-pointed, powerful, strong, of boundless vigor, Agni who knows the lofty hymn, kept secret

As the lost milch-cow's track, the doubly mighty,—he hath declared to me this hidden knowledge.

May he with sharpened teeth, the bounteous giver, Agni, consume with flame most fiercely glowing

Those who regard not Varuna's[33] commandments and the dear steadfast laws of sapient Mitra.[34]

Like youthful women without brothers, straying, like dames who hate their lords, of evil conduct,

They who are full of sin, untrue, unfaithful, they have engendered this abysmal station.

To me, weak, innocent, thou, luminous Agni, hast boldly given as 'twere a heavy burthen,

This Prishtha[35] hymn, profound and strong and mighty, of seven elements, and with offered dainties.

So may our song that purifies, through wisdom reach in a moment him the universal,

Established on the height, on earth's best station, above the beauteous grassy skin of Prisni.[36]

Of this my speech what shall I utter further? They indicate the milk stored up in secret

When they have thrown as 'twere the cows' stalls open. The bird[37] protects earth's best and well-loved station.

---

32 Common god of all Aryans.

33 Varuna is the god of the natural and the moral order.

34 A god of light.

35 Intended for midday oblations.

36 The earth. Prisni is also the cow whose milk is used in the oblation that Agni, the bull, devours.

37 The sun; it flies through heaven.

This is the great ones'[38] mighty apparition which from of old the radiant
    cow[39] hath followed.

This, shining brightly in the place of order, swift, hasting on in secret, she
    discovered.

He then who shone together with his parents remembered Prisni's fair and
    secret treasure,

Which, in the mother cow's most lofty station, the bull's[40] tongue, of the
    flame bent forward, tasted.

With reverence I declare the law, O Agni; what is, comes by thine order,
    Jatavedas.[41]

Of this, whate'er it be, thou art the sovereign; yea, all the wealth that is in
    earth or heaven.

What is our wealth therefrom, and what our treasure? Tell us, O Jatavedas,
    for thou knowest,

What is our best course in this secret passage: we, unreproached, have
    reached a place far distant.

What is the limit, what the rules, the guerdon? Like fleet-foot coursers speed
    we to the contest.

When will the goddesses, the immortal's spouses, the dawns, spread over us
    the sun-god's splendor?

Unsatisfied, with speech devoid of vigor, scanty and frivolous and inconclu-
    sive,

Wherefore do they address thee here, O Agni? Let these who have no weap-
    ons suffer sorrow.

The majesty of him the good, the mighty, aflame, hath shone for glory in the
    dwelling.

He, clothed in light, hath shone most fair to look on, wealthy in blessings, as
    a home shines with riches.

Hymn IV.6

Priest of our rite, stand up erect, O Agni, in the gods' service best of sacrifi-
    cers,

For over every thought thou art the ruler: thou furtherest e'en the wisdom
    of the pious.

He was set down 'mid men as priest unerring, Agni, wise, welcome in our
    holy synods.

Like Savitar.[42] he hath lifted up his splendor, and like a builder raised his
    smoke to heaven.

The glowing ladle, filled with oil, is lifted: choosing gods' service to the right
    he circles.

---

38   The sun's rays.

39   The dawn.

40   The bull is Agni in the form of the sun.

41   Omniscient Agni.

42   The sun as generator of life.

Eager he rises like the new-wrought pillar which, firmly set and fixed, anoints the victims.

When sacred grass is strewn and Agni kindled, the Adhvaryu[43] rises to his task rejoicing.

Agni the priest, like one who tends the cattle, goes three times round, as from of old he wills it.

Agni himself, the priest, with measured motion, goes round, with sweet speech, cheerful, true to order.

His fulgent flames run forth like vigorous horses: all creatures are affrighted when he blazes.

Beautiful and auspicious is thine aspect, O lovely Agni, terrible when spreading.

Thy splendors are not covered by darkness: detraction leaves no stain upon thy body.

Naught hindered his production, bounteous giver: his mother and his sire[44] were free to send him.

Then as a friend benevolent, refulgent, Agni shone forth in human habitations.

He, Agni, whom the twice-five sisters,[45] dwelling together, in the homes of men engendered,

Bright like a spear's tooth, wakened in the morning, with powerful mouth and like an axe well-sharpened.

These thy bay coursers, Agni, dropping fatness, ruddy vigorous, speeding straightly forward,

And red steeds, wonderful, of mighty muscle, are to this service of the gods invited:

These brightly shining flames of thine, O Agni, that move forever restless, all-subduing,

Like falcons basting eagerly to the quarry, roar loudly like the army of the Maruts.

To thee, O flaming God, hath prayer been offered. Let the priest laud thee: give to him who worships.

Men have established Agni as invoker, fain to adore the glory of the living.

Hymn X.5

He only is the sea, holder of treasures: born many a time he views the hearts within us.

He hides him in the secret couple's bosom. The bird dwells in the middle of the fountain.

Inhabiting one dwelling-place in common, strong stallions and the mares have come together.

---

43 The priest(s) who perform(s) the practical work of sacrifice.

44 Earth and heaven.

45 The priest's ten fingers that produce the fire from the drill.

The sages guard the seat of holy order, and keep the highest names concealed within them.

The holy pair, of wondrous power, have coupled: they formed the infant, they who bred produced him.

The central point of all that moves and moves not, the while they wove the sage's thread with insight.

For tracks of order and refreshing viands attend from ancient times the goodly infant.

Wearing him as a mantle, earth and heaven grow strong by food of pleasant drink and fatness.

He, calling loudly to the seven red sisters,[46] hath, skilled in sweet drink, brought them to be looked on.

He, born of old, in middle air, hath halted, and sought and found the covering robe of Pushan.[47]

Seven are the pathways which the wise have fashioned; to one of these may come the troubled mortal.

He standeth in the dwelling of the highest, a pillar, on sure ground where paths are parted.

Not being, being[48] in the highest heaven, in Aditi's bosom and in Daksha's[49] birthplace,

Is Agni, our first-born of holy order, the milch-cow and the bull in life's beginning.

Hymn X.51

Large was that covering, and firm of texture, folded wherein thou enteredst the waters.[50]

One deity alone, O Jatavedas Agni, saw all thy forms in sundry places. What god bath seen me? Who of all their number clearly beheld my forms in many places?

Where lie, then, all the sacred logs of Agni that lead him godward, Varuna and Mitra?

In many places, Agni Jatavedas, we sought thee hidden in the plants and waters.

Then Yama[51] marked thee, god of wondrous splendor! Effulgent from thy tenfold secret dwelling.

I fled in fear from sacrificial worship, Varuna, lest the gods should thus engage me.

---

46   The tongues of fire.

47   The sun-god as giver of prosperity and protector of travelers.

48   Both the existent and the nonexistent.

49   Aditi and Daksha are wife and husband. The former is infinite nature and the latter the creative power. The meaning here is that Agni is as yet undeveloped embryo and therefore is both male and female.

50   Fearing the fate of his three brothers, who had perished in the service of the gods, Agni once fled and hid himself in the waters. The gods discovered him and persuaded him to return to his sacred duties.

51   The god of the dead.

Thus were my forms laid down in many places. This, as my goal, I Agni saw
> before me.

Come; man is pious and would fain do worship; he waits prepared: in gloom
> thou, Agni, dwellest.

Make pathways leading godward clear and easy, and bear oblations with a
> kindly spirit.

This goal mine elder brothers once selected, as he who drives a car the way
> to travel.

So, Varuna, I fled afar through terror, as flies the wild bull from an archer's
> bowstring.

We give thee life unwasting, Jatavedas, so that, employed, thou never shalt
> be injured.

So, nobly born! shalt thou with kindly spirit bear to the gods their share of
> men's oblations.

Grant me the first oblations and the latter, entire, my forceful share of holy
> presents,

The soul of plants, the fatness of the waters, and let there be long life, ye
> gods, to Agni.

Thine be the first oblations and the latter, entire, thy forceful shares of holy
> presents.

Let all this sacrifice be thine, O Agni, and let the world's four regions bow
> before thee.

SOMA

HYMN IX.1

In sweetest and most gladdening stream flow pure, O Soma, on thy way,
Pressed out for Indra, for his drink.
Fiend-queller, friend of all men, he hath with the wood[52] attained unto
His place, his iron-fashioned home.[53]
Be thou best Vritra-slayer, best granter of bliss, most liberal:
Promote our wealthy princes' gifts.
Flow onward with thy juice unto the banquet of the mighty gods;
Flow hither for our strength and fame.
O Indu,[54] we draw nigh to thee, with this one object day by day:
To thee alone our prayers are said.
By means of this eternal fleece[55] may Surya's daughter[56] purify
Thy soma that is foaming forth.

---

52 Some wooden implement, perhaps a spoon.

53 A metal container for the soma juice.

54 Another name for soma, meaning "the moon," which was believed to contain the celestial nectar that it pours down
through the sieve of heaven.

55 The filter made of wool for filtering soma juice.

56 Faith.

Ten sister maids[57] of slender form seize him within the press and hold
Him firmly on the final day.[58]
The virgins send him forth: they blow the skin musician-like, and fuse
The triple foe-repelling meath.
Inviolable milch-kine round about him blend for Indra's drink,
The fresh young soma with their milk.
In the wild raptures of this draught, Indra slays all the Vritras: he,
The hero, pours his wealth on us.

HYMN IX.3

Here present this immortal god flies, like a bird upon her wings,
To settle in the vats of wood.
This god, made ready with the hymn, runs swiftly through the winding
      ways,
Inviolable as he flows.
This god while flowing is adorned, like a bay steed for war, by men
Devout and skilled in holy songs.
He, like a warrior going forth with heroes, as he flows along
Is fain to win all precious boons.
This god, as he is flowing on, speeds like a car and gives his gifts:
He lets his voice be heard of all.
Praised by the sacred bards, this god dives into waters, and bestows
Rich gifts upon the worshiper.
Away he rushes with his stream, across the regions, into heaven,
And roars as he is flowing on.
While flowing, meet for sacrifice, he bath gone up to heaven across
The regions, irresistible.
After the way of ancient time, this god, pressed out for deities,
Flows tawny to the straining-cloth.
This lord of many holy laws, even at his birth engendering strength,
Effused, flows onward in a stream.

HYMN IX.4

O Soma flowing on thy way, win thou and conquer high renown;
And make us better than we are.
Win thou the light, win heavenly light, and, Soma, all felicities;
And make us better than we are.
Win skillful strength and mental power.
O Soma, drive away our foes; And make us better than we are.
Ye purifiers, purify soma for Indra, for his drink:
Make thou us better than we are.
Give us our portion in the sun through thine own mental power and aids;
And make us better than we are.

---

57 The priest's fingers.

58 The day on which the soma is extracted.

Through thine own mental power and aid long may we look upon the sun;
Make thou us better than we are.
Well-weaponed Soma, pour to us a stream of riches doubly great;
And make us better than we are.
As one victorious, unsubdued in battle pour forth wealth to us;
And make us better than we are.
Well-weaponed Soma, pour to us a stream of riches doubly great;
And make us better than we are.
As one victorious, unsubdued in battle pour forth wealth to us;
And make us better than we are.
By worship, Pavamana![59] men have strengthened thee to prop the law:
Make thou us better than we are.
O Indu, bring us wealth in steeds, manifold, quickening all life;
And make us better than we are.

VARUNA

HYMN 11.28

This praise of the self-radiant wise Aditya[60] shall be supreme o'er all that is
    in greatness.
I beg renown of Varuna the mighty, the god exceeding kind to him who wor-
    ships.
Having extolled thee, Varuna, with thoughtful care may we have high for-
    tune in thy service,
Singing thy praises like the fires at coming, day after day, of mornings rich
    in cattle.
May we be in thy keeping, O thou leader wide-ruling Varuna, lord of many
    heroes.
O sons of Aditi, forever faithful, pardon us, gods, admit us to your friend-
    ship.
He made them flow, the Aditya, the sustainer: the rivers run by Varuna's
    commandment.
These feel no weariness, nor cease from flowing: swift have they flown like
    birds in air around us.
Loose me from sin as from a bond that binds me: may we swell, Varuna, thy
    spring of order.
Let not my thread, while I weave song, be severed, nor my work's sum, before
    the time, be shattered.
Far from me, Varuna, remove all danger: accept me graciously, thou holy
    sovereign.

---

59   The god Soma often is addressed as Pavamana, meaning "self-purifying." Soma juice undergoes purification as it
flows through the wool that is used as a strainer.

60   *Aditya*, meaning "son of Aditi," is a generic name for gods. It especially refers to the sun and Varuna.

Cast off, like cords that hold a calf, my troubles: I am not even mine eyelid's lord without thee.

Strike us not, Varuna, with those dread weapons which, Asura,[61] at thy bidding wound the sinner.

Let us not pass away from light to exile. Scatter, that we may live, the men who hate us.

O mighty Varuna, now and hereafter, even as of old, will we speak forth our worship.

For in thyself, invincible god, thy statutes ne'er to be moved are fixed as on a mountain.

Move far from me what sins I have committed: let me not suffer, king, for guilt of others.

Full many a morn remains to dawn upon us: in these, O Varuna, while we live direct us.

O king, whoever, be he friend or kinsman, hath threatened me affrighted in my slumber

If any wolf or robber fain would harm us, therefrom, O Varuna, give thou us protection.

May I not live, O Varuna, to witness my wealthy, liberal, dear friend's destitution.

King, may I never lack well-ordered riches. Loud may we speak, with heroes, in assembly.

HYMN V.85

Sing forth a hymn sublime and solemn, grateful to glorious Varuna, imperial ruler,

Who hath struck out, like one who slays the victim, earth as a skin to spread in front of Surya.

In the tree-tops the air he hath extended, put milk in kine and vigorous speed in horses,

Set intellect in hearts, fire in the waters, Surya in heaven and Soma on the mountain.

Varuna lets the big cask, opening downward, flow through the heaven and earth and air's mid-region.

Therewith the universe's sovereign waters earth as the shower of rain bedews the barley.

When Varuna is fain for milk he moistens the sky, the land, and earth to her foundation.

Then straight the mountains clothe them in the rain-cloud: the heroes,[62] putting forth their vigor, loose them.

I will declare this mighty deed of magic, of glorious Varuna the lord immortal,

---

61 Lord God. In this case, Varuna.

62 Maruts, Indra's soldiers.

Who standing in the firmament hath meted the earth out with the sun as
  with a measure.

None, verily, hath ever let or hindered this the most wise god's mighty deed
  of magic,

Whereby with all their flood, the lucid rivers fill not one sea wherein they
  pour their waters.

If we have sinned against the man who loves us, have ever wronged a brother,
  friend, or comrade,

The neighbor ever with us, or a stranger, O Varuna, remove from us the
  trespass.

If we, as gamesters cheat at play, have cheated, done wrong unwittingly or
  sinned of purpose,

Cast all these sins away like loosened fetters, and, Varuna, let us be thine
  own beloved.

HYMN VII.87

Varuna cut a pathway out for Surya, and led the watery floods of rivers onward.

The mares[63] as in a race, speed on in order. He made great channels for the
  days to follow.

The wind, thy breath, hath sounded through the region like a wild beast that
  seeks his food in pastures.

Within these two, exalted earth and heaven, O Varuna, are all the forms
  thou lovest.

Varuna's spies, sent forth upon their errand, survey the two world-halves
  well formed and fashioned.

Wise are they, holy, skilled in sacrifices, the furtherers of the praise-songs of
  the prudent.

To me who understand hath Varuna spoken, the names borne by the cow are
  three times seven.[64]

The sapient god, knowing the place's secret, shall speak as 'twere to teach the
  race that cometh.

On him three heavens rest and are supported, and the three earths are there
  in sixfold order.[65]

The wise King Varuna bath made in heaven that golden swing[66] to cover it
  with glory.

Like Varuna from heaven he sinks in Sindhu,[67] like a white-shining spark, a
  strong wild creature.

---

63 The swift rivers.

64 The cow here is a personification of both speech and written language. "Three times seven" refers to the twenty-one
meters of Sanskrit poetry.

65 Different regions of the world. Each of the three earths is seen as having two seasons.

66 The sun.

67 River Indus or the sea.

Ruling in depths and meting out the region, great saving power hath he, this world's controller.

Before this Varuna may we be sinless—him who shows mercy even to the sinner

While we are keeping Aditi's ordinances. Preserve us evermore, ye gods, with blessings.

HYMN VII.89

Let me not yet, King Varuna, enter into the house of clay:[68]

Have mercy, spare me, mighty lord.

When, thunderer! I move along tremulous like a wind-blown skin,

Have mercy, spare me, mighty lord.

O bright and powerful god, through want of strength I erred and went astray:

Have mercy, spare me, mighty lord.

Thirst found thy worshiper though he stood in the midst of water-floods:

Have mercy, spare me, mighty lord.

O Varuna, whatever the offence may be which we as men commit against the heavenly host,

When through our want of thought we violate thy laws, punish us not, O god, for that iniquity.

USHAS

HYMN 1.113

This light is come, amid all lights the fairest; born is the brilliant, far-extending brightness.

Night, sent away for Savitar's uprising, hath yielded up a birthplace for the morning.

The fair, the bright is come with her white offspring;[69] to her the dark one hath resigned her dwelling.

Akin, immortal, following each other, changing their colors both the heavens move onward.

Common, unending is the sisters'[70] pathway; taught by the gods, alternately they travel.

Fair-formed, of different hues and yet one-minded, night and dawn clash not, neither do they tarry.

Bright leader of glad sounds, our eyes behold her; splendid in hue she hath unclosed the portals.

She, stirring up the world, hath shown us riches: dawn hath awakened every living creature.

---

68 The grave.

69 The white clouds.

70 Night and day.

Rich dawn, she sets afoot the coiled-up sleeper, one for enjoyment, one for
wealth or worship,

Those who saw little for extended vision. All living creatures bath the dawn
awakened.

One to high sway, one to exalted glory, one to pursue his gain, and one his
labor:

All to regard their different vocations, all moving creatures hath the dawn
awakened.

We see her there, the child of heaven, apparent, the young maid, flushing in
her shining raiment.

Thou sovereign lady of all earthly treasure, flush on us here, auspicious dawn,
this morning.

She, first of endless moms to come hereafter, follows the path of moms that
have departed.

Dawn, at her rising, urges forth the living: him who is dead she wakes not
from his slumber.

As thou, dawn, hast caused Agni to be kindled,[71] and with the sun's eye hast
revealed creation.

And hast awakened men to offer worship; thou hast performed, for gods, a
noble service.

How long a time, and they shall be together,—dawns that have shone and
dawns to shine hereafter?

She yearns for former dawns with eager longing, and goes forth gladly shining with the others.

Gone are the men who in the days before us looked on the rising of the earlier morning.

We, we the living, now behold her brightness, and they come nigh who shall
hereafter see her.

Foe-chaser, born of law, the law's protectress, joy-giver, waker of all pleasant
voices,

Auspicious, bringing food for gods' enjoyment, shine on us here, most bright,
O dawn, this morning.

From days eternal hath dawn shone, the goddess, and shows this light today,
endowed with riches.

So will she shine on days to come; immortal she moves on in her own
strength, undecaying.

In the sky's borders hath she shone in splendor: the goddess bath thrown off
the veil of darkness.

Awakening the world with purple horses, on her well-harnessed chariot
dawn approaches.

Bringing all life-sustaining blessings with her, showing herself she sends
forth brilliant lustre.

Last of the countless mornings that have vanished, first of bright moms to
come hath dawn arisen.

71 Daybreak is the time for lighting sacrificial fires.

Arise! The breath, the life, again hath reached us: darkness hath passed away, and light approacheth.

She for the sun bath left a path to travel: we have arrived where men prolong existence.

Singing the praises of refulgent mornings with his hymn's web the priest, the poet, rises.

Shine then today, rich maid, on him who praises thee, shine down on us the gift of life and offspring.

Dawns giving sons all heroes, kine and horses, shining upon the man who brings oblations,

These let the soma-presser gain when ending his glad songs louder than the voice of Vayu.[72]

Mother of gods, Aditi's form of glory, ensign of sacrifice, shine forth exalt-ed.

Rise up, bestowing praise on our devotion: all-bounteous, make us chief among the people.

Whatever splendid wealth the dawns bring with them to bless the man who offers praise and worship,

Even that may Mitra, Varuna vouchsafe us, and Aditi and Sindhu, earth and heaven.

THE SACRIFICIAL HORSE

HYMN 1.163

What time, first springing into life, thou neighedst, proceeding from the sea or upper waters,

Limbs of the deer hadst thou, and eagle pinions. O steed, thy birth is high and must be praised.

This steed which Yama gave hath Trita[73] harnessed, and him, the first of all, bath Indra mounted.

His bridle the Gandharva[74] grasped. O Vasus,[75] from out the sun ye fash-ioned forth the courser.

Yama art thou, O horse; thou art Aditya; Trita art thou by secret operation.

Thou art divided thoroughly from Soma.[76] They say thou hast three bonds in heaven that hold thee.

Three bonds, they say, thou hast in heaven that bind thee, three in the waters, three within the ocean.

To me thou seemest Varuna, O courser, there where they say is thy sublimest birthplace.

---

72 The god of wind.

73 God of the remote birthplace of the sun. In this passage, *Yama* means "Agni" as a solar deity.

74 Gandharva is Visvavasu, a heavenly being who dwells in the region of the air and guards the celestial soma.

75 Means "good." Vasus are a class of gods, eight in number, who were at first personifications of natural phenomena.

76 Perhaps here the moon, but the meaning is obscure.

Here, courser, are the places where they groomed thee, here are the traces of thy hoofs as winner.

Here have I seen the auspicious reins that guide thee, which those who guard the holy law keep safely.

Thyself from far I recognized in spirit,—a bird that from below flew through the heaven.

I saw thy head still soaring, striving upward by paths unsoiled by dust, pleasant to travel.

Here I beheld thy form, matchless in glory, eager to win thee food at the cow's station.[77]

Whene'er a man brings thee to thine enjoyment, thou swallowest the plants, most greedy eater.

After thee, courser, come the car, the bridegroom, the kine come after, and the charm of maidens.

Full companies have followed for thy friendship: the pattern of thy vigor gods have copied.

Horns[78] made of gold hath he: his feet are iron: less fleet than he, though swift as thought, is Indra.

The gods have come that they may taste the oblation of him who mounted, first of all, the courser.

Symmetrical in flank, with rounded haunches, mettled like heroes, the celestial coursers

Put forth their strength, like swans in lengthened order, when they, the steeds, have reached the heavenly causeway.

A body formed for flight hast thou, O charger; swift as the wind in motion is thy spirit.

Thy horns are spread abroad in all directions: they move with restless beat in wildernesses.

The strong steed hath come forward to the slaughter, pondering with a mind directed godward.

The goat who is his kin is led before him: the sages and the singers follow after.

The steed is come unto the noblest mansion, is come unto his father and his mother.[79]

This day shall he approach the gods, most welcome: then he declares good gifts to him who offers.

77 The cow's station is the sacrificial altar.

78 Used figuratively to mean "mane." The sun's rays are probably the intended meaning.

79 Heaven and earth.

CREATION

HYMN X.129

Then was not nonexistent nor existent: there was no realm of air, no sky beyond it.

What covered in, and where? and what gave shelter? Was water there, unfathomed depth of water?

Death was not then, nor was there aught immortal: no sign was there, the day's and night's divider.

That one thing, breathless, breathed by its own nature: apart from it was nothing whatsoever.

Darkness there was: at first concealed in darkness this. All was indiscriminated chaos.

All that existed then was void and formless: by the great power of warmth was born that unit.

Thereafter rose desire in the beginning, desire, the primal seed and germ of spirit.

Sages who searched the heart's thought discovered the existent's kinship in the nonexistent.

Transversely was their severing line[80] extended: what was above it then, and what below it?

There were begetters, there were mighty forces, free action here and energy up yonder.

Who verily knows and who can here declare it, whence it was born and whence comes this creation?

The gods are later than this world's production. Who knows then whence it first came into being?

He, the first origin of this creation, whether he formed it all or did not form it,

Whose eye controls this world in highest heaven, he verily knows it, or perhaps he knows not.

PURUSHA (THE MACROCOSMIC PERSON)

HYMN X.90

A thousand heads hath Purusha, a thousand eyes, a thousand feet.

On every side pervading earth he fills a space ten fingers wide.

This Purusha is all that yet hath been and all that is to be;

The lord of immortality which waxes greater still by food.

So mighty is his greatness; yea, greater than this is Purusha.

All creatures are one-fourth of him, three-fourths eternal life in heaven.

With three-fourths Purusha went up: one-fourth of him again was here.

---

80   A line drawn by the ancient sages to divide the upper and lower worlds. It marked duality coming out of unity.

Thence he strode out to every side over what eats not and what eats.

From him Viraj[81] was born; again Purusha from Viraj was born.

As soon as he was born he spread eastward and westward o'er the earth.

When gods prepared the sacrifice with Purusha as their offering,

Its oil was spring, the holy gift was autumn; summer was the wood.

They balmed as victim on the grass Purusha born in earliest time.

With him, the deities and all Sadhyas[82] and Rishis sacrificed.

From that great general sacrifice the dripping fat was gathered up.

He formed the creatures of the air, and animals both wild and tame.

From that great general sacrifice Richas and Sama-hymns were born:

Therefrom were spells and charms produced; the yajus[83] had its birth from it.

From it were horses born, from it all cattle with two rows of teeth:

From it were generated kine, from it the goats and sheep were born.

When they divided Purusha how many portions did they make?

What do they call his mouth, his arms? What do they call his thighs and feet?

The Brahman was his mouth, of both his arms was the Rajanya made.

His thighs became the Vaisya, from his feet the Sudra[84] was produced.

The moon was gendered from his mind, and from his eye the sun had birth;

Indra and Agni from his mouth were born, and Vayu from his breath.

Forth from his navel came mid-air; the sky was fashioned from his head;

Earth from his feet, and from his ear the regions. Thus they formed the worlds.

Seven fencing-sticks[85] had he, thrice seven layers of fuel were prepared,

When the gods, offering sacrifice, bound, as their victim, Purusha.

Gods, sacrificing, sacrificed the victim: these were the earliest holy ordinances.

The mighty ones attained the height of heaven, there where the Sadhyas, gods of old, are dwelling.

---

81 The vital juice, sperm, ovum, or embryo.

82 A class of celestial beings, probably ancient divine sacrificers.

83 The hymns (richas or yajus) of the *Rig-Veda*, those of the *Sama-Veda*, and the compositions of the *Yajur-Veda* were created by the sacrifice of Purusha.

84 The four social classes—the Brahmans (priests), Rajanyas (rulers–warriors), the Vaisyas (commoners), and the Sudras (menials)—were born from Purusha's sacrifice.

85 Pieces of wood laid around the sacrificial fire to enclose it.

2
......

GITAGOVINDA
Jayadeva

Classical India was a land of great linguistic and political diversity, united by what anthropologists call the "great tradition." This consisted of the higher philosophical concepts, rituals, and mythology of Hinduism; the literary culture of the royal courts; the laws of the Brahmans; and the practices and customs of learned Brahmans themselves, which formed a model of behavior for the rest of society. The "little tradition" of village life, within which the great mass of the Indian population lived out their lives, encompassed the close interrelationships of family and friends, the familiarity with the fields and orchards, the cycle of seasons with their festivals of fertility and thanksgiving, and a general sense of harmony with the world of nature. These gave the individual peasant a sense of the rightness and stability of things. Local customs and traditions dominated Indian daily life, and Brahman families living within the village community linked the peasants with the more sophisticated traditions of Brahmanic legend and lore. It was the combination of these two traditions, and their mutual interaction, that gave Indian culture unity and continuity it would not otherwise have possessed. One of the important factors joining the great and little traditions was their common devotion to the great god Vishnu, in his earth-dwelling form of Krishna.

Vishnu appears in the Rig Veda only as the dwarf who measured the earth in three strides. In later centuries, this dwarf was considered to have been only one of Vishnu's ten avatars or incarnations, for Vishnu was a god who visited the earth. Some of these legendary incarnations, such as his appearance as a fish or as a boar, were probably myths originally unconnected with Vishnu. Other incarnations, such as Rama (of the epic poem The Ramayana) and Krishna, were probably heroic warrior-kings famed in legend long before they came to be identified as personifications of Vishnu.

By the seventh century, Vishnu began to gain greater importance in Indian religion, perhaps because he appeared as a god of love and kindness for humanity, and one who could be approached by the individual without the intermediation of a Brahman. Cults emphasizing personal devotion to Vishnu flourished in South India, and in succeeding centuries also gained followers in North India. Hindu devotionalism came to be expressed in terms of a reciprocal love between the worshipper and the god, and the acceptance of this concept by the Brahmans gave India a worship in which all could join as individuals and equals. Thus the effects of the caste system, the dominance of the Brahmans in religion and learning, and the great differences of wealth that characterized the Indian economic system were, in some measure, mitigated by a concept of a god who admitted all equally to his worship and his love. Moreover, Vishnu was not an abstract being, dwelling

From Love Song of the Dark Lord: Jayadeva's Gitagovinda, ed. and trans. Barbara Stoller Miller (New York: Columbia University Press, 1977), pp. 69, 72-74, 77, 122-25.

in a realm apart from his worshippers. To be with them, he took earthly form and lived among the men and women of India. Of all the forms he took, none was more beloved to the Indians than the fun-loving and ardent Krishna.

The life and deeds of Krishna are the theme of many myths and legends, from his birth and mischievous childhood to his role as the awesome charioteer in the Bhagavad Gita. In the tenth-century Bhagavata Purana, the most popular of the eighteen Sanskrit puranas, he appears in the form of a cowherd (govinda). In this tale, the young Krishna flirts and sports with a group of pretty cowherdesses (gopi), finally falling in love with Radha, one of their number. Krishna's choice of occupation and playmates in the Gitagovinda is in part a popular explanation for the sacredness of India's holy animal, the cow. In the Vedic Hymns, cattle signify wealth and the spoils of battle, and the Aryan nobles apparently protected this symbol of their wealth by forbidding anyone else to kill or harm one of them. This original secular restraint appears to have evolved into a religious tabu. Later, cows became sacrificial animals and were therefore dedicated to the gods. By the time of the Gitagovinda, they had come to symbolize maternal love and the spirit of devotion to Krishna. In the Gitagovinda, Jayadeva explains through myth why this came to be.

Jayadeva was a court poet in Bengal in the latter part of the twelfth century. The Gitagovinda, his greatest work, portrays personal devotion to God in terms of physical love. In the West, the poem has been criticized for its openly erotic character, but in India it remains one of the central works of devotion to Vishnu. It draws not only on earlier devotional literature, but also on Tantric ritual, the character of which is amply illustrated by the erotic themes in temple sculpture of the period. For the Indians of the time, it was only reasonable to describe abstract concepts in concrete terms through allegory. It seemed perfectly natural to them to describe their joyous love for their god in terms of the most ecstatic physical pleasure they knew.

The Gitagovinda has been translated into all modern Indian languages and is presented in theater, music, and dance throughout the country. The poem presents the story of the love of Radha and Krishna, and the only other character is another gopi who is Radha's confidante. The excerpts in this selection come from the beginning and from the end of the poem. The first excerpt is from Jayadeva's invocation, after which the narrative begins with Radha's description of how she observed Krishna's lovemaking with the other gopis. She hides in anger and jealousy; Krishna, realizing his love for Radha, searches unsuccessfully for her. He then waits for Radha to come to him. Radha wastes away from the anguish of separation and from the thought that Krishna no longer cares for her. Radha's friend passes back and forth between the two, describing the agony of the one to the other and urging each to overcome pride and to take the first step toward reconciliation. After a night and a day of separation, it is Krishna who comes to Radha and declares his love. He then returns to his home in the forest; Radha follows him to his hut, and the loveplay given here concludes the poem. Jayadeva stresses the cosmic significance of the relationship by referring to Krishna by various names that invoke Hindu mythology: Madhava (descendant of Madhu, or Spring), Hari (a demon), Narayana, and Yadu or Yadava (hero). Radha is called Sri, "radiance" or "beauty," which is another name of the goddess Laksmi, consort of Vishnu. To peasant worshippers, the allegory was clear; after a winter of short days, cold winds, and perhaps diminishing supplies of food, the god Vishnu arrives as Spring, a hero defeating death and Winter and, with joy and love, blesses humankind with the fruits of the season to come.

Questions

1. What does Jayadeva say are his motives for composing this work?
2. Some people claim that uninhibited eroticism, such as that demonstrated in the *Gitagovinda*, is a sign of decline in a civilization. What evidence for and against this argument can you find in this example?
3. The *Gitagovinda* is written in an ornate Sanskrit understood by few people, yet it was intended to be sung and danced publicly. How might ordinary Hindus have interpreted the story?

GITAGOVINDA

JOYFUL KRISHNA

"Clouds thicken the sky.
Tamala trees darken the forest.
The night frightens him.
Radha, you take him home!"
They leave at Nanda's order,
Passing trees in thickets on the way,
Until secret passions of Radha and Madhava

Triumph on the Jumna riverbank.
Jayadeva, wandering king of bards
Who sing at Padmavati's lotus feet,
Was obsessed in his heart
By rhythms of the goddess of speech,
And he made this lyrical poem
From tales of the passionate play
When Krishna loved Sri.

Umapatidhara is prodigal with speech,
Sarana is renowned for his subtle flowing sounds,
But only Jayadeva divines the pure design of words.
Dhoyi is famed as king of poets for his musical ear,
But no one rivals master Govardhana
For poems of erotic mood and sacred truth.
If remembering Hari enriches your heart,
If his arts of seduction arouse you,
Listen to Jayadeva's speech
In these sweet soft lyrical songs.
　　　　　　◆
Your beauty is fresh as rain clouds.
You hold the mountain to churn elixir from the sea.
Your eyes are night birds drinking from Sri's moon face.
　　Triumph, God of Triumph, Hari!

Poet Jayadeva joyously sings
This song of invocation
In an auspicious prayer.
     Triumph, God of Triumph, Hari!
As he rests in Sri's embrace,
On the soft slope of her breast,
The saffroned chest of Madhu's killer
Is stained with red marks of passion
And sweat from fatigue of tumultuous loving.
May his broad chest bring you pleasure too!
When spring came, tender-limbed Radha wandered
Like a flowering creeper in the forest wilderness,
Seeking Krishna in his many haunts.
The god of love increased her ordeal,
Tormenting her with fevered thoughts,
And her friend sang to heighten the mood.

When he quickens all things
To create bliss in the world,
His soft black sinuous lotus limbs
Begin the festival of love
And beautiful cowherd girls wildly
Wind him in their bodies.
Friend, in spring young Hari plays
Like erotic mood incarnate.
Winds from sandalwood mountains
Blow now toward Himalayan peaks,
Longing to plunge in the snows
After weeks of writhing
In the hot bellies of ground snakes.
Melodious voices of cuckoos
Raise their joyful sound
When they spy the buds
On tips of smooth mango branches.

"Joyful Krishna" is the first part in Gitagovinda

ECSTATIC KRISHNA

When her friends had gone,
Smiles spread on Radha's lips
While love's deep fantasies
Struggled with her modesty.
Seeing the mood in Radha's heart,
Hari spoke to his love;
Her eyes were fixed
On his bed of buds and tender shoots.

Leave lotus footprints on my bed of tender shoots, loving Radha!

Let my place be ravaged by your tender feet!
    Narayana is faithful now. Love me, Radhika!

I stroke your foot with my lotus hand—You have come far.
Set your golden anklet on my bed like the sun.
    Narayana is faithful now. Love me, Radhika!

Consent to my love; let elixir pour from your face!
To end our separation I bare my chest of the silk that bars your breast.
    Narayana is faithful now. Love me, Radhika!

Throbbing breasts aching for loving embrace are hard to touch.
Rest these vessels on my chest! Quench love's burning fire!
    Narayana is faithful now. Love me, Radhika!

Offer your lips' nectar to revive a dying slave, Radha!
His obsessed mind and listless body burn in love's desolation.
    Narayana is faithful now. Love me, Radhika!

Radha, make your jeweled girdle cords echo the tone of your voice!
Soothe the long torture my ears have suffered from cuckoo's shrill cries!
    Narayana is faithful now. Love me, Radhika!

Your eyes are ashamed now to see me tortured by baseless anger;
Glance at me and end my passion's despair!
    Narayana is faithful now. Love me, Radhika!

Each verse of Jayadeva's song echoes the delight of Madhu's foe.
Let emotion rise to a joyful mood of love in sensitive men!
    Narayana is faithful now. Love me, Radhika!

> Displaying her passion
> In loveplay as the battle began,
> She launched a bold offensive
> Above him
> And triumphed over her lover.
> Her hips were still,
> Her vine-like arm was slack,
> Her chest was heaving,
> Her eyes were closed.
> Why does a mood of manly force
> Succeed for women in love?

> Then, as he idled after passionate love,
> Radha, wanting him to ornament her,
> Freely told her lover,
> Secure in her power over him.

Yadava hero, your hand is cooler than sandalbalm on my breast;
Paint a leaf design with deer musk here on Love's ritual vessel!
    She told the joyful Yadu hero, playing to delight her heart.

Lover, draw kohl glossier than a swarm of black bees on my eyes!
Your lips kissed away the lampblack bow that shoots arrows of Love.

She told the joyful Yadu hero, playing to delight her heart.
My ears reflect the restless gleam of doe eyes, graceful Lord.
Hang earrings on their magic circles to form snares for love.
    She told the joyful Yadu hero, playing to delight her heart.

Pin back the teasing lock of hair on my smooth lotus face!
It fell before me to mime a gleaming line of black bees.
    She told the joyful Yadu hero, playing to delight her heart.

Make a mark with liquid deer musk on my moonlit brow!
Make a moon shadow, Krishna! The sweat drops are dried.
    She told the joyful Yadu hero, playing to delight her heart.

Fix flowers in shining hair loosened by loveplay, Krishna!
Make a flywhisk outshining peacock plumage to be the banner of Love.
    She told the joyful Yadu hero, playing to delight her heart.

My beautiful loins are a deep cavern to take the thrusts of love—
Cover them with jeweled girdles, cloths, and ornaments, Krishna!
    She told the joyful Yadu hero, playing to delight her heart.

Make your heart sympathetic to Jayadeva's splendid speech!
Recalling Hari's feet is elixir against fevers of this dark time.
    She told the joyful Yadu hero, playing to delight her heart.

> "Paint a leaf on my breasts!
> Put color on my cheeks!
> Lay a girdle on my hips!
> Twine my heavy braid with flowers!
> Fix rows of bangles on my hands
> And jeweled anklets on my feet!"
> Her yellow-robed lover
> Did what Radha said.

> His musical skills, his meditation on Vishnu,
> His vision of reality in the erotic mood,
> His graceful play in these poems,
> All show that master-poet Jayadeva's soul
> Is in perfect tune with Krishna—
> Let blissful men of wisdom purify the world
> By singing his *Gitagovinda*

> Bhojadeva's heir, Ramadevi's son, Jayadeva,
> Expresses the power of poetry
> In the *Gitagovinda*.
> Let his poem be in the voice
> Of devotees like sage Parasara.

"Ecstatic Krishna" is the twelfth part in Gitagovinda

Further Readings

There are many translations of the *Gitagovinda* in English, beginning with that of William Jones in 1792. The best known are the loose renderings of Edwin Arnold, *India's Song of Songs*, first published in 1875, and George Keyt, *Sri Jayadeva's Gita Govinda: The Loves of Krishna and Radha* (Bombay: Kutub-Popular, 1940). Hindu religious eroticism in general is discussed in Lee Siegel, *Sacred and Profane Dimensions of Love in Indian Traditions as Exemplified in the Gitagovinda of Jayadeva* (Delhi: Oxford University Press, 1978). Suniti Kumar Chatterji, *Jayadeva: Makers of Indian Literature* (New Delhi: Sahitya Akademi, 1973) is a biography of Jayadeva; worshippers of Vishnu regarded it as inspired. There is a splendid collection of scholarly essays on Krishna in Milton B. Singer, *Krishna: Myths, Rites, and Attitudes* (Honolulu: East-West Center, 1966). Two recent examples of American scholarship on Krishna in literature are Noel Sheth, *The Divinity of Krishna* (New Delhi: Munshiram Manorharlal, 1984), and John Stratton Hawley, *Krishna, the Butter Thief* (Princeton, NJ: Princeton University Press, 1983). Much Indian art centers on the figure of Krishna; this is beautifully illustrated in W. G. Archer, *The Loves of Krishna in Indian Painting and Poetry* (New York: Macmillan, 1957). Nigel Frith, *The Legend of Krishna* (New York: Schocken, 1976), provides popular narratives of many of the stories associated with Krishna.

3
......

THE BHAGAVAD GITA

The culture and civilization that developed in ancient India is nowhere more clearly reflected than in its two great epic poems, the Ramayana *and the* Mahabharata. *Transmitted orally for centuries, the two epics were reworked so frequently that today it is impossible to know which elements are the most ancient. The two poems were quite likely secular in origin but by the time they were placed in their final written form (ca. A.D. 200), they had become Scripture. These epics have had a profound influence on Indian society, both ancient and modern. They have provided the common ideas and ideals that have been instrumental in maintaining the unity and stability of Hindu life.*

The Mahabharata, *which in its present form consists of some 100,000 couplets, holds the distinction of being the world's longest poem. Part heroic tale and part religious lesson, it tells of a great battle fought on the plains near modern Delhi between the sons of a blind king and their cousins, the rightful heirs to the throne. Contained within this vast epic is the Bhagavad Gita ("Lord's Song"), a literary masterpiece universally regarded as the most important and influential of all Hindu scripture. The 1400 lines of the "Song" are not an integral part of the* Mahabharata *but were simply inserted into the epic at an appropriate place.*

The Bhagavad Gita *is a battlefield dialog between the prince Arjuna and Krishna, a god appearing in human form and serving as Arjuna's charioteer. Krishna consoles and instructs Arjuna as the prince prepares to go into battle against family and friends to defend his older brother's claim to the throne. Arjuna, a man renowned for his bravery and skill in war, recoils from the thought of killing relatives and friends and cries out to Krishna for help. Krishna, in his answer, touches on almost all the main themes of the "Song." Arjuna is told not to worry about slaying friends and relatives, for the soul is eternal and only the body dies. In fact, the souls of those killed in battle will only move on to the next life sooner than those who live to old age. Krishna further counsels the prince by pointing out that it is Arjuna's duty (dharma) as a member of the warrior class to fight and that he cannot obtain salvation unless he does his duty. Eventually, Arjuna is made to understand that, although he must do his duty, he must act selflessly in doing so. Arjuna must fight not for his own sake but for the welfare of all.*

The Bhagavad Gita *occupies a unique position in the ethical tradition of India. It stands out as a timeless, practical manual for daily life. The "Song" places human destiny solely in human hands. One's actions determine one's destiny. Individuals must fulfill their obligations but must do so without selfish attachment to personal satisfactions. It is the universality of these themes that has made the* Bhagavad Gita *one of India's most important contributions to world literature.*

Questions

1. According to the *Bhagavad Gita*, how should we conduct ourselves in our daily life? How can we obtain the highest good?
2. What questions does Arjuna ask Krishna regarding life and death? How does Krishna answer these questions? What effect does such knowledge have on everyday actions? What is the *Bhagavad Gita's* attitude toward war?

3. Describe the relationship between people and gods as expressed in this selection.
4. The *Bhagavad Gita* is said to have a universality that transcends time and place. What relevance does its message possess for you?

THE WAR WITHIN

DHRITARASHTRA

O Sanjaya, tell me what happened at Kurukshetra, the field of dharma,[1] where my family and the Pandavas gathered to fight.

SANJAYA

Having surveyed the forces of the Pandavas arrayed for battle, prince Duryodhana approached his teacher, Drona, and spoke, "O my teacher, look at this mighty army of the Pandavas, assembled by your own gifted disciple, Yudhishthira. There are heroic warriors and great archers who are the equals of Bhima and Arjuna: Yuyudhana, Virata, the mighty Drupada, Dhrishtaketu, Chekitana, the valiant king of Kashi, Purujit, Kuntibhoja, the great leader Shaibya, the powerful Yudhamanyu, the valiant Uttamaujas, and the son of Subhadra, in addition to the sons of Draupadi. All these command mighty chariots.

"O best of brahmins, listen to the names of those who are distinguished among our own forces: Bhishma, Karna, and the victorious Kripa; Ashvatthama, Vikarna, and the son of Somadatta. There are many others, too, heroes giving up their lives for my sake, all proficient in war and armed with a variety of weapons. Our army is unlimited and commanded by Bhishma; theirs is small and commanded by Bhima. Let everyone take his proper place and stand firm supporting Bhishma!"

Then the powerful Bhishma, the grandsire, oldest of all the Kurus, in order to cheer Duryodhana, roared like a lion and blew his conch horn. And after Bhishma, a tremendous noise arose of conchs and cowhorns and pounding on drums.

Then Sri Krishna and Arjuna, who were standing in a mighty chariot yoked with white horses, blew their divine conchs. Sri Krishna blew the conch named Panchajanya, and Arjuna blew that called Devadatta. The mighty Bhima blew the huge conch Paundra. Yudhishthira, the king, the son of Kunti, blew the conch Anatavijaya; Nakula and Sahadeva blew their conchs as well. Then the king of Kashi, the leading bowman, the great warrior Shikhandi, Dhrishtadyumna, Virata, the invincible Satyaki, Drupada, all the sons of Draupadi, and the strong-armed son of Subhadra

---

[1]The obligations of an individual; duty, responsibility.

From The Bhagavad Gita, translated by Eknath Easwaran (Petaluma, California: Nilgiri Press, 1985), pp. 52-56, 61-69, 75-79.

joined in, and the noise tore through the heart of Duryodhana's army. Indeed, the sound was tumultuous, echoing throughout heaven and earth.

Then, O Dhritarashtra, lord of the earth, having seen your son's forces set in their places and the fighting about to begin, Arjuna spoke these words to Sri Krishna:

ARJUNA

O Krishna, drive my chariot between the two armies. I want to see those who desire to fight with me. With whom will this battle be fought? I want to see those assembled to fight for Duryodhana, those who seek to please the evil-minded son of Dhritarashtra by engaging in war.

SANJAYA

Thus Arjuna spoke, and Sri Krishna, driving his splendid chariot between the two armies, facing Bhishma and Drona and all the kings of the earth, said: "Arjuna, behold all the Kurus gathered together."

And Arjuna, standing between the two armies, saw fathers and grandfathers, teachers, uncles, and brothers, sons and grandsons, in-laws and friends. Seeing his kinsmen established in opposition, Arjuna was overcome by sorrow. Despairing, he spoke these words:

ARJUNA

O Krishna, I see my own relations here anxious to fight, and my limbs grow weak; my mouth is dry, my body shakes, and my hair is standing on end. My skin burns, and the bow Gandiva has slipped from my hand. I am unable to stand; my mind seems to be whirling. These signs bode evil for us. I do not see that any good can come from killing our relations in battle. O Krishna, I have no desire for victory, or for a kingdom or pleasures. Of what use is a kingdom or pleasure or even life, if those for whose sake we desire these things-teachers, fathers, sons, grandfathers, uncles, in-laws, grandsons, and others with family ties—are engaging in this battle, renouncing their wealth and their lives? Even if they were to kill me, I would not want to kill them, not even to become ruler of the three worlds. How much less for the earth alone?

O Krishna, what satisfaction could we find in killing Dhritarashtra's sons? We would become sinners by slaying these men, even though they are evil. The sons of Dhritarashtra are related to us; therefore, we should not kill them. How can we gain happiness by killing members of our own family?

Though they are overpowered by greed and see no evil in destroying families or injuring friends, we see these evils. Why shouldn't we turn away from this sin? When a family declines, ancient traditions are destroyed. With them are lost the spiritual foundations for life, and the family loses its sense of unity. Where there is no sense of unity, the women of the family become corrupt; and with the corruption of its women, society is plunged into chaos. Social chaos is hell for the family and for those who have destroyed the family as well. It disrupts the process of spiritual evolution begun by our ancestors. The timeless spiritual foundations of family and society would be destroyed by these terrible deeds, which violate the unity of life.

It is said that those whose family dharma has been destroyed dwell in hell. This is a great sin! We are prepared to kill our own relations out of greed for the pleasures of a kingdom. Better for me if the sons of Dhritarashtra, weapons in hand, were to attack me in battle and kill me unarmed and unresisting.

ANJAYA

Overwhelmed by sorrow, Arjuna spoke these words. And casting away his bow and his arrows, he sat down in his chariot in the middle of the battlefield. . . .

THE ILLUMINED MAN

ANAYA

These are the words that Sri Krishna spoke to the despairing Arjuna, whose eyes were burning with tears of pity and confusion.

SRI KRISHNA

This despair and weakness in a time of crisis are mean and unworthy of you, Arjuna. How have you fallen into a state so far from the path to liberation? It does not become you to yield to this weakness. Arise with a brave heart and destroy the enemy.

ARJUNA

How can I ever bring myself to fight against Bhishma and Drona, who are worthy of reverence? How can 1, Krishna? Surely it would be better to spend my life begging than to kill these great and worthy souls! If I killed them, every pleasure I found would be tainted. I don't even know which would be better, for us to conquer them or for them to conquer us. The sons of Dhritarashtra have confronted us; but why would we care to live if we killed them? My will is paralyzed, and I am utterly confused. Tell me which is the better path for me. Let me be your disciple. I have fallen at your feet; give me instruction. What can overcome a sorrow that saps all my vitality? Even power over men and gods or the wealth of an empire seems empty.

SANJAYA

This is how Arjuna, the great warrior, spoke to Sri Krishna. With the words, "O Krishna, I will not fight," he fell silent.

As they stood between the two armies, Sri Krishna smiled and replied to Arjuna, who had sunk into despair.

SRI KRISHNA

You speak sincerely, but your sorrow has no cause. The wise grieve neither for the living nor for the dead. There has never been a time when you and I and the kings gathered here have not existed, nor will there be a time when we will cease to exist. As the same person inhabits the body through childhood, youth, and old age, so too at the time of death he attains another body. The wise are not deluded by these changes.

When the senses contact sense objects, a person experiences cold or heat, pleasure or pain. These experiences are fleeting; they come and go. Bear them patiently, Arjuna. Those who are not affected by these changes, who are the same in pleasure and pain, are truly wise and fit for immortality. Assert your strength and realize this!

The impermanent has no reality; reality lies in the eternal. Those who have seen the boundary between these two have attained the end of all knowledge. Realize that which pervades the universe and is indestructible; no power can affect this unchanging, imperishable reality. The body is mortal, but he who dwells in the body is immortal and immeasurable. Therefore, Arjuna, fight in this battle.

One man believes he is the slayer, another believes he is the slain. Both are ignorant; there is neither slayer nor slain. You were never born; you will never die. You have never changed; you can never change. Unborn, eternal, immutable, immemorial, you do not die when the body dies. Realizing that which is indestructible, eternal, unborn, and unchanging, how can you slay or cause another to slay?

As a man abandons worn-out clothes and acquires new ones, so when the body is worn out a new one is acquired by the Self, who lives within.

The Self cannot be pierced by weapons or burned by fire; water cannot wet it, nor can the wind dry it. The Self cannot be pierced or burned, made wet or dry. It is everlasing and infinite, standing on the motionless foundations of eternity. The Self is unmanifested, beyond all thought, beyond all change. Knowing this, you should not grieve.

O mighty Arjuna, even if you believe the Self to be subject to birth and death, you should not grieve. Death is inevitable for the living; birth is inevitable for the dead. Since these are unavoidable, you should not sorrow. Every creature is unmanifested at first and then attains manifestation. When its end has come, it once again becomes unmanifested. What is there to lament in this?

The glory of the Self is beheld by a few, and a few describe it; a few listen, but many without understanding. The Self of all beings, living within the body, is eternal and cannot be harmed. Therefore, do not grieve.

Considering your dharma, you should not vacillate. For a warrior, nothing is higher than a war against evil. The warrior confronted with such a war should be pleased, Arjuna, for it comes as an open gate to heaven. But if you do not participate in this battle against evil, you will incur sin, violating your dharma and your honor.

The story of your dishonor will be repeated endlessly: and for a man of honor, dishonor is worse than death. These brave warriors will think you have withdrawn from battle out of fear, and those who formerly esteemed you will treat you with disrespect. Your enemies will ridicule your strength and say things that should not be said. What could be more painful than this?

Death means the attainment of heaven; victory means the enjoyment of the earth. Therefore rise up, Arjuna, resolved to fight! Having made yourself alike in pain and pleasure, profit and loss, victory and defeat, engage in this great battle and you will be freed from sin.

You have heard the intellectual explanation of Sankhya, Arjuna; now listen to the principles of yoga.[2] By practicing these you can break through the bonds of karma.[3] On this path effort never goes to waste, and there is no failure. Even a little effort toward spiritual awareness will protect you from the greatest fear.

Those who follow this path, resolving deep within themselves to seek Me alone, attain singleness of purpose. For those who lack resolution, the decisions of life are many-branched and endless. There are ignorant people who speak flowery words and take delight in the letter of the law, saying that there is nothing else. Their hearts are full of selfish desires, Arjuna. Their idea of heaven is their own enjoyment, and the aim of all their activities is pleasure and power. The fruit of their actions is continual rebirth. Those whose minds are swept away by the pursuit of pleasure and power are incapable of following the supreme goal and will not attain samadhi.[4]

[2]Mental and physical discipline through which the individual attempts to reach the state of "pure soul," in which the soul is freed of both dharma and karma.

[3]The accumulated weight of past deeds and misdeeds on the individual soul.

[4]"The state of "pure soul"; also called nirvana.

The scriptures describe the three gunas. But you should be free from the action of the gunas,[5] established in eternal truth, self-controlled, without any sense of duality or the desire to acquire and hoard.

Just as a reservoir is of little use when the whole countryside is flooded, scriptures are of little use to the illumined man or woman, who sees the Lord everywhere.

You have the right to work, but never to the fruit of work. You should never engage in action for the sake of reward, nor should you long for inaction. Perform work in this world, Arjuna, as a man established within himself—without selfish attachments, and alike in success and defeat. For yoga is perfect evenness of mind.

Seek refuge in the attitude of detachment and you will amass the wealth of spiritual awareness. Those who are motivated only by desire for the fruits of action are miserable, for they are constantly anxious about the results of what they do. When consciousness is unified, however, all vain anxiety is left behind. There is no cause for worry, whether things go well or ill. Therefore, devote yourself to the disciplines of yoga, for yoga is skill in action.

The wise unify their consciousness and abandon attachment to the fruits of action, which binds a person to continual rebirth. Thus they attain a state beyond all evil.

When your mind has overcome the confusion of duality, you will attain the state of holy indifference to things you hear and things you have heard. When you are unmoved by the confusion of ideas and your mind is completely united in deep samadhi, you will attain the state of perfect yoga.

ARJUNA

Tell me of those who live established in wisdom, ever aware of the Self, O Krishna. How do they talk? How sit? How move about?

SRI KRISHNA

They live in wisdom who see themselves in all and all in them, who have renounced every selfish desire and sense craving tormenting the heart.

Neither agitated by grief nor hankering after pleasure, they live free from lust and fear and anger. Established in meditation, they are truly wise. Fettered no more by selfish attachments, they are neither elated by good fortune nor depressed by bad. Such are the seers. Even as a tortoise draws in its limbs, the wise can draw in their senses at will. Aspirants abstain from sense pleasures, but they still crave for them. These cravings all disappear

---

[5]The three elements or attributes of which all things and actions are composed: sat-Ira. the luminous, noble element; rains, the colored, passionate element; and tamas, the dark, indifferent element.

when they see the highest goal. Even of those who tread the path, the stormy senses can sweep off the mind. They live in wisdom who subdue their senses and keep their minds ever absorbed in me.

When you keep thinking about sense objects, attachment comes. Attachment breeds desire, the lust of possession that burns to anger. Anger clouds the judgment; you can no longer learn from past mistakes. Lost is the power to choose between what is wise and what is unwise, and your life is utter waste. But when you move amidst the world of sense, free from attachment and aversion alike, there comes the peace in which all sorrows end, and you live in the wisdom of the Self. The disunited mind is far from wise; how can it meditate? How be at peace? When you know no peace, how can you know joy? When you let your mind follow the call of the senses, they carry away your better judgment as storms drive a boat off its charted course on the sea.

Use all your power to free the senses from attachment and aversion alike, and live in the full wisdom of the Self. Such a sage awakes to light in the night of all creatures. That which the world calls day is the night of ignorance to the wise.

As rivers flow into the ocean but cannot make the vast ocean overflow, so flow the streams of the sense-world into the sea of peace that is the sage. But this is not so with the desirer of desires.

They are forever free who renounce all selfish desires and break away from the ego-cage of "I," "me," and "mine" to be united with the Lord. This is the supreme state. Attain to this, and pass from death to immortality. .   .

SELFLESS SERVICE

ARJUNA

O Krishna, you have said that knowledge is greater than action; why then do you ask me to wage this terrible war? Your advice seems inconsistent. Give me one path to follow to the supreme good.

SRI KRISHNA

At the beginning of time I declared two paths for the pure heart: jnana yoga, the contemplative path of spiritual wisdom, and karma yoga, the active path of selfless service. He who shirks action does not attain freedom; no one can gain perfection by abstaining from work. Indeed, there is no one who rests for even an instant; every creature is driven to action by his own nature.

Those who abstain from action while allowing the mind to dwell on sensual pleasure cannot be called sincere spiritual aspirants. But they excel who control their senses through the mind, using them for selfless service.

Fulfill all your duties; action is better than inaction. Even to maintain your body, Arjuna, you are obliged to act. Selfish action imprisons the world. Act selflessly, without any thought of personal profit.

At the beginning, mankind and the obligation of selfless service were created together. "Through selfless service, you will always be fruitful and find the fulfillment of your desires": this is the promise of the Creator.

Honor and cherish the devas[6] as they honor and cherish you; through this honor and love you will attain the supreme good. All human desires are fulfilled by the devas, who are pleased by selfless service. But anyone who enjoys the things given by the devas without offering selfless acts in return is a thief.

The spiritually minded, who eat in the spirit of service, are freed from all their sins; but the selfish, who prepare food for their own satisfaction, eat sin. Living creatures are nourished by food, and food is nourished by rain; rain itself is the water of life, which comes from selfless worship and service.

Every selfless act, Arjuna, is born from Brahman, the eternal, infinite Godhead. He is present in every act of service. All life turns on this law, O Arjuna. Whoever violates it, indulging his senses for his own pleasure and ignoring the needs of others, has wasted his life. But those who realize the Self are always satisfied. Having found the source of joy and fulfillment, they no longer seek happiness from the external world. They have nothing to gain or lose by any action; neither people nor things can affect their security.

It is better to strive in one's own dharma than to succeed in the dharma of another. Nothing is ever lost in following one's own dharma, but competition in another's dharma breeds fear and insecurity.

ARJUNA

What is the force that binds us to selfish deeds, O Krishna? What power moves us, even against our will, as if forcing us?

SRI KRISHNA

It is selfish desire and anger, arising from the guna of rajas; these are the appetites and evils which threaten a person in this life.

Just as a fire is covered by smoke and a mirror is obscured by dust, just as the embryo rests deep within the womb, knowledge is hidden by selfish desire-hidden, Arjuna, by this unquenchable fire for self-satisfaction, the inveterate enemy of the wise.

Selfish desire is found in the senses, mind, and intellect, misleading them and burying the understanding in delusion. Fight with all your strength,

[6]The gods, demigods, and spirits of Hindu belief

Arjuna! Controlling your senses, conquer your enemy, the destroyer of knowledge and realization.

The senses are higher than the body, the mind higher than the senses; above the mind is the intellect, and above the intellect is the Atman. Thus, knowing that which is supreme, let the Atman rule the ego. Use your mighty arms to slay the fierce enemy that is selfish desire.

Strive constantly to serve the welfare of the world; by devotion to selfless work one attains the supreme goal of life. Do your work with the welfare of others always in mind. It was by such work that Janaka[7] attained perfection; others, too, have followed this path.

What the outstanding person does, others will try to do. The standards such people create will be followed by the whole world. There is nothing in the three worlds for me to gain, Arjuna, nor is there anything I do not have; I continue to act, but I am not driven by any need of my own. If I ever refrained from continuous work, everyone would immediately follow my example. If I stopped working I would be the cause of cosmic chaos, and finally of the destruction of this world and these people.

The ignorant work for their own profit, Arjuna; the wise work for the welfare of the world, without thought for themselves. By abstaining from work you will confuse the ignorant, who are engrossed in their actions. Perform all work carefully, guided by compassion.

All actions are performed by the gunas of prakriti.[8] Deluded by his identification with the ego, a person thinks, "I am the doer." But the illumined man or woman understands the domain of the gunas and is not attached. Such people know that the gunas interact with each other; they do not claim to be the doer.

Those who are deluded by the operation of the gunas become attached to the results of their action. Those who understand these truths should not unsettle the ignorant. Performing all actions for my sake, completely absorbed in the Self, and without expectations, fight!—but stay free from the fever of the ego.

Those who live in accordance with these divine laws without complaining, firmly established in faith, are released from karma. Those who violate these laws, criticizing and complaining, are utterly deluded, and are the cause of their own suffering.

Even a wise man acts within the limitations of his own nature. Every creature is subject to prakriti; what is the use of repression? The senses have been conditioned by attraction to the pleasant and aversion to the unpleasant. Do not be ruled by them; they are obstacles in your path.

---

[7] King of Mithila who sacrificed to the gods personally, rather than through a Brahman priest, and thus became a Brahman through his own efforts. Janaka was also the father-in-law of Rama, hero of the epic, Ramayana.

[8] The material basis of the universe, as opposed to purusha, the spiritual basis.

Further Readings

Notable among the many commentaries on the Bhagavad Gita is Singh Balbir's Essence of the Bhagavad Gita (Atlantic Highlands, NJ: Humanities Press, 1981). A recent study of the comparative and intercultural aspects of the Gita, in particular, dealing with Western interpretations, is provided in Eric Sharpe's The Universal Gita (London: Duckworth, 1985). Prem Nath Bazaz' The Role of the Bhagavad Gita in Indian History (New Delhi: Sterling Publishers, 1975) is a critical examination of the Gita and its role in the historical development of India. Among the numerous works providing a general background for ancient India are Arthur L. Basham Aspects of Ancient Indian Culture (Bombay and New York: Asia Publishing House, 1966); Bridget All-chin, The Rise of Civilization in India and Pakistan (Cambridge and New York: Cambridge University Press, 1982); and Jeannine Auboyer, Daily Life in Ancient India (New York: Macmillan & Co., 1966).

WRITINGS ON BUDDHISM

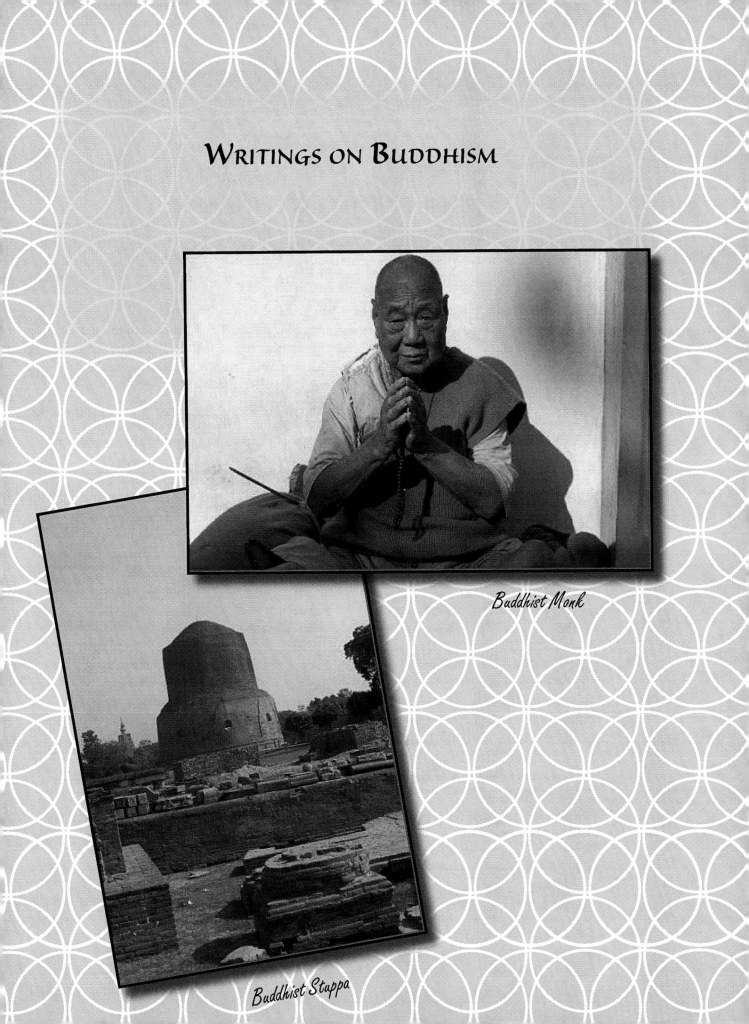

Buddhist Monk

Buddhist Stuppa

1

....

SERMON AT THE DEER PARK

SIDDHARTHA GAUTAMA BUDDHA

Religious reformers appeared in India in the middle of the first millennium B.C., contemporary with Confucius, the Hebrew prophets, the earliest Greek philosophers, and possibly Zoroaster in Persia. Among their contributions to Hinduism are a series of commentaries on, and explanations of, the Hindu faith. The most important of these are called Upanishads, some of which were written about 550 B.C. Most of the Upanishads speculate on the mechanics of transmigration, concluding that one's actions (karma) determine how one is reborn. If one's deeds are good, the soul (atman) is reborn into a higher status; if they are evil, one will live one's next lifetime in a lower status. Transmigration (samsara) is not mentioned in the early Vedas, but the Upanishads combined their concept of the brahman mentioned in the Vedic sacrifices with the atman or soul that transmigrates. The brahman was the "universal soul" and salvation was the reunification of the atman with brahman.

Karma and transmigration are the nearest things to religious dogma in Hinduism. By the sixth century B.C., the concept of karma increasingly came to mean ritually prescribed behavior; that is, karma was not so much a matter of good deeds as it was of fulfilling religious obligations. This enhanced the role of the Brahmans, since they were the only caste allowed to perform sacrifice, and other castes had to turn to them for assistance in fulfilling their religious debts. It was believed that only the Brahmans' sacrifices had the magical power to compel the gods to respond to human prayers. At the same time, individual duty (dharma) ceased being interpreted in broad human terms, and increasingly came to be defined in terms of caste occupation. In this way, the individual was removed from the center of religious activity in favor of the Brahmans, and individual morality tended to become merely a means of reinforcing a stratified and unequal social system.

The sages who wrote the Upanishads built on the foundations of the Vedas, accepting and elaborating their principles, but others rejected the authority of the Vedas with their emphasis on sacrifice and the inequality between classes and their neglect of personal moral responsibilities. Much of this heterodox thought appears to have come from tribal kingdoms on the fringes of the Ganges plain that had only recently and incompletely absorbed Aryan social institutions. One such kingdom, that of the Sakyas, lying in the foothills of the Himalayas, gave birth to the greatest challenger of Hindu orthodoxy, the founder of Buddhism, Gautama Siddhartha (c. 566-486 B.C.), the son of a Sakya chieftain.

The goal of religious effort in the Buddha's teachings was enlightenment (nirvana)—a release from the constant cycle of birth and rebirth and a cessation of any consciousness of

From *The Gospel of Buddha, According to Old Records*, told by Paul Carus, 4th rev. ed. (Chicago: Open Court Publishing Company, 1896), pp. 30-33, 37-43.

self. On the surface, this would appear quite similar to the Upanishads' view that salvation consists of the merging of individual and universal souls, but was really quite different. The Buddha explicitly denied the existence of the soul and explained transmigration as merely the movement of a life-force, like a flame passing from candle to candle. On a more institutional level, he also denied that the Brahmans had any special status or peculiar power in the cosmic order. In this sense, he founded a democratic and personal religion, in which each individual was to seek personal enlightenment.

The biography of the "historical Buddha" is an important part of Buddhist beliefs, particularly for Theravada Buddhists, for whom he is a model of the path of renunciation and moderation that leads to enlightenment. There is no full version of his life in early texts, and the following is summarized from later works. Prince Siddartha Gautama left his protected and pampered **life in his** father's court at the age of twenty-nine to become an ascetic. He practiced various systems of self-mortification and remained with the five ascetics mentioned in this selection for six years, practicing asceticism in an effort to understand the meaning of things and the path to enlightenment. He increased his psychic powers considerably in this fashion, but decided that this alone had not brought him any closer to enlightenment; that it had, in fact, prevented him from maintaining the inner calm necessary for successful meditation. The ascetics left him in disgust when he abandoned his extreme practices. He then meditated alone under the Tree of Wisdom at Gaya and repulsed the temptation from the demon Moral

The following selection describes his enlightenment and first actions as conceived by the sect of saffron-robed mendicants (bbikkhu) who followed his teachings in later centuries. He discovered the "Four Noble Truths" and became a buddha, or "enlightened one," and resumed to Benares, where he found the five ascetics who had been his disciples. In the Deer Park outside the city, he preached his first sermon, in which he set out the basic principles of his teachings. The Buddha chose not to pass into the state of nirvana, but remained on earth for forty more years, teaching and collecting disciples.

Questions

1. Why does the Buddha say that ignorance is the root of all evil?
2. How did the five ascetics greet the Buddha? Why?
3. What does the Buddha mean by "the instability of the ego"?

SERMON AT THE DEER PARK

Bodhisattva having put to flight Mara, gave himself up to meditation. All the miseries of the world, the evils produced by evil deeds and the sufferings arising therefrom passed before his mental eye, and he thought:

"Surely if living creatures saw the results of all their evil deeds, they would turn away from them in disgust. But selfhood blinds them, and they cling to their obnoxious desires.

"They crave for pleasure and they cause pain; when death destroys their individuality, they find no peace; their thirst for existence abides and their self hood reappears in new births.

"Thus they continue to move in the coil and can find no escape from the hell of their own making. And how empty are their pleasures, how vain are their endeavors! Hollow like the plantain-tree and without contents like the bubble.

"The world is full of sin and sorrow, because it is full of error. Men go astray because they think that delusion is better than truth. Rather than truth they follow error, which is pleasant to look at in the beginning but causes anxiety, tribulation, and misery."

And Bodhisattva began to expound the dharma. The dharma is the truth. The dharma is the sacred law. The dharma is religion. The dharma alone can deliver us from error, sin, and sorrow.

Pondering on the origin of birth and death, the Enlightened One recognized that ignorance was the root of all evil; and these are the links in the development of life, called the twelve nidanas:

"In the beginning there is existence blind and without knowledge; and in this sea of ignorance there are appetences formative and organising. From appetences, formative and organising, rises awareness or feelings. Feelings beget organisms that live as individual beings. These organisms develop the six fields, that is, the five senses and the mind. The six fields come in contact with things. Contact begets sensation. Sensation creates the thirst of individualised being. The thirst of being creates a cleaving to things. The cleaving produces the growth and continuation of selfhood. Selfhood continues in renewed births. The renewed births of selfhood are the cause of suffering, old age, sickness, and death. They produce lamentation, anxiety, and despair.

"The cause of all sorrow lies at the very beginning; it is hidden in the ignorance from which life grows. Remove ignorance and you will destroy the wrong appetences that rise from ignorance; destroy these appetences and you will wipe out the wrong perception that rises from them. Destroy wrong perception and there is an end of errors in individualised beings. Destroy errors in individualised beings and the illusions of the six fields will disappear. Destroy illusions and the contact with things will cease to beget misconception. Destroy misconception and you do away with thirst. Destroy thirst and you will be free of all morbid cleaving. Remove the cleaving and you destroy the selfishness of selfhood. If the selfishness of selfhood is destroyed you will be above birth, old age, disease, and death, and you escape all suffering."

The Enlightened One saw the four noble truths which point out the path that leads to Nirvana or the extinction of self:

"The first noble truth is the existence of sorrow. Birth is sorrowful, growth is sorrowful, illness is sorrowful, and death is sorrowful. Sad it is to be joined with that which we do not like. Sadder still is the separation from that which we love, and painful is the craving for that which cannot be obtained.

"The second noble truth is the cause of suffering. The cause of suffering is lust. The surrounding world affects sensation and begets a craving thirst, which clamors for immediate satisfaction. The illusion of self originates and manifests itself in a cleaving to things. The desire to live for the enjoyment of self entangles us in the net of sorrow. Pleasures are the bait and the result is pain.

"The third noble truth is the cessation of sorrow. He who conquers self will be free from lust. He no longer craves, and the flame of desire finds no material to feed upon. Thus it will be extinguished.

"The fourth noble truth is the eightfold path that leads to the cessation of sorrow. There is salvation for him whose self disappears before Truth, whose will is bent upon what he ought to do, whose sole desire is the performance of his duty. He who is wise will enter this path and make an end of sorrow.

"The eightfold path is (1) right comprehension; (2) right resolutions; (3) right speech; (4) right acts; (5) right way of earning a livelihood; (6) right efforts; (7) right thoughts; and (8) the right state of a peaceful mind."

This is the dharma. This is the truth.

Now the Blessed One thought: "To whom shall I preach the doctrine first? My old teachers are dead. They would have received the good news with joy. But my five disciples are still alive. I shall go to them, and to them shall I first proclaim the gospel of deliverance."

At that time the five bhikshus dwelt in the Deer Park at Benares, and the Blessed One not thinking of their unkindness in having left him at a time when he was most in need of their sympathy and help, but mindful only of the services which they had ministered unto him, and pitying them for the austerities which they practised in vain, rose and journeyed to their abode.

The five bhikshus saw their old teacher approach and agreed among themselves not to salute him, nor to address him as a master, but by his name only. "For," so they said, "he has broken his vow and has abandoned holiness. He is no bhikshu but Gautama, and Gautama has become a man who lives in abundance and indulges in the pleasures of worldliness."

But when the Blessed One approached in a dignified manner, they involuntarily rose from their seats and greeted him in spite of their resolution. Still they called him by his name and addressed him as "friend."

When they had thus received the Blessed One, he said: "Do not call the Tathagata by his name nor address him 'friend,' for he is Buddha, the Holy One. Buddha looks equally with a kind heart on all living beings and they therefore call him 'Father.' To disrespect a father is wrong; to despise him, is sin.

"The Tathagata," Buddha continued, "does not seek salvation in austerities, but for that reason you must not think that he indulges in worldly pleasures, nor does he live in abundance. The Tathagata has found the middle path.

"Neither abstinence from fish or flesh, nor going naked, nor shaving the head, nor wearing matted hair, nor dressing in a rough garment, nor covering oneself with dirt, nor sacrificing to Agni, will cleanse a man who is not free from delusions.

"Reading the Vedas, making offerings to priests, or sacrifices to the gods, self-mortification by heat or cold, and many such penances performed for the sake of immortality, these do not cleanse the man who is not free from delusions.

"Anger, drunkenness, obstinacy, bigotry, deception, envy, self-praise, disparaging others, superciliousness, and evil intentions constitute uncleanness; not verily the eating of flesh.

"Let me teach you, O bhikshus, the middle path, which keeps aloof from both extremes. By suffering, the emaciated devotee produces confusion and sickly thoughts in his mind. Mortification is not conducive even to worldly knowledge; how much less to a triumph over the senses!

"He who fills his lamp with water will not dispel the darkness, and he who tries to light a fire with rotten wood will fail.

"Mortifications are painful, vain, and profitless. And how can any one be free from self by leading a wretched life if he does not succeed in quenching the fires of lust.

"All mortification is vain so long as self remains, so long as self continues to lust after either worldly or heavenly pleasures. But he in whom self has become extinct is free from lust; he will desire neither worldly nor heavenly pleasures, and the satisfaction of his natural wants will not defile him. Let him eat and drink according to the needs of the body.

"Water surrounds the lotus-flower, but does not wet its petals.

"On the other hand, sensuality of all kind is enervating. The sensual man is a slave of his passions, and pleasure-seeking is degrading and vulgar.

"But to satisfy the necessities of life is not evil. To keep the body in good health is a duty, for otherwise we shall not be able to trim the lamp of wisdom, and keep our mind strong and clear.

"This is the middle path, O bhikshus, that keeps aloof from both extremes."

And the Blessed One spoke kindly to his disciples, pitying them for their errors, and pointing out the uselessness of their endeavors, and the ice of ill-will that chilled their hearts melted away under the gentle warmth of the Master's persuasion.

Now the Blessed One set the wheel of the most excellent law a-rolling, and he began to preach to the five bhikshus, opening to them the gate of immortality, and showing them the bliss of Nirvana.

And when the Blessed One began his sermon, a rapture thrilled through all the universes.

The devas left their heavenly abodes to listen to the sweetness of the truth; the saints that had parted from life crowded around the great teacher to receive the glad tidings; even the animals of the earth felt the bliss that rested upon the words of the Tathagata: and all the creatures of the host of sentient beings, gods, men, and beasts, hearing the message of deliverance, received and understood it in their own language.

Buddha said:

"The spokes of the wheel are the rules of pure conduct; justice is the uniformity of their length; wisdom is the tire; modesty and thoughtfulness are the hub in which the immovable axle of truth is fixed.

"He who recognises the existence of suffering, its cause, its remedy, and its cessation has fathomed the four noble truths. He will walk in the right path.

"Right views will be the torch to light his way. Right aims will be his guide. Right words will be his dwelling-place on the road. His gait will be straight, for it is right behavior. His refreshments will be the right way of earning his livelihood. Right efforts will be his steps: right thoughts his breath; and peace will follow in his footprints."

And the Blessed One explained the instability of the ego.

"Whatsoever is originated will be dissolved again. All worry about the self is vain; the ego is like a mirage, and all the tribulations that touch it will pass away. They will vanish like a nightmare when the sleeper awakes.

"He who has awakened is freed from fear; he has become Buddha; he knows the vanity of all his cares, his ambitions, and also of his pains.

"It easily happens that a man, when taking a bath, steps upon a wet rope and imagines that is is a snake. Horror will overcome him, and he will shake from fear, anticipating in his mind all the agonies caused by the serpent's venomous bite. What a relief does this man experience when he sees that the rope is no snake. The cause of his fright lies in his error, his ignorance, his illusion. If the true nature of the rope is recognised, his tranquillity of mind will come back to him; he will feel relieved; he will be joyful and happy.

"This is the state of mind of one who has recognised that there is no self, that the cause of all his troubles, cares, and vanities is a mirage, a shadow, a dream.

"Happy is he who has overcome all selfishness; happy is he who has attained peace; happy is he who has found the truth.

"The truth is noble and sweet; the truth can deliver you from evil. There is no saviour in the world except the truth.

"Have confidence in the truth, although you may not be able to comprehend it, although you may suppose its sweetness to be bitter, although you may shrink from it at first. Trust in the truth.

"The truth is best as it is. No one can alter it; neither can any one improve it. Have faith in the truth and live it.

"Errors lead astray; illusions beget miseries. They intoxicate like strong drinks; but they fade away soon and leave you sick and disgusted.

"Self is a fever; self is a transient vision, a dream; but truth is wholesome, truth is sublime, truth is everlasting. There is no immortality except in truth. For truth alone abideth forever."

And when the doctrine was propounded, the venerable Kaundinya, the oldest one among the five bhikshus, discerned the truth with his mental eye, and he said: "Truly, O Buddha, our Lord, thou hast found the truth."

And the devas and saints and all the good spirits of the departed generations that had listened to the sermon of the Tathagata, joyfully received the doctrine and shouted: "Truly, the Blessed One has founded the kingdom of righteousness. The Blessed One has moved the earth; he has set the wheel of Truth rolling, which by no one in the universe, be he god or man, can ever be fumed back. The kingdom of Truth will be preached upon earth; it will spread; and righteousness, good-will, and peace will reign among mankind."

FURTHER READINGS

Henry Clark Warren, *Buddhism in Translations* (New Delhi: Motilal Banarasidas, 1987) is a reprint of the 1896 edition of one of the pioneering works of Buddhist studies in the United States; there are well-edited selections of readings in Richard A. Gard, ed., *Buddhism* (New York: George Braziller, 1962) and Edward Conze, ed., *Buddhist Texts through the Ages* (Oxford: Cassirer, 1954). Richard F. Gombrich, *Theravada Buddhism: A Social History from Ancient Benares to Modern Colombo* (London: Routledge and Kegan Paul, 1988) briefly surveys the school of Buddhism that traces its origins to the earliest teachings of the Buddha. Jeannine Auboyer, *Buddha: A Pictorial History of His Life and Legacy* (New York: Crossroad, 1983), offers a superbly illustrated account of the life of Buddha. Edward Conze, *A Short History of Buddhism* (London: Allen & Unwin, 1980), provides an excellent and readable coverage of an extensive subject in a brief work. Arthur R. Wright, *Buddhism in Chinese History* (Stanford, CA: Stanford University Press, 1970) considers the introduction of Buddhism to China and the important role it occupies in the Chinese legacy.

2

......

THE PURE LAND SUTRA

As Buddhism moved out from India and into other areas, variations developed, with diverse sects creating their own styles of art, their own modes of worship, even their own doctrines. Those which taught the universal buddhahood of all believers came to be known collectively as Mahayana Buddhism, or The Greater Vehicle. The Pure Land sect, which began to flourish in China by the sixth century of our era taught that the Buddha was divine, that those who have been enlightened and worked their way up through the cycles of rebirth have the status of Bodhisattvas, or holy ones, who may delay their entrance into Nirvana as they assist those yet here in the world to develop their faith. Even the concept of Nirvana changed radically: early on, it was simply a mode of non-being, an escape from the suffering of this world; now there was conceived a happy land," filled with wonders and delights, which would prepare one to enter Nirvana. The very notion of squelching our desires, so important in early Buddhism, gave way to the notion of the satisfaction of desires—at least harmless satisfactions and worthwhile delights—in a sort of Buddhist heaven. Thus the Pure Land Sutra shows us something that is true of all religions which last a long time: they evolve over the course of time, so that the early proponents might even have trouble identifying the later practices and beliefs as being part of their same faith, though the later adherents, aware of the tradition, can identify the early practices and beliefs as being the sources of current ones.

In what ways does the "Pure Land" envisioned here cater to the wishes of its inhabitants? What does its geography suggest about the preferences,, and perhaps the actual habitation, of he members whor belong to this sect?

This world Sukhavati, Ananda,[1] which is the world system of the Lord Amitabha,[2] is rich and prosperous, comfortable, fertile, delightful and crowded with many Gods and men. And in this world system, Ananda, there are no hells, no animals, no ghosts, no Asuras[3] and none of the inauspicious places of rebirth. And in this our world no jewels make their appearance like those which exist in the world system Sukhavati.

And that world system Sukhavati, Ananda, emits many fragrant odors, it is rich in a great variety of flowers and fruits, adorned with jewel, trees, which are frequented by flocks of various birds with sweet voices, which the Tathagata's[4] miraculous power has conjured up. And these jewel trees, Ananda, have various colors, many colors, many hundreds of

---

1 Ananda was one of the Buddha's favorite disciples.

2 Amitabha was an Indian ascetic who, when seeking enlightenment, made a series of vows that helped him attain Buddhahood. Among those was the vow that if anyone approaching death would call on him by name, he would personally lead that one to rebirth in his own Buddha-world, Sukhavati. There it would be much easier for the believer to gain release from his human limitations.

3 Titanic beings who war constantly with the Gods.

4 A title of the Buddha.

thousands of colors. They are variously composed of the seven precious things, in varying combinations, i.e. of gold, silver, beryl, crystal, coral, red pearls or emerald. Such jewel trees, and clusters of banana trees and rows of palm trees, all made of precious things, grow everywhere in this Buddha-field. On all sides it is surrounded with golden nets, and all round covered with lotus flowers made of all the precious things. Some of the lotus flowers are half a mile in circumference, others up to ten miles. And from each jewel lotus issue thirty-six hundred thousand kotis[5] of rays. And at the end of each ray there issue thirty-six hundred thousand kotis of Buddhas, with golden-colored bodies, who bear the thirty-two marks of the superman, and who, in all the ten directions, go into countless world systems, and there demonstrate Dharma.

And further, Ananda, in this Buddha-field there are nowhere any mountains,—black mountains, jewel mountains, Sumerus, kings of mountains, circular mountains and great circular mountains. But the Buddha-field is everywhere even, delightful like the palm of the hand, and in all its parts the ground contains a great variety of jewels and gems.

And many kinds of rivers flow along in this world system Sukhavati. There are great rivers there, one mile broad, and up to fifty miles broad and twelve miles deep. And all these rivers flow along calmly, their water is fragrant with manifold agreeable odors, in them there are bunches of flowers to which various jewels adhere, and they resound with various sweet sounds. And the sound which issues from these great rivers is as pleasant as that of a musical instrument, which consists of hundreds of thousands of kotis of parts, and which, skillfully played, emits a heavenly music. It is deep, commanding, distinct, clear, pleasant to the ear, touching, the heart, delightful, sweet, pleasant, and one never tires of hearing it, it always agrees with one and one likes to hear it, like the words "Impermanent, peaceful, calm, and not-self" Such is the sound that reaches the ears of those beings.

And, Ananda, both the banks of those great rivers are lined with variously scented jewel trees, and from them bunches of flowers, leaves and branches of all kinds hang down. And if those beings wish to indulge in sports full of heavenly delights on those river-banks, then, after they have stepped into the water, the water in each case rises as high as they wish it to,—up to the ankles, or the knees, or the hips, or their sides, or their ears. And heavenly delights arise. Again, if beings wish the water to be cold, for them it becomes cold; if they wish it to be hot, for them it becomes hot; if they wish it to be hot and cold, for them it becomes hot and cold, to suit their pleasure. And those rivers flow along, full of water scented with the finest odors, and covered with beautiful flowers, resounding with the sounds of many birds, easy to ford, free from mud, and with golden sand at the bottom. And all the wishes those beings may think of, they all will be fulfilled, as long as they are rightful.

And as to the pleasant sound which issues from the water (of these rivers), that reaches all the parts of this Buddha-field. . . . And, hearing this, one gains the exalted zest and joyfulness, which is associated with detachment, dispassion, calm, cessation, Dharma, and brings about the state of mind which leads to the accomplishment of enlightenment. And nowhere in this world-system Sukhavati does one hear of anything unwholesome, nowhere of the hindrances, nowhere of the states of punishment, the, statesr of woe and the bad destinies, nowhere of suffering. Even of feelings which are neither pleasant nor unpleasant one does not hear here, how much less of suffering! And that, Ananda, is the rea-

5 A huge number.

son why this world-system is called the "Happy Land" (Sukhavati). But all this describes it only in brief, not in detail. One aeon might well reach its end while one proclaims the reasons for happiness in the world system Sukhavati, and still one could not come to the end of (the enumeration of) the reasons for happiness.

Moreover, Ananda, all the beings who have been reborn in this world-system Sukhavati, who are reborn in it, or who will be reborn in it, they will be exactly like the Paranirmitav-asavartin Gods: of the same color, strength, vigor, height and breadth, dominion, store of merit and keenness of super-knowledges; they enjoy the same dresses, ornaments, parks, palaces and pointed towers, the same kind of forms, sounds, smells, tastes and touchables, just the same kinds of enjoyments. And the beings in the world-system Sukhavati do not eat gross food, like soup or raw sugar; but whatever food they may wish for, that they perceive as eaten, and they become gratified in body and mind, without there being any further need to throw the food into the body, And if, after their bodies are gratified, they wish for certain perfumes, then the whole of that Buddha-field becomes scented with just that kind of heavenly perfumes. But if someone does not wish to smell that perfume, then the perception of it does not reach him. In the same way, whatever they may wish for, comes to them, be it musical instruments, banners, flags, etc.; or cloaks of different colors, or ornaments of various kinds. If they wish for a palace of a certain color, distinguishing marks, construction, height and width, made of various precious things, adorned with hundreds of thousands of pinnacles, while inside it various heavenly woven materials are spread out, and it is full of couches strewn with beautiful cushions,—then just such a palace appears before them. In those delightful palaces, surrounded and honored by seven times seven thousand Apsaras,[6] they dwell, play, enjoy and disport themselves.

And the beings who are touched by the winds, which are pervaded with various per fumes, are filled with a happiness as great as that of a monk who has achieved the cessation of suffering.

And in this Buddha-field one has no conception, at all of fire, sun, moon, planets, constellations, stars or blinding darkness, and no conception even of day and night, except (where they are mentioned) in the sayings of the Tathagata. There is nowhere a notion of monks possessing private parks for retreats.

And all the beings who have been born, who are born, who will be born in this Buddha-field, they all are fixed on the right method of salvation, until they have won Nirvana. And why? Because there is here no place for and no conception of the twor other groups, i.e., of those who are not fixed at all, and those who are fixed on wrong ways. For this reason also that world-system is called "Happy Land". . .

And further again, Ananda, in the ten directions, in each single direction, in Buddha-fields countless like the sands of the river Ganges, Buddhas and Lords countless like the sands of the river Ganges, glorify the name of the Lord Amitabha, of the Tathagata, praise him, proclaim his fame, extol his virtue. And why? Because all beings are irreversible from the supreme enlightenment if they hear the name of the Lord Amitabha, and, on hearing it, with one single thought only raise their hearts to him with a resolve connected with serene faith.

And if any beings, Ananda, again and again reverently attend to this Tathagata, if they will plant a large and immeasurable root of good, having raised their hearts to enlighten-

6 Beautiful divine nymphs.

ment, and if they vow to be reborn in that world system, then, when the hour of their death approaches, that Tathagata Amitabha, the Arhat, the fully Enlightened One, will stand before them, surrounded by hosts of monks. Then, having seen that Lord, and having died with hearts serene, they will be reborn in just that world-system Sukhavati. And if there are sons or daughters of good family, who may desire to see that Tathagata Amitabha in this very life, they should raise their hearts to the supreme enlightenment, they should direct their thought with extreme resoluteness and perseverance unto this Buddha-field and they should dedicate their store of merit to being reborn therein.

Translated by Edward Conze

3
......

THE DIAMOND SUTRA

The *term sutra has come to have a range of meanings in the context of Buddhist literature, from its narrowest definition as the sermons and discourses of the Buddha, to its widest definition as any Buddhist scripture. The word in the Sanskrit language originally meant "a thread, " and the contents of most of the sutras are "threaded" or strung together as narratives or portions of a doctrinal explanation. Those sutras that fall into the first category—sermons and discourses of the Gautama Buddha (see Selection 21)—were reputedly written down by one of the Buddha's ten great disciples, Ananda. They each characteristically begin with the formula "Thus have I heard," identify the place where the Buddha gave this sermon, and close with another formula to the effect that all who had heard these words "were filled with joy at his teaching, and, taking it sincerely to heart . . . went their ways."*

The Diamond Sutra, *which is substantially reproduced here, is one of the best known and most influential of these works. While Buddhism originated in Nepal and India, and for the first centuries of its development tended to spread toward the West, its greatest triumph as a missionary religion was ultimately in the Far East: China and the countries directly influenced by Chinese civilization—Japan, Korea, and Vietnam. Whereas Buddhism ceased to play a major role in the religious and cultural life of India, it became interwoven into the fabric of all lift and culture in the Far East as well as in Southeast Asia.*

The Diamond of the Perfection of Transcendental Wisdom, *to give it its full designation, probably was of Indian origin. It belongs to the literature of the Mahayana tradition of Buddhism, one of the two great divisions of the religion that came about toward the end of the first century A.D. This suggests that its origin, at least in this form, was much later than the life of the Gautama Buddha. Tradition has it that it was translated from Sanskrit into Chinese by the great missionary scholar–monk Kumarajiva about A.D. 400. The Diamond Sutra was a powerful factor in the spread of Buddhism in China and the zone of Chinese cultural influence. The oldest extant printed book in the world is a Chinese text of* The Diamond Sutra, *printedfrom carved wooden blocks in the ninth century.*

Mahayana Buddhism (represented here), far more than the Hinayana school, which forms the other branch of the divided Buddhist religion, is a popular faith that holds out to all human beings the hope of "salvation"—release from endless cycles of rebirth and death—through enlightenment. The sutras were written to be pleasant to read or hear, and relatively easy to recite. As the text of the following document (translated from Chinese) indicates, such reading and recitation was thought to convey great merit. The discourse between the Buddha and his disciple Subhuti seems to proceed slowly and to be characterized by frequent repetition. Yet the effect of the discourse is cumulative and progressive. The most basic Buddhist philosophical beliefs—the illusory nature of being, of ego, of all apparent perception—are, indeed, hard for the conventional Western mind to accept. The sutra leads the reader or hearer, step by often-repeated step,

From *The Diamond Sutra* and *The Sutra of Hui Neng,* translated by A. E Price and Wong Mou-Lam. Reprinted by arrangement with Shambhala Publications, Inc., P.O. Box 308, Boston, MA, 02117.

toward familiarity with these difficult concepts and eventually toward acceptance of them as the higher reality. And, by coupling their revelation with the hope of release from our imprisonment in this false non-world, the sutra makes the acceptance of these "hard" truths ultimately a matter of joy.

SECTION I: THE CONVOCATION OF THE ASSEMBLY

Thus have I heard. Upon a time Buddha sojourned in Anathapindika's Park by Shravasti[7] with great company of *bhikshus*,[8] even twelve hundred and fifty.

One day, at the time for breaking fast, the world-honored [the Buddha] enrobed, and carrying his bowl made his way into the great city of Shravasti to beg for his food. In the midst of the city he begged from door to door according to rule. This done, he returned to his retreat and took his meal. When he had finished he put away his robe and begging bowl, washed his feet, arranged his seat, and sat down.

SECTION II: SUBHUTI MAKES A REQUEST

Now in the midst of the assembly was the Venerable Subhuti. Forthwith he arose, uncovered his right shoulder, knelt upon his right knee, and, respectfully raising his hands with palms joined, addressed Buddha thus: "World-honored one, it is most precious how mindful the Tathagata[9] is of all the Bodhisattvas,[10] protecting and instructing them so well! World-honored one, if good men and good women seek the consummation of incomparable enlightenment, by what criteria should they abide and how should they control their thoughts?"

Buddha said: "Very good, Subhuti! Just as you say, the Tathagata is ever-mindful of all the Bodhisattvas, protecting and instructing them well. Now listen and take my words to heart: I will declare to you by what criteria good men and good women seeking the consummation of incomparable enlightenment should abide, and how they should control their thoughts."

Said Subhuti: "Pray, do, world-honored one. With joyful anticipation we long to hear."

SECTION III: THE REAL TEACHING OF THE GREAT WAY

Buddha said: "Subhuti, all the Bodhisattva-Heroes should discipline their thoughts as follows: All living creatures of whatever class, born from eggs, from wombs, from moisture, or by transformation, whether with form or without form, whether in a state of thinking or exempt from thought-necessity, or wholly beyond all thought realms—all these are caused by me to attain unbounded liberation nirvana.[11] Yet when vast, uncountable, im-

---

7   Located in northern India, near the border with Nepal. In Buddhist lore it is known as the "City of Wonders."

8   Begging monks of the order founded by the Gautama Buddha. Nuns of the order were called *bhikshunis*.

9   One of the many names for Buddha, one that denotes a realization of Buddha's closeness to ultimate truth. *The Diamond Sutra* gradually reveals the meaning of Tathagata, culminating in the dialogue in Section XIV below.

10   An advanced devotee of Buddhism, one who has approached enlightenment.

11   Nirvana is the goal of Buddhist enlightenment. A difficult concept to define, it is best understood as the final liberation not only from the physical self, but from the ego. Some Buddhists employed the analogy of a drop of rain "returning" to the sea, absorbed again into its element, losing all individuality.

measurable numbers of beings have thus been liberated, verily no being has been liberated. Why is this, Subhuti? It is because no Bodhisattva who is a real Bodhisattva cherishes the idea of ego-entity, a personality, a being, or a separated individuality."

SECTION IV: EVEN THE MOST BENEFICENT PRACTICES ARE RELATIVE

"Furthermore, Subhuti, in the practice of charity a Bodhisattva should be detached. That is to say, he should practice charity without regard to appearances; without regard to sound, odor, touch, flavor, or any quality. Subhuti, thus should the Bodhisattva practice charity without attachment. Wherefore? In such a case his merit is incalculable.

"Subhuti, what do you think? Can you measure all the space extending eastward?"

"No, world-honored one, I cannot."

"Then can you, Subhuti, measure all the space extending southward, westward, northward, or in any other direction, including nadir and zenith?" "No, world-honored one, I cannot."

"Well, Subhuti, equally incalculable is the merit of the Bodhisattva who practices charity without any attachment to appearances. Subhuti, Bodhisattvas should persevere one-pointedly in this instruction."

SECTION V: UNDERSTANDING THE ULTIMATE PRINCIPLE OF REALITY

"Subhuti, what do you think? Is the Tathagata to be recognized by some material characteristic?"

"No, world-honored one; the Tathagata cannot be recognized by any material characteristic. Wherefore? Because the Tathagata has said that material characteristics are not, in fact, material characteristics."

Buddha said: "Subhuti, wheresoever are material characteristics there is delusion; but whoso perceives that all characteristics are in fact no-characteristics, perceives the Tathagata."

• • •

SECTION VII: GREAT ONES, PERFECT BEYOND LEARN- ING, UTTER NO WORDS OF TEACHING

"Subhuti, what do you think? Has the Tathagata attained the consummation of incomparable enlightenment? Has the Tathagata a teaching to enunciate?"

Subhuti answered: "As I understand Buddha's meaning, there is no formulation of truth called consummation of incomparable enlightenment. Moreover, the Tathagata has no formulated teaching to enunciate. Wherefore? Because the Tathagata has said that truth is uncontainable and inexpressible. [12] It neither is nor is it *not*."

Thus it is that this unformulated principle is the foundation of the different systems of all the sages.

SECTION VIII: THE FRUITS OF MERITORIOUS ACTION

"Subhuti, what do you think? If anyone filled three thousand galaxies of worlds with the seven treasures[13] and gave all away in gifts of alms, would he gain great merit?"

Subhuti said: "Great indeed, world-honored one! Wherefore? Because merit partakes of the character of no-merit, the Tathagata characterized the merit as great."

Then Buddha said: "On the other hand, if anyone received and retained even only four lines of this discourse and taught and explained them to others, his merit would be the greater. Wherefore? Because, Subhuti, from this discourse issue forth all the Buddhas and the consummation of the incomparable enlightenment teachings of all the Buddhas.

"Subhuti, what is called 'the religion given by Buddha is not, in fact, Buddhareligion."[14]

• • •

SECTION XII: VENERATION OF THE TRUE DOCTRINE

"Furthermore, Subhuti, you should know that wheresoever this discourse is proclaimed, by even so little as four lines, that place should be venerated by the whole realms of gods, men and Titans, as though it were a Buddha-shrine. How much more is this so in the case of one who is able to receive and retain the whole and read and recite it throughout!

"Subhuti, you should know that such an one attains the highest and most wonderful truth. Wheresoever this sacred discourse may be found, there should you comport yourself as though in the presence of Buddha and disciples worthy of honor."

SECTION XIII: HOW THIS TEACHING SHOULD BE RECEIVED AND RETAINED

At that time Subhuti addressed Buddha, saying: "World-honored one, by what name should this discourse be known, and how should we receive and retain it?"

---

12 Compare this assertion about the inexpressibility of ultimate truth with that of the Chinese Taoist classic, the *Tao Te Ching* (Selection 30). As Buddhism was introduced from India into China in the early centuries A.D., it made an especially strong appeal to Taoists, whose own beliefs predisposed them to understand and accept such ideas.

13 Agate, cornelian, crystal, gold, lapis-lazuli, pearls, silver.

14 This paradox, apparently, can be explained by reference to the previous section (VII) of the sutra. Teaching, even the teaching of the Buddha, cannot encompass truth, but only can help one to set foot on the path toward enlightenment.

Buddha answered: "Subhuti, this discourse should be known as 'The Diamond[15] of the Perfection of Transcendental Wisdom'—thus should you receive and retain it. Subhuti, what is the reason herein? According to the Buddha-teaching the perfection of transcendental wisdom is not really such. 'Perfection of Transcendental Wisdom' is just the name given to it. Subhuti, what do you think? Has the Tathagata a teaching to enunciate?"

Subhuti replied to Buddha: "World-honored one, the Tathagata has nothing to teach."

"Subhuti, what do you think? Would there be many molecules in the composition of three thousand galaxies of worlds?"

Subhuti said: "Many, indeed, world-honored one!"

"Subhuti, the Tathagata declares that all these molecules are not really such; they are called 'molecules.' Furthermore, the Tathagata declares that the world is not really a world; it is called 'a world.'

"Subhuti, what do you think? May the Tathagata be perceived by the thirty-two physical peculiarities[16] of an outstanding sage?"

"No, world-honored one, the Tathagata may not be perceived by these thirty-two marks. Wherefore? Because the Tathagata has explained that the thirty-two marks are not really such; they are called 'the thirty-two marks.'"

"Subhuti, if, on the one hand, a good man or a good woman sacrifices as many lives as the sand-grains of the Ganges, and, on the other hand, anyone receives and retains even only four lines of this discourse, and teaches and explains them to others, the merit of the latter will be the greater."

SECTION XIV: PERFECT PEACE LIES IN FREEDOM FROM CHARACTERISTIC DISTINCTIONS

Upon the occasion of hearing this discourse Subhuti had an interior realization of its meaning and was moved to tears. Whereupon he addressed Buddha thus: "It is a most precious thing, world-honored one, that you should deliver this supremely profound discourse. Never have I heard such an exposition since of old my eye of wisdom first opened. World-honored one, if anyone listens to this discourse in faith with a pure, lucid mind, he will thereupon conceive an idea of fundamental reality. We should know that such an one establishes the most remarkable virtue. World-honored one, such an idea of fundamental reality is not, in fact, a distinctive idea; therefore the Tathagata teaches: 'Idea of Fundamental Reality' is merely a name.

"World-honored one, having listened to this discourse, I receive and retain it with faith and understanding. This is not difficult for me, but in ages to come—in the last five hun-

---

15　The choice of the title "Diamond" suggests not only the brilliance of the gem, but its hardness and power to cut through all other material, in this case to cut through false perceptions of the world.

16　A set of characteristics listed in Hindu scriptures. While we see Buddhism as a religion distinct from Hinduism because of the historical course it took, the Gautama Buddha came out of the same tradition as Hinduism. He was a deep believer in its doctrines, and doubtless thought of himself as a reformer rather than as a rebel.

dred years,[17] if there be men coming to hear this discourse who receive and retain it with faith and understanding, they will be persons of most remarkable achievement. Wherefore? Because they will be free from the idea of ego-entity, free from the idea of a personality, free from the idea of a being, and free from the idea of a separated individuality. And why? Because the distinguishing of an ego-entity is erroneous. Likewise the distinguishing of a personality, or a being, or a separated individuality is erroneous. Consequently, those who have left behind every phenomenal distinction are called Buddhas all."

Buddha said to Subhuti: "Just as you say! If anyone listens to this discourse and is neither filled with alarm nor awe nor dread, be it known that such an one is of remarkable achievement. Wherefore? Because, Subhuti, the Tathagata teaches that the first perfection, the perfection of charity, is not, in fact, the first perfection; such is merely a name.

"Subhuti, the Tathagata teaches likewise that the perfection of patience is not the perfection of patience: such is merely a name. Why so? It is shown thus, Subhuti: When the Rajah of Kalinga mutilated my body,[18] I was at that time free from the idea of ego-entity, a personality, a being, and a separated individuality. Wherefore? Because then when my limbs were cut away piece by piece, had I been bound by the distinctions aforesaid, feelings of anger and hatred would have been aroused within me. Subhuti, I remember that long ago, some time during my last past five hundred mortal lives, I was an ascetic practicing patience. Even then I was free from those distinctions of separated selfhood. Therefore, Subhuti, Bodhisattvas should leave behind all phenomenal distinctions and awaken the thought of the consummation of incomparable enlightenment by not allowing the mind to depend on notions evoked by the sensible world—by not allowing the mind to depend upon notions evoked by sounds, odors, flavors, touch-contacts, or any qualities. The mind should be kept independent of any thoughts which arise within it. If the mind depends upon anything it has no sure haven. This is why Buddha teaches that the mind of a Bodhisattva should not accept the appearance of things as a basis when exercising charity. Subhuti, as Bodhisattvas practice charity for the welfare of all living beings they should do it in this manner. Just as the Tathagata declares that characteristics are not characteristics, so he declares that all living beings are not, in fact, living beings.

"Subhuti, the Tathagata is he who declares that which is true; he who declares that which is fundamental; he who declares that which is ultimate. He does not declare that which is deceitful, nor that which is monstrous. Subhuti, that truth to which the Tathagata has attained is neither real nor unreal.

"Subhuti, if a Bodhisattva practices charity with mind attached to formal notions he is like unto a man groping sightless in the gloom; but a Bodhisattva who practices charity with mind detached from any formal notions is like unto a man with open eyes in the radiant glory of the morning, to whom all kinds of objects are clearly visible.

"Subhuti, if there be good men and good women in future ages, able to receive, read, and recite this discourse in its entirety, the Tathagata will clearly perceive and recognize them

---

17 Time references seem confusing, but what is meant here is the present age and the future.

18 An event in one of the hundreds of former incarnations of the Buddha.

by means of his Buddha-knowledge; and each one of them will bring immeasurable and incalculable merit to fruition."

• • •

SECTION XVI: PURGATION THROUGH SUFFERING THE RETRIBUTION FOR PAST SINS

"Furthermore, Subhuti, if it be that good men and good women, who receive and retain this discourse, are downtrodden, their evil destiny is the inevitable retributive result of sins committed in their past mortal lives.[19] By virtue of their present misfortunes, the reacting effects of their past will be, thereby, worked out, and they will be in a position to attain the consummation of incomparable enlightenment.

"Subhuti, I remember the infinitely remote past before Dipankara Buddha.[20] There were eighty-four thousand myriads of multimillion of Buddhas and to all these I made offerings; yes, all these I served without the least trace of fault. Nevertheless, if anyone is able to receive, retain, study, and recite this discourse at the end of the last five hundred-year period, he will gain such merit that mine in the service of all the Buddhas could not be reckoned as one-hundredth part of it, not even one-thousandth part of it, not even one thousand myriad multimillionth part of it—indeed, no such comparison is possible.

"Subhuti, if I fully detailed the merit gained by good men and good women coming to receive, retain, study, and recite this discourse in the last period, my hearers would be filled with doubt and might become disordered in mind, suspicious and unbelieving. You should know, Subhuti, that the significance of this discourse is beyond conception; likewise the fruit of its rewards is beyond conception."

SECTION XXV: THE ILLUSION OF EGO

"Subhuti, what do you think? Let no one say the Tathagata cherishes the idea: I must liberate all living beings. Allow no such thought, Subhuti. Wherefore? Because in reality there are no living beings to be liberated by the Tathagata. If there were living beings for the Tathagata to liberate, he would partake in the idea of selfhood, personality, entity, and separate individuality.

"Subhuti, although the common people accept the ego as real, the Tathagata declares that ego is not different from non-ego. Subhuti, whom the Tathagata referred to as 'common people' are not really common people; such is merely a name."

SECTION XXXII: THE DELUSION OF APPEARANCES

19 The doctrine of karma, which is common to several schools of Indian thought, holds that one's status in each life is a projection forward of the good or evil one has done in previous existences. Buddhism accepted this doctrine but pointed the way to an eventual escape from the "wheel of reincarnation," by the achievement of enlightenment (Buddhahood) and attainment of Nirvana.

20 Another earlier incarnation of the Buddha.

"Subhuti, someone might fill innumerable worlds with the seven treasures and give all away in gifts of alms, but if any good man or good woman awakens the thought of enlightenment and takes only four lines of this discourse, reciting, using, receiving, retaining, and spreading them abroad and explaining them for the benefit of others, it will be far more meritorious.

"Now in what manner may he explain them to others? By detachment from appearances—abiding in real truth. So I tell you

> Thus shall ye think of all this fleeting world;
> A star at dawn, a bubble in a stream;
> A flash of lightning in a summer cloud;
> A flickering lamp, a phantom, and a dream."

When Buddha finished this discourse the venerable Subhuti, together with the *bhikshus*, *bhikshunis*, lay-brothers and sisters, and the whole realms of gods, men, and Titans, were filled with joy by his teaching, and, taking it sincerely to heart they went their ways.

MODERN WRITINGS

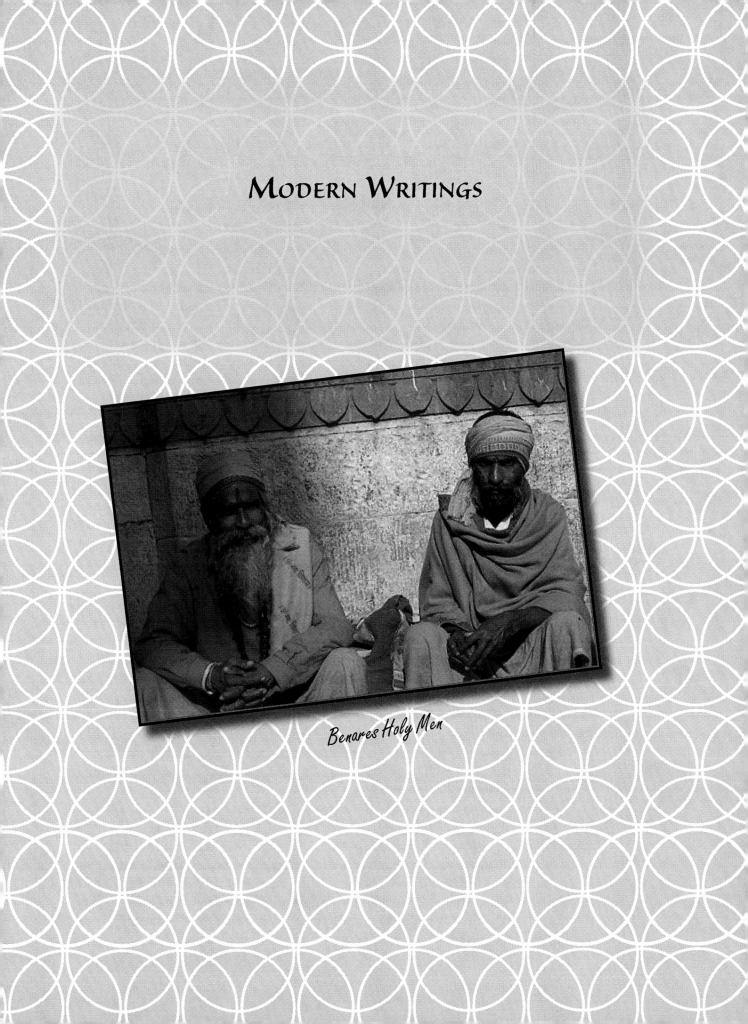

Benares Holy Men

1

......

THE ARYAN INVASION DEBATE

The Aryan Invasion of the Indus Valley and subsequently of north western Indian is a hotly debated topic. The original theory was proposed in the nineteenth century by European scholars who were using a biblical chronology and their own understanding of history, based on what were considered viable theories about the migrations and invasions of the so called Indo-Europeans out of Mesopotamian and into the western world. Because the Indo-Europeans were nomadic and had moved westward into Greece, Egypt, and Europe, these scholars felt that the same must have been true for eastward migrations and invasions. The nomads supposedly brought iron weapons and the chariot with them and easily conquered or slaughtered the local, agricultural civilizations with which they came in contact.

Since the nineteenth century, the theory has come into increasing debate. It was never really accepted or endorsed by Indians who see the Vedic tradition going back at least four thousand, if not seven or even ten thousand, years. As the theory has come under increased scrutiny, archaeologists have demonstrated that the Indus Valley in particular does not appear to have been the object of widespread violence from a conquest. The evidence of destruction or disturbances that has been found relates mostly to natural disasters and a gradual decline in city maintenance. It appears that the Indus River may have shifted causing floods and other destruction in the region and changing the climate so that the inhabitants of the Indus valley were forced to move east toward and into India.

Other misinterpretations rest on assumptions made about the wars between light and darkness mentioned in the Vedas. These wars between light and darkness were interpreted by scholars to refer to wars between the Aryans, who were assumed to be fair skinned like Europeans, and the darker skinned natives of the Indus Valley. There are descriptions of battles between light and darkness in other religious texts from around the world, yet these descriptions are not understood as referents to actual historical battles between light and dark skinned peoples. Furthermore, DNA testing has revealed that "the Y-chromosomal data consistently suggest a largely South Asian origin for Indian caste communities and therefore argue against any major influx, from regions north and west of India, of people associated either with the development of agriculture or the spread of the Indo-Aryan language family" (Renfrew, 1).

The Vedas make references to features of the Indus Valley that the Aryans appear to be quite familiar with, including the main rivers. More and more evidence is turning up to suggest that the Aryans were part of the Indus Valley culture all along. Settlements appear to the east of the Indus Valley along the dried up banks of the Saraswati and Drishadvati Rivers, where tradition says that Manu founded Vedic culture (Frawley, 6). The climate and the river courses changed through time, and eventually the Saraswati, which the Vedas describe as "endless in size" (Frawley, 6), dried up. Many scholars, including David Frawley, suggest that this event may have caused the end of the Indus culture.

The Aryan Invasion debate takes many forms. While traditional scholars date the Aryan Invasion to 1500 BC based on the biblical idea that the world began around 4,000 BC, other scholars have moved that date back, based on the migration of Indo-Europeans into the west around 6,000 BC. These scholars make the assumption that if migrations occurred westward into Greece, migrations must have also moved eastward into the Indus Valley area. However, there remains no real evidence of migrations or invasions in the Indus Valley.

David Frawley points out that much of the data and scholarship about the Indus Valley was written by white, Christian, European males who interpreted what they found in the nineteenth and early twentieth centuries without any real understanding of Hinduism or Indian culture. Frawley suggests that these assumptions were made in order to keep Indians divided against each other based on their supposed Aryan or Dravidian ancestry, to lend justification to the British conquest of India as the Brits were only following in the footsteps of the Aryans, and finally, to subordinate Hinduism and Indian Culture to the developments of religion, especially biblical religion, in the Middle East (11).

Svami B.V. Giri suggests that the Aryan Invasion supported a Christian influenced, western belief that there could not have been any areas of high civilization before the periods of Abraham or Moses. In "The Myth of the Aryan Invasion," Svami Giri states,

Most scholars of this period were neither archeologists nor historians in the strict sense of the word. Rather, they were missionaries paid by their governments to establish western cultural and racial superiority over the subjugated Indian citizens, through their study of indigenous religious texts. Consequently, for racial, political and religious reasons, early European indologists created a myth that still survives to this day. (1)

Further arguments against the Aryan Invasion point out that the word "Aryan" from Sanskrit refers to a person who is upright and noble (Giri, 3) and had nothing to do with race or blood. "This was a concoction by Max Mueller who, in 1853, introduced the word 'Arya' into the English language as referring a particular race and language" (Giri, 3), which in turn supported the Aryan Invasion theory. Unfortunately, those who did not understand the reference was originally to a language family and not to a race used the information to bolster their claims of a super race, the worst example being Hitler and the Nazi Government.

Until physical evidence of migration and conquest is found in the Indus Valley to support the Aryan Invasion theory, it remains unproved. The lack of evidence seems to support the opposing argument that the Indus Valley was inhabited by people who included those who followed the Vedas. As the climate changed, the rivers shifted, and trade declined, the Indus Valley inhabitants may have moved eastward into India looking for more hospitable regions to settle.

Works Cited

Frawley, David. "The Myth of the Aryan Invasion of India". http://www.hindunet.org/hindu_history/ancient/aryan/aryan_frawley.html

Giri, Svami B. V. "The Myth of the Aryan Invasion". http://www.gosai.com/chaitanya/saranagati/html/vedic-upanisads/aryan-invasion.html

Renfrew, Colin, Editor. "A prehistory of Indian Y chromosomes: Evaluating demic diffusion scenarios". PNAS. University of Cambridge, UK, January 13, 2006

2
......

INDIA 1750–1900

RAJA RAMMOHAN ROY: A SECOND CONFERENCE BETWEEN AN ADVOCATE FOR, AND AN OPPONENT OF, THE PRACTICE OF BURNING WIDOWS ALIVE (1820)

This is an imaginary dialogue arguing for and against sati, the practice of encouraging—and often forcing—widows to burn themselves alive on their husbands' funeral pyres, here referred to as "Concremation." This practice was outlawed by the British not long after the great Indian reformer Rammohan Roy made this argument, and is now extremely rare, as are the polygamous arrangements which he describes; but many of his comments on the burdens borne by women are applicable even today.

What are the main disadvantages to women that Roy sees in traditional marriage?

ADVOCATE

I alluded . . . to the real reason for our anxiety to persuade widows to follow their husbands, and for our endeavors to burn them pressed down with ropes: viz., that women are by nature of inferior understanding, without resolution, unworthy of trust, subject to passions, and void of virtuous knowledge; they, according to the precepts of the Sastra, are not allowed to marry again after the demise of their husbands, and consequently despair at once of all worldly pleasure; hence it is evident, that death to these unfortunate widows is preferable to existence; for the great difficulty which a widow may experience by living a purely ascetic life, as prescribed by the Shastras, is obvious; therefore, if she do not perform Concremation, it is probable that she may be guilty of such acts as may bring disgrace upon her paternal and maternal relations, and those that may be connected with her husband. Under these circumstances, we instruct them from their early life in the idea of Concremation, holding out to them heavenly enjoyments in company with their husbands, as well as the beatitude of their relations, both by birth and marriage, and their reputation in this world. From this many of them, on the death of their husbands, become desirous of accompanying them; but to remove every chance of their trying to escape from the blazing fire, in burning them we first tie them down to the pile.

OPPONENT

The reason you have now assigned for burning widows alive is indeed your true motive, as we are well aware; but the faults which you have imputed to women are not planted in their constitution by nature; it would be, therefore, grossly criminal to condemn that sex to death merely from precaution. By ascribing to them all sorts of improper conduct, you have indeed successfully persuaded the Hindu community to look down upon them as contemptible and mischievous creatures, whence they have been subjected to constant miseries. I have, therefore, to offer a few remarks on this head.

Women are in general inferior to men in bodily strength and energy; consequently the male part of the community, taking advantage of their corporeal weakness, have denied to them those excellent merits that they are entitled to by nature, and afterwards they are apt to say that women are naturally incapable of acquiring those merits. But if we give the subjects consideration, we may easily ascertain whether or not your accusation against them is consistent with justice. As to their inferiority in point of understanding, when did you ever afford them a fair opportunity of exhibiting their natural capacity? How then can you accuse them of want of understanding? If, after instruction in knowledge and wisdom, a person cannot comprehend or retain what has been taught him, we may consider him as deficient; but as you keep women generally void of education and acquirements, you cannot, therefore, in justice pronounce on their inferiority. On the contrary, Lilavati, Bhanumati, the wife of the prince of Karnat, and that of Kalidasa, are celebrated for their thorough knowledge of all the Shastras: moreover in the *Vrihadaranyaka Upanishhad* of the *Yajur Veda* it is clearly stated that Yajnavalkya imparted divine knowledge of the most difficult nature to his wife Maitreyi, who was able to follow and completely attain it!

Secondly. You charge them with want of resolution, at which I feel exceedingly surprised: for we constantly perceive, in a country where the name of death makes the male shudder, that the female, from her firmness of mind, offers to burn with the corpse of her deceased husband; and yet you accuse those women of deficiency in point of resolution.

Thirdly. With regard to their trustworthiness, let us look minutely into the conduct of both sexes, and we may be enabled to ascertain which of them is the most frequently guilty of betraying friends. If we enumerate such women in each village or town as have been deceived by men, and such men as have been betrayed by women, I presume that the number of the deceived women would be found ten times greater than that of the betrayed men. Men are, in general, able to read and write, and manage public affairs, by which means they easily promulgate such faults as women occasionally commit, but never consider as criminal the misconduct of men towards women. One fault they have, it must be acknowledged; which is, by considering others equally void of duplicity as themselves, to give their confidence too readily, from which they suffer much misery, even so far that some of them are misled to suffer themselves to be burnt to death.

In the fourth place, with respect to their subjection to the passions, this may be judged of by the custom of marriage as to the respective sexes; for one man may marry two or three, sometimes even ten wives and upwards; while a woman, who marries but one husband, desires at his death to follow him, forsaking all worldly enjoyments, or to remain leading the austere life of an ascetic.

Fifthly. The accusation of their want[1] of virtuous knowledge is an injustice. Observe what pain, what slighting, what contempt, and what afflictions their virtue enables them to support![2] How many Kulin Brahmans are there who marry ten or fifteen wives for the sake of money, that never see the greater number of them after the day of marriage, and visit others only three or four times in the course of their life. Still amongst those women, most, even without seeing or receiving any support from their husbands, living dependent on their fathers or brothers, and suffering much distress, continue to preserve their virtue; and when Brahmans, or those of other tribes, bring their wives to live with them, what misery do the women not suffer? At marriage the wife is recognized as half of her husband, but in after-conduct they are treated worse than inferior animals. For the woman is employed to do the work of a slave in the house, such as, in her turn, to clean the place very early in the morning, whether cold or wet, to scour the dishes, to wash the floor, to cook night and day, to prepare and serve food for her husband, father, mother-in-law, sisters-in-law, brothers-in-law, and friends and connections! (for amongst Hindus more than in other tribes relations long reside together, and on this account quarrels are more common amongst brothers respecting their worldly affairs). If in the preparation or serving up of the victuals they commit the smallest fault, what insult do they not receive from their husband, their mother-in-law, and the younger brothers of their husband? After all the male part of the family have satisfied themselves, the women content themselves with what may be left, whether sufficient in quantity or not. Where Brahmans or Kayasthas are not wealthy, their women are obliged to attend to their cows, and to prepare the cow-dung for firing. In the afternoon they fetch water from the river or tank, and at night perform the office of menial servants in making the beds. In case of any fault or omission in the performance of those labors they receive injurious treatment. Should the husband acquire wealth, he indulges in criminal amours to her perfect knowledge and almost under her eyes, and does not see her perhaps once a month. As long as the husband is poor, she suffers every kind of trouble, and when he becomes rich, she is altogether heart-broken. All this pain and affliction their virtue alone enables them to support. Where a husband takes two or three wives to live with him, they are subjected to mental miseries and constant quarrels. Even this distressed situation they virtuously endure. Sometimes it happens that the husband, from a preference for one of his wives, behaves cruelly to another. Amongst the lower classes, and those even of the better class who have not associated with good company, the wife, on the slightest fault, or even on bare suspicion of her misconduct, is chastised as a thief. Respect to virtue and their reputation generally makes them forgive even this treatment. If unable to bear such cruel usage, a wife leaves her husband's house to live separately from him, then the influence of the husband with the magisterial authority is generally sufficient to place her again in his hands; when, in revenge for her quitting him, he seizes every pretext to torment her in various ways, and sometimes even puts her privately to death. These are facts occurring every day, and not to be denied. What I lament is, that, seeing the women thus dependent and exposed to every misery, you feel for them no compassion, that might exempt them from being tied down and burnt to death.

1 Lack.

2 Bear.

3
......

WAITING FOR THE MAHATMA

R. K. NARAYAN

Mohandas Gandhi's reputation in India has never waned even though the nation's political course has taken directions he would have opposed, and scholars have interpreted and reinterpreted his contribution to Indian nationalism and the winning of independence. He is seen alternately as a saint, master political strategist, and utopian dreamer, but, in whatever guise, remains a figure of compelling interest in the Indian memory and imagination. A charismatic leader of such proportions is difficult to evaluate or analyze, and it is unlikely that historians and political scientists ever will succeed in mapping the true dimensions of his influence on India. It remains for the artists and creative writers to attempt to make an assessment. It is not unlikely that Gandhi will be transformed into a legend in the process, and the reader of this selection will be left to judge whether or not that transformation may not already be underway.

Several important novels have taken up the theme of Gandhi and his effect on India, including Raja Rao's Kanthapura (London: Allen & Unwin, 1938), and Mulk Raj Anand's Untouchable (Bombay: Jaico, 1956), but most attempt to portray Gandhi within a political context and thus lose something of the power of Gandhi's individual personality.

R. K. Narayan's *Waiting for the Mahatma* avoids this problem by largely ignoring the major political events of the time. The novel concentrates on depicting Gandhi as a real person among ordinary people, rather than as the saintly strategist of the independence movement. Narayan also avoids confronting Gandhi directly and thus being forced to describe and explain him. Gandhi appears frequently throughout the book, but he is described primarily in his relations to a young boy named Sriram and a young girl, Bharati, whom Sriram has fallen in love with. Sriram's caustic grandmother, other campaigners in the Indian independence movement, and various people who attempt to exploit Gandhi for their own ends are also included in the cast of characters. In this fashion the figure of Gandhi becomes a multifaceted reflection of a few people with whom he has come in contact. Moreover, this approach allows Narayan to present a realistic view of the lives and concerns of a few common people living in uncommon times. The novel thus offers us a different view of the last years of British rule in India.

Narayan is a major Indian novelist, and many of his stories are set in Malgudi, a fictional town resembling Mysore in South India. *Waiting for the Mahatma* (1955) initially had a mixed reception, partly due to the unconventional characterization of Gan-

From R. K. Narayan, *Waiting for the Mahatma* (Chicago: University of Chicago Press, 1981), pp. 62, 64-67, 69-72, 78-80, 84-85.

dhi, and partly because it appeared between his two most popular works, *The Financial Expert* (1953) and *The Guide* (1958). It is now considered one of his finest efforts.

Waiting *for the* Mahatma is the story of an introverted young man who is transformed by his ardent attachment to a disciple of Gandhi. The novel opens with the introduction of Sriram in about 1938, an orphan whose father had died in the service of the British in World War I and whose mother had died giving birth to him. Sriram has been raised by his Granny, who had saved his father's monthly pension payments and turned the bank account over to him on his twentieth birthday. With no need to work for a living, he leads an indolent and passionless life until meeting Bharati, a young girl whose devotion to the Mahatma leaves her no time for romantic involvement. In order to be near her, Sriram joins the nationalist movement and finally wins her when Gandhi approves their union on the day of his death in 1948. Despite this tragic conclusion, the novel is a richly humorous portrayal of middle-class Indian life in the last decade before independence.

In the following passage, Narayan portrays Sriram's conversion to Gandhi's movement, but leaves room for the reader to wonder what the young man's motivations truly are; perhaps he is not even sure of that himself. As the passage opens, the smitten Sriram has followed Bharati to a camp Gandhi has set up among the hovels of the untouchable city sweepers while on a visit to Malgudi. He offers to join the movement, and Bharati tells him to return at 3:00 A.M. When he does so, he unexpectedly finds himself face to face with Gandhi.

Questions

1. Does Sriram join with Gandhi exclusively because of his attraction to Bharati, or could he have other motives?
2. What does Sriram like and dislike about the life of Gandhi's volunteers?
3. How does Granny respond to Gandhi's campaign and to Sriram's intentions to take part in it?

WAITING FOR THE MAHATMA

Granny had slept fitfully. She had gone up to Kanni's shop five times during the evening to enquire if anyone had seen Sriram, and sent a boy who had come to make a purchase there to look for Sriram everywhere. At last the schoolmaster who lived up the street told her as he passed her house,

'Your pet is in Mahatma's camp. I saw him.'

'Ah! What was he doing there?' asked Granny alarmed. For her the Mahatma was one who preached dangerously, who tried to bring untouchables into the temples, and who involved people in difficulties with the police. She didn't like the idea. She wailed, 'Oh, master, why did you allow him to stay on there You should have brought him away. It is so late and he has not come home. As his old teacher you should have weaned him away.'

'Don't worry, madam, he is perfectly safe. How many of us could have the. privilege of being so near the Mahatma? You must be happy that he is doing so well! Our country needs more young men like him.'

Granny replied, 'It is teachers like you who have ruined our boys and this country,' and turned in, slamming the door.

He stood at the entrance to Mahatmaji's hut, holding his breath. It was very difficult to decide what he should do now. She had asked him to be present at the portals of the Great Presence, but perhaps she had been fooling him.

The door of Mahatmaji's hut was half open. Light streamed out through the gap. Sriram went towards it like a charmed moth. If he had paused to reflect he would not have believed himself to be capable of repeating a foolhardy act

second time. But through lack of sleep, and tension of nerves, a general recklessness had come over him, the same innocent charge that had taken him tumbling into the hut the previous evening took him there again now. He peeped in like a clown. The door was half open; he had over-estimated its width from a distance, for he could not peep in without thrusting his head through.

'Oh, there he is!' cried Bharati, with laughter in her voice. 'You may open the door if you wish to come in she said. Sriram felt again that the girl was making fun of him. Even in the great presence, she didn't seem to care. Here at least Sriram had hoped she would speak without the undertone of mischief. He felt so irritated at the thought that he replied with all the pungency he could muster in his tone: 'You have—I waited for you there—'

'Come in, come in' said the Mahatma. 'Why should you be standing there? You could have come straight in.'

'But she asked me to wait outside' said Sriram, stepping in gingerly. From the door to where the Mahatma sat the distance was less than ten feet, but he felt he was taking hours to cover it. His legs felt weak and seemed to intertwine, he seemed to be walking like a drunkard, a particularly dangerous impression to create in the Mahatma, who was out to persuade even the scavengers to give up drinking. In a flash it occurred to him that he ought to have a sensible answer ready if the Mahatma should suddenly turn round and ask, 'Have you been drinking toddy or whisky?'

But his trial came to an end, when Gandhi said, 'Bharati has just been mentioning you.' He spoke while his hands were busy fuming a spinning wheel, drawing out a fine thread. A man sitting in a comer, with a pad resting on his knee, was writing. Mahatmaji himself as always was doing several things at the same time. While his hands were spinning, his eyes perused a letter held before him by another, and he found it possible too to put in a word of welcome to Sriram. Through the back door of the hut many others were coming in and passing out. For each one of them Mahatmaji had something to say.

He looked up at Sriram and said: 'Sit down, young man. Come and sit as near me as you like.' There was so much unaffected graciousness in his tone that Sriram lost all fear and hesitation. He moved briskly up. He sat on the floor near Mahatmaji and watched with fascination the smooth fuming of the spinning wheel. Bharati went to an inner part of the hut, threw a swift look at Sriram, which he understood to mean, 'Remember not to make a fool of yourself.'

The Mahatma said, 'Nowadays I generally get up an hour earlier in order to be able to do this: spinning a certain length is my most important work: even my prayer comes only after that. I'd very much like you to take a vow to wear only cloth made out of your own hands each day.'

'Yes, I will do so: promised Sriram.

When the gong in the Taluk Office struck four, the Mahatma invited Sriram to go out with him for a walk.

During the last fifteen minutes of this walk the Mahatma said nothing) he walked in silence, looking at the ground before him. When the Mahatma was silent the others were even more so, the only movement they performed was putting one foot before another on the sand, keeping pace with him: some were panting hard and trying hard to suppress the sound. The Mahatma's silence was heavy and pervasive, and Sriram was afraid even to gulp or cough, although he very much wanted to clear his throat, cough, sneeze, swing his arms about. The only sound at the moment was the flowing of the river and the twitter of birds. Somewhere a cow was mooing. Even Bharati, the embodiment of frivolity, seemed to have become sombre. The Mahatma pulled out his watch, looked at it briefly and said, 'We will go back, that is all the walk I can afford today.' Sriram wanted to ask, 'Why?' But he held his tongue. The Mahatma turned to him as they were walking back, 'You have a grandmother, I hear, but no parents.'

'Yes. My grandmother is very old.'

'Yes, she must be, otherwise how can you call her a grandmother?' People laughed, Sriram too joined in this laughter out of politeness.

'Does she not miss you very much when you are away for so long?'

'Yes, very much. She gets very angry with me. I don't know what to do about it,' said Sriram courageously rushing ahead. He felt pleased at having said something of his own accord, but his only fear was that Bharati might step in and say something nasty and embarrassing, but he was happy to note that Bharati kept her peace.

Mahatmaji said: 'You must look after your granny too, she must have devoted herself to bringing you up.'

'Yes, but when I am away like this she is very much upset.'

'Is it necessary for you to be away from her so much?'

'Yes, Bapu, otherwise how can I do anything in this world?'

'What exactly do you want to do?'

It was now that Sriram became incoherent. He was seized with a rush of ideas and with all the confusion that too many ideas create. He said something, and the Mahatma watched him patiently, the others too held their breath and watched, and after a few moments of struggle for self expression, Sriram was able to form a cogent sentence. It was the unrelenting pressure of his subconscious desires that jerked the sentence out of his lips, and he said, 'I like to be where Bharati is.' The Mahatma said, 'Oh, is that so!' He patted Bharati's back and said, 'What a fine friend you have! You must be pleased to have such a devoted friend. How long have you known him?'

Bharati said like a shot, 'Since yesterday. I saw him for the first time sitting in your hut and I asked him who he was.'

Sriram interposed and added, 'But I knew her before, although I spoke to her only yesterday.'

The Mahatma passed into his hut, and went on to attend to other things. Many people were waiting for him. Bharati disappeared into the Mahatma's hut the moment they arrived. Sriram fell back and got mixed up with a crowd waiting outside. He felt jealous of Bharati's position. She sought him out later and said, 'You are probably unused to it, but in Bapu's presence we speak only the absolute truth and nothing less than that, and nothing more than that either.'

He took her to task: 'What will he think of me now when he knows that I have not known you long enough and yet—'

'Well, what?' she twitted him.

'And yet I wish to be with you and so on.'

'Why don't you go in and tell him you have been speaking nonsense and that you were blurting out things without forethought or self control? Why couldn't you have told him that you want to serve the country, that you are a patriot, that you want to shed your blood in order to see that the British leave the country? That is what most people say when they come near the Mahatma. I have seen hundreds of people come to him, and say the same thing.'

'And he believes all that?' asked Sriram.

'Perhaps not, but he thinks it is not right to disbelieve anyone.'

'But you say we must only speak the truth in his presence.'

'If you can, of course, but if you can't, the best thing to do is maintain silence.'

'Why are you so angry with me, is it not a part of your duty not to be angry with others?' asked Sriram pathetically.

'I don't care,' said Bharati, 'this is enough to irritate even the Mahatma. Now what will he think of me if he realizes I am encouraging a fellow like you to hang about the place, a fellow whom I have not known even for a full day yet!'

Sriram became reckless, and said breezily, 'What does it matter how long I have known you? Did you think I was going to lie to him if you had not spoken before I spoke?'

These bickerings were brought to an end by someone calling 'Bharati' from another hut. Bharati abandoned him and disappeared from the spot.

Bharati's words gave him an idea. He realized his own omission, and proposed to remedy it next time he walked with the Mahatma. Sriram's anxiety lest he fall asleep when the Mahatma was up kept him awake the whole night. He shared the space on the floor with one of the men in the camp. It was a strange feeling to lie down in a hut, and he felt he was becoming a citizen of an entirely new world. He missed the cosy room of his house in Kabir Lane, he missed the two pillows and the soft mattress and the carpet under it; even the street noises of Kabir Street added much to the domestic quality of life, and he missed it badly now. He had to adopt an entirely new mode of life. He had to live, of his own choice, in a narrow hut, with thatch above, with a dingy, sooty smell hanging about everything. The floor had been swept with cow dung and covered with a thin layer of sand. He had to snuggle his head on the crook of his arm for a pillow.

[Sriram spends a day in the camp and reams of the volunteers' commitment to poverty, nonviolence, self-suffering, and Indian independence, after which he felt ready to speak to Gandhi again.]

Sriram was told that he could accompany Mahatmaji in his tour of the villages on condition that he went home, and secured Granny's approval. Sriram tried to slur the matter over, he said it would not be necessary, he hinted he was an independent man used to such outings from home. The Mahatma's memory was better than that. He said with a smile, 'I remember you said that she didn't like to see you mixing with us.'

Sriram thought it over and said, 'Yes, master, but how can I for ever remain tied to her? It is not possible.'

'Are you quite sure that you want to change your style of life?' asked the Mahatma.

'I can think of nothing else,' Sriram said. 'How can I live as I have lived all these years?' He threw a quick glance at Bharati as she came in with some letters for the Mahatma. Her look prevented him from completing the sentence, which would have run, 'And I always wish to be with Bharati and not with my grandmother.'

The Mahatma said, 'I shall be happy to have you with us as long as you like, but you must first go home and tell your grandmother and receive her blessing. You must tell her frankly what you wish to do, but you must cause her no pain.'

Sriram hesitated. The prospect of facing Granny was unnerving. The thought of her was like the thought of an unreal troublesome world, one which he hoped he had left be-hind for ever: the real world for him now was the one of Bharati, Gorpad, unslaughtered naturally dying animals, the Mahatma, spinning wheels. He wanted to be here all the time; it seemed impossible for him to go back to Kabir Street, that *pyol,* and that shop, and those people there who treated him as if he were only eight years old. He stood before the Mahatma as if to appeal to him not to press him to go and face his grandmother, but the master was unrelenting. 'Go and speak to her. I don't think she is so unreasonable as to deny you your ambitions. Tell her that I would like to have you with me. If you tour with me the next two weeks, you will observe and learn much that may be useful to you later in life. Tell her she will feel glad that she let you go. Assure her that I will look after you safely.' Every word filled him with dread when he remembered the terms in which Granny referred to the Mahatma. He dared not even give the slightest indication as to how she would react. He felt a great pity for the Mahatma, so innocent that he could not dream of anyone talking ill of him. He felt angry at the thought of Granny, such an ill-informed, ignorant and bigoted personality! What business had she to complicate his existence in this way? If he could have had his will he would have ignored his grandmother, but he had to obey the Mahatma now.

He said, 'All right, sir. I will go and get my granny's blessing. I'll be back early tomor-row.'

[He summons up his courage and returns home. Apparently made anxious by his ab-sence, Granny feeds him delicacies and ridicules the lifestyle of the volunteers.]

Sriram was horrified. 'What do you take the Mahatma for! Do you know, he won't even wear sandals made of the hide of slaughtered animals!'

Granny was seized by a fit of laughter. Tears rolled down her cheeks. 'Won't wear san-dals!' she cried in uncontrollable laughter. 'Never heard of such a thing before! How do they manage it? By peeling off the skin of animals before they are slaughtered, is that it?'

'Shut up, Granny!' cried Sriram in a great rage. 'What an irresponsible gossip you are! I never thought you could be so bad!'

Granny for the first time noticed a fiery earnestness in her grandson, and gathered her-self up. She said: 'Oh! He is your God, is he?'

'Yes, he is, and I won't hear anyone speak lightly of him.'

'What else can I know, a poor ignorant hag like me! Do I read the newspapers? Do I listen to lectures? Am I told what is what by anyone? How should I know anything about that man Gandhi!'

'He is not a man; he is a Mahatma!' cried Sriram.

'What do you know about a Mahatma, anyway?' asked Granny.

Sriram fidgeted and rocked himself in his chair in great anger. He had not come prepared to face a situation of this kind. He had been only prepared to face a granny who might show sullenness at his absence, create difficulties for him when he wanted to go away and exhibit more sorrow and rage than levity. But here she was absolutely reckless, frivolous, and without the slightest sense of responsibility or respect. This was a situation which he had not anticipated, and he had no technique to meet it. It was no use, he realized, showing righteous indignation: that would only tickle the old lady more and more, and when the time came for him to take her permission and go, she might become too intractable.

Granny came back to her original mood after all these unexpected transitions. She said: 'You must eat your dinner, my boy,' very earnestly. She bustled about again as if for a distinguished visitor. She pulled a dining leaf out of a bundle in the kitchen rack, spread it on the floor, sprinkled a little water on it, and drew the bronze rice pot nearer, and sat down in order to be able to serve him without getting up again. The little lamp wavered in its holder. He ate in silence, took a drink of water out of the good old brass tumbler that was by his side; he cast a glance at the old bronze vessel out of which rice had been served to him for years. He suddenly felt depressed at the sight of it all. He was oppressed with the thought that he was leaving these old associations, that this was really a farewell party. He was going into an unknown life right from here. God knew what was in store for him. He felt very gloomy at the thought of it all. He knew it would be no good ever talking to his granny about his plans, or the Mahatma or Bharati. All that was completely beyond her comprehension. She would understand only edibles and dinner and fasting at night in order to impress a neighbour with her austerity. No use talking to her about anything. Best to leave in the morning without any fuss. He had obeyed Mahatmaji's mandate to the extent of seeing her and speaking to her. The Mahatma should be satisfied and not expect him to be able to bring about a conversion in the old lady's outlook, enough to earn her blessing.

Granny was very old, probably eighty, ninety, or a hundred. He had never tried to ascertain her age correctly. And she would not understand new things. At dead of night, after assuring himself that Granny was fast asleep, he got up, scribbled a note to her by the night lamp, and placed it under the brass pot containing water on the window sill, which she was bound to lift first thing in the morning. She could carry it to a neighbour and have it read to her if she had any difficulty in finding her glasses. Perhaps she might not like to have it read by the neighbours. She would always cry: 'Sriram, my glasses, where are the wretched glasses gone?' whenever anything came to her hand for reading, and it would be his duty to go to the cupboard, and fetch them. Now he performed the same duty in anticipation. He tip-toed to the almirah, took the glasses out of their case silently, and resumed to the hall, leaving the spectacle case open, because it had a tendency to close with a loud clap. He placed the glasses beside his letter of farewell, silently opened the door, and stepped into the night.

FURTHER READINGS

There are several literary critiques of Narayan's work, including William Walsh, *R. K. Narayan: A Critical Appreciation* (London: Heinemann, 1982), and M. K. Naik, *The Ironic Vision: A Study of the Fiction of R. K. Narayan* (New Delhi: Sterling, 1983). *R. K. Narayan, My Days* (New York: Viking, 1974) is a collection of autobiographical sketches. Of particular interest to students is his second novel, *The Bachelor of Arts* (1937, Chicago: The University of Chicago Press, 1980), which describes a young man's last year of college and first year after graduation. His experiences on a lecture tour of universities in the United States are humorously recounted in R. K. Narayan, *Reluctant Guru* (Delhi: Hind, 1974).

4

......

A HORSE AND TWO GOATS

R.K. NARAYAN

R. K. Narayan (1902–2001), one of India's best-known writers, was born in
Madras, India, and educated at Maharaja's College in Mysore, India.
Although Narayan's native language was Tamil, he wrote in English.
As suggested by their titles, many of his novels focus on characters
in India's middle class: *The Bachelor of Arts* (1937), *The English
Teacher* (1945), *The Financial Expert* (1952), and *The Sweet Ven-
dor* (1967). He retold many of India's legends in *Gods, Demons and
Others* (1964) and translated the great Sanskrit epics, *The Ramayana*
(1972) and *The Mahabharata* (1978). His short stories, many of them
published originally by his own press, Indian Thought Publications,
are set in a village, Malgudi, similar to Narayan's own childhood village, Mysore: *Malgudi Days* (1943), *A Horse and Two Goats* (1970),
and *The World of Malgudi* (2000). "A Horse and Two Goats," the
title story of the collection, presents a humorous encounter between a
poor farmer who does not understand English and an American who
does not understand Tamil.

Of the seven hundred thousand villages dotting the map of India, in which the majority of India's five hundred million live, flourish, and die, Kritam was probably the tiniest,
indicated on the district survey map by a microscopic dot, the map being meant more
for the revenue official out to collect tax than for the guidance of the motorist, who in
any case could not hope to reach it since it sprawled farfrom the highway at the end of a
rough track furrowed up by the iron-hooped wheels of bullock carts. But its size did not
prevent its giving itself the grandiose name Kri-tam, which meant in Tamil "coronet" or
"crown" on the brow of this subcontinent. The village consisted of less than thirty houses,
only one of them built with brick and cement. Painted a brilliant yellow and blue all over
with gorgeous carvings of gods and gargoyles on its balustrade, it was known as the Big
House. The other houses, distributed in four streets, were generally of bamboo thatch,
straw, mud, and other unspecified material. Muni's was the last house in the fourth street,
beyond which stretched the fields. In his prosperous days Muni had owned a flock of forty
sheep and goats and sallied forth every morning driving the flock to the highway a couple
of miles away. There he would sit on the pedestal of a clay statue of a horse while his
cattle grazed around. He carried a crook at the end of a bamboo pole and snapped foliage

from the avenue trees to feed his flock; he also gathered faggots and dry sticks, bundled them, and carried them home for fuel at sunset.

His wife lit the domestic fire at dawn, boiled water in a mud pot, threw into it a handful of millet flour, added salt, and gave him his first nourishment for the day. When he started out, she would put in his hand a packed lunch, once again the same millet cooked into a little ball, which he could swallow with a raw onion at midday. She was old, but he was older and needed all the attention she could give him in order to be kept alive.

His fortunes had declined gradually, unnoticed. From a flock of forty which he drove into a pen at night, his stock had now come down to two goats, which were not worth the rent of a half rupee a month the Big House charged for the use of the pen in their back yard. And so the two goats were tethered to the trunk of a drumstick tree which grew in front of his hut and from which occasionally Muni could shake down drumsticks. This morning he got six. He carried them in with a sense of triumph. Although no one could say precisely who owned the tree, it was his because he lived in its shadow.

She said, "If you were content with the drumstick leaves alone, I could boil and salt some for you."

"Oh, I am tired of eating those leaves. I have a craving to chew the drumstick out of sauce, I tell you."

"You have only four teeth in your jaw, but your craving is for big things. All right, get the stuff for the sauce, and I will prepare it for you. After all, next year you may not be alive to ask for anything. But first get me all the stuff, including a measure of rice or millet, and I will satisfy your unholy craving. Our store is empty today. Dhall, chili, curry leaves, mustard, coriander, gingelley oil, and one large potato. Go out and get all this." He repeated the list after her in order not to miss any item and walked off to the shop in the third street.

He sat on an upturned packing case below the platform of the shop. The shop-man paid no attention to him. Muni kept clearing his throat, coughing, and sneezing until the shopman could not stand it any more and demanded, "What ails you? You will fly off that seat into the gutter if you sneeze so hard, young man." Muni laughed inordinately, in order to please the shopman, at being called "young man." The shop-man softened and said, "You have enough of the imp inside to keep a second wife busy, but for the fact the old lady is still alive." Muni laughed appropriately again at this joke. It completely won the shopman over; he liked his sense of humour to be appreciated. Muni engaged his attention in local gossip for a few minutes, which always ended with a reference to the postman's wife who had eloped to the city some months before.

- The shopman felt most pleased to hear the worst of the postman, who had cheated him. Being an itinerant postman, he returned home to Kritam only once in ten days and every time managed to slip away again without passing the shop in the third street. By thus humouring the shopman, Muni could always ask for one or two items of food, promising repayment later. Some days the shopman was in a good mood and gave in, and sometimes he would lose his temper suddenly and bark at Muni for daring to ask for credit. This was such a day, and Muni could not progress beyond two items listed as essential components. The shopman was also displaying a remarkable memory for old facts and figures and took out an oblong ledger to support his observations. Muni felt impelled to rise and flee. But his self-respect kept him in his seat and made him listen to the worst things about himself. The shopman concluded, "If you could find five rupees and a quarter, you will have paid off an ancient debt and then could apply for admission to swarga. How much have you got now?"

"I will pay you everything on the first of the next month."

"As always, and whom do you except to rob by then?"

Muni felt caught and mumbled, "My daughter has sent word that she will be sending me money."

"Have you a daughter?" sneered the shopman. "And she is sending you money! For what purpose, may I know?"

"Birthday, fiftieth birthday," said Muni quietly.

"Birthday! How old are you?"

Muni repeated weakly, not being sure of it himself, "Fifty." He always calculated his age from the time of the great famine when he stood as high as the parapet around the village well, but who could calculate such things accurately nowadays with so many famines occurring? The shopman felt encouraged when other customers stood around to watch and comment. Muni thought helplessly, "My poverty is exposed to everybody. But what can I do?"

"More likely you are seventy," said the shopman. "You also forget that you mentioned a birthday five weeks ago when you wanted castor oil for your holy bath."

"Bath! Who can dream of a bath when you have to scratch the tank-bed for a bowl of water? We would all be parched and dead but for the Big House, where they let us take a pot of water from their well." After saying this Muni unobtrusively rose and moved off.

He told his wife, "That scoundrel would not give me anything. So go out and sell the drumsticks for what they are worth."

He flung himself down in a corner to recoup from the fatigue of his visit to the shop. His wife said, "You are getting no sauce today, nor anything else. I can't find anything to give you to eat. Fast till the evening, it'll do you good. Take the goats and be gone now," she cried and added, "Don't come back before the sun is down." He knew that if he obeyed her she would somehow conjure up some food for him in the evening. Only he must be careful not to argue and irritate her. Her temper was undependable in the morning but improved by evening time. She was sure to go out and work—grind corn in the Big House, sweep or scrub somewhere, and earn enough to buy foodstuff and keep a dinner ready for him in the evening.

Unleashing the goats from the drumstick tree, Muni started out, driving them ahead and uttering weird cries from time to time in order to urge them on. He passed through the village with his head bowed in thought. He did not want to look at anyone or be accosted. A couple of cronies lounging in the temple corridor hailed him, but he ignored their call. They had known him in the days of affluence when he lorded over a flock of fleecy sheep, not the miserable gawky goats that he had today. Of

course he also used to have a few goats for those who fancied them, but real wealth lay in sheep; they bred fast and people came and bought the fleece in the shearing season; and then that famous butcher from the town came over on the weekly market days bringing him betel leaves, tobacco, and often enough some *bhang*, which they smoked in a hut in the coconut grove, undisturbed by wives and well-wishers. After a smoke one felt light and elated and inclined to forgive everyone including that brother-in-law of his who had once tried to set fire to his home. But all this seemed like the memories of a previous birth. Some pestilence afflicted his cattle (he could of course guess who had laid his animals under curse), and even the friendly butcher would not touch one at half the price . . . and now here he was left with the two craggy creatures. He wished someone would rid him of their company too. The shopman had said that he was seventy. At seventy, one only waited to be summoned by God. When he was dead what would his wife do? They had lived in each other's company since they were children. He was told on their day of wedding that he was ten years old and she was eight. During the wedding ceremony they had had to recite their respective ages and names. He had thrashed her only a few times in their career, and later she had the upper hand. Progeny, none. Perhaps a large progeny would have brought him the blessing of the gods. Fertility brought merit. People with fourteen sons were always so prosperous and at peace with the world and themselves. He recollected the thrill he had felt when he mentioned a daughter to that shopman; although it was not believed, what if he did not have a daughter?—his cousin in the next village had many daughters, and any one of them was as good as his; he was fond of them all and would buy them sweets if he could afford it. Still, everyone in the village whispered behind their backs that Muni and his wife were a barren couple. He avoided looking at anyone; they all professed to be so high up, and everyone else in the village had more money than he. "I am the poorest fellow in our caste and no wonder that they spurn me, but I won't look at them either," and so he passed on with his eyes downcast along the edge of the street, and people left him also very much alone, commenting only to the extent, "Ah, there he goes with his two goats; if he slits their throats, he may have more peace of mind." "What has he to worry about anyway? They live on nothing and have none to worry about." Thus people commented when he passed through the village. Only on the outskirts did he lift his head and look up. He urged and bullied the goats until they meandered along to the foot of the horse statue on the edge of the village. He sat on its pedestal for the rest of the day. The advantage of this was that he could watch the highway and see the lorries and buses pass through to the hills, and it gave him a sense of belonging to a larger world. The pedestal of the statue was broad enough for him to move around as the sun traveled up and westward; or he could also crouch under the belly of the horse, for shade.

The horse was nearly life-size, moulded out of clay, baked, burnt, and brightly coloured, and reared its head proudly, prancing its forelegs in the air and flourishing its tail in a loop; beside the horse stood a warrior with scythe-like mustachios, bulging eyes, and aquiline nose. The old image-makers believed in indicating a man of strength by bulging out his eyes and sharpening his moustache tips, and also decorated the man's chest with beads which looked today like blobs of mud through the ravages of sun and wind and rain (when it came), but Muni would insist that he had known the beads to sparkle like the nine gems at one time in his life. The horse itself was said to have been as white as a dhobi-washed sheet, and had had on its back a cover of pure brocade of red and black lace, matching the multicoloured sash around the waist of the warrior. But none in the village remembered the splendour as no one noticed its existence. Even Muni, who spent all his waking hours at its foot, never bothered to look up. It was untouched even by the young vandals of the village who gashed tree trunks with knives and tried to topple off milestones and inscribed lewd designs on all walls. This statue had been closer to the population of the village at one time, when this spot bordered the village; but when the highway was laid through (or perhaps when the tank and wells dried up completely here) the village moved a couple of miles inland.

Muni sat at the foot of the statue, watching his two goats graze in the arid soil among the cactus and lantana bushes. He looked at the sun; it had tilted westward no doubt, but it was not the time yet to go back home; if he went too early his wife would have no food for him. Also he must give her time to cool off her temper and feel sympathetic, and then she would scrounge and manage to get some food. He watched the mountain road for a time signal. When the green bus appeared around the bend he could leave, and his wife would feel pleased that he had let the goats feed long enough.

He noticed now a new sort of vehicle coming down at full speed. It looked like both a motor car and a bus. He used to be intrigued by the novelty of such spectacles, but of late work was going on at the source of the river on the mountain and an assortment of people and traffic went past him, and he took it all casually and described to his wife, later in the day, everything he saw. Today, while he observed the yellow vehicle coming down, he was wondering how to describe it later to his wife when it sputtered and stopped in front of him. A red-faced foreigner, who had been driving it, got down and went round it, stooping, looking, and poking under the vehicle; then he straightened himself up, looked at the dashboard, stared in Muni's direction, and approached him. "Excuse me, is there a gas station nearby, or do I have to wait until another car comes—" He suddenly looked up at the clay horse and cried, "Marvellous," without completing his sentence. Muni felt he should get up and

away, and cursed his age. He could not readily put his limbs into action; some *years* ago he could outrun a cheetah, as happened once when he went to the forest to cut fuel and it was then that two of his sheep were mauled—a sign that bad times were coming. Though he tried, he could not easily extricate himself from his seat, and then there was also the problem of the goats. He could not leave them behind.

The red-faced man wore khaki clothes—evidently a policeman or a soldier. Muni said to himself, "He will chase or shoot if I start running. Some dogs chase only those who run—oh, Shiva protect me. I don't know why this man should be after me." Meanwhile the foreigner cried, "Marvellous!" again, nodding his head. He paced around the statue with his eyes fixed on it. Muni sat frozen for a while, and then fidgeted and tried to edge away. Now the other man suddenly pressed his palms together in a salute, smiled, and said, "Namaste! How do you do?"

At which Muni spoke the only English expressions he had learnt, "Yes, no." Having exhausted his English vocabulary, he started in Tamil: "My name is Muni.

These two goats are mine, and no one can gainsay it—though our village is full of slanderers these days who will not hesitate to say that what belongs to a man doesn't belong to him?' He rolled his eyes and shuddered at the thought of evil-minded men and women peopling his village.

The foreigner faithfully looked in the direction indicated by Muni's fingers, gazed for a while at the two goats and the rocks, and with a puzzled expression took out his silver cigarette case and lit a cigarette. Suddenly remembering the courtesies of the season, he asked, "Do you smoke?" Muni answered, "Yes, no." Whereupon the red-faced man took a cigarette and gave it to Muni, who received it with surprise, having had no offer of a smoke from anyone for years now. Those days when he smoked bhang were gone with his sheep and the large-hearted butcher. Nowadays he was not able to find even matches, let alone bhang. (His wife went across and borrowed a fire at dawn from a neighbour.) He had always wanted to smoke a cigarette; only once did the shopman give him one on credit, and he remembered how good it had tasted. The other flicked the lighter open and offered a light to Muni. Muni felt so confused about how to act that he blew on it and put it out. The other, puzzled but undaunted, flourished his lighter, presented it again, and lit Muni's cigarette. Muni drew a deep puff and started coughing; it was racking, no doubt, but extremely pleasant. When his cough subsided he wiped his eyes and took stock of the situation, understanding that the other man was not an Inquisitor of any kind. Yet, in order to make sure, he remained wary. No need to run away from a man who gave him such a potent smoke. His head was reeling from the effect of one of those strong American cigarettes made with roasted tobacco. The man said, "I come from New York," took out a wallet from his hip pocket, and presented his card.

Muni shrank away from the card. Perhaps he was trying to present a warrant and arrest him. Beware of khaki, one part of his mind warned. Take all the cigarettes or bhang or whatever is offered, but don't get caught. Beware of khaki. He wished he weren't seventy as the shopman had said. At seventy one didn't run, but surrendered to whatever came. He could only ward off trouble by talk. So he went on, all in the chaste Tamil for which Kritam was famous. (Even the worst detractors could not deny that the famous poetess Avvaiyar was born in this area, although no one could say whether it was in Kritam or Kuppam, the adjoining village.) Out of this heritage the Tamil language gushed through Muni in an unimpeded flow. He said, "Before God, sir, Bhagwan, who sees everything, I tell you, sir, that we know nothing of the case. If the murder was committed, whoever did it will not escape. Bhagwan is all-seeing. Don't ask me about it. I know nothing." A body had been found mutilated and thrown under a tamarind tree at the border between Kritam and Kuppam a few weeks before, giving rise to much gossip and speculation. Muni added an explanation. "Anything is possible there. People over there will stop at nothing." The foreigner nodded his head and listened courteously though he understood nothing.

"I am sure you know when this horse was made," said the red man and smiled ingratiatingly.

Muni reacted to the relaxed atmosphere by smiling himself, and pleaded, "Please go away, sir, I know nothing. I promise we will hold him for you if we see any bad character around, and we will bury him up to his neck in a coconut pit if he tries to escape; but our village has always had a clean record. Must definitely be the other village."

Now the red man implored, "Please, please, I will speak slowly, please try to understand me. Can't you understand even a simple word of English? Everyone in this country seems to know English. I have gotten along with English everywhere in this country but you don't speak it. Have you any religious or spiritual scruples against English speech?"

Muni made some indistinct sounds in his throat and shook his head. Encouraged, the other went on to explain at length, uttering each syllable with care and deliberation. Presently he sidled over and took a seat beside the old man, explaining, "You see, last August, we probably had the hottest summer in history, and I was working in shirt-sleeves in my office on the fortieth floor of the Empire State Building. We had a power failure one day, you know, and there I was stuck for four hours, no elevator, no air conditioning. All the way in the train I kept thinking, and the minute I reached home in Connecticut, I told my wife Ruth, 'We will visit India this winter, it's time to look at other civilizations.' Next day she called the travel agent first thing and told him to fix it, and so here I am. Ruth came with me but is staying back at Srinagar, and I am the one doing the rounds and joining her later."

Muni looked reflective at the end of this long oration and said, rather feebly, 'Yes, no,' as a concession to the other's language, and went on in Tamil, "When I was this high"—he indicated a foot high—" I had heard my uncle say .. ."

No one can tell what he was planning to say, as the other interrupted him at this stage to ask, "Boy, what is the secret of your teeth? How old are you?"

The old man forgot what he had started to say and remarked, "Sometimes we too lose our cattle. Jackals or cheetahs may sometimes carry them off, but sometimes it is just theft from over in the next village, and then we will know who has done it. Our priest at the temple can see in the camphor flame the face of the thief, and when he is caught .. ." He gestured with his hands a perfect mincing of meat.

The American watched his hands intently and said, "I know what you mean. Chop something? Maybe I am holding you up and you want to chop wood? Where is your axe? Hand it to me and show me what to chop. I do enjoy it, you know, just a hobby. We get a lot of driftwood along the backwater near my house, and on Sundays I do nothing but chop wood for the fireplace. I really feel different when I watch the fire in the fireplace, although it may take all the sections of the Sunday *New York Times* to get a fire started." And he smiled at this reference.

Muni felt totally confused but decided the best thing would be to make an attempt to get away from this place. He tried to edge out, saying, "Must go home," and turned to go. The other seized his shoulder and said desperately, "Is there no one, absolutely no one here, to translate for me?" He looked up and down the road, which was deserted in this hot afternoon; a sudden gust of wind churned up the dust and dead leaves on the roadside into a ghostly column and propelled it towards the mountain road. The stranger almost pinioned Muni's back to the statue and asked, "Isn't this statue yours? Why don't you sell it to me?"

The old man now understood the reference to the horse, thought for a second, and said in his own language, "I was an urchin this high when I heard my grandfather explain this horse and warrior, and my grandfather himself was this high when he heard his grandfather, whose grandfather . . ."

The other man interrupted him. "I don't want to seem to have stopped here for nothing. I will offer you a good price for this," he said, indicating the horse. He had concluded without the least doubt that Muni owned this mud horse. Perhaps he guessed by the way he sat on its pedestal, like other souvenir sellers in this country presiding over their wares.

Muni followed the man's eyes and pointing fingers and dimly understood the subject matter and, feeling relieved that the theme of the mutilated body had been abandoned at least for the time being, said again, enthusiastically, "I was this high when my grandfather told me about this horse and the warrior, and my grandfather was this high when he himself . . ." and he was getting into a deeper bog of reminiscence each time he tried to indicate the antiquity of the statue.

The Tamil that Muni spoke was stimulating even as pure sound, and the foreigner listened with fascination. "I wish I had my tape-recorder here," he said, assuming the pleasantest expression. "Your language sounds wonderful. I get a kick out of every word, you utter, here"—he indicated his ears—"but you don't have to waste your breath in sales talk. I appreciate the article. You don't have to explain its points."

"I never went to a school, in those days only Brahmin went to schools, but we had to go out and work in the fields morning till night, from sowing to harvest time . ◆ ◆ and when Pongal came and we had cut the harvest, my father allowed me to go out and play with others at the tank, and so I don't know the Parangi language you speak, even little fellows in your country probably speak the Parangi language, but here only learned men and officers know it. We had a postman in our village who could speak to you boldly in your language, but his wife ran away with someone and he does not speak to anyone at all nowadays. Who would if a wife did what she did? Women must be watched; otherwise they will sell themselves and the home." And he laughed at his own quip.

The foreigner laughed heartily, took out another cigarette, and offered it to Muni, who now smoked with ease, deciding to stay on if the fellow was going to be so good as to keep up his cigarette supply. The American now stood up on the pedestal in the attitude of a demonstrative lecturer and said, running his finger along some of the carved decorations around the horse's neck, speaking slowly and uttering his words syllable by syllable, "I could give a sales talk for this better than anyone else. . . . This is a marvelous combination of yellow and indigo, though faded now. . . . How do you people of this country achieve these flaming colours?"

Muni, now assured that the subject was still the horse and not the dead body, said, "This is our guardian, it means death to our adversaries. At the end of Kali Yuga, this world and all other worlds will be destroyed, and the Redeemer will come in the shape of a horse called 'Kalki'; this horse will come to life and gallop and trample down all bad men." As he spoke of bad men the figures of his shopman and his brother-in-law assumed concrete forms in his mind, and he reveled for a moment in the predicament of the fellow under the horse's hoof: served him right for trying to set fire to his home. . . .

While he was brooding on this pleasant vision, the foreigner utilized the pause to say, "I assure you that this will have the best home in the U.S.A. I'll push away the book-case, you know I love books and am a member of five book clubs, and the choice and bonus volumes mount up to a pile really in our living room, as high as this horse itself. But they'll have to go. Ruth may disapprove, but I will convince her. The T.V. may have to be shifted too. We can't have everything in the living room. Ruth will probably say what about when we have a party? I'm going to keep him right in the middle of the room. I don't see how that can interfere with the party—we'll stand around him and have our drinks."

Muni continued his description of the end of the world. "Our pundit discoursed at the temple once how the oceans are going to close over the earth in a huge wave and swallow us—this horse will grow bigger than the biggest wave and carry on its back only the good people and kick into the floods the evil ones—plenty of them about—" he said reflectively. "Do you know when it is going to happen?" he asked.

The foreigner now understood by the tone of the other that a question was being asked and said, "How am I transporting it? I can push the seat back and make room in the rear. That van can take in an elephant"—waving precisely at the back of the seat.

Muni was still hovering on visions of avatars and said again, "I never missed our pundit's discourses at the temple in those days during every bright half of the month, although he'd go on all night, and he told us that Vishnu is the highest god. Whenever evil men trouble us, he comes down to save us. He has come many times. The first time he incarnated as a great fish, and lifted the scriptures on his back when the floods and sea waves . . ."

"I am not a millionaire, but a modest businessman. My trade is coffee."

Amidst all this wilderness of obscure sound Muni caught the word "coffee" and said, "If you want to drink 'kapi,' drive further up, in the next town, they have Friday market, and there they open 'kapi-otels'—so I learn from passers-by. Don't think I wander about. I go nowhere and look for nothing." His thoughts went back to the avatars. "The first avatar was in the shape of a little fish in a bowl of water, but every hour it grew bigger and bigger and became in the end a huge whale which the seas could not contain, and on the back of the whale the holy books were supported, saved and carried." Once he had launched on the first avatar, it was inevitable that he should go on to the next, a wild boar on whose tusk the earth was lifted when a vicious conqueror of the earth carried it off and hid it at the bottom of the sea. After describing this avatar Muni concluded, "God will always save us whenever we are troubled by evil beings. When we were young we staged at full moon the story of the avatars. That's how I know the stories; we played them all night until the sun rose, and sometimes the European collector would come to watch, bringing his own chair. I had a good voice and so they always taught me songs and gave me the women's roles. I was always Goddess Lakshmi, and they dressed me in a brocade sari, loaned from the Big House . . ."

The foreigner said, "I repeat I am not a millionaire. Ours is a modest business; after all, we can't afford to buy more than sixty minutes of T.V. time in a month, which works out to two minutes a day, that's all, although in the course of time we'll maybe sponsor a one-hour show regularly if our sales graph continues to go up . . ."

Muni was intoxicated by the memory of his theatrical days and was about to explain how he had painted his face and worn a wig and diamond earrings when the visitor, feeling that he had spent too much time already, said, "Tell me, will you accept a hundred rupees or not for the horse? I'd love to take the whiskered soldier also but no space for him this year. I'll have to cancel my air ticket and take a boat home, I suppose. Ruth can go by air if she likes, but I will go with the horse and keep him in my cabin all the way if necessary." And he smiled at the picture of himself voyaging across the seas hugging this horse. He added, "I will have to pad it with straw so that it doesn't break . . ."

"When we played *Ramayana*, they dressed me as Sita," added Muni. "A teacher came and taught us the songs for the drama and we gave him fifty rupees. He incarnated himself as Rama, and He alone could destroy Ravana, the demon with ten heads who shook all the worlds; do you know the story of *Ramayana*?"

"I have my station wagon as you see. I can push the seat back and take the horse in if you will just lend me a hand with it."

"Do you know *Mahabharata*? Krishna was the eighth avatar of Vishnu, incarnated to help the Five Brothers regain their kingdom. When Krishna was a baby he danced on the thousand-hooded giant serpent and trampled it to death; and then he suckled the breasts of the demoness and left them flat as a disc though when she came to him her bosoms were large, like mounds of earth on the banks of a dug up canal." He indicated two mounds with his hands. The stranger was completely mystified by the gesture. For the first time he said, "I really wonder what you are saying because your answer is cmcial. We have come to the point when we should be ready to talk business."

"When the tenth avatar comes, do you know where you and I will be?" asked the old man.

"Lend me a hand and I can lift off the horse from its pedestal after picking out the cement at the joints. We can do anything if we have a basis of understanding."

At this stage the mutual mystification was complete, and there was no need even to carry on a guessing game at the meaning of words. The old man chattered away in a spirit of balancing off the credits and debits of conversational exchange, and said in order to be on the credit side, "Oh, honourable one, I hope God has blessed you with numerous progeny. I say this because you seem to be a good man, willing to stay beside an old man and talk to him, while all day I have none to talk to except when somebody stops by to ask for a piece of tobacco. But I seldom have it, tobacco is not what it used to be at one time, and I have given up chewing. I cannot afford it nowadays." Noting the other's interest in his speech, Muni felt encouraged to ask, "How many children have you?" with appropriate gestures with his hands. Realizing that a question was being asked, the red man replied, "I said a hundred," which encouraged Muni to go into details. "How many of your children are boys and how many girls? Where are they? Is your daughter married? Is it difficult to find a son-in-law in your country also?"

In answer to these questions the red man dashed his hand into his pocket and brought forth his wallet in order to take immediate advantage of the bearish trend in the market. He flourished a hundred-rupee currency note and said, "Well, this is what I meant."

The old man now realized that some financial element was entering their talk. He peered closely at the currency note, the like of which he had never seen in his life; he knew the five and ten by their colours although always in other people's hands, while his own earning at any time was in coppers and nickels. What was this man flourishing the note for? Perhaps asking for change. He laughed to himself at the notion of anyone coming to him for changing a thousand- or ten-thousand-rupee note. He said with a grin, "Ask our village headman, who is also a moneylender; he can change even a lakh of rupees in gold sovereigns if you prefer it that way; he thinks nobody knows, but dig the floor of his puja room and your head will reel at the sight of the hoard. The man disguises himself in rags just to mislead the public. Talk to the headman yourself because he goes mad at the sight of me. Someone took away his pumpkins with the creeper and he, for some reason, thinks it was me and my goats . . . that's why I never let my goats be seen anywhere near the farms.' His eyes travelled to his goats nosing about, attempting to wrest nutrition from minute greenery peeping out of rock and dry earth.

The foreigner followed his look and decided that it would be a sound policy to show an interest in the old man's pets. He went up casually to them and stroked their backs with every show of courteous attention. Now the truth dawned on the old man. His dream of a lifetime was about to be realized. He understood that the red man was actually making an offer for the goats. He had reared them up in the hope of selling them some day and, with the capital, opening a small shop on this very spot. Sitting here, watching towards the hills, he had often dreamt how he would put up a thatched roof here, spread a gunny sack out on the ground, and display on it fried nuts, coloured sweets, and green coconut for the thirsty and famished wayfarers on the highway, which was sometimes very busy. The animals were not prize ones for a cattle show, but he had spent his occasional savings to provide them some fancy diet now and then, and they did not look too bad. While he was reflecting thus, the red man shook his hand and left on his palm one hundred rupees in tens now, suddenly realizing that this was what the old man was asking. "It is all for you or you may share it if you have a partner."

The old man pointed at the station wagon and asked, "Are you carrying them off in that?"

"Yes, of course," said the other, understanding the transportation part of it.

The old man said, "This will be their first ride in a motor car. Carry them off after I get out of sight, otherwise they will never follow you, but only me even if I am traveling on the path of Yama Loka." He laughed at his own joke, brought his palms together in a salute, turned round and went off, and was soon out of sight beyond a clump of thicket.

The red man looked at the goats grazing peacefully. Perched on the pedestal of the horse, as the westerly sun touched off the ancient faded colours of the statue with a fresh splendour, he ruminated, "He must be gone to fetch some help, I suppose!" and settled down to wait. When a truck came downhill, he stopped it and got the help of a couple of men to detach the horse from its pedestal and place it in his station wagon. He gave them five rupees each, and for a further payment they siphoned off gas from the truck, and helped him to start his engine.

Muni hurried homeward with the cash securely tucked away at his waist in his dhoti. He shut the street door and stole up softly to his wife as she squatted before the lit oven wondering if by a miracle food would drop from the sky. Muni displayed his fortune for the day. She snatched the notes from him, counted them by the glow of the fire, and cried, "One hundred rupees! How did you come by it? Have you been stealing?"

"I have sold our goats to a red-faced man. He was absolutely crazy to have them, gave me all this money and carried them off in his motor car!"

Hardly had these words left his lips when they heard bleating outside. She opened the door and saw the two goats at her door. "Here they are!" she said. "What's the meaning of all this?"

He muttered a great curse and seized one of the goats by its ears and shouted, "Where is that man? Don't you know you are his? Why did you come back?" The goat only wriggled in his grip. He asked the same question of the other too. The goat shook itself off. His wife glared at him and declared, "If you have thieved, the police will come tonight and break your bones. Don't involve me. I will go away to my parents. . ."

Questions for Discussion

1. How does Muni's conversation with the shopman establish the tension in the story? How does Muni's negotiation with the American bring the story to a climax? How does Muni's wife bring the story to an ironic conclusion?

2. How does Muni characterize his former life as a "wealthy" man? What does his conversation about Indian legends reveal about his character? What does the American's decision to visit India reveal about his character?

3. How does Narayan establish the setting of Muni's village? How does the red-faced American interpret India's climate and culture?

4. How does Narayan present the conversation between Muni and the American? How does he reveal the humor in their strange conversation?

5. What does the story reveal about the power of language to create the basis for understanding or mutual mystification?

Three Writing Assignments

1. Respond to the story by describing your attempt to communicate with someone who did not speak your language.

2. Investigate India's caste system and village culture. Use your research to explain Muni's position in his village and the significance of his "new" wealth.
3. Create the cocktail story the red-faced American will tell about the horse once it is displayed in his home.

PART II:

China

photo courtesy of E. Frame

Ancient land of Dao
Wise, humble and contented
Teach us your secrets.
—Edward M. Frame

China

Tai Shan. One of the five sacred Mountains of China

Sitar Player

The Great Wall of China

The Great Wall of China

Historical Perspective of China

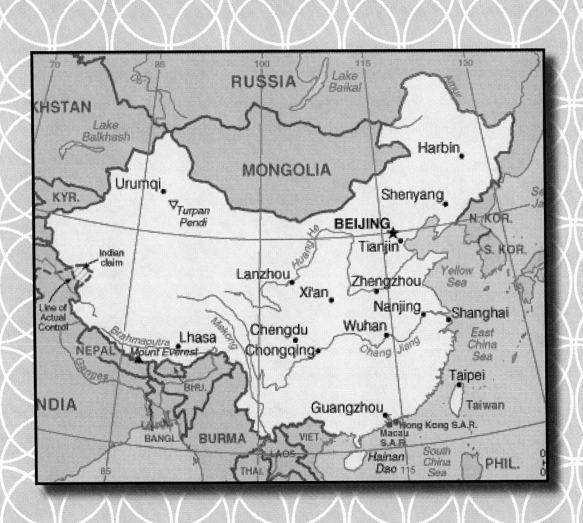

Courtesy of William J. Duiker

CHINA IN ANTIQUITY

FOCUS QUESTIONS

- How did geography influence the civilization that arose in China?
- What were the major tenets of Confucianism, Legalism, and Daoism, and what role did each play in Chinese civilization?
- What were the key aspects of social and economic life in early China?
- What role did nomadic peoples play in early Chinese history?
- ➤ What concepts of kingship and political and governmental institutions characterized each of the major dynasties of early China—the Shang, the Zhou, the Qin, and the Han?

he Master said: "If the government seeks to rule by decree, and to maintain order by the use of punishment, the people will seek to evade punishment and have no sense of shame. But if government leads by virtue and governs through the rules of propriety, the people will feel shame and seek to correct their mistakes."

That statement is from the *Analects*, a collection of remarks by the Chinese philosopher Confucius that were gathered together by his disciples and published after his death in the fifth century B.C.E. Confucius lived at a time when Chinese society was in a state of increasing disarray. The political principles that had governed society since the founding of the Zhou dynasty six centuries earlier were widely ignored, and squabbling principalities scuffled for primacy as the power of the Zhou court steadily declined. The common people groaned under the weight of an oppressive manorial system that left them at the mercy of their feudal lords.

In the midst of this turmoil, Confucius traveled the length of the kingdom observing events and seeking employment as a political counselor. In the process, he attracted a number of disciples, to whom he expounded a set of ideas that in later years served as the guiding principles for the Chinese empire. Some of his ideas are strikingly modern in their thrust. Among them is the revolutionary proposition that government depends on the will of the people.

The civilization that produced Confucius had originated more than fifteen hundred years earlier along the two great river systems of East Asia, the Yellow and the Yangtze. This vibrant new civilization, which we know today as ancient China, expanded gradually over its neighboring areas. By the third century B.C.E., it had emerged as a great empire, as well as the dominant cultural and political force in the entire region.

Like Sumer, Harappa, and Egypt, the civilization of ancient China began as a collection of autonomous villages cultivating food crops along a major river system. Improvements in agricultural techniques led to a food surplus and the growth of an urban civilization characterized by more complex political and social institutions, as well as new forms of artistic and intellectual creativity.

Like its counterparts elsewhere, ancient China faced the challenge posed by the appearance of pastoral peoples on its borders. Unlike Harappa, Sumer, and Egypt, however, ancient China was able to surmount that challenge, and many of its institutions and cultural values survived intact down to the beginning of the twentieth century. For that reason, Chinese civilization is sometimes described as the oldest continuous civilization on earth. •

THE LAND AND PEOPLE OF CHINA

According to Chinese legend, Chinese society was founded by a series of rulers who brought the first rudiments of civilization to the region nearly five thousand years ago. The first was Fu Xi (Fu Hsi), the ox-tamer, who "knotted cords for hunting and fishing," domesticated animals, and introduced the beginnings of family life. The second was Shen Nong (Shen Nung), the divine farmer, who "bent wood for plows and hewed wood for plowshares." He taught the people the techniques of agriculture. Last came Huang Di (Huang Ti), the Yellow Emperor, who "strung a piece of wood for the bow, and whittled little sticks of wood for the arrows." Legend credits Huang Di with creating the Chinese system of writing, as well as with inventing the bow and arrow.[1] Modern historians, of course, do not accept the literal accuracy of such legends but view them instead as part of the process whereby early peoples attempt to make sense of the world and their role in it. Nevertheless, such re-creations of a mythical past often contain an element of truth. Although there is no clear evidence that the "three sovereigns" actually existed, their achievements do symbolize some of the defining characteristics of Chinese civilization: the interaction between nomadic and agricultural peoples, the importance of the family as the basic unit of Chinese life, and the development of a unique system of writing.

Human communities have existed in China for several hundred thousand years. Sometime around the eighth millennium B.C.E., the early peoples living along the riverbanks of northern China began to master the cultivation of crops. A number of these early agricultural settlements were in the neighborhood of the Yellow River, where they gave birth to two Neolithic societies known to archaeologists as the Yangshao and the Longshan cultures (sometimes identified in terms of their pottery as the painted and black pottery cultures). Similar communities have been found in the Yangtze valley in central China and along the coast to the south. The southern settlements were based on the cultivation of rice rather than dry crops such as millet, barley, and wheat, but they were as old as those in the north. Thus agriculture, and perhaps other elements of early civilization, may have developed spontaneously in several areas of China rather than radiating outward from one central region.

At first, these simple Neolithic communities were hardly more than villages, but as the inhabitants mastered the rudiments of agriculture, they gradually gave rise to more sophisticated and complex societies. In a pattern that we have already seen elsewhere, civilization gradually spread from these nuclear settlements in the valleys of the Yellow and Yangtze Rivers to other lowland areas of eastern and central China. The two great river valleys, then, can be considered the core regions in the development of Chinese civilization.

Although these densely cultivated valleys eventually became two of the great food-producing areas of the ancient world, China is more than a land of fertile fields. In fact, only 12 percent of the total land area is arable, compared with 23 percent in the United States. Much of the remainder consists of mountains and deserts that ring the country on its northern and western frontiers.

This often arid and forbidding landscape is a dominant feature of Chinese life and has played a significant role in Chinese history. The geographical barriers served to isolate the Chinese people from advanced agrarian societies in other parts of Asia. The frontier regions in the Gobi Desert, Central Asia, and the Tibetan plateau were sparsely inhabited by peoples of Mongolian, Indo-European, or Turkish extraction. Most were pastoral societies, and like the other river valley civilizations, their contacts with the Chinese were often characterized by mutual distrust and conflict. Although less numerous than the Chinese, many of these peoples possessed impressive skills in war and were sometimes aggressive in seeking

wealth or territory in the settled regions south of the Gobi Desert. Over the next two thousand years, the northern frontier became one of the great fault lines of conflict in Asia as Chinese armies attempted to protect precious farmlands from marauding peoples from beyond the frontier. When China was unified and blessed with capable rulers, it could usually keep the nomadic intruders at bay and even bring them under a loose form of Chinese administration. But in times of internal weakness, China was vulnerable to attack from the north, and on several occasions, nomadic peoples succeeded in overthrowing native Chinese rulers and setting up their own dynastic regimes.

From other directions, China normally had little to fear. To the east lay the China Sea, a lair for pirates and the source of powerful typhoons that occasionally ravaged the Chinese coast but otherwise rarely a source of concern. South of the Yangtze River was a hilly region inhabited by a mixture of peoples of varied language and ethnic stock who lived by farming, fishing, or food gathering. They were gradually absorbed in the inexorable expansion of Chinese civilization.

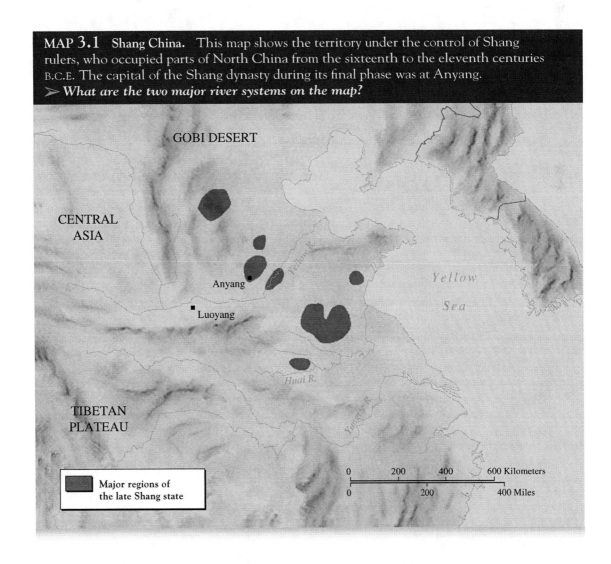

MAP **3.1** **Shang China.** This map shows the territory under the control of Shang rulers, who occupied parts of North China from the sixteenth to the eleventh centuries B.C.E. The capital of the Shang dynasty during its final phase was at Anyang.
➤ *What are the two major river systems on the map?*

Major regions of the late Shang state

A TREATISE ON THE YELLOW RIVER AND ITS CANALS

Sima Qian (Szu-ma Ch'ien) was a famous historian of the Han dynasty who lived during the second and first centuries B.C.E. In his most famous work, titled Historical Records, he describes the public works projects undertaken during the Xia dynasty to convert the dangerous waters of the Yellow River to human use. Although the identification of irrigation with Yu may be apocryphal, irrigation works were under way in central China at least as early as the sixth century B.C.E., and China later became one of the foremost hydraulic societies in the ancient world.

SIMA QIAN, *HISTORICAL RECORDS*

The documents on the Hsia dynasty tell us that Emperor Yu spent thirteen years controlling and bringing an end to the floods, and during that period, though he passed by the very gate of his own house, he did not take the time to enter. On land he traveled in a cart and on water in a boat; he rode a sledge to cross the mud and wore cleated shoes in climbing the mountains. In this way he marked out the nine provinces, led the rivers along the bases of the mountains, decided what tribute was appropriate for each region in accordance with the quality of its soil, opened up the nine roads, built embankments around the nine marshes, and made a survey of the nine mountains.

Of all the rivers, the Yellow River caused the greatest damage to China by overflowing its banks and inundating the land, and therefore he turned all his attention to controlling it. Thus he led the Yellow River in a course from Chi-shih past Lung-men and south to the northern side of Mount Hua; from there eastward along the foot of Ti-chu Mountain, past the Meng Ford and the confluence of the Lo River to Ta-p'ei. At this point Emperor Yu decided that, since the river was descending from high ground and the flow of the water was rapid and fierce, it would be difficult to guide it over level ground without danger of frequent disastrous breakthroughs. He therefore divided the flow into two channels, leading it along the higher ground to the north, past the Chiang River and so to Ta-lu. There he spread it out to form the Nine Rivers, brought it together again to make the Backward-Flowing River [i.e., tidal river], and thence led it into the Gulf of Pohai. When he had thus opened up the rivers of the nine provinces and fixed the outlets of the nine marshes, peace and order were brought to the lands of the Hsia, and his achievements continued to benefit the Three Dynasties which followed.

THE DAWN OF CHINESE CIVILIZATION: THE SHANG DYNASTY

Historians of China have traditionally dated the beginning of Chinese civilization to the founding of the Xia (Hsia) dynasty more than four thousand years ago. Although the precise date for the rise of the Xia is in dispute, recent archaeological evidence confirms its existence. Legend maintains that the founder was a ruler named Yu, who is also credited with introducing irrigation and draining the floodwaters that periodically threatened to inundate the northern China plain (see the box above). The Xia dynasty was replaced by a second dynasty, the Shang, around the sixteenth century B.C.E. (see Map 3.1). The late Shang capital at Anyang, just north of the Yellow River in north-central China, has been excavated by archaeologists. Among the finds were thousands of so-called oracle bones, ox and chicken bones or turtle shells that were used by Shang rulers for divination and to communicate with the gods. The inscriptions on these oracle bones are the earliest known form of Chinese writing and provide much of our information about the beginnings of civilization in China. They describe a culture gradually emerging from the Neolithic to the early Bronze Age.

Political Organization

China under the Shang dynasty was a predominantly agricultural society ruled by an aristocratic class whose major occupation was war. One ancient chronicler complained that "the big affairs of state consist of sacrifice and soldiery."[2] Combat was carried on by means of two-horse chariots. The appearance of chariots in China in the mid-second millennium B.C.E. coincides roughly with similar developments elsewhere, leading some historians to suggest that the Shang ruling class may originally have invaded China from elsewhere in Asia. But items found in Shang burial mounds are similar to Longshan pottery, implying that the Shang ruling elites were linear descendants of the indigenous Neolithic peoples in the area. If that was the case, the Shang may have acquired their knowledge of horse-drawn chariots through contact with the peoples of neighboring regions.

Some recent support for that assumption has come from evidence unearthed in the sandy wastes of Xinjiang, China's far-northwestern province. There archaeologists have discovered corpses dating back as early as the second millennium B.C.E. with physical characteristics that are clearly European. They are also clothed in textiles similar to those worn at the time in Europe, suggesting that they may have been members of an Indo-European migration from areas much farther to the west. If that is the case, they

THE ASIAN READER ◆ China in Antiquity 129

Werner Forman Archive, British Library/Art Resource, NY

≫ SHELL AND BONE WRITING. The earliest known form of true writing in China dates back to the Shang dynasty and was inscribed on shells or animal bones. Questions for the gods were scratched on bones, which cracked after being exposed to fire. The cracks were then interpreted by sorcerers. The questions often expressed practical concerns: Will it rain? Will the king be victorious in battle? Will he recover from his illness? Originally composed of pictographs and ideographs four thousand years ago, Chinese writing has evolved into an elaborate set of symbols that combine meaning and pronunciation in a single character.

were probably familiar with advances in chariot making that occurred a few hundred years earlier in southern Russia and Kazakstan. By about 2000 B.C.E., spoked wheels were being deposited at grave sites in the Ukraine and also in the Gobi Desert, just north of the great bend of the Yellow River. It is thus likely that the new technology became available to the founders of the Shang dynasty and may have aided their rise to power in northern China.

The Shang king ruled with the assistance of a central bureaucracy in the capital city. His realm was divided into a number of territories governed by aristocratic chieftains, but the king appointed these chieftains and could apparently depose them at will. He was also responsible for the defense of the realm and controlled large armies that often fought on the fringes of the kingdom. The transcendent importance of the ruler was graphically displayed in the ritual sacrifices undertaken at his death, when hundreds of his retainers were buried with him in the royal tomb.

As the inscriptions on the oracle bones make clear, the Chinese ruling elite believed in the existence of super-

natural forces and thought that they could communicate with those forces to obtain divine intervention on matters of this world. In fact, the purpose of the oracle bones was to communicate with the gods. This evidence also suggests that the king was already being viewed as an intermediary between heaven and earth. In fact, an early Chinese character for king (王) consists of three horizontal lines connected by a single vertical line; the middle horizontal line represents the king's place between human society and the divine forces in nature.

The early Chinese also had a clear sense of life in the hereafter. Though some of the human sacrifices discovered in the royal tombs were presumably intended to propitiate the gods, others were meant to accompany the king or members of his family on the journey to the next world. From this conviction would come the concept of the veneration of ancestors (commonly known in the West as "ancestor worship") and the practice, which continues to the present day in many Chinese communities, of burning replicas of physical objects to accompany the departed on their journey to the next world.

Social Structures

In the Neolithic period, the farm village was apparently the basic social unit of China, at least in the core region of the Yellow River valley. Villages were organized by clans rather than by nuclear family units, and all residents probably took the common clan name of the entire village. In some cases, a village may have included more than one clan. At Banpo (Pan P'o), an archaeological site near modern Xian that dates back at least eight thousand years, the houses in the village are separated by a ditch, which some scholars think may have served as a divider between two clans. The individual dwellings at Banpo housed nuclear families, but a larger building in the village was apparently used as a clan meeting hall. The tribal origins of Chinese society may help explain the continued importance of the joint family in traditional China, as well as the relatively small number of family names in Chinese society. Even today there are only about four hundred commonly used family names in a society of more than one billion people.

By Shang times, the classes were becoming increasingly differentiated. It is likely that some poorer peasants did not own their farms but were obliged to work the land of the chieftain and other elite families in the village (see the box on p. 65). The aristocrats not only made war and served as officials (indeed, the first Chinese character for *official* originally meant "warrior"), but they were also the primary landowners. In addition to the aristocratic elite and the peasants, there were a small number of merchants and artisans, as well as slaves, probably consisting primarily of criminals or prisoners taken in battle.

The Shang are perhaps best known for their mastery of the art of bronze casting. Utensils, weapons, and ritual

LIFE IN THE FIELDS

The following passage is from The Book of Songs, *a classic written during the early Zhou dynasty. This excerpt describes the calendar of peasant life on an estate in ancient China and indicates the various types of service that peasants provided for their lord.*

THE BOOK OF SONGS

In the seventh month the Fire Star passes the meridian;
In the ninth month clothes are given out.
In the days of [our] first month, the wind blows cold;
In the days of [our] second, the air is cold.
Without coats, without garments of hair,
How could we get to the end of the year?
In the days of [our] third month we take our plows in hand;
In the days of [our] fourth we make our way to the fields.
Along with wives and children,
We eat in those south-lying acres.
The surveyor of the fields comes and is glad.

In the seventh month the Fire Star passes the meridian;
In the ninth month clothes are given out.
With the spring days the warmth begins,
And the oriole utters its song.
The young women take their deep baskets
And go along the small paths,
Looking for the tender [leaves of the] mulberry trees
As the spring days lengthen out,
They gather in crowds the white southern wood.
The girl's heart is wounded with sadness,
For she will soon be going with one of the young lords.

. . .

In the eighth month spinning is begun;
We make dark fabrics and yellow,
"With our red dye so bright,
We make robes for our young lords."

In the ninth month we prepare the stockyard,
And in the tenth we bring in the harvest.
The millets, the early and the late,
Together with paddy and hemp, beans and wheat.

. . .

Now we go up to work in the manor.
"In the day you gather the thatch-reeds;
In the evening twist them into rope;
Go quickly on to the roofs;
Soon you are to sow the grain."

In the days of [our] second month we cut the ice with
    tingling blows;
In the days of [our] third month [it is] stored in the
    icehouse.
In the days of [our] fourth month, very early,
A lamb with scallions is offered in sacrifice.
In the ninth month are shrewd frosts;
In the tenth month the stockyard is cleared.
With twin pitchers we hold the feast,
Killed for it is a young lamb.
Up we go into the lord's hall,
Raise the cup of buffalo horn;
"Long life for our lord; may he live forever and ever!"

objects made of bronze have been found in royal tombs in urban centers throughout the area known to be under Shang influence (see "Metalwork and Sculpture" later in this chapter). It is also clear that the Shang had achieved a fairly sophisticated writing system that would eventually spread throughout East Asia and evolve into the written language that is still used in China today.

THE ZHOU DYNASTY

In the eleventh century B.C.E., the Shang dynasty was overthrown by an aggressive young state located somewhat to the west of Anyang, the Shang capital, and near the great bend of the Yellow River as it begins to flow directly eastward to the sea. The new dynasty, which called itself the Zhou (Chou), survived for about eight hundred years and was thus the longest-lived dynasty in the history of China. According to tradition, the last of the Shang rulers was a tyrant who oppressed the people (Chinese sources assert that he was a degenerate who built "ponds of wine" and ordered the composing of lustful music that "ruined the morale of the nation"),[3] leading the ruler of the principality of Zhou to revolt and establish a new dynasty.

The Zhou located their capital in their home territory, near the present-day city of Xian. Later they established a second capital city at modern Luoyang, farther to the east, to administer new territories captured from the Shang. This established a pattern of eastern and western capitals that would endure off and on in China for nearly two thousand years.

Political Structures

The Zhou dynasty (1045–221 B.C.E.) adopted the political system of its predecessors, with some changes. The Shang practice of dividing the kingdom into a number of territories governed by officials appointed by the king was continued under the Zhou. At the apex of the government hierarchy was the Zhou king, who was served by a bureaucracy of growing size and complexity. It now included several ministries responsible for rites, education,

© Bradley D. Appleby

➤ **MUSIC IN THE CONFUCIAN ERA.** This set of bronze bells was discovered in a recent excavation of the tomb of a Zhou dynasty nobleman. Also found in the pit were several tons of bronze weaponry and ritual vessels, along with the bones of twenty-one attendants, consorts, and musicians, who had presumably been sacrificed to serve their lord in the afterlife. Weighing over 2 tons and covering a range of five octaves, the sixty-five bells required five performers standing on either side. Each bell contained a written inscription, providing the most complete written record of musical systems used in ancient China. Bronze bells have not been found in any other contemporary civilization and are considered one of the great cultural achievements of antiquity. The largest known bell dating from the Roman Empire, for example, is only 6 centimeters high.

law, and public works. Beyond the capital, the Zhou kingdom was divided into a number of principalities, governed by members of the hereditary aristocracy, who were appointed by the king and were at least theoretically subordinated to his authority.

But the Zhou kings also introduced some innovations. According to the *Rites of Zhou*, one of the oldest surviving documents on statecraft, the Zhou dynasty ruled China because it possessed the "mandate of Heaven." According to this concept, Heaven (viewed as an impersonal law of nature rather than as an anthropomorphic deity) maintained order in the universe through the Zhou king, who thus ruled as a representative of Heaven but not as a divine being. The king, who was selected to rule because of his talent and virtue, was then responsible for governing the people with compassion and efficiency. It was his duty to propitiate the gods in order to protect the people from natural calamities or bad harvests. But if the king failed to rule effectively, he could, theoretically at least, be overthrown and replaced by a new ruler. As noted earlier, this idea was used to justify the Zhou conquest of the Shang. Eventually, the concept of the heavenly mandate would become a cardinal principle of Chinese statecraft.[4] Each founder

of a new dynasty would routinely assert that he had earned the mandate of Heaven, and who could disprove it except by overthrowing the king? As a pragmatic Chinese proverb put it: "He who wins is the king; he who loses is the rebel."

By the sixth century B.C.E., the Zhou dynasty began to decline. As the power of the central government disintegrated, bitter internal rivalries arose among the various principalities, where the governing officials had succeeded in making their positions hereditary at the expense of the king. As the power of these officials grew, they began to regulate the local economy and seek reliable sources of revenue for their expanding armies, such as a uniform tax system and government monopolies on key commodities such as salt and iron.

Economy and Society

During the Zhou dynasty, the essential characteristics of Chinese economic and social institutions began to take shape. The Zhou continued the pattern of land ownership that had existed under the Shang: the peasants worked on lands owned by their lord but also had land of their own that they cultivated for their own use. The practice was called the "well field system," since the Chinese character for well (井) resembles a simplified picture of the division of the farmland into nine separate segments. Each peasant family tilled an outer plot for its own use and then joined with other families to work the inner one for the hereditary lord (see the box on p. 65). How widely this system was used is unclear, but it represented an ideal described by Confucian scholars of a later day. As the following poem indicates, life for the average farmer was a difficult one. The "big rat" is probably a reference to the high taxes imposed on the peasants by the government or lord.

> Big rat, big rat
> Do not eat my millet!
> Three years I have served you,
> But you will not care for me.
> I am going to leave you
> And go to that happy land;
> Happy land, happy land,
> Where I will find my place.[5]

Trade and manufacturing were carried out by merchants and artisans, who lived in walled towns under the direct control of the local lord. Merchants did not operate independently but were considered the property of the local lord and on occasion could even be bought and sold like chattels. A class of slaves performed a variety of menial tasks and perhaps worked on local irrigation projects. Most of them were probably prisoners of war captured during conflicts with the neighboring principalities. Scholars do not know how extensive slavery was in ancient times, but slaves probably did not constitute a large portion of the total population.

The period of the later Zhou, from the sixth to the third century B.C.E., was an era of significant economic growth and technological innovation, especially in agriculture. During that time, large-scale water control projects were undertaken to regulate the flow of rivers and distribute water evenly to the fields, as well as to construct canals to facilitate the transport of goods from one region to another (see the box on p. 63). Perhaps the most impressive technological achievement of the period was the construction of the massive water control project on the Min River, a tributary of the Yangtze. This system of canals and spillways, which was put into operation by the state of Qin a few years prior to the end of the Zhou dynasty, diverted excess water from the river into the local irrigation network and watered an area populated by as many as five million people. The system is still in use today, over two thousand years later.

Food production was also stimulated by a number of advances in farm technology. By the mid-sixth century B.C.E., the introduction of iron had led to the development of iron plowshares, which permitted deep plowing for the first time. Other innovations dating from the later Zhou were the use of natural fertilizer, the collar harness, and

the technique of leaving land fallow to preserve or replenish nutrients in the soil (see the box on p. 68). By the late Zhou dynasty, the cultivation of wet rice had become one of the prime sources of food in China. Although rice was difficult and time-consuming to produce, it replaced other grain crops in areas with a warm climate because of its good taste, relative ease of preparation, and high nutritious value.

The advances in agriculture, which enabled the population of China to rise as high as twenty million people during the late Zhou era, were also undoubtedly a major factor in the growth of commerce and manufacturing. During the late Zhou, economic wealth began to replace noble birth as the prime source of power and influence. Utensils made of iron became more common, and trade developed in a variety of useful commodities, including cloth, salt, and various manufactured goods.

One of the most important items of trade in ancient China was silk. There is evidence of silkworm raising as early as the Neolithic period. Remains of silk material have been found on Shang bronzes, and a large number of fragments have been recovered in tombs dating from the mid-Zhou era. Silk cloth was used not only for clothing and quilts but also to wrap the bodies of the dead prior to burial. Fragments have been found throughout Central Asia and as far away as Athens, suggesting that the famous "Silk Road" stretching from central China westward to the Middle East and the Mediterranean Sea was in operation as early as the fifth century B.C.E. (see Map 3.4 on p. 79; see also Chapter 10).

With the development of trade and manufacturing, China began to move toward a money economy. The first form of money may have been seashells (the Chinese character for goods or property contains the ideographic symbol for "shell"), but by the Zhou dynasty, pieces of iron shaped like a knife or round coins with a hole in the middle so they could be carried in strings of a thousand were being used. Most ordinary Chinese, however, simply used a system of barter. Taxes, rents, and even the salaries of government officials were normally paid in grain.

The Hundred Schools of Ancient Philosophy

In China, as in other great river valley societies, the birth of civilization was accompanied by the emergence of an organized effort to comprehend the nature of the cosmos and the role of human beings within it. Speculation over such questions began in the very early stages of civilization and culminated at the end of the Zhou era in the "hundred schools" of ancient philosophy, a wide-ranging debate over the nature of human beings, society, and the universe.

The first hint of religious belief in ancient China comes from relics found in royal tombs of Neolithic times. By then, the Chinese had already developed a religious sense

ENVIRONMENTAL CONCERNS IN ANCIENT CHINA

Even in antiquity, China possessed a large population that often stretched the limits of the productive potential of the land. In the following excerpt, the late Zhou philosopher Mencius appeals to his sovereign to adopt policies that will conserve precious resources and foster the well-being of his subjects. Clearly, Mencius was concerned that environmental needs were being neglected. Unfortunately, his advice has not always been followed, and environmental degradation remains a problem in China today. The destruction of the forests, for example, has deprived China of much of its wood resources, and the present government has launched an extensive program to plant trees.

THE BOOK OF MENCIUS

If you do not interfere with the busy season in the fields, then there will be more grain than the people can eat; if you do not allow nets with too fine a mesh to be used in large ponds, then there will be more fish and turtles than they can eat; if hatchets and axes are permitted in the forests on the hills only in the proper seasons, then there will be more timber than they can use. When the people have more grain, more fish and turtles than they can eat, and more timber than they can use, then in the support of their parents when alive and in the mourning of them when dead, they will be able to have no regrets over anything left undone. This is the first step along the Kingly way.

If the mulberry is planted in every homestead of five mu of land, then those who are fifty can wear silk; if chickens, pigs, and dogs do not miss their breeding season, then those who are seventy can eat meat; if each lot of a hundred mu is not deprived of labor during the busy seasons, then families with several mouths to feed will not go hungry. Exercise due care over the education provided by the village schools, and discipline the people by teaching them the duties proper to sons and younger brothers, and those whose heads have turned gray will not be carrying loads on the roads. When those who are seventy wear silk and eat meat and the masses are neither cold nor hungry, it is impossible for their prince not to be a true King.

Now when food meant for human beings is so plentiful as to be thrown to dogs and pigs, you fail to realize that it is time for garnering, and when men drop dead from starvation by the wayside, you fail to realize that it is time for distribution. When people die, you simply say, "It is none of my doing. It is the fault of the harvest." In what way is that different from killing a man by running him through, while saying all the time, "It is none of my doing. It is the fault of the weapon." Stop putting the blame on the harvest and the people of the whole Empire will come to you.

beyond the primitive belief in the existence of spirits in nature. The Shang had begun to believe in the existence of one transcendent god, known as Shang Di, who presided over all the forces of nature. As time went on, the Chinese concept of religion evolved from a vaguely anthropomorphic god to a somewhat more impersonal symbol of universal order known as Heaven (*Tian*, or *T'ien*). There was also much speculation among Chinese intellectuals about the nature of the cosmic order. One of the earliest ideas was that the universe was divided into two primary forces of good and evil, light and dark, male and female, called the *yang* and the *yin*, represented symbolically by the sun (*yang*) and the moon (*yin*). According to this theory, life was a dynamic process of interaction between the forces of *yang* and *yin*. Early Chinese could attempt only to understand the process and perhaps to have some minimal effect on its operation. They could not hope to reverse it. It is sometimes asserted that this belief has contributed to the heavy element of fatalism in Chinese popular wisdom. The Chinese have traditionally believed that bad times will be followed by good times, and vice versa.

The belief that there was some mysterious "law of nature" that could be interpreted by human beings led to various attempts to predict the future, such as the Shang oracle bones and other methods of divination. Philosophers invented ways to interpret the will of nature, while shamans, playing a role similar to the *brahmins* in India, were employed at court to assist the emperor in his policy deliberations until at least the fifth century C.E. One of the most famous manuals used for this purpose was the *Yi Jing* (*I Ching*), known in English as the *Book of Changes*.

CONFUCIANISM

Such efforts to divine the mysterious purposes of Heaven notwithstanding, Chinese thinking about metaphysical reality also contained a strain of pragmatism, which is readily apparent in the ideas of the great philosopher Confucius. Confucius (the name is the Latin form of his honorific title, Kung Fuci, or K'ung Fu-tzu, meaning Master Kung) was born in the state of Lu (in the modern province of Shandong) in 551 B.C.E. After reaching maturity, he apparently hoped to find employment as a political adviser in one of the principalities into which China was divided at that time, but he had little success in finding a patron. Nevertheless, he made an indelible mark on history as

THE WAY OF THE GREAT LEARNING

Few texts exist today that were written by Confucius himself. Most were written or edited by his disciples. The following text, titled The Great Learning, *was probably written two centuries after Confucius' death, but it illustrates his view that good government begins with the cultivation of individual morality and proper human relationships at the basic level. This conviction that to bring peace to the world, you must cultivate your own person continued to win general approval down to modern times. There are interesting similarities between such ideas and the views expressed in the Indian treatise* Arthasastra, *discussed in Chapter 2.*

THE GREAT LEARNING

The Way of the Great Learning consists in clearly exemplifying illustrious virtue, in loving the people, and in resting in the highest good.

Only when one knows where one is to rest can one have a fixed purpose. Only with a fixed purpose can one achieve calmness of mind. Only with calmness of mind can one attain serene repose. Only in serene repose can one carry on careful deliberation. Only through careful deliberation can one have achievement. Things have their roots and branches; affairs have their beginning and end. He who knows what comes first and what comes last comes himself near the Way.

The ancients who wished clearly to exemplify illustrious virtue throughout the world would first set up good government in their states. Wishing to govern well their states, they would first regulate their families. Wishing to regulate their families, they would first cultivate their persons. Wishing to cultivate their persons, they would first rectify their minds. Wishing to rectify their minds, they would first seek sincerity in their thoughts. Wishing for sincerity in their thoughts, they would first extend their knowledge. The extension of knowledge lay in the investigation of things. For only when things are investigated is knowledge extended; only when knowledge is extended are thoughts sincere; only when thoughts are sincere are minds rectified; only when minds are rectified are our persons cultivated; only when our persons are cultivated are our families regulated; only when families are regulated are states well governed; and only when states are well governed is there peace in the world.

From the emperor down to the common people, all, without exception, must consider cultivation of the individual character as the root. If the root is in disorder, it is impossible for the branches to be in order. To treat the important as unimportant and to treat the unimportant as important—this should never be. This is called knowing the root; this is called the perfection of knowledge.

---

an independent (and somewhat disgruntled) political and social philosopher.

In conversations with his disciples contained in the *Analects*, Confucius often adopted a detached and almost skeptical view of Heaven. "You are unable to serve man," he commented on one occasion, "how then can you hope to serve the spirits? While you do not know life, how can you know about death?" In many instances, he appeared to advise his followers to revere the deities and the ancestral spirits but to keep them at a distance. Confucius believed it was useless to speculate too much about metaphysical questions. Better by far to assume that there was a rational order to the universe and then concentrate one's attention on ordering the affairs of this world.[6]

Confucius' interest in philosophy, then, was essentially political and ethical. The universe was constructed in such a way that if human beings could act harmoniously in accordance with its purposes, their own affairs would prosper. Much of his concern was with human behavior. The key to proper behavior was to behave in accordance with the *Dao* (Way). Confucius assumed that all human beings had their own *Dao*, depending on their individual role in life, and it was their duty to follow it. Even the ruler had his own *Dao*, and he ignored it at his peril, for to do so could mean the loss of the mandate of Heaven. The idea of the *Dao* is reminiscent of the concept of *dharma* in

ancient India and played a similar role in governing the affairs of society.

Two elements in the Confucian interpretation of the *Dao* are particularly worthy of mention. The first is the concept of duty. It was the responsibility of all individuals to subordinate their own interests and aspirations to the broader need of the family and the community. Confucius assumed that if each individual worked hard to fulfill his or her assigned destiny, the affairs of society as a whole would surely prosper as well. In this respect, it was important for the ruler to set a good example. If he followed his "kingly way," the beneficial effects would radiate throughout society (see the box above).

The second key element is the idea of humanity, sometimes translated as "human-heartedness." This concept involves a sense of compassion and empathy for others. It is similar in some ways to Christian concepts, but with a subtle twist. Where Christian teachings call on human beings to "behave toward others as you would have them behave toward you," the Confucian maxim is put in a different way: "Do not do unto others what you would not wish done to yourself." To many Chinese, this attitude symbolizes an element of tolerance in the Chinese character that has not always been practiced in other societies.[7]

Confucius may have considered himself a failure because he never attained the position he wanted, but many of his contemporaries found his ideas appealing, and in the generations after his death, his message spread widely throughout China. Confucius was an outspoken critic of his times and lamented the disappearance of what he regarded as the Golden Age of the early Zhou.

In fact, however, Confucius was not just another disgruntled Chinese conservative mourning the passing of the good old days; rather, he was a revolutionary thinker, many of whose key ideas looked forward rather than backward. Perhaps his most striking political idea was that the government should be open to all men of superior quality, not limited to those of noble birth. As one of his disciples reports in the *Analects:* "The Master said, by nature, men are nearly alike; by practice, they get to be wide apart."[8] Confucius undoubtedly had himself in mind as one of those "superior" men, but the rapacity of the hereditary lords must have added strength to his convictions.

The concept of rule by merit was, of course, not an unfamiliar idea in the China of his day; the *Rites of Zhou* had clearly stated that the king himself deserved to rule because of his talent and virtue, rather than as the result of noble birth. In practice, however, aristocratic privilege must often have opened the doors to political influence, and many of Confucius' contemporaries must have regarded his appeal for government by talent as both exciting and dangerous. Confucius did not explicitly question the right of the hereditary aristocracy to play a leading role in the political process, nor did his ideas have much effect in his lifetime. Still, they introduced a new concept that was later implemented in the form of a bureaucracy selected through a civil service examination (see "Confucianism and the State" later in this chapter).

Confucius' ideas, passed on to later generations through the *Analects* as well as through writings attributed to him, had a strong impact on Chinese political thinkers of the late Zhou period, a time when the existing system was in disarray and open to serious question. But as with most great thinkers, Confucius' ideas were sufficiently ambiguous to be interpreted in very contradictory ways. Some, like the philosopher Mencius (370–290 B.C.E.), stressed the humanistic side of Confucian ideas, arguing that human beings were by nature good and hence could be taught their civic responsibilities by example. He also stressed that the ruler had a duty to govern with compassion:

> It was because Chieh and Chou lost the people that they lost the empire, and it was because they lost the hearts of the people that they lost the people. Here is the way to win the empire: win the people and you win the empire. Here is the way to win the people: win their hearts and you win the people. Here is the way to win their hearts: give them and share with them what they like, and do not do to them what they do not like. The people turn to a human ruler as water flows downward or beasts take to wilderness.[9]

Here is a prescription for political behavior that could win wide support in our own day. Other thinkers, however,

rejected Mencius' rosy view of human nature and argued for a different approach.

LEGALISM

One school of thought that became quite popular during the "hundred schools" era in ancient China was the philosophy of Legalism. Taking issue with the view of Mencius and other disciples of Confucius that human nature was essentially good, the Legalists argued that human beings were by nature evil and would follow the correct path only if coerced by harsh laws and stiff punishments. These thinkers were referred to as the School of Law because they rejected the Confucian view that government by "superior men" could solve society's problems and argued instead for a system of impersonal laws.

The Legalists also disagreed with the Confucian belief that the universe has a moral core. They therefore believed that only firm action by the state could bring about social order. Fear of harsh punishment, more than the promise of material reward, could best motivate the common people to serve the interests of the ruler. Because human nature was essentially corrupt, officials could not be trusted to carry out their duties in a fair and evenhanded manner, and only a strong ruler could create an orderly society. All human actions should be subordinated to the effort to create a strong and prosperous state subject to his will.

DAOISM

One of the most popular alternatives to Confucianism was the philosophy of Daoism (frequently spelled Taoism). According to Chinese tradition, the Daoist school was founded by a contemporary of Confucius popularly known as Lao Tzu (Lao Zi), or the Old Master. Many modern scholars, however, are skeptical that Lao Tzu actually existed.

Obtaining a clear understanding of the original concepts of Daoism is difficult because its primary document, a short treatise known as the *Dao De Jing* (sometimes translated as *The Way of the Tao*), is an enigmatic book whose interpretation has baffled scholars for centuries. The opening line, for example, explains less what the *Dao* is than what it is not: "The Tao [Way] that can be told of is not the eternal Tao. The name that can be named is not the eternal name."[10]

Nevertheless, the basic concepts of Daoism are not especially difficult to understand. Like Confucianism, Daoism does not anguish over the underlying meaning of the cosmos. Rather, it attempts to set forth proper forms of behavior for human beings here on earth. In most other respects, however, Daoism presents a view of life and its ultimate meaning that is almost diametrically opposed to that of Confucianism. Where Confucian doctrine asserts that it is the duty of human beings to work hard to improve life here on earth, Daoists contend that the

THE DAOIST ANSWER TO CONFUCIANISM

he Dao De Jing (The Way of the Dao) is the great classic of philosophical Daoism (Taoism). Traditionally attributed to the legendary Chinese philosopher Lao Tzu (Old Master), it was probably written sometime during the era of Confucius. This opening passage illustrates two of the key ideas that characterize Daoist belief: it is impossible to define the nature of the universe, and "inaction" (not Confucian "action") is the key to ordering the affairs of human beings.

THE WAY OF THE DAO

The Tao that can be told of is not the eternal Tao;
The name that can be named is not the eternal name.
The Nameless is the origin of Heaven and Earth;
The Named is the mother of all things.

Therefore let there always be nonbeing, so we may see their
* subtlety.*
And let there always be being, so we may see their
* outcome.*
The two are the same,
But after they are produced, they have different names.
They both may be called deep and profound.

Deeper and more profound,
The door of all subtleties!
When the people of the world all know beauty as beauty,
There arises the recognition of ugliness.
When they all know the good as good,
There arises the recognition of evil.
Therefore:
Being and nonbeing produce each other;
Difficult and easy complete each other;
Long and short contrast each other;
High and low distinguish each other;
Sound and voice harmonize each other;
Front and behind accompany each other.

Therefore the sage manages affairs without action
And spreads doctrines without words.
All things arise, and he does not turn away from them.
He produces them but does not take possession of them.
He acts but does not rely on his own ability.
He accomplishes his task but does not claim credit for it.
It is precisely because he does not claim credit that his
* accomplishment remains with him.*

---

true way to interpret the will of Heaven is not action but inaction (*wu wei*). The best way to act in harmony with the universal order is to act spontaneously and let nature take its course (see the box above).

Such a message could be very appealing to those who were uncomfortable with the somewhat rigid flavor of the Confucian work ethic and preferred a more individualistic approach. This image would eventually find graphic expression in Chinese landscape painting, which in its classical form would depict naturalistic scenes of mountains, water, and clouds and underscore the fragility and smallness of individual human beings.

Daoism achieved considerable popularity in the waning years of the Zhou dynasty. It was especially popular among intellectuals, who may have found it appealing as an escapist antidote in a world characterized by growing disorder.

POPULAR BELIEFS

Daoism also played a second role as a loose framework for popular spiritualistic and animistic beliefs among the common people. Popular Daoism was less a philosophy than a religion; it comprised a variety of rituals and forms of behavior that were regarded as a means of achieving heavenly salvation or even a state of immortality on earth. Daoist sorcerers practiced various types of mind- or body-training exercises in the hope of achieving power, sexual

prowess, and long life. It was primarily this form of Daoism that survived into a later age.

The philosophical forms of Confucianism and Daoism did not provide much meaning to the mass of the population, for whom philosophical debate over the ultimate meaning of life was not as important as the daily struggle for survival. Even among the elites, interest in the occult and in astrology was high, and magicoreligious ideas coexisted with the interest in natural science and humanistic philosophy throughout the ancient period.

For most Chinese, Heaven was not a vague, impersonal law of nature, as it was for many Confucian and Daoist intellectuals, but a terrain peopled with innumerable gods and spirits of nature, both good and evil, who existed in trees, mountains, and streams as well as in heavenly bodies. As human beings mastered the techniques of farming, they called on divine intervention to guarantee a good harvest. Other gods were responsible for the safety of fishers, transportation workers, or prospective mothers.

Another aspect of popular religion was the belief that the spirits of deceased human beings lived in the atmosphere for a time before ascending to heaven or descending to hell. During that period, surviving family members had to care for the spirits through proper ritual, or they would become evil spirits and haunt the survivors.

Thus in ancient China, human beings were offered a variety of interpretations of the nature of the universe.

Confucianism satisfied the need for a rational doctrine of nation building and social organization at a time when the existing political and social structure was beginning to disintegrate. Philosophical Daoism provided an alternative to Confucianism and a framework for a set of diverse animistic beliefs at the popular level. But neither could satisfy the deeper emotional needs that sometimes inspire the human spirit. Neither could effectively provide solace in a time of sorrow or the hope of a better life in the hereafter. Something else would be needed to fill the gap.

THE RISE OF THE CHINESE EMPIRE: THE QIN AND THE HAN

During the last two centuries of the Zhou dynasty (the fourth and third centuries B.C.E.), the authority of the king became increasingly nominal, and several of the small principalities into which the Zhou kingdom had been divided began to evolve into powerful states that presented a potential challenge to the Zhou ruler himself. Chief among these were Qu (Ch'u) in the central Yangtze valley, Wu in the Yangtze delta, and Yue (Yueh) along the southeastern coast. At first, their mutual rivalries were in check, but by the late fifth century B.C.E., competition intensified into civil war, giving birth to the so-called Period of the Warring States (see the box on p. 73). Powerful principalities vied with each other for preeminence and largely ignored the now purely titular authority of the Zhou court (see Map 3.2). New forms of warfare also emerged with the invention of iron weapons and the introduction of the foot soldier. Cavalry, too, made its first appearance, armed with the powerful crossbow.

Eventually, the relatively young state of Qin, located in the original homeland of the Zhou, became a key player in these conflicts. Benefiting from a strong defensive position in the mountains to the west of the great bend of the Yellow River, as well as from their control of the rich Sichuan

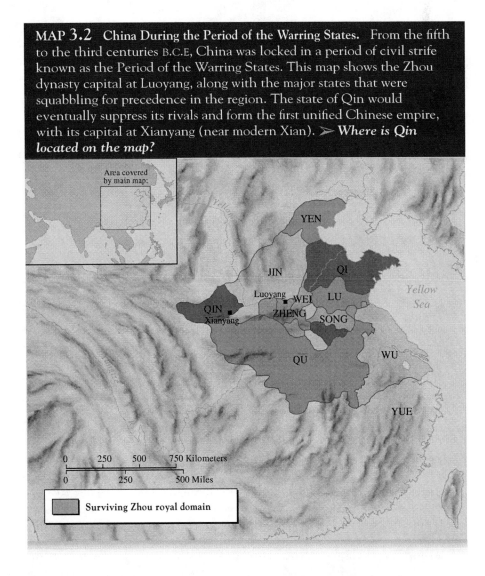

MAP 3.2 China During the Period of the Warring States. From the fifth to the third centuries B.C.E, China was locked in a period of civil strife known as the Period of the Warring States. This map shows the Zhou dynasty capital at Luoyang, along with the major states that were squabbling for precedence in the region. The state of Qin would eventually suppress its rivals and form the first unified Chinese empire, with its capital at Xianyang (near modern Xian). ➤ **Where is Qin located on the map?**

THE ART OF WAR

With the possible exception of the nineteenth-century German military strategist Karl von Clausewitz, there is probably no more famous or respected writer on the art of war than the ancient Chinese thinker Sun Tzu. Yet surprisingly little is known about him. Recently discovered evidence suggests that he lived sometime in the fifth century B.C.E., during the chronic conflict of the Period of Warring States, and that he was an early member of an illustrious family of military strategists who advised Zhou rulers for more than two hundred years. But despite the mystery surrounding his life, there is no doubt of his influence on later generations of military planners. Among his most avid followers in our century have been the revolutionary leaders Mao Zedong and Ho Chi Minh, as well as the Japanese military strategists who planned the attacks on Port Arthur and Pearl Harbor.

The following brief excerpt from his classic The Art of War provides a glimmer into the nature of his advice, still so timely today.

SELECTIONS FROM SUN TZU

Sun Tzu said:

"In general, the method for employing the military is this: . . . Attaining one hundred victories in one hundred battles is not the pinnacle of excellence. Subjugating the enemy's army without fighting is the true pinnacle of excellence. . . .

"Thus the highest realization of warfare is to attack the enemy's plans; next is to attack their alliances; next to attack their army; and the lowest is to attack their fortified cities.

"This tactic of attacking fortified cities is adopted only when unavoidable. Preparing large movable protective shields, armored assault wagons, and other equipment and devices will require three months. Building earthworks will require another three months to complete. If the general cannot overcome his impatience but instead launches an assault wherein his men swarm over the walls like ants, he will kill one-third of his officers and troops, and the city will still not be taken. This is the disaster that results from attacking [fortified cities].

"Thus one who excels at employing the military subjugates other people's armies without engaging in battle, captures other people's fortified cities without attacking them, and destroys others people's states without prolonged fighting. He must fight under Heaven with the paramount aim of 'preservation.' . . .

"In general, the strategy of employing the military is this: If your strength is ten times theirs, surround them; if five, then attack them; if double, then divide your forces. If you are equal in strength to the enemy, you can engage him. If fewer, you can circumvent him. If outmatched, you can avoid him. . . .

"Thus there are five factors from which victory can be known:

"One who knows when he can fight, and when he cannot fight, will be victorious.

"One who recognizes how to employ large and small numbers will be victorious.

"One whose upper and lower ranks have the same desires will be victorious.

"One who, fully prepared, awaits the unprepared will be victorious.

"One whose general is capable and not interfered with by the ruler will be victorious.

"These five are the Way (Tao) to know victory. . . .

"Thus it is said that one who knows the enemy and knows himself will not be endangered in a hundred engagements. One who does not know the enemy but knows himself will sometimes be victorious, sometimes meet with defeat. One who knows neither the enemy nor himself will invariably be defeated in every engagement."

---

plains, the Qin gradually subdued their main rivals through conquest or diplomatic maneuvering. In 221 B.C.E., the Qin ruler declared the establishment of a new dynasty, the first truly unified government in Chinese history.

The Qin Dynasty (221–206 B.C.E.)

One of the primary reasons for the triumph of the Qin was probably the character of the Qin ruler, known to history as Qin Shi Huangdi (Ch'in Shih Huang Ti), or the First Emperor of Qin. A man of forceful personality and immense ambition, Qin Shi Huangdi had ascended to the throne of Qin in 246 B.C.E. at the age of thirteen. Described by the famous Han dynasty historian Sima Qian as having "the chest of a bird of prey, the voice of a jackal, and the heart of a tiger," the new king of Qin found the Legalist views of his adviser Li Su (Li Ssu) only too appealing. In 221 B.C.E., Qin Shi Huangdi defeated the last of Qin's rivals and founded a new dynasty with himself as emperor.

The Qin dynasty transformed Chinese politics. Philosophical doctrines that had proliferated during the late Zhou period were prohibited, and Legalism was adopted as the official ideology. Those who opposed the policies of the new regime were punished and sometimes executed, while books presenting ideas contrary to the official orthodoxy were publicly put to the torch, perhaps the first example of book burning in history (see the box on p. 74).

Legalistic theory gave birth to a number of fundamental administrative and political developments, some of

MEMORANDUM ON THE BURNING OF BOOKS

*L*i Su, the author of the following passage, was a chief minister of the First Emperor of Qin. An exponent of Legalism, Li Su hoped to eliminate all rival theories on government. His recommendation to the emperor on the subject was recorded by the Han dynasty historian Sima Qian. The emperor approved the proposal and ordered all books contrary to the spirit of Legalist ideology to be destroyed on pain of death. Fortunately, some texts were preserved by being hidden or even memorized by their owners and were thus available to later generations. For centuries afterward, the First Emperor of Qin and his minister were singled out for criticism because of their intolerance and their effort to control the very minds of their subjects. Totalitarianism, it seems, is not exclusively a modern concept.

SIMA QIAN, *HISTORICAL RECORDS*

In earlier times the empire disintegrated and fell into disorder, and no one was capable of unifying it. Thereupon the various feudal lords rose to power. In their discourses they all praised the past in order to disparage the present and embellished empty words to confuse the truth. Everyone cherished his own favorite school of learning and criticized what had been instituted by the authorities. But at present Your Majesty possesses a unified empire, has regulated the distinctions of black and white, and has firmly established for yourself a position of sole supremacy. And yet these independent schools, joining with each other, criticize the codes of laws and instructions. Hearing of the promulgation of a decree, they criticize it, each from the standpoint

of his own school. At home they disapprove of it in their hearts; going out they criticize it in the thoroughfare. They seek a reputation by discrediting their sovereign; they appear superior by expressing contrary views, and they lead the lowly multitude in the spreading of slander. If such license is not prohibited, the sovereign power will decline above and partisan factions will form below. It would be well to prohibit this.

Your servant suggests that all books in the imperial archives, save the memoirs of Ch'in, be burned. All persons in the empire, except members of the Academy of Learned Scholars, in possession of the *Book of Odes*, the *Book of History*, and discourses of the hundred philosophers should take them to the local governors and have them indiscriminately burned. Those who dare to talk to each other about the *Book of Odes* and the *Book of History* should be executed and their bodies exposed in the marketplace. Anyone referring to the past to criticize the present should, together with all members of his family, be put to death. Officials who fail to report cases that have come under their attention are equally guilty. After thirty days from the time of issuing the decree, those who have not destroyed their books are to be branded and sent to build the Great Wall. Books not to be destroyed will be those on medicine and pharmacy, divination by the tortoise and milfoil, and agriculture and arboriculture. People wishing to pursue learning should take the officials as their teachers.

---

which would survive the Qin and serve as a model for future dynasties. In the first place, unlike the Zhou, the Qin was a highly centralized state. The central bureaucracy was divided into three primary ministries: a civil authority, a military authority, and a censorate, whose inspectors surveyed the efficiency of officials throughout the system. This would later become standard administrative procedure for future Chinese dynasties.

Below the central government were two levels of administration: provinces and counties. Unlike the Zhou system, officials at these levels did not inherit their positions but were appointed by the court and were subject to dismissal at the emperor's whim. Apparently, some form of merit system was used, although there is no evidence that selection was based on performance in an examination. The civil servants may have been chosen on the recommendation of other government officials. A penal code provided for harsh punishments for all wrongdoers. Officials were watched by the censors, who reported directly to the throne. Those guilty of malfeasance in office were executed.

Qin Shi Huangdi, who had a passion for centralization, unified the system of weights and measures, standardized the monetary system and the written forms of Chinese characters, and ordered the construction of a system of roads extending throughout the empire. He also attempted to eliminate the remaining powers of the landed aristocrats and divided their estates among the peasants, who were now taxed directly by the state. He thus elimi-

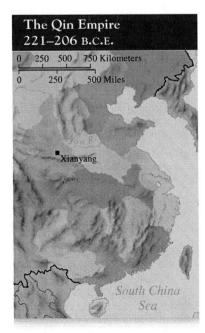

The Qin Empire 221–206 B.C.E.

0   250   500   750 Kilometers

0   250   500 Miles

Xianyang

Yellow River

South China Sea

秦 始 皇 帝

➤ **QIN SHI HUANGDI.** Qin Shi Huangdi, the First Emperor of Qin, who reigned from 221 to 210 B.C.E., was one of the most influential figures in the history of China. Although considered ruthless by many historians, he created the first unified Chinese state, ordered the construction of a system of roads throughout the country, standardized the Chinese currency and written language, and brought together the scattered defensive battlements into what we now know as the Great Wall.

nated potential rivals and secured tax revenues for the central government. Members of the aristocratic clans were required to live in the capital city at Xianyang (Hsienyang), just north of modern Xian, so that the court could monitor their activities. Such a system may not have been advantageous to the peasants in all respects, however, since the central government could now collect taxes more effectively and mobilize the peasants for military service and for various public works projects.

The Qin dynasty was equally unsympathetic to the merchants, whom it viewed as parasites. Private commercial activities were severely restricted and heavily taxed, and many vital forms of commerce and manufacturing, including mining, wine making, and the distribution of salt, were placed under a government monopoly.

Qin Shi Huangdi was equally aggressive in foreign affairs. His armies continued the gradual advance to the south that had taken place during the final years of the Zhou dynasty, extending the border of China to the edge of the Red River in modern Vietnam. To supply the Qin armies operating in the area, a canal was dug that provided direct inland navigation from the Yangtze River in central China to what is now the modern city of Guangzhou (Canton) in the south.

BEYOND THE FRONTIER: THE NOMADIC PEOPLES AND THE GREAT WALL OF CHINA

The main area of concern for the Qin emperor, however, was in the north, where a nomadic people, known to the Chinese as the Xiongnu (Hsiung-nu) and possibly related to the Huns (see Chapter 5), had become increasingly active in the area of the Gobi Desert. The area north of the Yellow River had been sparsely inhabited since prehistoric times. During the Qin period, the climate of North China was somewhat milder and moister than it is today, and parts of the region were heavily forested. The local population probably lived by hunting and fishing, practicing limited forms of agriculture, or herding animals such as cattle or sheep.

As the climate gradually became drier, people were forced to rely increasingly on animal husbandry as a means of livelihood. Their response was to master the art of riding on horseback and to adopt the nomadic life. Organized loosely into communities consisting of a number of kinship groups, they ranged far and wide in search of pasture for their herds of cattle, goats, or sheep. As they moved seasonally from one pasture to another, they often traveled several hundred miles carrying their goods and their circular felt tents, called *yurts*.

But the new way of life presented its own challenges. Increased food production led to a growing population, which in times of drought outstripped the available resources. Rival groups then competed for the best pastures. After they mastered the art of fighting on horseback sometime during the middle of the first millennium B.C.E., territorial warfare became commonplace throughout the entire frontier region from the Pacific Ocean to Central Asia.

By the end of the Zhou dynasty in the third century B.C.E., the nomadic Xiongnu posed a serious threat to the security of China's northern frontier, and a number of Chinese principalities in the area began to build walls and fortifications to keep them out. But warriors on horseback possessed significant advantages over the infantry of the Chinese.

Qin Shi Huangdi's answer to the problem was to strengthen the walls to keep the marauders out. In Sima Qian's words:

[The] First Emperor of the Ch'in dispatched Meng T'ien to lead a force of a hundred thousand men north to attack the barbarians. He seized control of all the lands south of the Yellow River and established border defenses along the river, constructing forty-four walled district cities overlooking the river and manning them with convict laborers transported to the border for garrison duty. Thus he utilized the natural mountain barriers to establish the border defenses, scooping out the valleys and constructing ramparts and building installations at other points where they were needed. The whole line of defenses stretched over ten thousand *li* [a *li* is one-third of a mile] from Lin-t'ao to Liao-tung and even extended across the Yellow River and through Yang-shan and Pei-chia.[11]

Today, of course, we know Qin Shi Huangdi's project as the Great Wall, which extends nearly 4,000 miles from the sandy wastes of Central Asia to the sea. It is constructed of massive granite blocks and is wide enough on top to provide a roadway for horse-drawn chariots. Although the wall that appears in most photographs today was built 1,500 years after the Qin, during the Ming dynasty, some of the walls built by the Qin remain standing. Their construction was a massive project that required the efforts of thousands of laborers, many of whom met their deaths there and, according to legend, are now buried within the wall.

THE FALL OF THE QIN

The Legalist system put in place by the First Emperor of Qin was designed to achieve maximum efficiency as well as total security for the state. It did neither. Qin Shi

Huangdi was apparently aware of the dangers of factions within the imperial family and established a class of eunuchs (males whose testicles have been removed) who served as personal attendants for himself and female members of the royal family. The original idea may have been to restrict the influence of male courtiers, and the eunuch system later became a standard feature of the Chinese imperial system. But as confidential advisers to the royal family, eunuchs were in a position of influence. The rivalry between the "inner" imperial court and the "outer" court of bureaucratic officials led to tensions that persisted until the end of the imperial system.

By ruthlessly gathering control over the empire into his own hands, Qin Shi Huangdi had hoped to establish a rule that, in the words of Sima Qian, "would be enjoyed by his sons for ten thousand generations." In fact, his centralizing zeal alienated many key groups. Landed aristocrats and Confucian intellectuals, as well as the common people, groaned under the censorship of thought and speech, harsh taxes, and forced labor projects. "He killed men," recounted the historian, "as though he thought he could never finish, he punished men as though he were afraid he would never get around to them all, and the whole world revolted against him."[12] Shortly after the emperor died in 210 B.C.E., the dynasty quickly descended into factional rivalry, and four years later it was overthrown.

The disappearance of the Qin brought an end to an experiment in absolute rule that later Chinese historians would view as a betrayal of humanistic Confucian principles. But in another sense, the Qin system was a response—though somewhat extreme—to the problems of administering a large and increasingly complex society. Although later rulers would denounce Legalism and enthrone Confucianism as the new state orthodoxy, in practice they would make use of a number of the key tenets of Legalism to administer the empire and control the behavior of their subjects.

The Glorious Han Dynasty (202 B.C.E.–221 C.E.)

The fall of the Qin was followed by a brief period of civil strife as aspiring successors competed for hegemony. Out of this strife emerged one of the greatest and most durable dynasties in Chinese history—the Han (see Map 3.3). The Han dynasty would later become so closely identified with the advance of Chinese civilization that even today the Chinese sometimes refer to themselves as "people of Han" and to their language as the "language of Han."

The founder of the Han dynasty was Liu Bang (Liu Pang), a commoner of peasant origin who would be known historically by his title of Han Gaozu (Han Kao Tsu, or Exalted Emperor of Han). Under his strong rule and that of his successors, the new dynasty quickly moved to consolidate its control over the empire and promote the welfare of its subjects. Efficient and benevolent, at least by the

⋙ **THE GREAT WALL.**   The section of the Great Wall that is often visited by tourists today is not the work of the First Emperor of Qin but was built at the order of a Ming ruler many centuries later. The original walls were often composed of loose stone, dirt, or piled rubble and posed little obstacle to invading nomads from the north. The section illustrated here is located north of the city of Dunhuang in Central Asia.

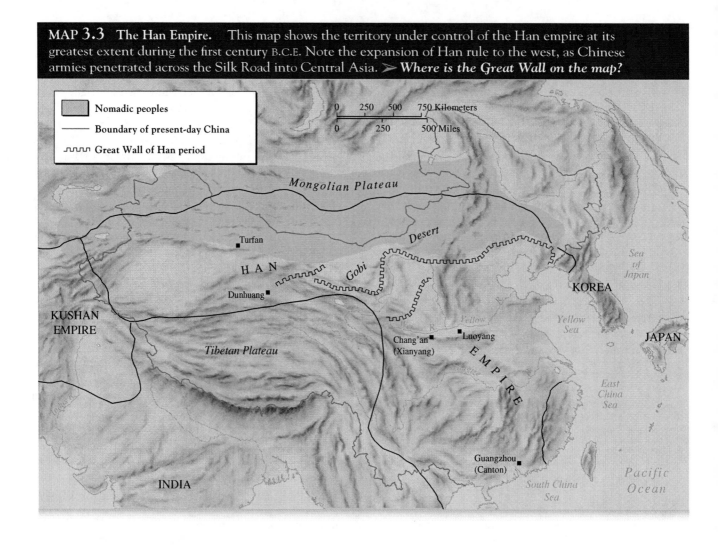

MAP 3.3 The Han Empire.   This map shows the territory under control of the Han empire at its greatest extent during the first century B.C.E. Note the expansion of Han rule to the west, as Chinese armies penetrated across the Silk Road into Central Asia. ➤ *Where is the Great Wall on the map?*

standards of the time, Gaozu maintained the centralized political institutions of the Qin but abandoned their harsh Legalistic approach to law enforcement. Han rulers also reversed the effort by the First Emperor of Qin to enforce a single ideology and discovered in Confucian principles a useful foundation for the creation of a new state philosophy. Under the Han, Confucianism began to take on the character of an official ideology.

CONFUCIANISM AND THE STATE

The integration of Confucian doctrine with Legalist practice, creating a system generally known as State Confucianism, did not take long to accomplish. Although the founding Han ruler declared his intention to discard the harsh methods adopted by the Qin, he and his successors found it convenient to retain many of the institutions introduced by the First Emperor of Qin. For example, they borrowed the tripartite division of the central government into civilian and military authorities and a censorate. The government was headed by a "grand coun-

cil" including representatives from all three segments of government. The Han also retained the system of local government, dividing the empire into provinces and districts.

Finally, and perhaps most important, the Han continued the Qin system of selecting government officials on the basis of merit rather than birth. Shortly after founding the new dynasty, Emperor Gaozu decreed that local officials would be asked to recommend promising candidates for public service. Thirty years later, in 165 B.C.E., the first known civil service examination was administered to candidates for positions in the bureaucracy. Shortly after that, an academy was established to train candidates. Nevertheless, the first candidates were almost all from aristocratic or other wealthy families, and the Han bureaucracy itself was still dominated by the traditional hereditary elite. Still, the principle of selecting officials on the basis of talent had been established and would eventually become standard practice.

Under the Han dynasty, the population increased rapidly—by some estimates rising from about twenty million to over sixty million at the height of the dynasty—creating a growing need for a large and efficient bureaucracy to maintain the state in proper working order. Unfortunately, the Han were unable to resolve all of the problems left over from the past. Factionalism at court remained a serious problem and undermined the efficiency of the central government. Equally important, despite their efforts, the Han rulers were never able to restrain the great aristocratic families, who continued to play a dominant role in political and economic affairs. The failure to curb the power of the wealthy clans eventually became a major factor in the collapse of the dynasty.

SOCIETY AND ECONOMY IN THE HAN EMPIRE

Han rulers also retained some of the economic and social policies of their predecessors. In particular, they saw that a free peasantry paying taxes directly to the state would both limit the wealth and power of the great noble families and increase the state's revenues. The Han had difficulty preventing the recurrence of the economic inequities that had characterized the last years of the Zhou, however. The land taxes were relatively light, but the peasants also faced a number of other exactions, including military service and forced labor of up to one month annually. Although the use of iron tools brought new lands under the plow and food production increased steadily, the trebling of the population under the Han eventually reduced the average size of the individual farm plot to about one acre per capita, barely enough for survival. As time went on, many poor peasants were forced to sell their land and become tenant farmers, paying rents ranging up to half of the annual harvest. Thus land once again came to be concentrated in the hands of the powerful landed clans, which often owned thousands of acres worked by tenants and mustered their own military forces to bully free farmers into becoming tenants.

Although such economic problems contributed to the eventual downfall of the dynasty, in general the Han era was one of unparalleled productivity and prosperity. The period was marked by a major expansion of trade, both domestic and foreign. This was not necessarily due to official encouragement. In fact, the Han were as suspicious of private merchants as their predecessors had been and levied stiff taxes on trade in an effort to limit commercial activities. Merchants were also subject to severe social constraints. They were disqualified from seeking office, restricted in their place of residence, and viewed in general as parasites providing little true value to Chinese society.

The state itself directed much trade and manufacturing; it manufactured weapons, for example, and operated shipyards, granaries, and mines. The government also moved cautiously into foreign trade, mostly with neighboring areas in Central and Southeast Asia, although trade relations were established with countries as far away as

India and the Mediterranean (see Map 3.4). Some of this long-distance trade was carried by sea through southern ports like Guangzhou, but more was transported by overland caravans on the Silk Road (see Chapter 10) and other routes that led westward into Central Asia. Some of the trade was organized in the form of tribute missions, with neighboring countries providing local specialties like tropical products and precious stones in return for Chinese silks, glazed pottery (an early form of porcelain), and various manufactured products. China often gave more than it received to ensure that neighboring monarchs would accept China's benevolent protection and not harbor its enemies.

New technology contributed to the economic prosperity of the Han era. Significant progress was achieved in

© Christopher Lui

⇝ **A PRIZED POSSESSION.** Horse-drawn chariots were first used by nomadic peoples in the steppes of Central Asia and made their appearance in China late in the second millennium B.C.E. They quickly assured local rulers of military superiority on the battlefield, while their mobility proved useful during big game hunts at a time when the heavily forested plains of northern China were filled with tigers, elephants, and even rhinoceros. Like the pharaohs in Egypt, Chinese rulers filled their tombs with prized possessions deemed useful in the next world. Here we see the remains of a chariot and horses in a burial pit in Hebei province that dates from the early Zhou dynasty.

such areas as textile manufacturing, water mills, and iron casting; skill at ironworking led to the production of steel a few centuries later. Paper was invented under the Han, and the development of the rudder and fore-and-aft rigging permitted ships to sail into the wind for the first time. Thus equipped, Chinese merchant ships carrying heavy cargoes could sail throughout the islands of Southeast Asia and into the Indian Ocean.

Finally, the Han emperors continued the process of territorial expansion and consolidation that had begun under the Zhou and the Qin. Han rulers, notably Han Wudi (Han Wu Ti, or Martial Emperor of Han), successfully completed the assimilation into the empire of the regions south of the Yangtze River, including the Red River delta in what is today northern Vietnam. Han armies also marched westward as far as the Caspian Sea, pacifying nomadic tribal peoples and extending China's boundary far into Central Asia. The Han continued to have problems with the Xiongnu beyond the Great Wall to the north. Nomadic raids on Chinese territory continued intermittently to the end of the dynasty, once reaching almost to the gates of the capital city, now located at Chang'an (Ch'ang An, or Eternal Peace), on the site of modern Xian.

MAP 3.4   Trade Routes of the Ancient World. This map shows the various land and maritime routes that extended from China toward other civilizations that were located to the south and west of the Han empire. The various goods that were exchanged are identified at the bottom of the map.

➤ *What were the major goods exported by China?*

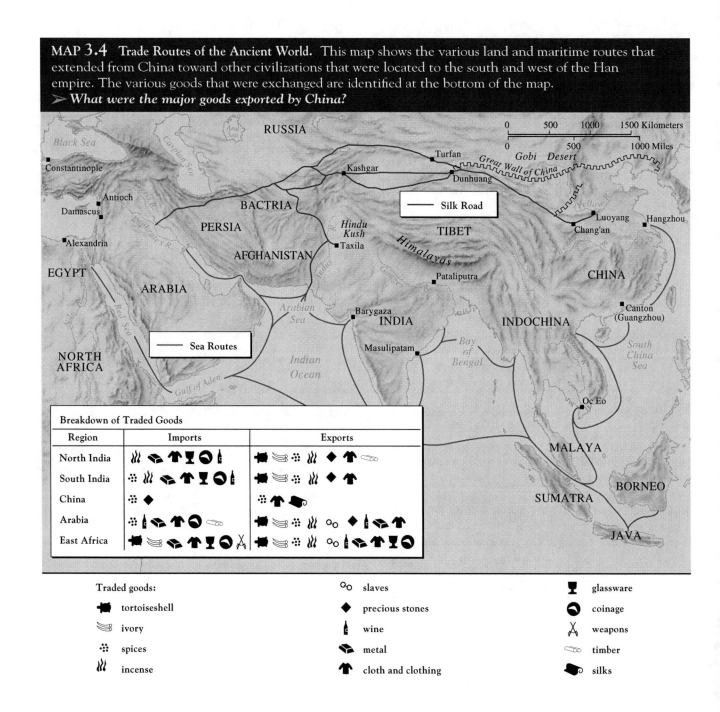

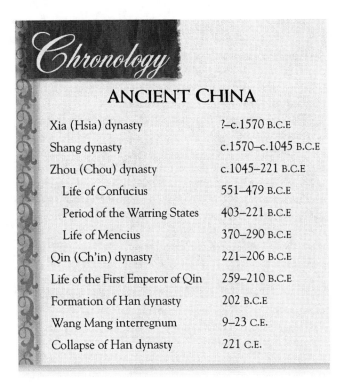

THE DECLINE AND FALL OF THE HAN

In 9 C.E., the reformist official Wang Mang, who was troubled by the plight of the peasants, seized power from the Han court and declared the foundation of a new Xin (New) dynasty. The empire had been crumbling for decades. As frivolous or depraved rulers amused themselves with the pleasures of court life, the power and influence of the central government began to wane, and the great noble families filled the vacuum, amassing vast landed estates and transforming free farmers into tenants. Wang Mang tried to confiscate the great estates, restore the ancient well field system, and abolish slavery. In so doing, however, he alienated powerful interests, who conspired to overthrow him. In 23 C.E., beset by administrative chaos and a collapse of the frontier defenses, Wang Mang was killed in a coup d'état.

For a time, strong leadership revived some of the glory of the early Han. The court did attempt to reduce land taxes and carry out land resettlement programs. The growing popularity of nutritious crops like rice, wheat, and soybeans, along with the introduction of new crops such as alfalfa and grapes, helped boost food production. But the monopoly of land and power by the great landed families continued. Weak rulers were isolated within their imperial chambers and dominated by eunuchs and other powerful figures at court. Official corruption and the concentration of land in the hands of the wealthy led to widespread peasant unrest. The population of the empire, which had been estimated at about sixty million in China's first census in the year 2 C.E., had shrunk to less than one-third that number two hundred years later. In the early third century C.E., the dynasty was finally brought to an end when power was seized by Cao Cao (Ts'ao Ts'ao), a general known to later generations as one of the main

characters in the famous Chinese epic *The Romance of the Three Kingdoms*. But Cao Cao was unable to consolidate his power, and China entered a period of almost constant anarchy and internal division, compounded by invasions by northern tribal peoples. The next great dynasty did not arise until the beginning of the seventh century, four hundred years later.

DAILY LIFE IN ANCIENT CHINA

Few social institutions have been as closely identified with China as the family. As in most agricultural civilizations, the family served as the basic economic and social unit in society. In traditional China, however, it took on an almost sacred quality as a microcosm of the entire social order.

In Neolithic times, the farm village, organized around the clan, was the basic social unit in China, at least in the core region of the Yellow River valley. Even then, however, the smaller family unit was becoming more important, at least among the nobility, who attached considerable significance to the ritual veneration of their immediate ancestors.

During the Zhou dynasty, the family took on increasing importance, in part because of the need for cooperation in agriculture. The cultivation of rice, which had become the primary crop along the Yangtze River and in the provinces to the south, is highly labor-intensive. The seedlings must be planted in several inches of water in a nursery bed and then transferred individually to the paddy beds, which must be irrigated constantly. During the harvest, the stalks must be cut and the kernels carefully separated from the stalks and husks. As a result, children—and the labor they supplied—were considered essential to the survival of the family, not only during their youthful years but also later, when sons were expected to provide for their parents. Loyalty to family members came to be considered even more important than loyalty to the broader community or the state. Confucius commented that it is the mark of a civilized society that a son should protect his father even if the latter has committed a crime against the community.

At the crux of the concept of family was the idea of filial piety, which called on all members of the family to subordinate their needs and desires to the patriarchal head of the family. More broadly, it created a hierarchical system in which every family member had his or her place. All Chinese learned the "five relationships" that were the key to a proper social order. The son was subordinate to the father, the wife to her husband, the younger brother to the older brother, and all were subject to their king. The final relationship was the proper one between friend and friend.

Courtesy of William J. Duiker

FLOODED RICE FIELDS.   Rice, which was first cultivated in China as long as seven or eight thousand years ago, is a very labor-intensive crop that requires many workers to plant the seedlings and organize the distribution of water. Initially, the fields are flooded to facilitate the rooting of the rice seedlings and to add nutrients to the soil. Fish breeding in the flooded fields help keep mosquitoes and other insects in check. As the plants mature, the fields are drained, and the plants complete their four-month growing cycle in dry soil. Shown here is an exmple of ter-racing on a hillside to preserve water for the nourishment of young seedlings.

Only if all members of the family and the community as a whole behaved in a properly filial manner would society function effectively.

A stable family system based on obedient and hard-working members can serve as a bulwark for an efficient government, but putting loyalty to the family and the clan over loyalty to the state can also present a threat to a centralizing monarch. For that reason, the Qin dynasty attempted to destroy the clan system in China and assert the primacy of the state. Legalists even imposed heavy taxes on any family with more than two adult sons in order to break down the family concept. The Qin reportedly also originated the practice of organizing several family units into larger groups of five and ten families that would exercise mutual control and surveillance. Later dynasties continued the practice under the name of the *Bao-jia* (*Pao-chia*) system.

But the efforts of the Qin to eradicate or at least reduce the importance of the family system ran against tradition and the dynamics of the Chinese economy, and under the Han, the family revived and increased in importance. With official encouragement, the family system began to take on the character that it would possess until our own day. The family was not only the basic economic unit; it was also the basic social unit for education, religious observances, and training in ethical principles.

We know much more about the lifestyle of the elites than that of the common people in ancient China. The first houses were probably constructed of wooden planks, but later Chinese mastered the art of building in tile and brick. By the first millennium B.C.E., most public buildings and the houses of the wealthy were probably constructed in this manner. By Han times, most Chinese probably lived in simple houses of mud, wooden planks, or brick with thatch or occasionally tile roofs. But in some areas, especially the loess (pronounced "less," a type of soil common in North China) regions of North China, cave dwelling remained common down to modern times. The most famous cave dweller of modern times was Mao Zedong, who lived in a cave in Yan'an during his long struggle against Chiang Kai-shek.

Chinese houses usually had little furniture; most people squatted or sat with their legs spread out on the packed mud floor. Chairs were apparently not introduced until the sixth or seventh century C.E. Clothing was simple, consisting of cotton trousers and shirts in the summer and wool or burlap in the winter.

The staple foods were millet in the north and rice in the south. Other common foods were wheat, barley, soybeans, mustard greens, and bamboo shoots. In early times, such foods were often consumed in the form of porridge, but by the Zhou dynasty, stir-frying in a wok was becoming common. When possible, the Chinese family would vary its diet of grain foods with vegetables, fruit (including pears, peaches, apricots, and plums), and fish or meat; but for most, such additions to the daily plate of rice, millet, or soybeans were a rare luxury.

Alcohol in the form of ale was drunk at least by the higher classes and by the early Zhou era had already begun to inspire official concern. According to the *Book of History*, "King Wen admonished . . . the young nobles . . . that they should not ordinarily use spirits; and throughout all the states he required that they should be drunk only on occasion of sacrifices, and that then virtue should preside so that there might be no drunkenness."[13]

Most Chinese, then as now, lived in the countryside. But as time went on, cities began to play a larger role in Chinese society. The first towns were little more than forts for the local aristocracy; they were small in size and limited in population. By the Zhou era, however, larger towns, usually located on the major trade routes, began to combine administrative and economic functions, serving as regional markets or manufacturing centers. Such cities were usually surrounded by a wall and a moat, and a raised platform might be built within the walls to provide a place for ritual ceremonies and housing for the ruler's family.

By the Han, the major city in China was Chang'an, the imperial capital. The city covered a total area of nearly 40 square kilometers and was enclosed by a 12-foot earthen wall surrounded by a moat. Twelve gates provided entry into the city, and eight major avenues ran east-west or north-south. Each avenue was 45 meters wide; a center strip in each avenue was reserved for the emperor, whose palace and gardens occupied nearly half the southern and central part of the city.

The Humble Estate: Women in Ancient China

Female subservience was a key element in the social system of ancient China. As in many traditional societies, the male was considered of transcendent importance because of his role as food procurer or, in the case of farming communities, food producer. In ancient China, men worked in the fields and women raised children and served in the home. The Chinese written language graphically demonstrates how ancient Chinese society regarded the sexes. The character for man (男) combines the symbols for strength and a rice field, whereas the character for woman (女) represents a person in a posture of deference and respect. The character for peace (安) is a woman under a roof. A wife is symbolized by a woman with a broom.

Confucian thought, while not denigrating the importance of women as mothers and homemakers, accepted the dual roles of men and women in Chinese society. Men governed society. They carried on family ritual through the veneration of ancestors. They were the warriors, scholars, and ministers. Their dominant role was firmly enshrined in the legal system. Men were permitted to have more than one wife and to divorce a spouse who did not produce a male child. Women were denied the right to own property, and there was no dowry system in ancient China that would have provided the wife with a degree of financial security from her husband and his family. As the third-century C.E. woman poet Fu Xuan lamented:

> How sad it is to be a woman
> Nothing on earth is held so cheap.
> No one is glad when a girl is born.
> By her the family sets no store.
> No one cries when she leaves her home
> Sudden as clouds when the rain stops.[14]

Not surprisingly women were taught to accept their secondary role in life. Ban Zhao, a prominent female historian of the Han dynasty whose own career was an exception to the rule, described that role as follows:

> To be humble, yielding, respectful and reverential; to put herself after others . . . these qualities are those exemplifying woman's low and humble estate. To retire late and rise early; not to shirk exertion from dawn to dark . . . this is called being diligent. To behave properly and decorously in serving her husband; to be serene and self-possessed, shunning jests and

© Michael Holford, London

❧ **HAN POTTERY HOUSE.** During the Han dynasty, the Chinese people thought that even in heaven one could still be surrounded by one's earthly possessions, such as family, servants, and house. Since such material goods could not accompany one directly into the afterworld, pottery models such as the one shown here were made and then placed in tombs with the dead.

laughter . . . this is called being worthy of continuing the husband's lineage. If a woman possess the above-mentioned three qualities, then her reputation shall be excellent.[15]

Some women did become a force in politics, especially at court, where wives of the ruler or other female members of the royal family were often influential in palace intrigues. Such activities were frowned on, however, as the following passage from the *Book of Songs* attests:

> A clever man builds a city,
> A clever woman lays one low;
> With all her qualifications, that clever woman
> Is but an ill-omened bird.
> A woman with a long tongue
> Is a flight of steps leading to calamity;
> For disorder does not come from heaven,
> But is brought about by women.
> Among those who cannot be trained or taught
> Are women and eunuchs.[16]

CHINESE CULTURE

Modern knowledge about artistic achievements in ancient civilizations is limited because often little has survived the ravages of time. Fortunately, many ancient civilizations, such as Egypt and Mesopotamia, were located in relatively arid areas where many artifacts were preserved, even over thousands of years. In more humid regions, such as China and South Asia, the cultural residue left by the civilizations of antiquity has been adversely affected by climate.

As a result, relatively little remains of the cultural achievements of the prehistoric Chinese aside from Neolithic pottery and the relics found at the site of the Shang dynasty capital at Anyang. In recent years, a rich trove from the time of the Qin Empire has been unearthed near the tomb of Qin Shi Huangdi near Xian in central China and at Han tombs nearby. But little remains of the literature of ancient China and almost none of the painting, architecture, and music.

Metalwork and Sculpture

Discoveries at archaeological sites indicate that ancient China was a society rich in cultural achievement. The pottery found at Neolithic sites such as Longshan and Yangshao exhibits a freshness and vitality of form and design, and the ornaments, such as rings and beads, show a strong aesthetic sense.

The pace of Chinese cultural development began to quicken during the Shang dynasty, which ruled in northern China from the sixteenth to the eleventh century B.C.E. At that time, objects cast in bronze began to appear. A variety of bronze vessels were produced for use in preparing and serving food and drink in the ancestral rites. Later vessels were used for decoration or for dining at court.

The method of casting used was one reason for the extraordinary quality of Shang bronze work. Bronze workers in most ancient civilizations used the lost-wax method, where a model was first made in wax. After a clay mold had been formed around it, the model was heated so that the wax would disappear, and the empty space was filled with molten metal. In China, clay molds composed of several sections were tightly fitted together prior to the introduction of the liquid bronze. This technique,

which had evolved from ceramic techniques used during the Neolithic period, enabled the artisans to apply the design directly to the mold and thus contributed to the clarity of line and rich surface decoration of the Shang bronzes.

Bronze casting became a large-scale business, and more than ten thousand vessels of an incredible variety of form and design survive today. The art of bronze working continued into the Zhou and the Han dynasties, but the quality and originality declined. The Shang bronzes remain the pinnacle of creative art in ancient China.

One reason for the decline of bronze casting in China was the rise in popularity of iron. Ironmaking developed in China around the ninth or eighth century B.C.E., much later than in the Middle East, where it had been mastered almost a millennium earlier. Once familiar with the process, however, the Chinese quickly moved to the forefront. Ironworkers in Europe and the Middle East, lacking the technology to achieve the high temperatures necessary to melt iron ore for casting, were forced to work with wrought iron, a cumbersome and expensive process. By the fourth century B.C.E., the Chinese had invented the technique of the blast furnace, powered by a person operating a bellows. They were therefore able to manufacture cast-iron ritual vessels and agricultural tools centuries before an equivalent technology appeared in the West.

Another reason for the deterioration of the bronze-casting tradition was the development of cheaper materials such as lacquerware and ceramics. Lacquer, obtained from a resinous

➤ **A SHANG WINE VESSEL.**
Used initially as food containers in royal ceremonial rites during the Shang dynasty, Chinese bronzes were the product of an advanced technology unmatched by any contemporary civilization. This wine vessel displays a deep green patina as well as a monster motif, complete with large globular eyes, nostrils, and fangs, typical of many Shang bronzes. Known as the *taotie*, this fanciful beast is normally presented in silhouette as two dragons face-to-face so that each side forms half of the mask. Although the *taotie* presumably served as a guardian force against evil spirits, scholars are still not aware of its exact significance for early Chinese peoples.

Courtesy of William J. Duiker

QIN SHI HUANGDI'S TOMB. The First Emperor of Qin ordered the construction of an elaborate mausoleum, an underground palace complex protected by an army of terra-cotta soldiers and horses to accompany him on his journey to the afterlife. This massive formation of six thousand life-size armed soldiers, discovered accidentally by farmers in 1974, reflects Qin Shi Huangdi's grandeur and power.

substance deposited on trees by the *lac* insect, had been produced since Neolithic times, and by the Han era it had become a popular method of applying a hard coating to objects made of wood or fabric. Pottery, too, had existed since early times, but technological advances during the Han led to the production of a high-quality form of pottery covered with a brown or gray-green glaze, the latter known popularly as celadon. During the Han, both lacquerware and pottery replaced bronze in popularity and value.

In 1974, in a remarkable discovery, farmers digging a well about 35 miles east of Xian unearthed a number of terra-cotta figures in an underground pit about one mile east of the burial mound of the First Emperor of Qin. Chinese archaeologists sent to work at the site discovered a vast terra-cotta army that they believed was a re-creation of Qin Shi Huangdi's imperial guard, which was to accompany the emperor on his journey to the next world.

One of the astounding features of the terra-cotta army is its size. The army is enclosed in four pits that were originally encased in a wooden framework, which has since disintegrated. More than a thousand figures have already been unearthed in the first pit, along with horses, wooden chariots, and seven thousand bronze weapons. Archaeologists estimate that there are more than six thousand figures in that pit alone.

Equally impressive is the quality of the work. Slightly larger than life-size, the figures were molded of finely textured clay, then fired and painted. The detail on the uniforms is realistic and sophisticated, but the most striking feature is the individuality of the facial features of the soldiers. Apparently, ten different head shapes were used and

were then modeled further by hand to reflect the variety of ethnic groups and personality types in the army.

The discovery of the terra-cotta army also shows that the Chinese had come a long way from the human sacrifices that had taken place at the death of Shang sovereigns more than a thousand years earlier. But the project must have been ruinously expensive and is additional evidence of the burden the Qin ruler imposed on his subjects. One historian has estimated that one-third of the national income in Qin and Han times may have been spent on preparations for the ruler's afterlife. The emperor's mausoleum has not yet been unearthed, but it is enclosed in a mound nearly 250 feet high and is surrounded by a rectangular wall nearly 4 miles around. According to the Han historian Sima Qian, the ceiling is a replica of the heavens, while the floor contains a relief model of the entire Qin kingdom, with rivers flowing in mercury. According to tradition, traps were set within the mausoleum to prevent intruders, and the workers applying the final touches were buried alive in the tomb with its secrets.

Qin Shi Huangdi's ambitious effort to provide for his immortality became a pattern for his successors during the Han dynasty, although apparently on a somewhat more modest scale. In 1990, Chinese workers discovered a similar underground army for a Han emperor of the second century B.C.E. Like the imperial guard of the First Qin Emperor, the underground soldiers were buried in parallel pits and possessed their own weapons and individual facial features. But they were smaller—only one-third the height of the average human adult—and were armed with wooden weapons and dressed in silk clothing, now decayed. A burial pit nearby indicates that as many as ten thousand workers, probably slaves or prisoners, died in the process of building the emperor's mausoleum, which took an estimated ten years to construct.

Language and Literature

Precisely when writing developed in China cannot be determined, but certainly by Shang times, as the oracle bones demonstrate, the Chinese had developed a simple but functional script. Like many other languages of antiquity, it was primarily ideographic and pictographic in form. Symbols, usually called "characters," were created to represent an idea or to form a picture of the object to be represented. For example, the Chinese characters for mountain (山), the sun (日), and the moon (月) were meant to represent the objects themselves. Other characters, such as "big" (大) (a man with his arms outstretched), represent an idea. The word "east" (東) symbolizes the sun coming up behind the trees.

Each character, of course, would be given a sound by the speaker when pronounced. In other cultures, this process led to the abandonment of the system of ideographs and the adoption of a written language based on phonetic symbols. The Chinese language, however, has never entirely abandoned its original ideographical format, although the phonetic element has developed into a significant part of the individual character. In that sense, the Chinese written language is virtually unique in the world today.

One reason the language retained its ideographic quality may have been the aesthetic quality of the written characters. By the time of the Han dynasty, if not earlier, the written language came to be seen as an art form as well as a means of communication, and calligraphy became one of the most prized forms of painting in China.

Even more important, if the written language had developed in the direction of a phonetic alphabet, it could no longer have served as the written system for all the peoples of an expanding civilization. Although the vast majority spoke a tongue derived from a parent Sinitic language (a system distinguished by its tonal nature, a characteristic that gives Chinese its lilting quality even today), the languages spoken in various regions of the country differed from each other in pronunciation and to a lesser degree in vocabulary and syntax; for the most part, they were (and are today) mutually unintelligible.

The Chinese answer to this problem was to give all the spoken languages the same writing system. Although any character might be pronounced differently in different regions of China, that character would be written the same way (after the standardization undertaken under the Qin) no matter where it was written. This system of written characters could be read by educated

➤ **SOLDIER IN QIN SHI HUANGDI'S TOMB.** This is one of the six thousand soldiers guarding the underground palace complex of Emperor Qin Shi Huangdi's tomb. Incredibly, each soldier has individualized facial features and expressions. Originally, they carried real weapons, and their uniforms were painted in brilliant colors. They are a most majestic and foreboding sight, individually and collectively.

Chinese from one end of the country to the other. It became the language of the bureaucracy and the vehicle for the transmission of Chinese culture to all Chinese from the Great Wall to the southern border and even beyond. The written language, however, was not identical with the spoken. Written Chinese evolved a totally separate vocabulary and grammatical structure from the spoken tongues. As a result, those who used it required special training.

The earliest extant form of Chinese literature dates from the Zhou dynasty. It was written on silk or strips of bamboo and consisted primarily of historical records such as the *Rites of Zhou*, philosophical treatises such as the *Analects* and *The Way of the Dao*, and poetry, as recorded in *The Book of Songs* and the *Song of the South* (see the box on p. 86). In later years, when Confucian principles had

LOVE SPURNED IN ANCIENT CHINA

The Book of Songs is an anthology of about three hundred poems written during the early Zhou dynasty. According to tradition, they were selected by Confucius from a much larger collection. In later years, many were given political interpretations. The poem reprinted here, however, expresses a very human cry of love spurned.

THE BOOK OF SONGS: THE ODES

You seemed a guileless youth enough,
Offering for silk your woven stuff;
But silk was not required by you;
I was the silk you had in view.
With you I crossed the ford, and while
We wandered on for many a mile
I said, "I do not wish delay,
But friends must fix our wedding-day. . . .
Oh, do not let my words give pain,
But with the autumn come again."

And then I used to watch and wait
To see you passing through the gate;
And sometimes, when I watched in vain,
My tears would flow like falling rain;
But when I saw my darling boy,
I laughed and cried aloud for joy.
The fortune-tellers, you declared,
Had all pronounced us duly paired;
"Then bring a carriage," I replied,
"And I'll away to be your bride."

The mulberry tree upon the ground,
Now sheds its yellow leaves around.

Three years have slipped away from me
Since first I shared your poverty;
And now again, alas the day!
Back through the ford I take my way.

My heart is still unchanged, but you
Have uttered words now proved untrue;
And you have left me to deplore
A love that can be mine no more.

For three long years I was your wife,
And led in truth a toilsome life;
Early to rise and late to bed,
Each day alike passed o'er my head.
I honestly fulfilled my part,
And you—well, you have broke my heart.
The truth my brothers will not know,
So all the more their gibes will flow.
I grieve in silence and repine
That such a wretched fate is mine.

Ah, hand in hand to face old age!—
Instead, I turn a bitter page.
O for the riverbanks of yore;
O for the much-loved marshy shore;
The hours of girlhood, with my hair
Ungathered, as we lingered there.
The words we spoke, that seemed so true,
I little thought that I should rue;
I little thought the vows we swore
Would some day bind us two no more.

been elevated to a state ideology, the key works identified with the Confucian school were integrated into a set of so-called Confucian Classics. These works became required reading for generations of Chinese schoolchildren and introduced them to the forms of behavior that would be required of them as adults.

Under the Han dynasty, although poetry and philosophical essays continued to be popular, historical writing became the primary form of literary creativity. Historians such as Sima Qian and Ban Gu (the dynasty's official historian and the older brother of the female historian Ban Zhao) wrote works that became models for later dynastic histories. These historical works combined political and social history with biographies of key figures. Like so much literary work in China, their primary purpose was moral and political—to explain the underlying reasons for the rise and fall of individual human beings and dynasties.

Music

From early times in China, music was viewed not just as an aesthetic pleasure but also as a means of achieving political order and refining the human character. In fact, music may have originated as an accompaniment to sacred rituals at the royal court. According to the *Historical Records*, a history written during the Han dynasty: "When our sage-kings of the past instituted rites and music, their objective was far from making people indulge in the . . . amusements of singing and dancing. . . . Music is produced to purify the heart, and rites introduced to rectify the behavior."[17] Eventually, however, music began to be appreciated for its own sake as well as to accompany singing and dancing.

A wide variety of musical instruments were used, including flutes, various stringed instruments, bells and chimes, drums, and gourds. Bells cast in bronze were first used as musical instruments in the Shang period; they were hung in rows and struck with a wooden mallet. The finest were produced during the mid-Zhou era and are considered among the best examples of early bronze work in China.

By the late Zhou era, bells had begun to give way as the instrument of choice to strings and wind instruments, and the purpose of music shifted from ceremony to entertainment. This led conservative critics to rail against the onset of an age of debauchery.

Ancient historians stressed the relationship between music and court life, but it is highly probable that music, singing, and dancing were equally popular among the common people. The *Book of History*, purporting to describe conditions in the late third millennium B.C.E., suggests that ballads emanating from the popular culture were welcomed at court. Nevertheless, court music and popular music differed in several respects. Among other things, popular music was more likely to be motivated by the desire for pleasure than for the purpose of law and order and moral uplift. Those differences continued to be reflected in the evolution of music in China down to modern times.

CONCLUSION

Of the great classical civilizations discussed in Part I of this book, China was the last to come into full flower. By the time the Shang began to emerge as an organized state, the societies in Mesopotamia and the Nile valley had already reached an advanced level of civilization. Unfortunately, not enough is known about the early stages of these civilizations to allow us to determine why some developed earlier than others, but one likely reason for China's late arrival was that it was virtually isolated from other emerging centers of culture elsewhere in the world and thus was compelled to develop essentially on its own. Only at the end of the first millennium B.C.E. did the Han dynasty come into regular contact with other civilizations in South Asia, the Middle East, and the Mediterranean.

Once embarked on its own path toward the creation of a complex society, however, China achieved results that were in all respects the equal of its counterparts elsewhere. During the glory years of the Han dynasty, China extended the boundaries of its empire far into the sands of Central Asia and southward along the coast of the South China Sea into what is now Vietnam. The doctrine of State Confucianism provided an effective ideology for the state, and Chinese culture appeared unrivaled. In many respects, its scientific and technological achievements were unsurpassed.

One reason for China's striking success was undoubtedly that unlike its contemporary civilizations, it long was able to fend off the danger from nomadic peoples (along the northern frontier). By the end of the second century B.C.E., however, the Xiongnu were looming ominously, and tribal warriors began to nip at the borders of the empire. While the dynasty was strong, the problem was manageable, but when internal difficulties began to corrode the unity of the state, China became increasingly vulnerable to the threat from the north and entered its own time of troubles.

During the glory years of the Han, another great civilization was beginning to take form on the northern shores of the Mediterranean Sea. Unlike China and the other ancient societies discussed thus far, this new civilization in Europe was based as much on trade as on agriculture. Yet the political and cultural achievements of ancient Greece were the equal of any of the great human experiments that had preceded it and soon began to exert a significant impact on the rest of the ancient world.

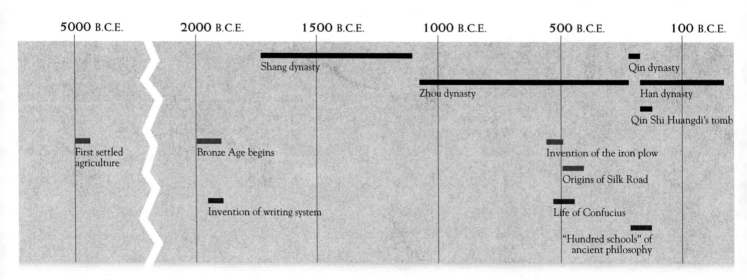

| 5000 B.C.E. | 2000 B.C.E. | 1500 B.C.E. | 1000 B.C.E. | 500 B.C.E. | 100 B.C.E. |

Shang dynasty

Zhou dynasty

Qin dynasty

Han dynasty

Qin Shi Huangdi's tomb

First settled agriculture

Bronze Age begins

Invention of the iron plow

Origins of Silk Road

Invention of writing system

Life of Confucius

"Hundred schools" of ancient philosophy

CHAPTER NOTES

1. *Book of Changes*, quoted in Chang Chi-yun, *Chinese History of Fifty Centuries*, vol. 1, *Ancient Times* (Taipei, 1962), pp. 15, 31, and 65.
2. Ibid., p. 381.
3. Quoted in E. N. Anderson, *The Food of China* (New Haven, Conn., 1988), p. 21.
4. According to Chinese tradition, the *Rites of Zhou* was written by the duke of Zhou himself near the time of the founding of the Zhou dynasty. However, modern historians believe that it was written much later, perhaps as late as the fourth century B.C.E.
5. From *The Book of Songs*, quoted in Sebastian de Grazia, ed., *Masters of Chinese Political Thought: From the Beginnings to the Han Dynasty* (New York, 1973), pp. 40–41.
6. *Confucian Analects* (Lun Yu), ed. James Legge (Taipei, 1963), 11:11 and 6:20.
7. Ibid., 15:23.
8. Ibid., 17:2.
9. *Book of Mencius* (Meng Zi), 4 A:9, quoted in William Theodore de Bary et al., eds., *Sources of Chinese Tradition* (New York, 1960), p. 107.
10. Quoted in de Bary, *Sources of Chinese Tradition*, p. 53.
11. Burton Watson, *Records of the Grand Historian of China* (New York, 1961), vol. 2, pp. 155, 160.
12. Ibid., pp. 32, 53.
13. Clae Waltham, *Shu Ching: Book of History* (Chicago, 1971), p. 154.
14. Arthur Waley, ed., *Chinese Poems* (London, 1983), p. xx.
15. Lloyd E. Eastman, *Family, Fields, and Ancestors: Constancy and Change in China's Social and Economic History, 1550–1949* (New York, 1988), p. 19.
16. Quoted in Herbert A. Giles, *A History of Chinese Literature* (New York, 1923), p. 19.
17. Chang Chi-yun, *Chinese History of Fifty Centuries*, vol. 1, p. 183.

SUGGESTED READING

Several general histories of China provide a useful overview of the period of antiquity. Perhaps the best known is the classic *East Asia: Tradition and Transformation* (Boston, 1973), by J. K. Fairbank, E. O. Reischauer, and A. M. Craig. For an authoritative overview of the ancient period, see M. Loewe and E. L. Shaughnessy, *The Cambridge History of Ancient China from the Origins of Civilization to 221 B.C.* (Cambridge, 1999). Political and social maps of China can be found in A. Herrmann, *A Historical Atlas of China* (Chicago, 1966).

The period of the Neolithic era and the Shang dynasty has received increasing attention in recent years. For an impressively documented and annotated overview, see Kwang-chih Chang, *Shang Civilization* (New Haven, Conn., 1980) and *Studies in Shang Archaeology* (New Haven, Conn., 1982). D. Keightley, *The Origins of Chinese Civilization* (Berkeley, Calif., 1983), presents a number of interesting articles on selected aspects of the period.

The Zhou and Qin dynasties have also received considerable attention. The former is exhaustively analyzed in Cho-yun Hsu and J. M. Linduff, *Western Zhou Civilization* (New Haven, Conn., 1988), and Li Xueqin, *Eastern Zhou and Qin Civilizations* (New Haven, Conn., 1985). The latter is a translation of an original work by a mainland Chinese scholar and is especially interesting for its treatment of the development of the silk industry and the money economy in ancient China. On bronze casting, see E. L. Shaughnessy, *Sources of Eastern Zhou History* (Berkeley, Calif., 1991). Also of value for its treatment of the formation of social classes is Cho-yun Hsu, *Ancient China in Transition* (Stanford, Calif., 1965).

There are a number of useful books on the Han dynasty. Zhong-shu Wang, *Han Civilization* (New Haven, Conn., 1982), presents recent evidence from the mainland on recent excavations from Han tombs and the old imperial capital of Chang'an. M. Loewe, *Everyday Life in Early Imperial China During the Han Period, 202 B.C.–220 A.D.* (London, 1968), contains useful material on religious beliefs and the development of social classes during the Han. Also see the lavishly illustrated *Han Civilization of China* (Oxford, 1982) by M. P. Serstevens. For a firsthand view, see B. Watson, *Records of the Grand Historian of China* (New York, 1961), a translation of key passages from Sima Qian's history of the period.

The philosophy of ancient China has attracted considerable attention from Western scholars. Some standard works include A. Waley, *Three Ways of Thought in Ancient China* (New York, 1939); H. G. Creel, *Chinese Thought: From Confucius to Mao Tse-Tung* (Chicago, 1953); Feng Yu-lan, *A Short History of Chinese Philosophy* (New York, 1960); and F. Mote, *Intellectual Foundations of China*, 2d ed. (New York, 1989). On Confucius, see H. G. Creel, *Confucius: The Man and the Myth* (London, 1951), a sympathetic treatment that emphasizes the humanistic side of Confucian philosophy.

For works on general culture and science, consult the illustrated work by R. Temple, *The Genius of China: 3000 Years of Science, Discovery, and Invention* (New York, 1986), and J. Needham, *Science in Traditional China: A Comparative Perspective* (Boston, 1981). See also E. N. Anderson, *The Food of China* (New Haven, Conn., 1988).

The most comprehensive collection of original writings is W. T. de Bary and Irene Bloom, *Sources of Chinese Tradition*, 2d ed. (New York, 1999), which includes excerpts from most of the ancient texts. The complete translations of the Confucian Classics are in J. Legge, *The Chinese Classics*, 5 vols. (Hong Kong, 1960), with critical and exegetical notes. For a modernized edition of the *Book of History*, see C. Waltham, *Shu Ching: Book of History* (Chicago, 1971). For an annotated version of Lao Tzu, see Wing-Tsit Chan, *The Way of Lao Tzu* (Indianapolis, 1963).

For an introduction to classical Chinese literature, consult the three standard anthologies: Liu Wu-Chi, *An Introduction to Chinese Literature* (New York, 1961); V. H. Mair, ed., *The Columbia Anthol-*

ogy of *Traditional Chinese Literature* (New York, 1994); and S. Owen, ed., *An Anthology of Chinese Literature: Beginnings to 1911* (New York, 1996). For a comprehensive introduction to Chinese art, consult M. Sullivan, *The Arts of China*, 4th ed. (Berkeley, Calif., 1999), with good illustrations in color. Also see M. Tregear, *Chinese Art*, rev. ed. (London, 1997), and *Art Treasures in China* (New York, 1994). Also of interest is P. B. Ebrey, *The Cambridge Illustrated History of China* (Cambridge, 1999). On music, see J. F. So, ed., *Music in the Age of Confucius* (Washington, D. C., 2000).

INFOTRAC COLLEGE EDITION

For additional reading, go to InfoTrac College Edition, your online research library at
http://web1.infotrac-college.com

Enter the search terms "Confucius or Confucian" using Keywords.

Enter the search terms "Taoism or Daoism" using the Subject Guide.

Enter the search terms "Han dynasty" using Keywords.

Enter the search terms "China history" using Keywords.

WRITINGS ON CONFUCIANISM

1

......

CHINA, 479 B.C.

THE CONFUCIAN TRADITION[1] IN CHINESE HISTORY

TIT WEI-MING

Iron metallurgy came late to China, but its social and political effects were devastating. The chariot-driving Bronze Age aristocracy was replaced by cavalry and peasant infantry, and the Chou dynasty (ca. 1100 B. c. -403 B. c:) disintegrated, leaving in its wake a number of petty contending principalities. This was the beginning of the Age of Warring States (403 B.c.-218 B. C.). In China as elsewhere, the collapse of the Bronze Age empires and the fall of their priestly castes left people to explain to themselves what had befallen them and to devise personal rules to guide them in the new and tumultuous times. The result was the rise of teachers such as Buddha in India, Joel in Israel, and Hesiod in Greece, and the spread of their doctrines.

K'ung-fu-tzu, Master K'ung, or Confucius, was the leading teacher in China. ignoring the imperial pantheon of deities of early times, he concentrated on the ethics of human actions as the means of bringing order into an age of chaos. He taught that leaders should be motivated by service to others, righteousness, integrity, conscientiousness, and, above humanity. They should strive to combine these inner virtues with outer culture and—for want of a better term—manners. The logical extension of this doctrine was that power should be wielded in a humane manner by individuals who displayed both inner and outer merit. This vision proved so strong that Confucius's teachings formed the basis of education in China for the next 2,500 years.

Tu Wei-ming discusses the importance of the Confucian ethic to both China and the various cultures around it. No one can study Eastern civilization without quickly becoming aware of the deep and continuing influence that the teachings of Master K'ung continue to exert upon all aspects of life and thought.

READING QUESTIONS

1. What was the purpose of education for Confucius?
2. What is the *Analects* and what is its importance?
3. How did Confucius define the quality of humanity?
4. What is filial piety and why was it considered so important by Confucius?

---

1 From Tu Wei-ming, "The Confucian Tradition in Chinese History," in Paul S. Ropp, rd., *Heritage Qf China: Contemporary Perspectives On Chinese Civilization* (Berkeley: University of California Press, 1990), pp. 112-117.

Confucianism, a generic Western term that has no counterpart in Chinese, is a world-view, a social ethic, a political ideology, a scholarly tradition, and a way of life.[2] Although Confucianism is often grouped together with Buddhism, Christianity, Hinduism, Islam, Judaism, and Taoism as a major historical religion, it is not an organized religion. Yet it has exerted profound influence on East Asian political culture as well as East Asian spiritual life. Both in theory and practice Confucianism has made an indelible mark on the governments, societies, educational practices, and family life of East Asia. It is an exaggeration to characterize traditional Chinese life and culture as "Confucian," but for well over two thousand years Confucian ethical values have served as a source of inspiration as well as the court of appeal for human interaction at all levels—individual, communal, and national—in the Sinic world.

Confucianism was not an organized missionary tradition, but by the first century B.C. it had spread to those East Asian countries that were under the influence of Chinese literate culture. In the centuries following the Confucian revival of Sung times (A.D. 960-1279), Confucianism was embraced in Chosön dynasty Korea beginning in the fifteenth century and in. Tokugawa Japan beginning in the seventeenth century. Prior to the arrival of the Western powers in East Asia in the mid nineteenth century the Confucian persuasion was so predominant in the art of governance, the form and conduct of elite education, and the moral discourse of the populace that China, Korea, and Japan were all distinctively "Confucian" states. In Southeast Asia, Vietnam and Singapore were also influenced by Confucianism.

THE LIFE OF CONFUCIUS

Considering Confucius's tremendous importance, his life seems starkly undramatic, or as a Chinese expression has it, "plain and real." The plainness and reality of Confucius's life, however, illustrate his humanity not as a revealed truth but as an expression of self-cultivation, the ability of human effort to persevere in the endless but ennobling tasks of self-improvement and humanitarian service. The faith in the possibility that ordinary human beings can become awe-inspiring sages and worthies is deeply rooted in the Confucian heritage and the insistence that human beings are teachable, improvable, and perfectible through personal and communal endeavor is typically Confucian.

Confucius was born in 551 B.C. in Ch'ii-fu in the small feudal state of Lu (in modern Shantung province), which was noted for its preservation of the traditions of ritual and music of the Chou civilization. Confucius's ancestors were probably members of the aristocracy who had become virtual poverty-stricken commoners by the time of this birth. His father died when Confucius was only three years old. Instructed first by his mother, Confucius distinguished himself as an indefatigable learner in his teens. He recalled toward the end of his life that his heart was set on learning at fifteen (2.4, that is, book 2, chapter 4 of the *Analects*).

---

2 The adjective "Confucian" derives from "Confucius," the Latinization of Kung Fu-tzu, or Master Kung. The term "Confucianism" was coined in Europe only in the eighteenth century. It is used, not entirely accurately, to translate the Chinese termju-chia. which literally means "family of scholars," signifying a genealogy, a school, or a tradition of learning. Please note that my citations from the *Analects* are given by book and verse number and thus are the same for any edition.

Confucius served in minor government posts managing stables and keeping books for granaries before he married a woman of similar background when he was nineteen. He may already have acquired a reputation as a multitalented scholar at an early age. Confucius's mastery of the six arts—ritual, music. archery, charioteering, calligraphy, and arithmetic—and his familiarity with the classical traditions, notably poetry and history, enabled him to start a brilliant teaching career in his thirties.

Confucius is known as the first private teacher in China, for he was instrumental in establishing the art of teaching as a vocation, indeed as a way of life. Before Confucius aristocratic families hired tutors to educate their sons and government officials instructed their subordinates in the necessary techniques, but he was the first person to devote his whole life to learning and teaching for the purpose of transforming and improving society.

For Confucius the primary function of education is to provide the proper way of training noblemen (china-tzu), a process that involves constant self-improvement and continuous social interaction. Although he emphatically noted (14.25) that learning is "for the sake of the self" and that the end of learning is self-realization. he found public service a natural consequence of true education. Confucius confronted learned hermits who challenged the validity of his desire to serve the world; he resisted the temptation to "herd with birds and animals" (18.6), to live apart from the human community, and opted to try to transform the world from within. For decades Confucius was actively involved in the political arena wishing to put his humanist ideas into practice through governmental channels.

In his late forties and early fifties Confucius served first as a magistrate, then as an assistant minister of public works, and eventually as minister of justice in the state of Lu. But his political career was short-lived. At fifty-six, when he realized that his superiors were uninterested in his policies, he left the state of Lu in an attempt to find another feudal state in which to render his service. Despite his political frustration he was accompanied by a growing circle of students during this self-imposed exile of almost thirteen years. His reputation as a man of vision and mission spread. At the age of sixty-seven, he returned home to teach and to preserve his cherished classical traditions by writing and editing. He died in 479 B.C. at the age of seventy-three. According to the *Records of the Historian* seventy-two of his students mastered the "six arts," and three thousand people claimed to be his followers.

THE *ANALECTS* AS THE EMBODIMENT
OF CONFUCIAN IDEAS

The *Analects (Lun-ya)*, the most revered sacred text in the Confucian tradition, was probably compiled by the second generation of Confucius's disciples.[3] Based primarily on the master's sayings, which were preserved in both oral and written transmissions, the *Analects* captures the Confucian spirit in form and content in the same way that the Platonic dialogues underscore the Socratic pedagogy. The purpose in compiling this digest of Confucius's statements seems not to have been to present an argument or to record an event but to offer an invitation to its readers to take part in an ongoing conversation. Dialogue

3   For a good translation of the *Analects* see D. C. Lau, trans. *The Analects* (Ilarmondsworth: Penguin, 1979).

is used to show Confucius in thought and action, not as an isolated individual, but as a center of human relationships.

Confucius's life as a student and teacher exemplified the Confucian idea that education is a ceaseless process of self-realization. When one of his students reportedly had difficulty describing him. Confucius came to his aid: "Why did you not simply say something to this effect: he is the sort of man who forgets to eat when he engages himself in vigorous pursuit of learning, who is so full of joy that he forgets his worries, and who does not notice that old age is coming on?" (7.18).

The community that Confucius created through his inspiring personality was a scholarly fellowship of like-minded men of different ages and different backgrounds from different states. They were attracted to Confucius because they shared his vision and in varying degrees took part in his mission to bring moral order to an increasingly fragmented polity. This mission was difficult and even dangerous. The master himself suffered from joblessness, homelessness, starvation, and, occasionally, life-threatening violence. Yet, his faith in the survivability of the culture that he cherished and the workability of the approach to teaching that he propounded was so steadfast that he convinced his followers as well as himself that Heaven was on their side. When Confucius's life was threatened in K'uang, he said: "Since the death of King Wen [founder of the Chou dynasty], does not the mission of culture (*wen*) rest here in me? If Heaven intends this culture to be destroyed, those who come after me will not be able to have any part of it. If Heaven does not intend this culture to be destroyed, then what can the men of K'uang do to me?" (9.5).

This expression of self-confidence may give the impression that there was presumptuousness in Confucius's self-image. However, Confucius made it explicit that he was far from attaining sagehood and that all he really excelled in was "love of learning" (5.28). In this sense Confucius was neither a prophet with privileged access to the divine nor a philosopher who has already seen the truth, but a teacher of humanity who is an advanced fellow traveler on the way to self-realization.

As a teacher of humanity, Confucius stated his ambition in terms of human care: "To bring comfort to the old, to have trust in friends, and to cherish the young" (5.26). Confucius's vision of the way to develop a moral community began with a holistic reflection on the human condition. Instead of dwelling on abstract ideas, such as the state of nature, Confucius sought to understand the actual situation of a given time and use this understanding as a point of departure. His aim was to restore trust in government and to transform society into a moral community by cultivating a sense of human caring in politics and society. To achieve this aim, the creation of a scholarly community, the fellowship of *chlin-tzu* (noblemen), was essential. In the words of Confucius's disciple, Tseng Tzu, the true nobleman "must be broad-minded and resolute, for his burden is heavy and his road is long. He takes humanity as his burden. Is that not heavy? Only with death does his road come to an end. Is that not long?" (8.7). However, the fellowship of *chtin-tzu*, as moral vanguards of society, did not seek to establish a radically different order. Its mission was to reformulate and revitalize those institutions that were believed to have maintained social solidarity and enabled people to live in harmony and prosperity for centuries.

An obvious example of such an institution is the family. The role and function of the family was related in the *Analects* when Confucius was asked why he did not take part in government. He responded (2.21) by citing a passage from an ancient classic, the *Book qf Documents*, "Simply by being a good son and friendly to his brothers a man can exert an influence upon government!" This passage shows that what one does in the confines of one's private home is politically significant. This position is predicated on the Confucian conviction that the self-cultivation of each person is the root of social order and that social order is the basis for political stability and universal peace. The assertion that family ethics are politically efficacious must be seen in the context of the Confucian conception of politics as "rectification" (cheng). In this conception rulers are supposed to govern by moral leadership and exemplary teaching rather than by force. The government's responsibility is not only to provide food and security but also to educate the people. Law and punishment are the minimum requirements for order; but social harmony can only be attained by virtue, which is achieved through ritual performance. To perform ritual is to take part in a communal act to promote mutual understanding.

One of the fundamental Confucian values that ensures the integrity of ritual performance is filial piety. Confucius believed that filial piety was the first step toward moral excellence. He seemed to contend that the way to enhance personal dignity and identity is not to alienate ourselves from our family but to cultivate our genuine feelings for our parents. To learn to embody the family in our minds and hearts is to enable ourselves to move beyond self-centeredness or, to borrow from modern psychology, to transform the enclosed private ego into an open self. Indeed, the cardinal Confucian virtue, *jen* (humanity), is the result of self-cultivation. The first test for our self-cultivation is our ability to establish meaningful relationships with our family members. Filial piety does not demand unconditional submissiveness to parental authority; rather it demands recognition of and reverence for our source of life.

The purpose of filial piety, as the Greeks would have it, is "human flourishing" for both parent and child. Confucians see it as an essential way of learning to be human. They are fond of applying the family metaphor to the community, the country, and the universe. They prefer to address the emperor as the Son of Heaven, the king as ruler-father, and the magistrate as the "father-mother official" because they assume that implicit in the family-centered nomenclature is a political vision. When Confucius responded that taking care of family affairs is itself active participation in politics. he made it clear that family ethics are not merely a private, personal concern. Rather, family ethics make possible the realization of the public good.

In response to a question from his favorite disciple, Yen Hui, Confucius defined humanity as "conquer yourself and return to ritual" (12.1). This interplay between inner spiritual self-transformation (the master is said to have freed himself from four things: "opinionatedness, dogmatism. obstinacy, and egoism" (9.41) and social participation enabled Confucius to be "loyal" (chung) to himself and "considerate" (shu) of others (4.15). Understandably, the Confucian golden rule is "Do not do unto others what you would not want other to do unto you" (15.23). Confucius's legacy, laden with profound ethical implications, is captured by his "plain and real" appreciation that learning to be human is a communal enterprise: "A man of humanity, wishing to establish himself, also establishes others, and wishing to enlarge himself, also enlarges others. The ability to take as analogy what is near at hand can be called the method of humanity" (6.28). ❖

RECOMMENDED READINGS

Fung Yu-lang, A *Short History of Chinese Philosophy*, ed. Derk Bodde (New York: Macmillan, 1948), provides an excellent general introduction to Chinese philosophy; Arthur F.

Wright, *The Confucian Persuasion* (Palo Alto, CA: Stanford University Press, (1960), offers some stimulating insights into Confucianism in particular. Arthur F. Waley sets Confucianism in its wider cultural and social context in *Confucianism and Chinese Civilization* (Stanford: Stanford University Press, 1975). The standard English translation of the basic Confucian text is still Arthur F. Waley, *The Analects of Confucius* (New York: Allen & Unwin, 1938), although there are now several others available. Ch'u Chai and Winberg Ch'ai, eds. and trans., offer a representative sampling of later Confucian texts in *The Sacred Books of Confucius and Other Confucian Classics* (New York: Bantam, 1965). There are several biographies of Confucius, all of which are as much legend as fact. Raymond S. Dawson, *Confucius* (New York: Hill & Wang, 1982), provides one of the more recent of these. The reader who wishes to pursue Confucianism further would do well to turn to David L. Hall, *Thinking Through Confucius* (Albany: State University of New York Press, 1987).

2

......

THE CLASSIC OF FILIAL PIETY⁴

HSIAO CHING

K'ung Fu-tzu, commonly known in the West as Confucius, was the greatest of the Chinese sages and is generally regarded as having done more than any other single individual to shape Chinese character and culture over the centuries. His life spanned the years 551 to 478 B.C., years of turmoil and unrest in China. The Chou dynasty had lost all real power some two centuries earlier, and attempts to maintain a measure of peace and political unity through a "concert of princes" was failing. The intricate social and political relations, the highly developed religious ritual, and the sophisticated culture that had evolved over the preceding thousand years were disintegrating. Ancient values and attitudes provided the people with little sense of purpose and direction as China continued towards the period known as the "era of the warring states" (453-221 B.C.).

K'ung entered the civil service of the prince of Lu, a state in what is now the province of Shantung. He soon began teaching, and quickly gathered numerous disciples. He taught that the welfare of the people and the good of the state depend on individuals conducting themselves properly in their relations with others, and that the virtuous individual teaches others by example. Virtue is its own reward, and proper conduct ennobles the individual more certainly than high birth. Although K'ung wrote little, his disciples copied down his discourses and spread his reputation far and wide. Nevertheless, as would later be the case with Plato, although the princes admired and honored him, none was willing to accept him as counsellor.

Though his followers were persecuted and scattered, Confucian teachings survived and were adopted as doctrine by the great Han emperors as they once again brought unity to China (206 B.C.–A.D. 220). *The Classic of Filial Piety* (*Hsiao Ching*), although ascribed to Confucius's disciple Tseng Tzu, was probably written much later than Confucius's time and is a good example of how Confucian teachings reached Han China. Although K'ung Fu-tzu himself does not seem to have emphasized filial piety to such a degree, in this work it becomes the fundamental social virtue upon which all other relationships rest. The *Hsiao Ching* was not only the manual of conduct for every educated individual of Han China, but a required elementary textbook in all schools.

It is characteristic of the Confucians that they paid little attention to metaphysics and theology. If virtue is its own reward, there is little reason to speculate about the gods and the afterlife. In this little piece, which takes the form of a dialogue between Tseng Tzu and K'ung, there are no hidden doctrines or complex theorizing. Social and political obliga-

---

4 From *The Humanist Way in Ancient China*, ed. and trans. Ch'u Chai and Winberg Chai (New York: Bantam, 1965), pp. 326–334.

tions on the one hand, and the Chinese tradition of the veneration of ancestors on the other, are brought together in a single and practical doctrine.

Questions

1. How is filial piety defined in this work?
2. How does filial piety lead the individual to a concern for his own welfare?
3. What is the *Tao* that is frequently mentioned?
4. What is the purpose of the frequent quotations from the *Shih King,* a collection of ancient poems compiled by K'ung Fu-tzu?

THE CLASSIC OF FILIAL PIETY

THE GENERAL THEME

Chung'ni[5] was at leisure, and Tseng Tzu attended him. The Master said: "The early kings possessed the supreme virtue and the basic Tao for the regulation of the world. On account of this, the people lived in peace and harmony; neither superiors nor inferiors had any complaints. Do you know this?"

Tseng Tzu rose from his seat and said: "How can Sheng,[6] dull of intelligence, know this?"

The Master said: "Filial piety is the basis of virtue and the source of culture. Sit down again, and I will explain it to you. The body and the limbs, the hair and the skin, are given to one by one's parents, and to them no injury should come; this is where filial piety begins. To establish oneself and practice the Tao is to immortalize one's name and thereby to glorify one's parents; this is where filial piety ends. Thus, filial piety commences with service to parents; it proceeds with service to the sovereign; it is completed by the establishment of one's own personality.

"In the *Shih* it is said:

> May you think of your ancestors,
> And so cultivate their virtues!"

THE SON OF HEAVEN

The Master said: "One who loves one's parents does not dare to hate others. One who reveres one's parents does not dare to spurn others. When love and reverence are thus cherished in the service of one's parents, one's moral influence transforms the people, and one becomes a pattern to all within the four seas. This is the filial piety of the Son of Heaven.

"In the *Fu Code,* it is said:

> When the One Man has blessings,
> The millions of people rely on him."

THE FEUDAL PRINCES

---

5 Confucius.

6 Tseng Tzu's name: this was a courteous way of addressing seniors.

When the prince is not proud and arrogant, he will be secure in his position, however high it may be. When the prince is frugal and prudent, he will keep his wealth, however abundant it may be. When he secures himself in his high position, he will remain unimpaired in his dignity; when he keeps his abundant wealth, he will remain rich. And thus, preserving his wealth and dignity, he will be able to protect his country and pacify his people. This is the filial piety of feudal princes.

In the *Shih* it is said:

> In fear and trembling,
> With caution and care,
> As if standing by a deep abyss,
> As if treading on thin ice.

THE HIGHT OFFICERS

They do not presume to be in costume not prescribed by the early kings; they do not presume to use words not sanctioned by the early kings; they do not presume to act contrary to the virtuous conduct of the early kings. Thus, none of their words [is] contrary to sanctions, and none of their actions [is] not in accordance with the Tao. Their words are not improper; nor are their actions indecent. Their words spread over the world, and yet no fault is found in them. Their actions spread over the world, and yet no complaint is caused by them. When these three things are properly observed, they will be able to preserve their ancestral temples. This is the filial piety of high officers.

In the *Shih* it is said:

> Day and night, never slacken
> In the service of the One Man.

THE SCHOLARS

One serves one's mother in the same manner in which one serves one's father, and the love toward them is the same. One serves one's prince in the same manner in which one serves one's father, and the reverence toward them is the same. Thus, to the mother one shows love and to the prince one shows reverence, but to the father one shows both love and reverence. Therefore, to serve the prince with filial piety is to show loyalty; to serve the senior with reverence is to show obedience. Not failing in loyalty and obedience in the service of ones superiors, one will be able to preserve one's emolument and position and to carry on one's family sacrifices. This is the filial piety of scholars.

In the *Shih* it is said:

> Rise early and go to sleep late;
> Never disgrace those who bore you.

THE COMMON PEOPLE

In order to support their parents, they follow the Tao of Heaven; they utilize the earth in accordance with the quality of its soil, and they are prudent and frugal in their expenditure. This is the filial piety of the common people.

Therefore, from the Son of Heaven down to the common people, there has never been one on whom, if filial piety was not pursued from the beginning to end, disasters did not befall.

THE TRINITY—HEAVEN, EARTH, AND MAN

Tseng Tzu said: "How great is filial piety!" The Master said: "Filial piety is the basic principle of Heaven, the ultimate standard of earth, and the norm of conduct for the people. Men ought to abide by the guiding principle of Heaven and earth as the pattern of their lives, so that by the brightness of Heaven and the benefits of earth they would be able to keep all in the world in harmony and in unison. On this account, their teachings, though not stringent, are followed, and their government, though not rigorous, is well ordered. The early kings, knowing that their teachings could transform the people, made themselves an example of practicing all-embracing love; thereby the people did not neglect their parents. They expounded the virtuous and righteous conduct, and the people enthusiastically complied. They made of themselves an example of respectful and prudent behavior, and the people were not contentious. They guided themselves with *li*[7] and music, and the people lived in concord. They verified the distinction between good and evil, and the people knew restraint.

"In the *Shih* it is said:

> Oh, majestic Master Yin,
> The people all look up to thee!"

GOVERNMENT BY FILIAL PIETY

The Master said: "Formerly the enlightened kings governed the world by filial piety. They did not dare to neglect the ministers of small states—to say nothing of the dukes, marquises, earls, viscounts, and barons! They thereby gained the good will of all the states to serve their early kings.

"Those who governed the states did not dare to ignore the widows and widowers—to say nothing of scholars and the people! They thereby gained the good will of all the subjects to serve their former princes.

"Those who regulated their families did not dare to mistreat their servants and concubines—to say nothing of their wives and children! They thereby gained the good will of others who served their parents.

"Accordingly, while living, the parents enjoyed comfort; after their death, sacrifices were offered to their spirits. In this way the world was kept in peace; disasters did not arise, nor did riots occur. Such was the way in which the early enlightened governed the world by filial piety.

"In the *Shih* it is said:

> Glorious was his virtuous conduct,
> And all states submitted themselves."

GOVERNMENT BY THE SAGE

Tseng Tzu said: "I venture to ask whether in the virtue of the sage there is anything that surpasses filial piety."

The Master said: "It is the nature of Heaven and earth that man is the most honorable of all beings. Of all human conduct none is greater than filial piety. In filial piety nothing is greater than to revere one's father. In revering one's father, nothing is greater than making him a peer of Heaven. The Duke of Chou did this. Formerly the Duke of Chou sacrificed

---

7 Order, propriety; the rules of proper conduct.

to Hou Chi in the suburbs as the peer of Heaven. He sacrificed to King Wen [his father] at the Ming T'ang [Bright Temple] as the peer of Shang Ti [Supreme Being]. Therefore, all the feudal princes within the four seas came, each with his tribute, to join in the sacrifices. How can there be anything in the virtue of the sage that surpasses filial piety?

"Affection is fostered by parents during childhood, and from there springs the child's reverence, which grows daily, while sustaining his parents. The sage was to follow this innate development by teaching reverence and to follow this piety. In filial piety nothing is greater than to revere one's father. In revering innate feeling of affection by teaching love. Thus, the teachings of the sage, though not stringent, were followed, and his government, though not rigorous, was well ordered. All this was brought about because of this innate disposition.

"The *Tao* of father and son is rooted in the Heaven-endowed nature, and develops into the equity between sovereign and ministers. Parents give one life; no bond is stronger. They bring up and care for their child; no kindness is greater. Therefore, one who does not love one's parents, but others, acts to the detriment of virtue. One who does not revere one's parents, but others, acts to the detriment of *li*. Should the rules of conduct be modeled on such perversity, the people would have no true norm by which to abide. Therein is found no goodness but only evil. Although such a person may gain a high position, the *chün-tzu* will not esteem him.

The *chün-tzu* is not like this. His speech is consistent with the Tao, his action with what is good. His virtuous equity is respected; his administration is commendable; his demeanor is pleasing; his movements are proper. In this way he governs the people, and therefore they look upon him with awe and love—make him their model and follow him. Thus he is able to realize his virtuous teachings and to carry out his edicts and orders.

"In the *Shih* it is said:

> The *chun-tzu*[8] our princely lord
> His fine demeanor is without fault."

THE PRACTICE OF FILIAL PIETY

The Master said: "In serving his parents, a filial son reveres them in daily life; he makes them happy while he nourishes them; he takes anxious care of them in sickness; he shows great sorrow over their death and he sacrifices to them with solemnity. When he has performed these five duties, he has truly served his parents.

"He who really serves his parents will not be proud in a high position; he will not be rebellious in an inferior position; among the multitude he will not be contentious. To be proud in a high position is to be ruined; to be rebellious in an inferior position is to incur punishment; to be contentious among the multitude is to bring about violence. As long as these three evils are not discarded, a son cannot be called filial, even though he treats his parents daily with the three kinds of meat."[9]

THE FIVE PUNISHMENTS

The Master said: "There are five punishments for three thousand offenses, and of these offenses there is no greater crime than lack of filial piety. To intimidate the sovereign is to

---

8 "Masterly scion": an enlightened member of the ruling class.

9 Beef, lamb, and pork.

defy a superior; to denounce the sage is to disregard the law; to decry filial piety is to not acknowledge parents. This is the way of great chaos."

ILLUSTRATION OF THE BASIC TAO

The Master said: "There is nothing better than filial piety to teach the people love for one another. There is nothing better than brotherly deference to teach the people propriety and prudence. There is nothing better than music to transform their manners and to change customs. There is nothing better than *li* to safeguard the sovereign and to govern the people.

"*Li* is but reverence. When the parents are revered, the son is pleased; when the elder brother is revered, the younger brother is pleased; when the sovereign is revered, the ministers are pleased; when the One Man is revered, the millions of men are pleased. Thus, those who are revered are few, but those who are pleased are many. This is said to be the 'basic *Tao*.'"

ILLUSTRATION OF THE SUPREME VIRTUE

The Master said: "The *chun-tzu* in teaching filial piety need not go daily to visit the families. He need only teach filial piety and he will show reverence due to all the fathers of the world. He need only teach brotherly deference and thereby show reverence due to all the elder brothers of the world. He need only teach the duties of ministers and thereby show reverence due to all the sovereigns of the world.

"In the *Shih* it is said:

> The princely man, cheerful and pleasant,
> Is the father and mother of the people!

"Without possessing the supreme virtue how can he keep the people in such harmony?"

ILLUSTRATION OF PERPETUATING THE NAME

The Master said: "The *chun-tzu* serves his parents with filial piety: thus his loyalty can be transferred to his sovereign. He serves his elder brother with brotherly deference; thus his respect can be transferred to his superiors. He orders his family well; thus his good order can be transferred to his public administration.

"Therefore, when one cultivates one's conduct within oneself, one's name will be perpetuated for future generations."

THE DUTY OF ADMONITION

Tseng Tzu said: "I have heard about parental love, loving respect, cherishing care for parents, and making their name known. I venture to ask whether a son, by obeying every command of his father, can be called filial?"

The Master said, "What are you talking about? What are you talking about? In the old days, the Son of Heaven,[10] who had seven ministers to admonish him, would not have lost his world, even if he were devoid of virtue. A state prince, who had five officers to admonish him, would not have lost his state, even if he were devoid of virtue. A minister,

---

10 The emperor in the era of the Chou dynasty.

who had three assistants to admonish him, would not have lost his family, even if he were devoid of virtue.

"Thus, if a scholar has a friend to admonish him, he will not deviate from his good name. If a father has a son to admonish him, he will not commit gross wrong. In case of gross wrong, the son should never fail to admonish his father against it; nor should the minister fail to admonish his sovereign. Hence when there is gross wrong, there should be admonition. How can a son, by obeying the command of his father, be called filial?"

INFLUENCE AND EFFECT

The Master said: "Formerly the enlightened kings were filial in the service of their fathers and thereby became enlightened in the service of Heaven. They were filial in the service of their mothers and thereby became discreet in the service of earth. When the young deferred to the elders, superiors governed inferiors well. When they were enlightened and discreet in the service of Heaven and earth, the blessings of spirits were manifest.

"Hence, even the Son of Heaven has someone to honor—his father. He has someone to respect—his elder brothers. He sacrifices at the ancestral temple, lest he forget his parents. He cultivates his person and acts with prudence, lest he disgrace his elders. He pays reverence, at the ancestral temples, to the spirits and ghosts, so as to enjoy their blessings. When his filial piety and brotherly deference reach perfection, he is endowed with divine enlightenment. His virtuous influence illuminates the four seas and penetrates far and wide.

"In the *Shih* it is said:

> From the west to the east,
> From the south to the north,
> None thought of not submitting."

SERVING THE SOVEREIGN

The Master said: "In serving his sovereign, the *chun-tzu* endeavors to be utterly loyal when he is in office; he contemplates, in retirement, to remedy his shortcomings. Then he tries to conform to what is good in the sovereign, and to rectify what is wrong in him. In this way a mutual affection will be fostered between superiors and inferiors.

"In the *Shih* it is said:

> In my heart I love him,
> Why should I not tell it?
> I keep him in my heart,
> When shall I forget him?"

MOURNING FOR PARENTS

The master said: "In mourning for his parents, a filial son weeps without wailing, he observes funeral rites without heeding his personal appearance, he speaks without regard for eloquence, he finds no comfort in fine clothing, he feels no joy on hearing music, he has no appetite for good food; all this is the innate expression of grief and sorrow. After three days, he breaks his fast, so as to teach the people that the dead should not hurt the living and that disfigurement should not destroy life; this is the rule of the sages. Mourning only extends to the period of three years, so as to show the people that sorrow comes to an end.

"The body, dressed in fine robes, is placed in the encased coffin. The sacrificial vessels are set out with grief and sorrow. Beating the breasts and stamping the feet, weeping and wailing, the mourners escort the coffin to the resting-place selected by divination. A shrine is built, and there offerings are made to the spirits. Spring and autumn sacrificial rites are performed, for the purpose of thinking about them at the proper season.

"When parents are alive, they are served with love and reverence; when they are dead, they are mourned with grief and sorrow. This is the performance of man's supreme duty, fulfillment of the mutual affection between the living and the dead, and the accomplishment of the filial son's service to his parents."

FURTHER READINGS

For the history of China, the multivolume Denis Twitchett and John K. Fairbanks, eds., *Cambridge History of China* (Cambridge: Cambridge University Press, 1978–), is an excellent scholarly reference. Arthur F. Wright discusses Confucian philosophy generally in *The Confucian Persuasion* (Palo Alto: Stanford University Press, 1960). The standard English translation of the basic work of Confucian thought is still Arthur Waley, trans. *The Analects of Confucius*, (New York: George Allen and Unwin, 1938).

Michael Lowe, *Chinese Ideas of Life and Death: Faith, Myth and Reason in the Han Period* (London: Allen & Unwin, 1982) examines some intellectual and religious beliefs of the Ch'in and Han periods. Hugh Baker, *Chinese Family and Kinship* (New York: Macmillan, 1979) and Paul Chao, *Chinese Kinship* (London: Kegan Paul, 1983) each offer informative material on the importance of filial piety in Chinese society. Benjamin I. Schwartz, *The World of Thought in Ancient China* (Cambridge, MA: Harvard University Press, 1985) provides information on the relationship between moral quality and the family. A brief examination of the Confucian emphasis on filial piety is included in Yu-lan Feng, *A Short History of Chinese Philosophy*, ed. Derk Bodde (New York: Macmillan, 1948) and Herrlee Creel, *Confucius and the Chinese Way* (New York: Harper, 1960). A brief but informative section on family life in China is included in Herrlee Creel, *The Birth of China, a Study of the Formative Period of Chinese Civilization* (New York: Reynal & Hitchcock, 1937).

3

BAN ZHAO: LESSONS FOR WOMEN

(1ST CENTURY CE)

Ban Zhao was the sister of a famous Han historian, and became his assistant when her husband died. So brilliant was she that after her brother's death the emperor appointed her court historian in his place. Despite her own unconventional and distinguished career; the book she wrote teaching women how they should behave followed traditional Confucian values, urging submissiveness.

On what one subject does Ban Zhao insist on the rights of women? Does she hold a romantic view of marriage? Which of er demands on women do you object to the most? Are there any you approve of?

HUMILITY

On the third day after the birth of a girl the ancients observed three customs: [first] to place the baby below the bed; [second] to give her a potsherd with which to play; and [third] to announce her birth to her ancestors by an offering. Now to lay the baby below the bed plainly indicated that she is lowly and weak, and should regard it as her primary duty to humble herself before others. To give her potsherds with which to play indubitably signified that she should practice labor and consider it her primary duty to be industrious. To announce her birth before her ancestors clearly meant that she ought to esteem as her primary duty the continuation of the observance of worship in the home. . . .

Let a woman modestly yield to others; let her respect others; let her put others first, herself last. Should, she do something good, let her not mention it; should she do some thing bad, let her not deny it. Let her bear disgrace; let her even endure when others speak or do evil to her. Always let her seem to tremble and to fear. . . .

Let a woman retire late to bed, but rise early to duties let her not dread tasks by day or by night. Let her not refuse to perform domestic duties whether easy or difficult.

EDUCATION

Yet only to teach men and not to teach women—is that not ignoring the essential relation between them? According to the "Rites," it is the rule to begin to teach children to read at the age of eight years, and by the age of fifteen years they ought then to be ready for cultural training. Only why should it not be [that girls' education as well as boys' be] according to this principle?

RESPECT AND CAUTION

If husband and wife have the habit of staying together, never leaving one another, and following each other around within the limited space of their own rooms, then they will lust after and take liberties with one another. From such action improper language will arise between the two. This kind of discussion may lead, to licentiousness. Out of licentiousness will be born a heart of disrespect to the husband. Such a result comes from not knowing that one should stay in one's proper place.

BE "WOMANLY"

A woman ought to have four qualifications: [1] womanly virtue; [2] womanly words; [3] womanly bearing; and [4] womanly work. Now what is called womanly virtue need not be brilliant ability, exceptionally different from others. Womanly words need be neither clever in debate nor keen in conversation. Womanly appearance requires neither a pretty nor a perfect face and form. Womanly work need not be work done more skillfully than that of others.

To guard carefully her chastity; to control her behavior; in every motion to exhibit modesty; and to model each act in the best usage, this is womanly virtue.

To choose her words with care; to avoid vulgar language; to speak at appropriate times; and not to weary others [with much conversation], may be called the characteristics of womanly words.

To wash and scrub filth away; to keep clothes and ornaments fresh and clean; to wash the head and bathe the body regularly, and to keep the person free from disgraceful filth, may be called the characteristics of womanly bearing.

With whole-hearted devotion to sew and to weave; to love not gossip and silly laughter; In cleanliness and order [to prepare] the wine and food for serving guests, may be called the characteristics of womanly work.

WHOLE-HEARTED DEVOTION

Now in the Rites is written the principle that a husband may marry again, but there is no [law] that authorizes a woman to be married the second time. Therefore it is said of husbands as of Heaven, that as certainly as people cannot run away from Heaven, so surely a wife cannot leave [a husband's home].

IMPLICIT OBEDIENCE

Now to "win the love of one man is the crown of a woman's life; to lose the love of one man *is* her eternal disgrace." This saying advises a fixed will and a whole-hearted devotion for a woman. Ought she then to lose the hearts of her father- and mother-in-law? ... Whenever the mother-in-law says, "Do not do that," and if what she says is right, unquestionably the daughter-in-law obeys. Whenever the mother-in-law says, "Do that," even if what, she says is wrong, still the daughter-in-law submits unfailingly to the command.

Translated by Nancy Lee Swann

WRITINGS ON TAOISM

1

......

TAO TE CHING[1]

LAO TZU

Few books are as enigmatic, or as intriguing, as the Chinese classic, *Tao te ching*, sometimes translated as "The Classic of the Way and the Power." Scholars argue about the date of its writing, although they generally are willing to admit that it was composed sometime between 600 and 200 B.C. They dispute whether it is the product of a single mind or simply a collection of adages drawn from various ancient sources. Students of the work have viewed it variously as a metaphysical, mystical, or ethical treatise, a manual of administrative methods, or even a book of hidden meanings that, if properly understood, can give the reader power over the forces of nature and enable him to gain immortality. And yet, even without any general agreement on its nature or purpose, this little book has exerted a compelling influence over the centuries. Chinese scholars have written literally hundreds of commentaries on it, attempting to fathom its mysteries. A body of popular belief and ritual has grown up around it that continues to be practiced as one of the major religions in China today. Its attraction is not confined to the East, however, but extends to Westerners. It is said to be the most translated book, after the Bible, in history.

According to tradition, Lao Tzu was born in the province of Honan and was court archivist in the kingdom of Chou. K'ung Fu-tzu supposedly visited him, an encounter that has become famous in Chinese legend and art. The interview was brief; Lao Tzu suggested that K'ung should attempt to rid himself of arrogant airs and selfish desires, and bade him goodbye. Lao Tzu finally became disgusted with the kings of Chou, and decided to leave for the West. Reaching a pass on the border of the kingdom, he was stopped by the frontier guard, who begged him to write a book of instruction before he departed forever. Lao Tzu sat down by the roadside, wrote the five thousand characters that comprise the *Tao te ching*, and, handing them over to the guard, disappeared to the west.

It is difficult to discuss Taoist philosophy; the opening line of the *Tao te ching* can be translated as, "The Way that can be talked about is not the real Way." Basically, however, it would appear that the early Taoists regarded rational knowledge or, indeed, any knowledge at all, of physical nature as unattainable. Because all physical aspects of things are purely relative, they are indistinguishable and indescribable: "Water is life for a fish, death for a man." Moreover, the relativity is such that all things exist only in reference to their opposites: "It is only because everyone thinks that beauty exists that they think that ugliness exists." Even existence is a reflection of nonexistence: a house is a house only because of the holes that comprise the doors and windows; a wheel is a wheel only because of the empty space where the axle is fitted; a jug is useful only because it contains an empti-

---

1 From *The Way and the Power*, trans. Arthur Waley (London: Allen & Unwin, 1934), pp. 141, 143, 145-147, 149-152, 154, 159, 166, 180.

ness, and that emptiness is significant only because it can be filled. All things that exist eventually pass into nothingness, and out of this nothingness, new things emerge. Thus all of nature, being and nothingness, is all mixed up together. The Universe is essentially a single whole and is in reality indivisible. This being so, it is humanly incomprehensible. Since knowledge of the universe is unattainable by reason, reason is of no use to anyone. Human knowledge is only an illusion. Wisdom is the realization of realizing this illusion, accepting that one cannot control nature, and learning to become a part of it. By refusing to struggle against the natural course of things, one gains power. By flowing along with nature, rather than swimming against the current, one's ends can be achieved without effort or action.

Though knowledge of the external world cannot be acquired, this is not necessarily true of the inner world of the mind. It must be remembered, however, that inner knowledge cannot be achieved through reason or analysis, and bears no relationship to any external reality. How it is to be gained is therefore impossible to describe in words. A later Taoist poet suggested that one forget everything one ever knew and "work on it." What "it" is, is, unfortunately, also impossible to describe.

Taoism flourished in early China in part because it provided a complement to Confucianism, which was essentially a social and moral philosophy, lacking any transcendent vision of the universe and making little provision for the satisfaction of human emotional needs. Confucianism was directed almost entirely towards the external world and stressed proper action as the means to achieve success. Obviously, however, not everyone in the world can, or even wants to, succeed. Taoism provided an alternative to those who were unable, or who refused to try, to prosper within the existing social and economic system.

As a consequence, Taoism proved attractive to the peasant masses. Seizing on the idea that one could achieve power through harmony with nature, they evolved a popular form of Taoism that mixed superstition, the shamanistic practices of China's northern neighbors, and ancient fertility rituals. Popular Taoism found it easy to borrow some of the practices of Indian Yoga, and to seek herbs that would not only exalt the spirit but gain one immortality. Even some educated Taoists came to believe that self-knowledge could gain one immortality and the power to control natural phenomena. Taoism thus eventually gave rise to the practice of magic, alchemy, and foretelling the future. At the popular level, at least, the teachings of the *Tao te ching* were perverted from what appears to have been their original intent.

And yet, Taoism continued to hold a fascination for the Chinese and, in recent times, for Westerners. The secret of its durability and attraction lies in the *Tao te ching* itself. Its five thousand characters are a mass of dense and ambiguous meanings, and the reader feels compelled to discover its message. Each brings his or her own individual needs and desires to the task, and each finds a message that seems personally right and true. Tao is described as an uncarved block, in which all things are potentially present. The same could be said of the *Tao te ching*; this may account for its enduring appeal.

Questions

1. How does Taoism describe the relativity of the physical universe?
2. What are the various characteristics of the Way?
3. How does the Sage exert power?

4. What is the Taoist view of how to govern?

TAO TE CHING

1

The Way that can be told of is not an Unvarying Way;
The names that can be named are not unvarying names.
It was from the Nameless that Heaven and Earth sprang;
The named is but the mother that rears the ten thousand creatures,[2] each
  after its kind.
Truly, "Only he that rids himself forever of desire can see the Secret Es-
  sences";
He that has never rid himself of desire can see only the Outcomes.
These two things issued from the same mould, but nevertheless are different
  in name.
This "same mould" we can but call the Mystery,
Or rather the "Darker than any Mystery,"
The Doorway whence issued all Secret Essences.

2

It is because every one under Heaven recognizes beauty as beauty, that the
  idea of ugliness exists.
And equally if every one recognized virtue as virtue, this would merely create
  fresh conceptions of wickedness.
For truly "Being and Not-being grow out of one another;
Difficult and easy complete one another.
Long and short test one another;

High and low determine one another.
Pitch and mode give harmony to one another.
Front and back give sequence to one another."
Therefore the Sage relies on actionless activity,
Carries on wordless teaching,
But the myriad creatures are worked upon by him; he does not disown
  them.
He rears them, but does not lay claim to them,
Controls them, but does not lean upon them,
Achieves his aim, but does not call attention to what he does;
And for the very reason that he does not call attention to what he does
He is not ejected from fruition of what he has done.

3

2 The physical world in general, humankind in particular.

If we stop looking for "persons of superior morality" (*hsien*) to put in power, there will be no more jealousies among the people. If we cease to set store by products that are hard to get, there will be no more thieves. If the people never see such things as excite desire, their hearts will remain placid and undisturbed. Therefore the Sage rules

By emptying their hearts
And filling their bellies,
Weakening their intelligence
And toughening their sinews
Ever striving to make the people knowledgeless and desireless.
Indeed he sees to it that if there be any who have knowledge, they dare not
　　interfere. Yet through his actionless activity all things are duly regu-
　　lated.

4

The Way is like an empty vessel
That yet may be drawn from
Without ever needing to be filled.
It is bottomless; the very progenitor of all things in the world.
In it all sharpness is blunted,
All tangles untied,
All glare tempered,
All dust smoothed.
It is like a deep pool that never dries.
Was it too the child of something else? We cannot tell.
But as a substanceless image it existed before the Ancestor.[3]

5

Heaven and Earth are ruthless;
To them the Ten Thousand Things are but as straw dogs.[4]
The Sage too is ruthless;
To him the people are but as straw dogs.
Yet Heaven and Earth and all that ties between
Is like a bellows
In that it is empty, but gives a supply that never fails.
Work it, and more comes out.
Whereas the force of words is soon spent.
Far better is it to keep what is in the heart.

6

The Valley Spirit never dies. It is named the Mysterious Female.
And the Doorway of the Mysterious Female

---

3 The "Ancestor" separated the heavens from the earth and thus created the world as we know it.
4 Dolls made of straw to be used in celebrations and then disgarded; things without souls or worth.

Is the base from which Heaven and Earth sprang.
It is there within us all the while;
Draw upon it as you will, it never runs dry.

7

Heaven is eternal, the Earth everlasting.
How come they to be so? It is because they do not foster their own lives;
That is why they live so long.
Therefore the Sage
Puts himself in the background; but is always to the fore.
Remains outside; but is always there.
Is it not just because he does not strive for any personal end
That all his personal ends are fulfilled?

8

The highest good is like that of water. The goodness of water is that it benefits the ten thousand creatures; yet itself does not scramble, but is content with the places that all men disdain.[5] It is this that makes water so near to the Way.
And if men think the ground the best place for building a house upon,
If among thoughts they value those that are profound,
If in friendship they value gentleness,

In words, truth; in government, good order;
In deeds, effectiveness; in actions, timeliness
In each case it is because they prefer what does not lead to strife,
And therefore does not go amiss.

9

Stretch a bow[6] to the very full,
And you will wish you had stopped in time;
Temper a sword-edge to its very sharpest,
And you will find it soon grows dull.
When bronze and jade fill your hall
It can no longer be guarded.
Wealth and place breed insolence
That brings ruin in its train.
When your work is done, then withdraw!
Such is Heaven's Way.

10

Can you keep the unquiet physical-soul from straying, hold fast to the Unity,
        and never quit it?

---

5 Water naturally seeks the lowest place, while people generally strive for the heights.
6 A fully stretch bow may snap.

Can you, when concentrating your breath, make it soft like that of a little
    child?
Can you wipe and cleanse your vision of the Mystery till all is without blur?
Can you love the people and rule the land, yet remain unknown?
Can you in opening and shutting the heavenly gates play always the female
    part?[7]
Can your mind penetrate every corner of the land, but you yourself never
    interfere?
Rear them, then, feed them,
Rear them, but do not lay claim to them.
Control them, but never lean upon them;
Be chief among them, but do not manage them.
This is called the Mysterious Power.

11

We put thirty spokes together and call it a wheel;
But it is on the space where there is nothing that the usefulness of the wheel
    depends.[8]
We turn clay to make a vessel;
But it is on the space where there is nothing that the usefulness of the vessel
    depends.
We pierce doors and windows to make a house;
And it is on these spaces where there is nothing that the usefulness of the
    house depends.
Therefore just as we take advantage of what is, we should recognize the use-
    fulness of what is not.

14

Because the eye gazes but can catch no glimpse of it,
It is called elusive.
Because the ear listens but cannot hear it,
It is called the rarefied.
Because the hand feels for it but cannot find it,
It is called the infinitesimal.
These three, because they cannot be further scrutinized,
Blend into one.
Its rising brings no light;
Its sinking, no darkness.
Endless the series of things without name
On the way back to where there is nothing.
They are called shapeless shapes;
Forms without form;
Are called vague semblances.

---

7 Passivity.
8 The hub, where the axel is placed.

Go towards them, and you can see no front;
Go after them, and you see no rear.
Yet by seizing on the Way that was
You can ride[9] the things that are now.
For to know what once there was, in the Beginning,
This is called the essence of the Way.

19

Banish wisdom, discard knowledge,
And the people will be benefited a hundredfold.
Banish human kindness, discard morality,
And the people will be dutiful and compassionate.
Banish skill, discard profit,
And thieves and robbers will disappear.

If when these three things are done they find life too plain and unadorned,
Then let them have accessories;
Give them Simplicity to look at, the Uncarved Block to hold, Give them
  selflessness and fewness of desires.

20

He who by Tao purposes to help a ruler of men
Will oppose all conquest by force of arms;
For such things are wont to rebound.
Where armies are, thorns and brambles grow.
The raising of a great host
Is followed by a year of dearth.
Therefore a good general effects his purpose and then stops; he does not take
  further advantage of his victory.
Fulfils his purpose and does not glory in what he has done;
Fulfils his purpose and does not boast of what he has done;
Fulfils his purpose, but takes no pride in what he has done;
Fulfils his purpose, but only as a step that could not be avoided.
Fulfils his purpose, but without violence;
For what has a time of vigour also has a time of decay.
This is against Tao,[10]
And what is against Tao will soon perish.

Further Readings

Numerous introductions to the history of Taoist philosophy and religion are available, but three of the best are Holmes Welch, Taoism: The Parting of the Way (Boston: Beacon Press, 1957); Max Kaltenmark, Lao Tzu and Taoism, trans. Roger Greaves (Stanford: Stanford University Press, 1969); and Liu Da, The Tao and Chinese Civilization (New

9 Control, dominate.
10 Violence is against the Way, as is all action, negative or positive.

York: Schocken Books, 1979). As has been noted, there are a large number of English translations of the Tao te ching (sometimes entitled *Lao Tzu*). That of one of the leaders of the rise of Victorian interest in Taoism has been reprinted as James Legge, *The Tao te ching: The Writings of Chuang-tzu; the Thai-Shan Tractate of Actions and Their Retributions* (Taipei: World Book, 1963). Arthur Waley, *The Way and the Power* (London: Allen & Unwin, 1934), did much to encourage modern interest. Dim C. Lau, *Tao te ching* (Baltimore: Penguin, 1963), is perhaps the most easily available, while Gia-fu Feng and Jane English, *Tao te ching* (New York: Vintage Books, 1972), is one of the more luxurious. Art photographs and calligraphic presentations of each section appear on facing pages. Wang Pi, *Commentary on the "Lao Tzu,"* trans. Ariane Rump (Honolulu: University Press of Hawaii, 1979), presents the text of the *Tao te ching*, together with the commentary of Wang Pi (A.D. 226–249), author of the oldest surviving commentary on Lao Tzu, of which several hundred have been written. This is not a book for a beginner, nor is Paul J. Lin, *A Translation of Lao Tzu's "Tao te ching" and Wang Pi's "Commentary"* (Ann Arbor: Center for Chinese Studies, University of Michigan, 1977). Lin provides a scholarly translation of the *Tao te ching*, with Wang Pi's commentary as footnotes, together with Ssu-ma Ch'ien's biography of Lao Tzu and Ho Shao's biography of Wang Pi. Ch'en Ku-ying, *Lao Tzu: Text Notes, and Comments*, trans. and adapted by Rhett Y. W. Young and Roger T. Ames (San Francisco: Chinese Materials Center, 1977), is probably the fullest available presentation of the *Tao te ching*, being a translation of the Chinese edition of 1970. It offers an extensive introduction, an excellent English translation, the full Chinese text, and notes taken from the major commentators on the *Tao te ching*. An appendix lists and discusses these major commentators. An early Taoist classic is provided in Huai nan-tzu, *The Huai nan-tzu, Book Eleven: Behavior, Culture, and the Cosmos*, trans. Benjamin E. Wallacker (New Haven, CT: American Oriental Society, 1962). Chuang Tzu, a major contributor to Taoist scripture, who probably wrote in the early third century B.C., is the subject of Michael R. Saso, *The Teachings of Taoist Master Chuang* (New Haven, CT: Yale University Press, 1978), and Wu Kuang-ming, *Chuang tzu: World Philosopher at Play* (New York: Crossroad, 1982). The literature of Taoism is very large, and this list of important works could be extended considerably. The bewildered reader is advised to turn to Benjamin Hoff, *The Tao of Pooh* (New York: Dutton, 1982), for a welcome diversion.

2
......

THE CHUANG TZU

CHUANG TZU

We have little knowledge of Chuang Tzu's lift beyond his given name, Chou, and the fact that he once held minor public office. It is believed that he was a contemporary of Mencius (Selection 28), which means that he was active in the last half of the fourth century B. C. and into the early years of the third. The single book attributed to him typically uses his name as its title. The traditional view is that Chuang Tzu, interpreting Taoist thought two and a half centuries after Lao Tzu (Selection 30), bore a relationship to the "Old Philosopher" analogous to that which Mencius had with Confucius (Selection 26). Chuang Tzu does invoke the name of Lao Tzu in his writing, but his thought is not always in accord with that of the Tao Te Ching, and scholars in the last century have suggested that the two great Taoist texts may be more nearly contemporary, and may have drawn from a common source now lost.

The Chuang Tzu is certainly a different sort of bookfrom the Tao Te Ching. Most obvious is the different form of the work, a collection of thirty-three chapters composed of prose essays and anecdotes. Many of the latter are philosophical "tall tales" in which Lao Tzu encounters Confucius, or Chuang Tzu encounters Mencius or some other philosopher of the time. In each of these invented conversations, the Taoist comes off as wiser and more intellectually agile, clearly the winner in a friendly contest of wits, while Confucius (or whoever) goes away a bit befuddled the bubble of his intellectual and moral pretensions burst. Other fictional meetings involve a "simple" craftsman who responds to pompous questioning from a king or duke about his skill. The answer the craftsman gives demonstrates the shallowness of the questioner's mind but also makes a point about the seamless relationship between a craftsman and his material, a metaphor for that central Taoist belief in mankind's oneness with all nature.

While this Taoist theme, which some have called a "nature mysticism," is a prominent motif of The Chuang Tzu; its governing passion is the quest for freedom, a freedom so far-reaching in its conception as to approach philosophical anarchy. The Tao Te Ching also has unconventional things to say about the approach to and uses of political power, but it lies within the scope of those works of the Hundred Schools which see the maintenance of political order as a central problem. Chuang Tzu's view of public responsibility, on the other hand, is that it is a trap that the wise will avoid. In later years, in the troubled times that came again and again throughout Chinese history, this frankly anti-political strain in Chuang Tzu's thinking made his book a haven for the politically dispossessed, and the platform for a new life of retirement from the world.

Even beyond this anti-political element, however, the stories and essays of The Chuang Tzu are a call to intellectual freedom, to liberation of the mindfrom all conventional ways of seeing

From *The Complete Works of Chuang Tzu*, trans. Burton Watson (New York: Columbia University Press, 1968), pp. 35, 49, 116, 131, 152-153, 165-166, 187-189, 191-192, 193-194, 205-206, 244-245, 269, 357. Reprinted with permission of the publisher.

the world and of living and working in it. A number of passages in this selection illustrate this radical mode of thinking, perhaps none more so than those that deal with death. Chuang Tzu should not be understood as preaching a gospel of an afterlife in which, as in the Christian view, we are rewarded for our sufferings or virtues in this life. Rather, he sees death as the turning of another corner in a life characterized by many such turnings. One does not know what lies beyond that corner, but should approach it with a calm mind and without fear.

Hui Tzu[11] said to Chuang Tzu, "I have a big tree of the kind men call *shu*. Its trunk is too gnarled and bumpy to apply a measuring line to, its branches too bent and twisty to match up to a compass or square. You could stand it by the road and no carpenter would look at it twice. Your words, too, are big and useless, and so everyone alike spurns them!"

Chuang Tzu said, "Maybe you've never seen a wildcat or a weasel. It crouches down and hides, watching for something to come along. It leaps and races east and west, not hesitating to go high or low—until it falls into the trap and dies in the net. Then again there's the yak, big as a cloud covering the sky. It certainly knows how to be big, though it doesn't know how to catch rats. Now you have this big tree and you're distressed because it's useless. Why don't you plant it in

Not-Even-Anything Village, or the field of Broad-and-Boundless, relax and do nothing by its side, or lie down for a free and easy sleep under it? Axes will never shorten its life, nothing can ever harm it. If there's no use for it, how can it come to grief or pain?"

• • •

Once Chuang Chou[12] dreamt he was a butterfly, a butterfly flitting and fluttering around, happy with himself and doing as he pleased. He didn't know he was Chuang Chou. Suddenly he woke up and there he was, solid and unmistakable Chuang Chou. But he didn't know if he was Chuang Chou who had dreamt he was a butterfly, or a butterfly dreaming he was Chuang Chou. Between Chuang Chou and a butterfly there must be *some* distinction! This is called the transformation of things.

• • •

Ts'ui Chu was questioning Lao Tan.[13] "If you do not govern the world, then how can you improve men's minds?"

Lao Tan said, "Be careful—don't meddle with men's minds! Men's minds can be forced down or boosted up, but this downing and upping imprisons and brings death to the mind. Gentle and shy, the mind can bend the hard and strong; it can chisel and cut away, carve and polish. Its heat is that of burning fire, its coldness that of solid ice, its swiftness such that, in the time it takes to lift and lower the head, it has twice swept over the four

11 Hui Tzu, a friend of Chuang Tzu, was one of the School of Logicians. He represents, in *The Chuang Tzu*, a stolid intellectualism in contrast to the claims of the imagination that Chuang Tzu advances. Yet the next-to-last excerpt in this selection is a touching posthumous tribute to Hui Tzu as a friend and worthy intellectual sparring partner.

12 That is, Chuang Tzu. This passage uses his given name, Chou, rather than the honorific Tzu, which means "master."

13 That is, Lao Tzu.

seas and beyond. At rest, it is deep-fathomed and still; in movement, it is far-flung as the heavens, racing and galloping out of reach of all bonds. This indeed is the mind of man!"

♦ ♦ ♦

When Yao[14] ruled the world, Po-ch'eng Tzu-kao was granted land as one of his noblemen. But when Yao passed the throne to Shun, and Shun passed it to Yu,[15] Po-ch'eng Tzu-kao relinquished his title and took up farming. Yu went to see him and found him working in the fields. Yu scurried forward in the humblest manner, came to a halt, and said, "In former times, when Yao ruled the world, sir, you served as one of his noblemen. But when Yao passed the throne to Shun, and Shun passed it to me, you relinquished your title and took up farming. May I be so bold as to ask why?"

Tzu-kao said, "In former times, when Yao ruled the world, he handed out no rewards and yet the people worked hard; he handed out no punishments and yet the people were cautious. Now you reward and punish, and still the people fail to do good. From now on virtue will decay, from now on penalties will prevail. The disorder of future ages will have its beginning here! You had better be on your way now—don't interrupt my work!" Busily, busily, he proceeded with his farm work, never turning to look back.

♦ ♦ ♦

Duke Huan[16] was in his hall reading a book. The wheelwright P'ien, who was in the yard below chiseling a wheel, laid down his mallet and chisel, stepped up into the hall, and said to Duke Huan, "This book Your Grace is reading—may I venture to ask whose words are in it?"

"The words of the sages," said the duke.

"Are the sages still alive?"

"Dead long ago," said the duke.

"In that case, what you are reading there is nothing but the chaff and dregs of the men of old!"

"Since when does a wheelwright have permission to comment on the books I read?" said Duke Huan. "If you have some explanation, well and good. If not, it's your life!"

Wheelwright P'ien said, "I look at it from the point of view of my own work. When I chisel a wheel, if the blows of the mallet are too gentle, the chisel slides and won't take hold. But if they're too hard, it bites in and won't budge. Not too gentle, not too hard— you can get it in your hand and feel it in your mind. You can't put it into words, and yet there's a knack to it somehow. I can't teach it to my son, and he can't learn it from me. So I've gone along for seventy years, and at my age, I'm still chiseling wheels. When the men

14 See Selection 10, *The Book of History*.

15 Yu was another early emperor, credited with founding the Hsia Dynasty (2205?-1766? B.C.) and with devising a system to contain the devastating floods that afflicted China in his time. Unlike Yao and Shun, whose historical reality is questionable, Yu probably was an historical figure.

16 Duke Huan of Ch'i, who reigned from 685 to 643 B.C., was among the first of the aggressive feudal rulers. He appears in four anecdotes of *The Chuang Tzu*. His imperious speech in this excerpt is in keeping with his reputed character.

of old died, they took with them the things that couldn't be handed down. So what you are reading there must be nothing but the chaff and dregs of the men of old."

● ● ●

Confucius said to Lao Tzu, "I have been studying the six classics—the Odes, the Documents, the Ritual, the Music, the Changes, and the Spring and Autumn, for what I would call a long time, and I know their contents through and through. But I have been around to seventy-two different rulers with them, expounding the ways of the former kings and making clear the path trod by the Dukes of Chou and Shao, and yet not a single ruler has found anything to excite his interest. How difficult it is to persuade others, how difficult to make clear the way!"

Lao Tzu said, "It's lucky you didn't meet with a ruler who would try to govern the world as you say. The six classics are the old worn-out paths of the former kings—they are not the thing which walked the path. What you are expounding are simply those paths. Paths are made by shoes that walk them, they are by no means the shoes themselves!

"The white fish hawk has only to stare unblinking at its mate for fertilization to occur. With insects, the male cries on the wind above, the female cries on the wind below, and there is fertilization. The creature called the *lei* is both male and female and so it can fertilize itself. Inborn nature cannot be changed, fate cannot be altered, time cannot be stopped, the way cannot be obstructed. Get hold of the way and there's nothing that can't be done; lose it and there's nothing that *can* be done."

Confucius stayed home for three months and then came to see Lao Tzu once again. "I've got it," he said. "The magpie hatches its young, the fish spit out their milt, the slim-waisted wasp has its stages of transformation, and when baby brother is born, big brother howls. For a long time now I have not been taking my place as a man along with the process of change. And if I do not take my own place as a man along with the process of change, how can I hope to change other men?"

Lao Tzu said, "Good, Ch'iu—now you've got it!"

● ● ●

Once, when Chuang Tzu was fishing in the P'u River, the king of Ch'u[17] sent two officials to go and announce to him: "I would like to trouble you with the administration of my realm."

Chuang Tzu held onto the fishing pole and, without turning his head, said, "I have heard that there is a sacred tortoise in Ch'u that has been dead for three thousand years. The king keeps it wrapped in cloth and boxed, and stores it in the ancestral temple. Now would this tortoise rather be dead and have its bones left behind and honored? Or would it rather be alive and dragging its tail in the mud?"

"It would rather be alive and dragging its tail in the mud," said the two officials.

Chuang Tzu said, "Go away! I'll drag my tail in the mud!"

17 Ch'u was the largest of the warring states. The king is mentioned several times in *The Chuang Tzu*, more for his symbolism *as* a powerful figure than for any reflection on his character.

Chuang Tzu and Hui Tzu were strolling along the dam of the Hao River when Chuang Tzu said, "See how the minnows come out and dart around where they please? That's what fish really enjoy!"

Hui Tzu said, "You're not a fish—how do you know what fish enjoy?" Chuang Tzu said, "You're not I, so how do you know I don't know what fish enjoy?"

Hui Tzu said, "I'm not you, so I certainly don't know what you know. On the other hand, you're certainly not a fish—so that still proves you don't know what fish enjoy!"

Chuang Tzu said, "Let us go back to your original question, please. You asked me *how* I know what fish enjoy—so you already knew I knew it when you asked the question. I know it by standing here beside the Hao."

♦♦♦

Chuang Tzu's wife died. When Hui Tzu went to convey his condolences, he found Chuang Tzu sitting with his legs sprawled out, pounding on a tub and singing. "You lived with her, she brought up your children and grew old," said Hui Tzu. "It should be enough simply not to weep at her death. But pounding on a tub and singing—this is going too far, isn't it?"

Chuang Tzu said, "You're wrong. When she first died, do you think I didn't grieve like anyone else? But I looked back to her beginning and the time before she was born. Not only the time before she was born, but the time before she had a body. Not only the time before she had a body, but the time before she had a spirit. In the midst of the jumble of wonder and mystery a change took place and she had a spirit. Another change and she had a body. Another change and she was born. Now there's been another change and she's dead. It's just like the progression of the four seasons: spring, summer, fall, and winter.

"Now she's going to lie down peacefully in a vast room. If I were to follow after her bawling and sobbing, it would show that I don't understand anything about fate. So I stopped."

♦♦♦

When Chuang Tzu went to Ch'u, he saw an old skull, all dry and parched. He poked it with his carriage whip and then asked, "Sir, were you greedy for life and forgetful of reason, and so came to this? Was your state overthrown and did you bow beneath the axe, and so came to this? Did you do some evil deed and were you ashamed to bring disgrace upon your parents and family, and so came to this? Was it through the pangs of cold and hunger that you came to this? Or did your springs and autumns pile up until they brought you to this?"

When he had finished speaking, he dragged the skull over and, using it for a pillow, lay down to sleep.

In the middle of the night, the skull came to him in a dream and said, "You chatter like a rhetorician and all your words betray the entanglements of a living man. The dead know nothing of these! Would you like to hear a lecture on the dead?"

"Indeed," said Chuang Tzu.

The skull said, "Among the dead there are no rulers above, no subjects below, and no chores of the four seasons. With nothing to do, our springs and autumns are as endless as heaven and earth. A king facing south on his throne could have no more happiness than this!"

Chuang Tzu couldn't believe this and said, "If I got the arbiter of fate to give you a body again, make you some bones and flesh, return you to your parents and family and your old home and friends, you would want that, wouldn't you?"

The skull frowned severely, wrinkling up its brow. "Why would I throw away more happiness than that of a king on a throne and take on the troubles of a human being again?" it said.

◆◆◆

Woodworker Ch'ing carved a piece of wood and made a bell stand, and, when it was finished, everyone who saw it marveled, for it seemed to be the work of gods or spirits. When the marquis of Lu[18] saw it, he asked, "What art is it you have?"

Ch'ing replied, "I am only a craftsman—how would I have any art? There is one thing, however. When I am going to make a bell stand, I never let it wear out my energy. I always fast in order to still my mind. When I have fasted for three days, I no longer have any thought of congratulations or rewards, of titles or stipends. When I have fasted for five days, I no longer have any thought of praise or blame, of skill or clumsiness. And when I have fasted for seven days, I am so still that I forget I have four limbs and a form and body. By that time, the ruler and his court no longer exist for me. My skill is concentrated and all outside distractions fade away. After that, I go into the mountain forest and examine the heavenly nature of the trees. If I find one of superlative form, and I can see a bell stand there,[19] I put my hand to the job of carving; if not, I let it go. This way I am simply matching up 'heaven' with 'heaven.' That's probably the reason that people wonder if the results were not made by spirits."

The grand marshall's bucklemaker was eighty years old, yet he had not lost the tiniest part of his dexterity. The grand marshall said, "What skill you have! Is there a special way to this?"

"I have a way. From the time I was twenty I have loved to forge buckles. I never look at other things—if it's not a buckle, I don't bother to examine it."

Using this method of deliberately *not* using other things, he was able, over the years, to get some use out of it. And how much greater would a man be if, by the same method, he reached the point where there was nothing that he did not use! All things would come to depend on him.

◆◆◆

18 The feudal state of Lu was Confucius's home. Chuang Tzu's references to "the marquis of Lu" probably include several men who held this title over the years until Lu finally lost its independence and identity to larger, more aggressive states.

19 This idea finds a fascinating parallel in the Neoplatonic belief of the Renaissance sculptor Michelangelo, that the figures he carved were virtually imprisoned within the marble, and that he was liberating them with his chisel.

Chuang Tzu was accompanying a funeral when he passed by the grave of Hui Tzu. Turning to his attendants, he said, "There was once a plasterer who, if he got a speck of mud on the tip of his nose no thicker than a fly's wing, would get his friend Carpenter Shih to slice it off for him. Carpenter Shih, whirling his hatchet with a noise like the wind, would accept the assignment and proceed to slice, removing every bit of mud without injury to the nose, while the plasterer just stood there completely unperturbed. Lord Yuan of Sung, hearing of this feat, summoned Carpenter Shih and said, 'Could you try performing it for me?' But Carpenter Shih replied, 'It's true that I was once able to slice like that—but the material I worked on has been dead these many years.' Since you died, Master Hui, I have had no material to work on. There's no one I can talk to any more."

◆◆◆

Duke Ai of Lu said to Yen Ho,[20] "If I were to make Confucius my pillar and stanchion, do you think it would improve the health of the state?"

"Beware—that way lies danger! Confucius will deck things out in feathers and paint, and conduct his affairs with flowery phrases, mistaking side issues for the crux. He is willing to distort his inborn nature in order to make himself a model for the people, not even realizing that he is acting in bad faith. He takes everything to heart, submits all to the judgment of the spirit—how could such a man be worth putting in charge of the people? Does he meet with your approval? Would you like to provide for his support? It would be a mistake, but you may do it if you like. Yet one who would induce the people to turn their backs on reality and study hypocrisy is hardly fit to be made a model for the people. If we are to take thought for later ages, it would be best to drop the scheme." . . .

20 A scholar of Lu in the early fifth century B.C. whom Chuang Tzu admired for his humility and good sense.

WRITINGS ON BUDDHISM

1

·······

JOURNEY TO THE WEST[1]

WU CH'IENG-EN

Buddhism, like Christianity and Islam, is composed of various sects. The two major divisions within Buddhism are the Theravada, or Hinayana, and the Mahayana schools. The Theravada sect codified its versions of the teachings of Buddha in what was called the Pali Canon. This was transmitted orally until it was finally written down in about 400 B.C. in Sri Lanka. Theravada Buddhism is generally felt to be the less hopeful philosophy, holding that the individual can achieve salvation only through the slow process of accumulating merit in life after life. Nevertheless, it is still the form of Buddhism that is dominant in Sri Lanka, Burma, and Thailand. Mahayana Buddhism derived from those early teachers who engaged in metaphysical debates with Hindus and, in the process, developed a complex and subtle set of religious doctrines. Mahayana Buddhism teaches that there have been numerous Buddhas and Buddha-figures, some of whom are devoted to aiding the devout in the attainment of salvation. The Pure Land sect, whose teachings in *The Pure Land* appear in Part II, is derived from Mahayana belief. It was Mahayana Buddhism that eventually took root in China.

The spread of Buddhism in China was a slow process, made difficult by the lack of reliable books of Buddhist teachings available to Chinese scholars. Chinese and Sanskrit are vastly different languages, and accurate translation between the two is a demanding business at best. The early process of translation was complex and prone to error. A given text was translated orally from Sanskrit into spoken Chinese, and then Chinese scholars translated the spoken version into acceptable literary Chinese. In the process much of the meaning was distorted, particularly when the Chinese attempted to understand these Sanskrit texts in terms of Chinese culture and institutions.

From about A.D. 200 to 600, China was in a state of turmoil, and communication with India was broken by Chinese withdrawal from Central Asia. Buddhism flourished in China during the period, but scholars were quite aware that the texts they were using were unreliable. One of the great intellectual adventures of this period was the effort by Chinese Buddhist scholars to produce authoritative translations of Buddhist texts. A key figure in this process was the captive monk Kumarajiva (350-409). Of mixed Indian and Central Asian descent, Kumarajiva became a monk at the age of seven and eventually became a famous translator. In about 380, a Chinese military expedition captured him and spirited him off to China where he spent the last thirty years of his life translating texts into a beautiful literary Chinese that is still studied and admired. Despite the difficulties of his

---

1 From *Monkey: Folk Novel of China* by Wu Ch'eng-en, trans. Arthur Waley (New York: Grove, 1958), pp. 119, 126-27, 279, 282-84.

task, he managed to convey the subtleties of the original Sanskrit, although it is recorded that he was never satisfied with his translations.

Chinese scholars were still not content with the texts they had, and, over the years, about a hundred Chinese pilgrims made the arduous and dangerous trek to India to collect better ones. The most famous of these pilgrims was the monk Hsuan Tsang (c. 596-664), who had mastered the doctrines taught in the various Chinese schools of Buddhism and decided that only in India could he further his understanding of the faith. Setting out in the autumn of 629, he reached India and traveled widely throughout the country, staying for a time with the great king Harsha (r. 606-641). His account of his trip, Journey to the West (Hsi-yu Chi), is not only an adventurous tale, but an important source for the history and geography of India during this period. He finally returned to China in 645 and for the remainder of his life headed a translation bureau that rendered over seventy Sanskrit works into classical Chinese.

His exploits and accomplishments made Hsuan Tsang a celebrity in his own time and a legendary hero in centuries to come. Over time, fabulous legends became attached to his journey and were better known than the facts themselves. These stories were passed down as folk tales until the scholar Wu Ch'eng-en (c. 1500-1582) wrote a long novel with the same title as Hsuan Tsang's original work. He wrote the novel in popular rather than literary Chinese, and it has remained a favorite of the Chinese ever since. In the novel, Hsuan Tsang is called Tripitaka, literally "three baskets," the Sanskrit term for the canon of Buddhist scripture. Tripitaka is accompanied on his long journey by a monkey, who becomes the center of many humorous episodes, and they are joined later by a pig, a dragon transformed into a horse, and a monster named Sandy.

In addition to being a set of rollicking tales, *The Journey to the West* is also a satire on the religion and bureaucracy of the later Ming dynasty. Scholars also have read allegorical meaning into the adventures of the pilgrims, but these need not detain the reader. The selection begins as Tripitaka sets off on his journey.

Questions

1. The historical Hsuan Tsang was actually denied permission to leave China and was technically a fugitive on his pilgrimage. Why would later legends represent the journey as an embassy sent by the emperor?
2. How does India appear to the pilgrims?
3. What criticisms of China does the author have the Buddha make?

JOURNEY TO THE WEST

CHAPTER XIII

It was three days before the full moon, in the ninth month of the thirteenth year of Cheng Kuan, when Tripitaka, seen off by the Emperor and all his ministers, left the gates of Ch'ang-an. After a day or two of hard riding, he reached the Temple of the Law Cloud. The abbot and some five hundred priests, drawn up in two files, ushered him into the temple. After supper, sitting by lamplight, they discussed questions of religion and the purpose of Tripitaka's quest. Some spoke of how wide the rivers were that he must cross and how high the mountains that he must climb. Some spoke of the roads being infested by panthers and tigers, some of precipices hard to circumvent and demons impossible to overcome. Tripitaka said nothing, but only pointed again and again at his own heart. The priests did not understand what he meant, and when at last they asked him to explain, he said, 'It is the heart alone that can destroy them. I made a solemn vow, standing before the Buddha's image, to carry through this task, come what may. Now that I have started I cannot go back till I have reached India, seen Buddha, got the Scriptures, and turned the wheel of the Law, that our holy sovereign's great dynasty may forever be secure.'

CHAPTER XIV

After going downhill for some way they came to the stone box, in which there was really a monkey. Only his head was visible, and one paw, which he waved violently through the opening, saying, 'Welcome, Master! Welcome! Get me out of here, and I will protect you on your journey to the West.' The hunter stepped boldly up, and removing the grasses from Monkey's hair and brushing away the grit from under his chin, 'What have you got to say for yourself?' he asked. 'To you, nothing,' said Monkey. 'But I have something to ask of that priest. Tell him to come here.' 'What do you want to ask me?' said Tripitaka. 'Were you sent by the Emperor of T'ang to look for Scriptures in India?' asked Monkey. 'I was,' said Tripitaka. 'And what of that?' 'I am the Great Sage Equal of Heaven,' said Monkey. 'Five hundred years ago I made trouble in the Halls of Heaven, and Buddha clamped me down in this place. Not long ago the Bodhisattva Kuan-yin, whom Buddha had ordered to look around for someone to fetch Scriptures from India, came here and promised me that if I would amend my ways and faithfully protect the pilgrim on his way, I was to be released, and afterwards would find salvation. Ever since then I have been waiting impatiently night and day for you to come and let me out. I will protect you while you are going to get Scriptures and follow you as your disciple.'

CHAPTER XXVIII

They travelled westward for many months, and at last began to be aware that the country through which they were now passing was different from any that they had seen. Everywhere they came across gem-like flowers and magical grasses, with many ancient cypresses and hoary pines. In the villages through which they passed every family seemed to devote itself to the entertainment of priests and other pious works. On every hill were hermits practicing austerities, in every wood pilgrims chanting holy writ. Finding hospitality each night and starting again at dawn, they journeyed for many days, till they came at last within a sudden sight of a cluster of high eaves and towers. 'Monkey, that's a fine place,' said Tripitaka, pointing to it with his whip. 'Considering,' said Monkey, 'how often you have insisted upon prostrating yourself at the sight of false magicians' palaces and arch impostors' lairs, it is strange that when at last you see before you Buddha's true citadel, you should not even dismount from your horse.' At this Tripitaka in great excitement sprang from his saddle, and walking beside the horse was soon at the gates of the high building. A young Taoist came out to meet them. 'Aren't you the people who have come from the east to fetch scriptures?' he asked. Tripitaka hastily tidied his clothes and looking up saw that the boy was clad in gorgeous brocades and carried a bowl of jade dust in his hand. Monkey knew him at once. 'This,' he said to Tripitaka, 'is the Golden Crested Great Immortal of the Jade Truth Temple at the foot of the Holy Mountain.' Tripitaka at once advanced bowing. 'Well, here you are at last!' said the Immortal. 'The Bodhisattva misinformed me. Ten years ago she was told by Buddha to go to China and find someone who would fetch scriptures from India. She told me she had found someone who would arrive here in two or three years. Year after year I waited, but never a sign! This meeting is indeed a surprise.' 'I cannot thank you enough, Great Immortal, for your patience,' said Tripitaka.

Near the top of the hill they came upon a party of Upasakas filing through the green pinewoods, and under a clump of emerald cedars they saw bands of the Blessed. Tripitaka hastened to bow down to them. Worshippers male and female, monks and nuns pressed together the palms of their hands, crying, 'Holy priest, it is not to us that your homage should be addressed. Wait till you have seen Sakyamuni, and afterwards come and greet us each according to his rank.' 'He's always in too much of a hurry,' laughed Monkey. 'Come along at once and let us pay our respects to the people at the top.' Twitching with excitement Tripitaka followed Monkey to the gates of the Temple. Here they were met by the Vajrapani of the Four Elements. 'So your Reverence has at last arrived!' he exclaimed. 'Your disciple Hsuan Tsang has indeed arrived,' said Tripitaka, bowing. 'I must trouble you to wait here a moment, till your arrival has been announced,' said the Vajrapani. He then gave instructions to the porter at the outer gate to tell the porter at the second gate that the Vajrapani wished to report that the priest from China had arrived. The porter at the second gate sent word to the porter at the third gate. At this gate were holy priests with direct access to the Powers Above. They hurried to the Great Hall and informed the Tathagata, the Most Honoured One, even Sakyamuni Buddha himself that the priest from the Court of China had arrived at the Mountain to fetch scriptures.

Father Buddha was delighted. He ordered the Bodhisattva, Vajrapanis, Arhats, Protectors, Planets and Temple Guardians to form up in two lines. Then he gave orders that the priest of T'ang was to be shown in. Again the word was passed along from gate to gate: 'The priest of T'ang is to be shown in.' Tripitaka, Monkey, Pigsy and Sandy, carefully following the rules of etiquette prescribed to them, all went forward, horse and baggage following. When they reached the Great Hall they first prostrated themselves before the Tathagata and then bowed to right and left. This they repeated three times, and then knelt before the Buddha and presented their passports. He looked through them one by one and handed them back to Tripitaka, who bent his head in acknowledgment, saying, 'The disciple Hsuan Tsang has come by order of the Emperor of the great land of T'ang, all the way to this Holy Mountain, to fetch the true scriptures which are to be the salvation of all mankind. May the Lord Buddha accord this favour and grant me a quick return to my native land.'

Hereupon the Tathagata opened the mouth of compassion and gave vent to the mercy of his heart: 'In all the vast and populous bounds of your Eastern Land, greed, slaughter, lust and lying have long prevailed. There is no respect for Buddha's teaching, no striving towards good works. So full and abundant is the measure of the people's sins that they go down forever into the darkness of Hell, where some are pounded in mortars, some take on animal form, furry and horned. In which guise they are done by as they did on earth, their flesh becoming men's food. Confucius stood by their side teaching them all the virtues, king after king in vain corrected them with fresh penalties and pains. No law could curb their reckless debauches, no ray of wisdom penetrate their blindness.

'But I have three Baskets of Scripture that can save mankind from its torments and afflictions. One contains the Law, which tells of Heaven, one contains the Discourses, which speak of Earth, one contains the Scriptures, which save the dead. They are divided into thirty-five sections and are written upon fifteen thousand one hundred and forty-four scrolls. They are the path to Perfection, the gate that leads to True Good. In them may be learnt all the motions of the stars and divisions of earth, all that appertains to man, bird, beast, flower, tree and implement of use; in short, all that concerns mankind is found therein. In consideration of the fact that you have come so far, I would give you them all to take back. But the people of China are foolish and boisterous; they would mock at my mysteries and would not understand the hidden meaning of our Order . . . Ananda, Kasyapa,' he cried, 'take these four to the room under the tower, and when they have refreshed themselves, open the doors of the Treasury, and select from each of the thirty-five sections a few scrolls for these priests to take back to the East, to be a boon there forever.'

FURTHER READINGS

Arthur Waley's *Monkey: Folk Novel of China by Wu Ch'eng-en* includes translations of only thirty of the one hundred chapters of the novel. There is a full translation in Wu Ch'eng-en, *The Journey to the West*, trans. Anthony C. Yu, 4 vols. (Chicago: University of Chicago Press, 1977). Hsuan Tsang's account of his journey is translated in Samual Beal, trans., *Si Yu Ki: Buddhist Records of the Western World*, 2 vols. (London: Trubner, 1883). His Chinese biography is translated in Thomas Watters, *On Yuan Chwang* (London: Royal Asiatic Society, 1905). Arthur Waley also authored a biography in *The Real Tripitaka and Other Pieces* (London: Allen & Unwin, 1952). Arthur F. Wright, *Buddhism in Chinese History* (Stanford, CA: Stanford University Press, 1959) is an excellent brief introduction to the subject.

CHINESE WRITING

1
......

EMPRESS WU TSE T'IEN

BY ED FRAME, PROFESSOR OF HUMANITIES,

VALENCIA COMMUNITY COLLEGE

Wu Tse t'ien (624-705) was the only woman in Chinese history to assume the title of Emperor although there were many other women who held power through the control of their husbands or sons. Contrary to many of the popular myths, which paint a very negative picture of Empress Wu, modern research has begun to paint a somewhat more complementary picture of Empress Wu. Recent research has proven that although the Empress was certainly ruthless in her struggle for power, she was a product of the time and most likely her actions were on par with most other power seekers of the time period.

Wu Tse t'ien was definitely a product of the Tang Dynasty (618-907), which is considered to be among the greatest dynasties of ancient China. This was a period of history when China had an open door policy to foreign people with not only the Silk Road but also seven other roads and marine ways leading to various countries. The capital of Chang'an had a population of 1,000,000 (the largest city in the world at that time) and 100,000 were foreigners. The canals of the Sui dynasty (the dynasty before the Tang Dynasty) allowed the people to transport goods from south to north and horses had become incredibly important with 700,000 on record. The T'ang's implementation of land distribution gave life plots to the peasant families and helped increase the production of rice. Most important of all, for the future Empress, was the fact that the women of the Tang Dynasty were granted the same right to, and opportunities for, education as men. Tang women during this period were also allowed to learn military skills and historical records show there were even detachments of women with women generals. These skills would prove valuable when Wu Tse-t'ien assumes the full power of being Emperor.

Wu Tse t'ien's father was a successful merchant who reached ministerial ranks and her mother was of aristocratic birth with both Chinese and Turkic blood. The future Empress became a concubine of Emperor Taizong at the age of 13 and risked the death penalty by having an affair with the crown prince and her stepson, the later emperor, Gaozong (r.649-683). When Taizong died, Wu Tse t'ien joined a Buddhist nunnery, shaved her head, as required by tradition but later was returned to the palace at the request of, not the new emperor (Gaozong), but of his wife, the empress. This move later proved to be tragic for the official wife of Gaozong. When Wu Tse t'ien moved back to the palace she and Gaozong almost immediately became involved once again and she soon had a daughter, and later sons by the emperor. Her rise to power is one of the most fascinating in the long history of China and she showed the shrewdness of a woman and the ruthlessness of the males of that time period.

Many stories are common concerning Wu Tse t'ien's rise to power including the famous story of the taming of the horse and the killing of her own daughter. In the story of the horse legend paints a picture of a personality that might actually fit Wu Tse t'ien. In this story the emperor has a horse that cannot be tamed and asks for volunteers for help. No one steps forward except for Wu Tse t'ien and she is quoted as saying "First give me an iron whip and if that doesn't work, give me a hammer and I will hit it. If this does not work, give me a knife and I will kill it". In the second story the death of her first born child, a daughter, was blamed on the Empress and caused the Emperor to get rid of her. Myth says that the emperor was particularly fond of this daughter and Wu Tse t'ien allowed the empress to visit the daughter. After the empress left she entered the nursery, killed her own daughter and reported to the emperor that the empress had committed this act due to jealousy.

Historically, research has shown that the rise to power of Wu Tse t'ien involved manipulations, murders, and the support of the intellectual and religious establishments. However, modern research has also shown that many of the later gruesome stories were most likely the product of Confucian scholars that wanted to be sure that China never again had a woman rise to the power of Emperor. Not only did she rise to the power of the emperor but was the only woman in Chinese history to actually gain the official title of Emperor. The question that needs to be asked is "who wrote the history". The answer of course is that the history of this powerful lady was written by males who did not believe that women should gain so much power. Therefore, the historical accounts must be carefully re-examined and that is what modern researchers in China, Japan and America have recently been doing. The major work consulted for this article was by R.W.L. Guisso called: "Wu Tse t'ien and the Politics of Legitmation in T'ang China". This work is a doctoral thesis and extremely well documented with over 25 pages of works consulted.

The historical record clearly shows that Empress Wu continued the legacy of prosperity of her husband. She improved the imperial examination system which further guaranteed that no man of ability should be excluded due to his lowly birth. Records show that she personally interviewed candidates for important government positions. Her list of achievements is extensive and since she had the support of the people of China, are most likely true. Of considerable importance was the fact that taxes were reduced because of her policy of increasing the land under cultivation. For the lower classes this allowed for more money in their pockets and less money going to the federal government. Empress Wu encouraged gifted scholars to settle in China and because of her support of Buddhism, great Buddhist temples were built throughout the country. Her knowledge of the arts was extensive and for a ceremony in 693 she composed the music for 900 dancers. During her reign she also began to send male members of the royal family to marry the daughters and aunts of the tribal chieftains at the empire's borders. This was a complete reversal of tradition and contrary to tradition since normally female brides were sent to form these political alliances. Perhaps the most important achievement of all was the fact that she encouraged scholars to write stories about famous women, thus showing everyone that women were every bit as capable as men. Many of these stories have found their way into our own time period and are popular, not only in the East, but also in the Western countries.

In summary, history shows that the reign of the empress was a time of internal peace and prosperity for the people of China. Although she named her period of power the Chou Dynasty, this lasted but a short period of time and power was restored to the T'ang before her death. The Chou dynasty is best seen as a caretaker regime and the Empress Wu may best be seen as a caretaker Emperor.

Works Cited

- Guisso, R.W.L. <u>Wu Tse-T'ien and the Politics of Legitmation in T'ang China</u>. 1st ed. Bellingham: Western Washington, 1978.
- "T'ang Dynasty." 14 Aug. 2005 <http//www.mnsu.edu/edu/emuseum/Prehistory/china/classicalimperial china/china/tang.html>.
- Thorp and Vinograd, . <u>Chinese Art and Culture</u>. 1st ed. New York: Harry N. Abrams, Inc., 2001.
- Watson, William. <u>The Arts of China To AD 900</u>. 1st ed. London: Yale University Press, 1995.
- "Woman of the Tang Dynasty." 14 Aug. 2005 <http//www.chinavoc.com/History/tang/women.htm>.
- "Wu Zetian, Empress of China." 14 Aug. 2005 <http//www.nationmaster.com/encyclopedia/Wu-Zetian,-Empress-of-China>.
- "Wu Tse-t'ien ." <u>Women in World History</u>. 1st ed. Waterford, CT: Yorkin Publications, 1999.

2
......

THE BOOK OF SONGS

Chinese literature begins with the *Shih Ching*, or *Book of Songs*, one of the world's great collections of poetry. This ancient treasury of traditional songs dates from a period between the twelfth and seventh centuries B.C., during the Chou dynasty. Like the earliest classics of other ancient civilization—such as the *Vedic Hymns* of India, the *Epic of Gilgamesh* of Mesopotamia, and the *Iliad* of Greece—the songs of the *Shih Ching* represent an oral tradition written down, sometime around the seventh century B.C., only after centuries of modification and sophistication of both form and language. The collection was originally accompanied by music and was known to the Chinese as the *Shih*, or "song words." Later it became known as the *Shih Ching*, or "classic of song-words."

The source of Chinese poetry and the inspiration for much of Eastern philosophy, the *Book of Songs* occupies a primary place in Chinese literary history. No other single work in the Chinese language has been more powerful and significant in shaping what is essentially a Iyrical tradition. In it are found most of the themes that recur throughout the long and distinguished Chinese poetic heritage.

Tradition credits Confucius with the compilation of the 305 songs that comprise the *Book of Songs*. In the Analecrs, the Sage expresses the deepest respect for the *Book of Songs* and ascribes the deepest moral and ethical significance to its contents. His followers frequently employed the songs as texts for moral instruction and as examples of the highest wisdom. With the passage of time, the anthology became numbered among the Five Confucian Classics[1] and became one of the basic texts of Chinese education. An educated person was expected to have memorized the *Book of Songs* and to be able to recognize an allusion drawn from any poem in the collection.

Poetry has always occupied an important place in Chinese life and society. Poems are composed to express friendship, as entertainment at banquets or parties, as intellectual exercises, or simply for the fun of it. Anything can inspire a poem: a flower or mountain, a desire to praise one's ancestors, the joys of love and courtship, the sorrow of parting, the sight of snow, or dissatisfaction with government policy. Poetry expresses the personal and intimate side of Chinese life and thought as does no other genre, and the results are interwoven into the history of the Chinese people.

The *Book of Songs* already displays the human and individual character of Chinese poetry as well as the vast variety of topics it treats. The *Songs* vividly portray much of daily life and, as a result, afford invaluable glimpses into village life and human activi-

---

1 The others are *The Book of Changes (I Ching)*, *The Classic of History*, *The Spring and Autumn Annals*, and *The Book of Rites*. A now-lost *Classic of Music* was sometimes added to form the Six Classics.

From The Book of Songs, trans. Arthur Waley (New York: Grove Press, 1960), pp. 25, 35, 60, 67–68, 71, 113, 153, 161–162, 177, 193, 204–205, 209–211, 227, 233, 324.

ties during ancient times. Besides songs about working the fields and gathering the harvests, there are songs about hunting, feasting, performing sacrifices, honoring the emperors, and making love and war. All are charming in their freshness and surprising in their frankness. The sixteen selections that follow present some of the common topics in the *Book of Songs* and exhibit the qualities of China's most ancient and revered literary treasure.

Questions

1. Western literature often glorifies war in the form of the epic poem. What is the attitude towards war in the *Book of Songs?*
2. The *Book of Songs* is a valuable aid in the reconstruction of daily life in ancient China. After reading these poems, discuss the various social and economic activities typical of the period.
3. The ideal Chinese female was often characterized in literature by a humble, yielding, and respectful attitude towards males. Do the love poems of the *Book of Songs* also reflect this view?

THE BOOK OF SONGS

COURTSHIP

Elms of the Eastern Gate,
Oaks of the Hollow Mound—
The sons of the Tzu-chung
Trip and sway beneath them.

It is a lucky morning, hurrah!
The Yuan girls from the southern side
Instead of twisting their hemp
In the market trip and sway.

It is a fine morning at last!
"Let us go off to join the throng."
"You are lovely as the mallow."
"Then give me a handful of pepper-seed!"

Mao #137

SECRET COURTSHIP

I beg of you, Chung Tzu,
Do not climb into our homestead,
Do not break the willows we have planted.
Not that I mind about the willows,
But I am afraid of my father and mother.
Chung Tzu I dearly love;

But of what my father and mother say
Indeed I am afraid.

I beg of you, Chung Tzu,
Do not climb over our wall,
Do not break the mulberry-trees we have planted.
Not that I mind about the mulberry-trees,
But I am afraid of my brothers.
Chung Tzu I dearly love;
But of what my brothers say
Indeed I am afraid.

I beg of you, Chung Tzu,
Do not climb into our garden,
Do not break the hard-wood we have planted.
Not that I mind about the hard-wood,
But I am afraid of what people will say.
Chung Tzu I dearly love;
But of all that people will say
Indeed I am afraid.

Mao #76

The rural lover in China frequently visited his lady at night. He was expected to display his courage and resourcefulness by cleverly and quietly overcoming all obstacles in reaching her side. Although sometimes difficult, he was obligated to leave her home by daylight.

COURTSHIP AND SEDUCTION

In the wilds there is a dead doe;
With white rushes we cover her.
There was a lady longing for the spring;
A fair knight seduced her.
In the wood there is a clump of oaks,
And in the wilds a dead deer
With white rushes well bound;
There was a lady fair as jade.

"Heigh, not so hasty, not so rough;
Heigh, do not touch my handkerchief.[2]
Take care, or the dog will bark."

Mao #23

If people find a dead deer in the woods, they cover it piously with rushes. But there are men who "kill" a girl, in the sense that they seduce her and then fail to "cover up" the dam-

---

2 Which was worn at the girdle.

age by marrying her. Such is the burden in the preceding poem, its last three lines calling up "elliptically" the scene of the seduction.

MARRIAGE

Over the southern hill so deep
The male fox drags along,
But the way to Lu is easy and broad
For this Ch'i lady on her wedding-way.
Yet once she has made the journey,
Never again must her fancy roam.

Fibre shoes, five pairs;
Cap ribbons, a couple.[3]
The way to Lu is easy and broad
For this lady of Ch'i to use.
But once she has used it,
No way else must she ever go.

When we plant hemp, how do we do it?
Across and along we put the rows.
When one takes a wife, how is it done?
The man must talk with her father and mother.
And once he has talked with them,
No one else must he court.

When we cut firewood, how do we do it?
Without an axe it would not be possible.
When one takes a wife, how is it done?
Without a match-maker he cannot get her.
But once he has got her,
No one else must he ever approach.[4]

Mao #101

MARRIAGE

Tossed is that cypress boat,
Wave-tossed it floats.
My heart is in turmoil, I cannot sleep.
But secret is my grief.
Wine I have, all things needful
For play, for sport.

My heart is not a mirror,
To reflect what others will.

---

3 Marriage gifts.

4 With a view to marriage. It does not, of course, mean that he may not have concubines.

Brothers too I have;
I cannot be snatched away.
But lo, when I told them of my plight
I found that they were angry with me.

My heart is not a stone;
It cannot be rolled.
My heart is not a mat;
It cannot be folded away.
I have borne myself correctly
In rites more than can be numbered.

My sad heart is consumed,
I am harassed
By a host of small men.
I have borne vexations very many,
Received insults not few.
In the still of night I brood upon it;
In the waking hours I rend my breast.

Oh sun, ah, moon,
Why are you changed and dim?
Sorrow clings to me
Like an unwashed dress.
In the still of night I brood upon it,
Long to take wing and fly away.

                                                      Mao #26

This is the song of a lady whose friends tried to marry her against her inclinations.

BLESSINGS

The fish caught in the trap
Were yellow-jaws and sand eels.
Our lords have wine
Good and plentiful.

The fish caught in the trap
Were bream and tench.
Our lords have wine
Plentiful and good.

The fish caught in the trap
Were mud fish and carp.
Our lords have wine
Good and to spare.

Things they have in plenty,
Only because their ways are blessed.
Things they have that are good,
Only because they are at peace with one another.
Things they have enough and to spare,
Only because their ways are lovely.

Mao #170

WELCOME

The red bow is unstrung,
When one is given it, one puts it away.
I have a lucky guest;
To the depths of my heart I honour him.
The bells and drums are all set;
The whole morning I feast him.

The red bow is unstrung,
When one is given it, one stores it.
I have a lucky guest;
To the depths of my heart I delight in him.
The bells and drums are all set;
The whole morning I ply him.

The red bow is unstrung,
When one is given it, one puts it in its press.
I have a lucky guest;
To the depths of my heart I love him.
The bells and drums are all set;
The whole morning I drink pledges with him.

Mao #175

THE CLAN FEAST

Ting, ting goes the woodman's axe;
Ying, ying cry the birds,
Leave the dark valley,
Mount to the high tree. "Ying" they cry,
Each searching its mate's voice.

Seeing then that even a bird
Searches for its mate's voice,
How much the more must man
Needs search out friends and kin.
For the spirits are listening
Whether we are all friendly and at peace.

"Heave ho," cry the woodcutters.
I have strained my wine so clear,
I have got a fatted lamb
To which I invite all my fathers.[5]
Even if they choose not to come
They cannot say I have neglected them.

Spick and span I have sprinkled and swept,
I have set out the meats, the eight dishes of grain.
I have got a fatted ox,
To which I invite all my uncles,
 And even if they choose not to come
They cannot hold me to blame.

They are cutting wood on the bank.
Of strained wine I have good store;
The dishes and trays are all in rows.
Elder brothers and younger brothers, do not stay afar!
If people lose the virtue that is in them,
It is a dry throat that has led them astray.

When we have got wine we strain it, we!
When we have none, we buy it, we!
Bang, bang we drum, do we!
Nimbly step the dance, do we!
And take this opportunity
Of drinking clear wine.

Mao #165

AGRICULTURE

Abundant is the year, with much millet, much rice;
But we have tall granaries,
To hold myriads, many myriads and millions of grain.
We make wine, make sweet liquor,
We offer it to ancestor, to ancestress,
We use it to fulfill all the rites,
To bring down blessings upon each and all.

Mao #279

AGRICULTURE

They clear away the grass, the trees;
Their ploughs open up the ground.
In a thousand pairs they tug at weeds and roots,
 Along the low grounds, along the ridges.

---

5 Paternal uncles.

There is the master and his eldest son,
There the headman and overseer.
They mark out, they plough.
Deep the food-baskets that are brought;
Dainty are the wives,
The men press close to them.
And now with shares so sharp
They set to work upon the southern acre.
They sow the many sorts of grain,
The seeds that hold moist life.
How the blade shoots up,
How sleek, the grown plant;
Very sleek, the young grain!
Band on band, the weeders ply their task.
Now they reap, all in due order;
Close- packed are their stooks[6]—
Myriads, many myriads and millions,
To make wine, make sweet liquor,
As offering to ancestor and ancestress,
For fulfillment of all the rites.
"When sweet the fragrance of offering,
Glory shall come to the fatherland.
When pungent the scent,
The blessed elders are at rest."[7]
Not only here is it like this,
Not only now is it so.
From long ago it has been thus.

Mao #290

DYNASTIC SONG

The charge that Heaven gave
Was solemn, was for ever.
And ah, most glorious
King Wen in plentitude of power!
With blessings he has whelmed us;
We need but gather them in.
 High favours has King Wen[8] vouchsafed to us;
May his descendants hold them fast.

Mao #267

6 Bundles of grain.

7 Or, "are reassured."

8 Father of King Wu, who conquered the Yin. The standard chronology puts his accession in 1134 B.C. The twenty-six kings from 770 to 249 B.C. had an average reign-length of twenty years. If we apply this average to the twelve kings who preceded them, the date 1134 works out as a hundred years too early.

Kings rule by virtue of a charge (*ming*), an appointment assigned to them by Heaven.

DYNASTIC SONG

Pity me, your child,
Inheritor of a House unfinished,
Lonely and in trouble.
O august elders,
All my days I will be pious,
Bearing in mind those august forefathers
That ascend and descend in the courtyard.
Yes, I your child,
Early and late will be reverent.
O august kings,
The succession shall not stop!

Mao #286

A song from the legend of King Ch'eng. It is said that when he came to the throne he was a mere child and had to be helped in his rule by his uncle, the Duke of Chou. He also had wicked uncles, who rebelled against him, making common cause with the son of the last Shang king. The story in its main features is probably historical. But the part played by the Duke of Chou has perhaps been exaggerated by the Confucians, who made the duke into a sort of patron saint of their school.

WARRIOR SONG

How few of us are left, how few!
Why do we not go back?
Were it not for our prince and his concerns,
What should we be doing here in the dew?

How few of us are left, how few!
Why do we not go back?
Were it not for our prince's own concerns,
What should we be doing here in the mud?

Mao #36

WARRIOR SONG

How can you plead that you have no wraps?
I will share my rug with you.
The king is raising an army;
I have made ready both axe and spear;
You shall share them with me as my comrade.
How can you plead that you have no wraps?
I will share my under-robe with you.
The king is raising an army,
I have made ready both spear and halberd;
You shall share them with me when we start.

How can you plead that you have no wraps?
I will share my skirt[9] with you.
The king is raising an army,
I have made ready both armour and arms;
You shall share them with me on the march.

Mao #133

LAMENTATION

Oh, the flowers of the bignonia,
Gorgeous is their yellow!
The sorrows of my heart,
How they stab!

Oh, the flowers of the bignonia,
And its leaves so thick!
Had I known it would be like this,
Better that I should never have been born!

As often as a ewe has a ram's head,
As often as Orion is in the Pleiads,
Do people to-day, if they find food at all,
Get a chance to eat their fill.

Mao #233

SACRIFICE

Thick grows the star-thistle;
We must clear away its prickly clumps.
From of old, what have we been doing?
We grow wine-millet and cooking-millet,
Our wine-millet, a heavy crop;
Our cooking-millet doing well.
Our granaries are all full,
For our stacks were in their millions,
To make wine and food,
To make offering, to make prayer-offering,
That we may have peace, that we may have ease,
That every blessing may be vouchsafed.
In due order, treading cautiously,
We purify your oxen and sheep.
We carry out the rice-offering, the harvest offering,
Now baking, now boiling,
 Now setting out and arranging,
Praying and sacrificing at the gate.

9 As a rug at night.

Very hallowed was this service of offering;
Very mighty the forefathers.
The Spirits and Protectors[10] have accepted;
The pious descendant shall have happiness,
They will reward him with great blessings,
With span of years unending.

We mind the furnaces, treading softly;
Attend to the food-stands so tall,
For roast meat, for broiled meat.
Our lord's lady hard at work
Sees to the dishes, so many,
Needed for guests, for strangers.
Healths and pledges go the round,
Every custom and rite is observed,
Every smile, every word is in place.
The Spirits and Protectors will surely come
And requite us with great blessings,
Countless years of life as our reward.

Very hard have we striven
That the rites might be without mistake.
The skilful recitant conveys the message,
Goes and gives it to the pious son:

"Fragrant were your pious offerings,
The Spirits enjoyed their drink and food.
They assign to you a hundred blessings.
According to their hopes, to their rules,
All was orderly and swift,
All was straight and sure.
For ever they will bestow upon you good store;
Myriads and tens of myriads."

The rites have all been accomplished,
The bells and drums are ready.
The pious son goes to his seat
And the skilful recitant conveys the message.
"The Spirits are all drunk."
The august Dead One then rises
And is seen off with drums and bells;
The Spirits and protectors have gone home.
Then the stewards and our lord's lady
Clear away the dishes with all speed,

10 An ancestor.

While the uncles and brothers
All go off to the lay feast.

The musicians go in and play,
That after-blessings may be secured.
Your viands are passed round;
No one is discontented, all are happy;
They are drunk, they are sated.
Small and great all bow their heads:
"The Spirits," they say, "enjoyed their drink and food
And will give our lord a long life.
He will be very favoured and blessed,
And because nothing was left undone,
By son's sons and grandson's grandsons
Shall his line for ever be continued."

                                                                              Mao #209

At Chinese sacrifices a young man, usually the grandson of the sacrificer, impersonated the ancestor to whom the sacrifice was being made. For the time being the spirit of the ancestor entered into him. It was, however, no frenzied "possession"; . . . on the contrary, the demeanor of the Dead One was extremely quiet and restrained.

FURTHER READINGS

The multivolume Dennis Twitchett and John K. Fairbanks, eds., *Cambridge History of China* (Cambridge, UK: Cambridge University Press, 1978–), is the standard reference work on Chinese history. Edward H. Shaefer, *Ancient China* (New York: Time, 1967), is a finely illustrated overview of early Chinese history. Joseph R. Levenson and Franz Schurmann, *China: An Interpretive History* (Berkeley: University of California Press, 1969), covers Chinese history from the earliest times to the end of the Han dynasty. Henri Maspero, *China in Antiquity*, trans. Frank A. Kierman, Jr. (Amherst: University of Massachusetts Press, 1978), offers a sound presentation of the development of Chinese literature and philosophy from primitive times to the founding of the Ch'in dynasty. Notable among numerous general works on ancient China are William Watson, *China before the Han Dynasty* (New York: Frederick Praeger, 1961), David N. Keightley, *The Origins of Chinese Civilization* (Berkeley: University of California Press, 1983), Leonard Cottrell, *The Tiger of Ch'in: The Dramatic Emergence of China as a Nation* (New York: Holt, Rinehart and Winston, 1962), Kwang-chih Chang, *Shang Civilization* (New Haven, CT: Yale University Press, 1980), and Jacques Gernet, *Ancient China from the Beginnings to the Empire*, trans. Raymond Rudorff (London: Faber and Faber, 1968).

William Naughton, *The Book of Songs* (New York: Twayne, 1971), provides an excellent critical analysis of both the subjects and style of the Songs. C. H. Wang, *The Bell and the Drum: Shih Ching as Formulaic Poetry in an Oral Tradition* (Berkeley: University of California Press, 1974), and W. A. Dobson, *The Language of the Book of Songs* (Toronto: University of Toronto Press, 1968), are two helpful linguistic studies. Burton Watson, *Early Chinese Literature* (New York: Columbia University Press, 1961), provides a critical study of early Chinese literature in general.

Cyril Birch, ed., *Anthology of Chinese Literature from Early Times to the Fourteenth Century* (New York: Grove Press, 1965), affords an excellent sampling of a vast field. Wu-chi Liu and Irving Yucheng Lo, eds., *Sunflower Splendor: Three Thousand Years of Chinese Poetry* (Bloomington, IN: Indiana University Press, 1975), is a comprehensive anthology of Chinese poetry from ancient times to the present. The text provides helpful background material and bibliographies for poets and poems. A third useful anthology is Burton Watson, ed. and trans., *The Columbia Book of Chinese Poetry* (New York: Columbia University Press, 1984), a work that begins with the *Book of Songs*.

PART III:

Japan, Korea, and Vietnam

photo courtesy of E. Frame

Land of the Kami,
Nature and man become one.
Cherry Blossoms speak.
–Edward M. Frame

Historical Perspective
Japan, Korean and Vietnam

© Kyoto National Museum, Kyoto, Japan with permission from the Kozan-ji Temple, Kyoto

THE EAST ASIAN RIMLANDS: EARLY JAPAN, KOREA, AND VIETNAM

FOCUS QUESTIONS

- What centralizing and decentralizing forces were at work in Japan before 1500, and how did they influence the political and governmental structures that arose?
- What were the main characteristics of economic and social life in early Japan?
- What were the most important cultural achievements of early Japan, and how do they illustrate the Japanese ability to blend indigenous and imported elements?
- What were the main developments in Korean and Vietnamese history before 1500?
- ➤ How did Chinese civilization influence the civilizations that arose in Japan, Korea, and Vietnam?

These people, the exasperated official complained, are like birds and beasts. "They wear their hair tied up and go barefoot, while for clothing they simply cut a hole in a piece of cloth for their head or they fasten their garments on the left side [in barbarian style]." Their women are untrustworthy "and promiscuously wander about." In some areas, "men and women go naked without shame" and are little better than bugs.[1]

The speaker was Xue Tong, a Chinese administrator stationed in northern Vietnam at the end of the Han dynasty. His comments vividly reflected the frustration of Chinese bureaucrats faced with what they regarded as the uncivilized behavior of the untutored peoples living along the frontiers of the Chinese Empire. To Xue Tong and other upright Confucian officials like him, it was hopeless to try to civilize these people.

Such comments should not surprise us. During ancient times, China was the most technologically advanced society in East Asia. To the north and west were nomadic pastoral peoples whose military exploits were often impressive but whose political and cultural attainments were still limited, at least by comparison with the great river valley civilizations of the day. In inland areas south of the Yangtze River were scattered clumps of rice farmers and hill peoples, most of whom had not yet entered the era of state building and certainly had little knowledge of the niceties of Confucian ethics.

But Xue Tong and officials like him were being a little too hasty in their judgments. Along the fringes of Chinese civilization were a number of other agricultural societies that were beginning to follow a pattern of development similar to that of China, although somewhat later in time. One of these was in the islands of Japan, where an organized agricultural society was beginning to take shape just about the time Xue Tong was complaining about the barbarian peoples in the south. These developments may have been hastened by events on the Korean peninsula, where an advanced Neolithic society had begun to develop a few centuries earlier. Even in the Red River valley, where Xue Tong viewed the local inhabitants with such disdain, a relatively advanced civilization had been in existence for several hundred years before the area was conquered by the Han dynasty in the second century B.C.E.

All of these early agricultural societies were eventually influenced to some degree by their great neighbor China. Vietnam remained under Chinese rule for a thousand years. Korea retained its separate existence but was long a tributary state of China and in many ways followed the cultural example of its larger patron. Only Japan retained both its political independence and its cultural uniqueness. Yet even the Japanese were strongly influenced by the glittering culture of their powerful neighbor, and today many Japanese institutions and customs still bear the imprint of several centuries of borrowing from the Middle Kingdom. In this chapter, we will take a closer look at these emerging societies along the Chinese rimlands and consider how their cultural achievements reflected or contrasted with those of the Chinese Empire. ●

JAPAN: LAND OF THE RISING SUN

The geographical environment helps explain some of the historical differences between Chinese and Japanese society. Whereas China is a continental civilization, Japan is an island country. It consists of four main islands (see Map 11.1): Hokkaido in the north, the main island of Honshu in the center, and the two smaller islands of Kyushu and Shikoku in the southwest. Its total land area is about 146,000 square miles, about the size of the state of Montana. Japan's main islands are at approximately the same latitude as the eastern seaboard of the United States.

Like the eastern United States, Japan is blessed with a temperate climate. It is slightly warmer on the east coast, which is washed by the Pacific Current that sweeps up from the south, and has a number of natural harbors that provide protection from the winds and high waves of the Pacific Ocean. As a consequence, in recent times, the majority of the Japanese people have tended to live along the east coast, especially in the flat plains surrounding the cities of Tokyo, Osaka, and Kyoto. In these favorable environmental conditions, Japanese farmers have been able to harvest two crops of rice annually since early times.

SIXTH-CENTURY WAREHOUSE. During the sixth century C.E., an organized society was just beginning to form in the central valley around the modern cities of Kyoto and Osaka. Shown here is a twentieth-century model of a warehouse located in downtown Osaka. On this site, one of Japan's early rulers ordered the construction of sixteen such structures to hold grain and perhaps other foodstuffs. Each warehouse measured about 30 by 35 feet and was supported by several massive wooden posts. Thatched-roof structures built on wooden pilings such as this one were quite common throughout the region.

Courtesy of William J. Duiker

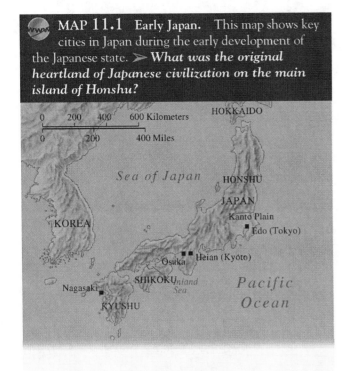

MAP 11.1 **Early Japan.** This map shows key cities in Japan during the early development of the Japanese state. ➤ *What was the original heartland of Japanese civilization on the main island of Honshu?*

By no means, however, is Japan an agricultural paradise. Like China, much of the country is mountainous, with only about 20 percent of the total land area suitable for cultivation. These mountains are of volcanic origin, since the Japanese islands are located at the juncture of the Asian and Pacific tectonic plates. This location is both an advantage and a disadvantage. Volcanic soils are extremely fertile, which helps explain the exceptionally high productivity of Japanese farmers. At the same time, the area is prone to earthquakes, such as the famous earthquake of 1923, which destroyed almost the entire city of Tokyo.

The fact that Japan is an island country has had a significant impact on Japanese history. As we have seen, the continental character of Chinese civilization, with its constant threat of invasion from the north, had a number of consequences for Chinese history. One effect was to make the Chinese more sensitive to the preservation of their culture from destruction at the hands of non-Chinese invaders. Proud of their own considerable cultural achievements and their dominant position throughout the region, the Chinese have traditionally been reluctant to dilute the purity of their culture with foreign innovations. Culture more than race is a determinant of the Chinese sense of identity.

By contrast, the island character of Japan probably had the effect of strengthening the Japanese sense of ethnic and cultural distinctiveness. Although the Japanese view of themselves as the most ethnically homogeneous people in East Asia may not be entirely accurate (the modern Japanese probably represent a mix of peoples, much like their neighbors on the continent), their sense of racial and

cultural homogeneity has enabled them to import ideas from abroad without worrying that the borrowings will destroy the uniqueness of their own culture.

A Gift from the Gods: Prehistoric Japan

According to an ancient legend recorded in historical chronicles written in the eighth century C.E., the islands of Japan were formed as a result of the marriage of the god Izanagi and the goddess Izanami. After giving birth to Japan, Izanami gave birth to a sun goddess whose name was Amaterasu. A descendant of Amaterasu later descended to earth and became the founder of the Japanese nation. This Japanese creation myth is reminiscent of similar beliefs in other ancient societies, which often saw themselves as the product of a union of deities. What is interesting about the Japanese version is that it has survived into modern times as an explanation for the uniqueness of the Japanese people and the divinity of the Japanese emperor, who is still believed by some Japanese to be a direct descendant of the sun goddess Amaterasu (see the box on p. 293).

Modern scholars have a more prosaic explanation for the origins of Japanese civilization. According to archaeological evidence, the Japanese islands have been occupied by human beings for at least 100,000 years. The earliest known Neolithic inhabitants, known as the Jomon people from the cord pattern of their pottery, lived in the islands as much as 10,000 years ago. They lived by hunting, fishing, and food gathering and probably had not mastered the techniques of agriculture.

Agriculture probably first appeared in Japan sometime during the first millennium B.C.E., although some archaeologists believe that the Jomon people had already learned how to cultivate some food crops considerably earlier than that. About 400 B.C.E., rice cultivation was introduced, probably by immigrants from the mainland by way of the Korean peninsula. Until recently, historians believed that these immigrants drove out the existing inhabitants of the area and gave rise to the emerging Yayoi culture (named for the site near Tokyo where pottery from the period was found). It is now thought, however, that Yayoi culture was a product of a mixture between the Jomon people and the new arrivals, enriched by imports such as wet-rice agriculture, which had been brought by the immigrants from the mainland. In any event, it seems clear that the Yayoi peoples were the ancestors of the vast majority of present-day Japanese.

At first, the Yayoi lived primarily on the southern island of Kyushu, but eventually they moved northward onto the main island of Honshu, conquering, assimilating, or driving out the previous inhabitants of the area, some of whose descendants, known as the Ainu, still live in the northern islands. Finally, in the first centuries C.E., the Yayoi settled in the Yamato plain in the vicinity of the modern cities of Osaka and Kyoto. Japanese legend recounts the story of

THE EASTERN EXPEDITION OF EMPEROR JIMMU

Japanese myths maintained that the Japanese nation could be traced to the sun goddess Amaterasu, who was the ancestor of the founder of the Japanese imperial family, Emperor Jimmu. This passage from the Nihon Shoki *(The Chronicles of Japan) describes the campaign in which the "divine warrior" Jimmu occupied the central plains of Japan, symbolizing the founding of the Japanese nation. Legend dates this migration to about 660 B.C.E., but modern historians believe that it took place much later (perhaps as late as the fourth century C.E.) and that the account of the "divine warrior" may represent an effort by Japanese chroniclers to find a local equivalent to the Sage Kings of prehistoric China.*

THE CHRONICLES OF JAPAN

Emperor Jimmu was forty-five years of age when he addressed the assemblage of his brothers and children: "Long ago, this central land of the Reed Plains was bequeathed to our imperial ancestors by the heavenly deities, Takamimusubi-no-Kami and Amaterasu Omikami. . . . However, the remote regions still do not enjoy the benefit of our imperial rule, with each town having its own master and each village its own chief. Each of them sets up his own boundaries and contends for supremacy against other masters and chiefs."

"I have heard from an old deity knowledgeable in the affairs of the land and sea that in the east there is a beautiful land encircled by blue mountains. This must be the land from which our great task of spreading our benevolent rule can begin, for it is indeed the center of the universe. . . . Let us go there, and make it our capital. . . . "

In the winter of that year . . . the Emperor personally led imperial princes and a naval force to embark on his eastern expedition. . . .

When Nagasunehiko heard of the expedition, he said: "The children of the heavenly deities are coming to rob me of my country." He immediately mobilized his troops and intercepted Jimmu's troops at the hill of Kusaka and engaged in a battle. . . . The imperial forces were unable to advance. Concerned with the reversal, the Emperor formulated a new divine plan and said to himself: "I am the descendant of the Sun Goddess, and it is against the way of heaven to face the sun in attacking my enemy. Therefore our forces must retreat to make a show of weakness. After making sacrifice to the deities of heaven and earth, we shall march with the sun on our backs. We shall trample down our enemies with the might of the sun. In this way, without staining our swords with blood, our enemies can be conquered." . . . So, he ordered the troops to retreat to the port of Kusaka and regroup there. . . .

[After withdrawing to Kusaka, the imperial forces sailed southward, landed at a port in the present-day Kita peninsula, and again advanced north toward Yamato.]

The precipitous mountains provided such effective barriers that the imperial forces were not able to advance into the interior, and there was no path they could tread. Then one night Amaterasu Omikami appeared to the Emperor in a dream: "I will send you the Yatagarasu, let it guide you through the land." The following day, indeed, the Yatagarasu appeared flying down from the great expanse of the sky. The Emperor said: "The coming of this bird signifies the fulfillment of my auspicious dream. How wonderful it is! Our imperial ancestor, Amaterasu Omikami, desires to help us in the founding of our empire."

---

a "divine warrior" (in Japanese, *Jimmu*) who led his people eastward from the island of Kyushu to establish a kingdom in the Yamato plain (see the box above).

In central Honshu, the Yayoi set up a tribal society based on a number of clans, called *uji*. Each *uji* was ruled by a hereditary chieftain, who provided protection to the local population in return for a proportion of the annual harvest. The population itself was divided between a small aristocratic class and the majority of the population, composed of rice farmers, artisans, and other household servants of the aristocrats. Yayoi society was highly decentralized, although eventually the chieftain of the dominant clan in the Yamato region, who claimed to be descended from the sun goddess Amaterasu, achieved a kind of titular primacy. There is no evidence, however, of a central ruler equivalent in power to the Chinese rulers of the Shang and the Zhou eras.

The Rise of the Japanese State

Although the Japanese had been aware of China for centuries, they paid relatively little attention to their more advanced neighbor until the early seventh century, when the rise of the centralized and expansionistic Tang dynasty presented a challenge. The Tang began to meddle in the affairs of the Korean peninsula, conquering the southwestern coast and arousing anxiety in Japan. Yamato rulers attempted to deal with the potential threat posed by the Chinese in two ways. First, they sought alliances with the remaining Korean states. Second, they attempted to centralize their authority so that they could mount a more effective resistance in the event of a Chinese invasion. The key figure in this effort was Shotoku Taishi (572–622), a leading aristocrat in one of the dominant clans in the Yamato region. Prince Shotoku sent missions

THE SEVENTEEN-ARTICLE CONSTITUTION

The following excerpt from the Nihon Shoki *(The Chronicles of Japan) is a passage from the seventeen-article constitution promulgated in 604 C.E. Although the opening section reflects Chinese influence in its emphasis on social harmony, there is also a strong focus on obedience and hierarchy. The constitution was put into practice during the reign of the famous Prince Shotoku.*

THE CHRONICLES OF JAPAN

Summer, 4th month, 3rd day [12th year of Empress Suiko, 604 C.E.]. The Crown Prince personally drafted and promulgated a constitution consisting of seventeen articles, which are as follows:

I. Harmony is to be cherished, and opposition for opposition's sake must be avoided as a matter of principle. Men are often influenced by partisan feelings, except a few sagacious ones. Hence there are some who disobey their lords and fathers, or who dispute with their neighboring villages. If those above are harmonious and those below are cordial, their discussion will be guided by a spirit of conciliation, and reason shall naturally prevail. There will be nothing that cannot be accomplished.

II. With all our heart, revere the three treasures. The three treasures, consisting of Buddha, the Doctrine, and the Monastic Order, are the final refuge of the four generated beings, and are the supreme objects of worship in all countries. Can any man in any age ever fail to respect these teachings? Few men are utterly devoid of goodness, and men can be taught to follow the teachings. Unless they take refuge in the three treasures, there is no way of rectifying their misdeeds.

III. When an imperial command is given, obey it with reverence. The sovereign is likened to heaven, and his subjects are likened to earth. With heaven providing the cover and earth supporting it, the four seasons proceed in orderly fashion, giving sustenance to all that which is in nature. If earth attempts to overtake the functions of heaven, it destroys everything. . . . If there is no reverence shown to the imperial command, ruin will automatically result. . . .

VII. Every man must be given his clearly delineated responsibility. If a wise man is entrusted with office, the sound of praise arises. If a wicked man holds office, disturbances become frequent. . . . In all things, great or small, find the right man, and the country will be well governed. . . . In this manner, the state will be lasting and its sacerdotal functions will be free from danger.

to the Tang capital of Chang'an to learn about the political institutions already in use in the relatively centralized Tang kingdom (see Map 11.2).

EMULATING THE CHINESE MODEL

Shotoku Taishi then launched a series of reforms to create a new system based roughly on the Chinese model. In the so-called seventeen-article constitution, he called for the creation of a centralized government under a supreme ruler and a merit system for selecting and ranking public officials (see the box above). His objective was to limit the powers of the hereditary nobility and enhance the prestige and authority of the Yamato ruler, who claimed divine status and was now emerging as the symbol of the unique character of the Japanese nation. In reality, there is evidence that places the origins of the Yamato clan on the Korean peninsula.

After Shotoku Taishi's death in 622, his successors continued to introduce reforms based on the Chinese model to make the government more efficient. In a series of so-called Taika ("great change") reforms that began in the mid-seventh century, the Grand Council of State was established, presiding over a cabinet of eight ministries. To the traditional six ministries of Tang China were added ministers representing the central secretariat and the imperial household. The territory of Japan was divided into administrative districts on the Chinese pattern. The rural village, composed ideally of fifty households, was the basic unit of government. The village chief was responsible for "the maintenance of the household registers, the assigning of the sowing of crops and the cultivation of mulberry trees, the prevention of offenses, and the requisitioning of taxes and forced labor." A law code was introduced, and a new tax system was established; now all farmland technically belonged to the state, so taxes were paid directly to the central government rather than through the local nobility, as had previously been the case.

As a result of their new acquaintance with China, the Japanese also developed a strong interest in Buddhism. Some of the first Japanese to travel to China during this period were Buddhist pilgrims hoping to learn more about the exciting new doctrine and bring back scriptures. Buddhism became quite popular among the aristocrats, who endowed wealthy monasteries that became active in

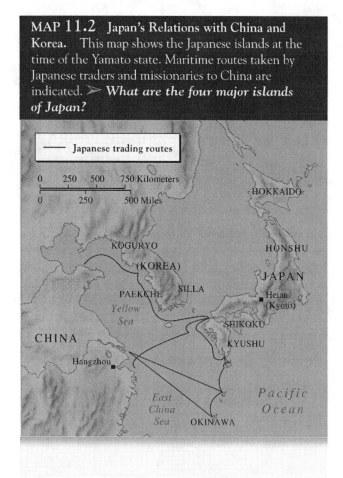

MAP 11.2 Japan's Relations with China and Korea. This map shows the Japanese islands at the time of the Yamato state. Maritime routes taken by Japanese traders and missionaries to China are indicated. ➤ *What are the four major islands of Japan?*

the allegedly divine character of the ruling family, the mandate remained in perpetuity in the imperial house rather than being bestowed on an individual who was selected by Heaven because of his talent and virtue, as was the case in China.

Had these reforms succeeded, Japan might have followed the Chinese pattern and developed a centralized bureaucratic government. But as time passed, the central government proved unable to curb the power of the aristocracy. Unlike in Tang China, the civil service examinations in Japan were not open to all but were restricted to individuals of noble birth. Leading officials were awarded large tracts of land, and they and other powerful families were able to keep the taxes from the lands for themselves. Increasingly starved for revenue, the central government steadily lost power and influence.

In 794, the emperor moved the capital to his family's original power base at nearby Heian, on the site of present-day Kyoto. The new capital was laid out in the now familiar Chang'an checkerboard pattern, but on a larger scale than at Nara. Now increasingly self-confident, the rulers ceased to emulate the Tang and sent no more missions to Chang'an. At Heian, the emperor—as the royal line descended from the sun goddess was now styled—continued to rule in name, but actual power was in the hands of the Fujiwara clan, which had managed through intermarriage to link its fortunes closely with the imperial family. A senior member of the clan began to serve as regent (in practice, the chief executive of the government) for the emperor.

What was occurring was a return to the decentralization that had existed prior to Shotoku Taishi. The central government's attempts to impose taxes directly on the rice lands failed, and rural areas came under the control of powerful families whose wealth was based on the ownership of tax-exempt farmland (called *shoen*). To avoid paying taxes, peasants would often surrender their lands to a local aristocrat, who would then allow the peasants to cultivate the lands in return for the payment of rent. To obtain protection from government officials, these local aristocrats might in turn grant title of their lands to a more powerful aristocrat with influence at court. In return, these individuals would receive inheritable rights to a portion of the income from the estate.

With the decline of central power at Heian, local aristocrats tended to take justice into their own hands and increasingly used military force to protect their interests. A new class of military retainers called the *samurai* emerged whose purpose was to protect the security and property of their patron. They frequently drew their leaders from disappointed aristocratic office seekers, who thus began to occupy a prestigious position in local society, where they often served an administrative as well as a military function. The samurai lived a life of simplicity and

Japanese politics. At first, the new faith did not penetrate to the masses, but eventually, popular sects such as the Pure Land sect, an import from China, won many adherents among the common people.

THE NARA AND HEIAN PERIODS

Initial efforts to build a new state modeled roughly after the Tang state were successful. After Shotoku Taishi's death in 622, political influence fell into the hands of the powerful Fujiwara clan, which managed to marry into the ruling family and continue the reforms Shotoku had begun. In 710, a new capital, laid out on a grid similar to the great Tang city of Chang'an, was established at Nara, on the eastern edge of the Yamato plain. The Yamato ruler began to use the title "son of Heaven" in the Chinese fashion. In deference to

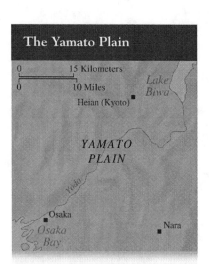

The Yamato Plain

Chronology

FORMATION OF THE JAPANESE STATE

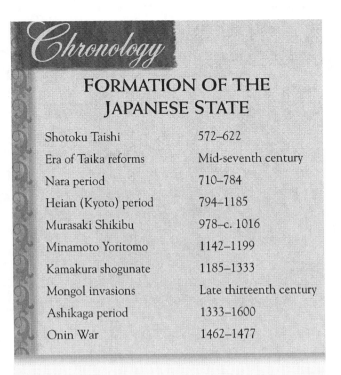

Shotoku Taishi	572–622
Era of Taika reforms	Mid-seventh century
Nara period	710–784
Heian (Kyoto) period	794–1185
Murasaki Shikibu	978–c. 1016
Minamoto Yoritomo	1142–1199
Kamakura shogunate	1185–1333
Mongol invasions	Late thirteenth century
Ashikaga period	1333–1600
Onin War	1462–1477

self-sacrifice and were expected to maintain an intense and unquestioning loyalty to their lord. Bonds of loyalty were also quite strong among members of the samurai class, and homosexuality was common. Like the knights of medieval Europe, the samurai fought on horseback (although a samurai carried a sword and a bow and arrows rather than lance and shield) and were supposed to live by a strict warrior code, known in Japan as *Bushido*, or "way of the warrior" (see the box on p. 297). As time went on, they became a major force and almost a surrogate government in much of the Japanese countryside.

THE KAMAKURA SHOGUNATE AND AFTER

By the end of the twelfth century, as rivalries among noble families led to almost constant civil war, once again centralizing forces asserted themselves. This time the instrument was a powerful noble from a warrior clan named Minamoto Yoritomo (1142–1199), who defeated several rivals and set up his power base on the Kamakura peninsula, south of the modern city of Tokyo. To strengthen the state, he created a more centralized government (the *bakufu*, or "tent government") under a powerful military leader, known as the shogun (general). The shogun attempted to increase the powers of the central government while reducing rival aristocratic clans to vassal status. This "shogunate system," in which the emperor was the titular authority while the shogun exercised actual power, served as the political system in Japan until the second half of the nineteenth century.

The system worked effectively, and it was fortunate that it did, because during the next century, Japan faced the most serious challenge it had confronted yet. The Mongols, who had destroyed the Song dynasty in China, were now attempting to assert their hegemony throughout all of Asia (see Chapter 10). In 1266, Emperor Khubilai Khan demanded tribute from Japan. When the Japanese refused, he invaded with an army of over 30,000 troops. Bad weather and difficult conditions forced a retreat, but the Mongols tried again in 1281. An army nearly 150,000 strong landed on the northern coast of Kyushu. The Japanese were able to contain them for two months until virtually the entire Mongol fleet was destroyed by a massive

➤ **SAMURAI.** During the Kamakura period, painters began to depict the adventures of the new warrior class. Here is an imposing mounted samurai warrior, the Japanese equivalent of the medieval knight in fief-holding Europe. Like his European counterpart, the samurai was supposed to live by a strict moral code and was expected to maintain an unquestioning loyalty to his liege lord. Above all, a samurai's life was one of simplicity and self-sacrifice.

JAPAN'S WARRIOR CLASS

The samurai was the Japanese equivalent of the medieval European knight. Like the knight, he was expected to adhere to a strict moral code. Although this passage comes from a document dating only to the seventeenth century, it shows the importance of hierarchy and duty in a society influenced by the doctrine of Confucius. Note the similarity with Krishna's discourse on the duties of an Indian warrior in Chapter 2.

THE WAY OF THE SAMURAI

The master once said: . . . Generation after generation men have taken their livelihood from tilling the soil, or devised and manufactured tools, or produced profit from mutual trade, so that peoples' needs were satisfied. Thus the occupations of farmer, artisan, and merchant necessarily grew up as complementary to one another. However, the samurai eats food without growing it, uses utensils without manufacturing them, and profits without buying or selling. . . . The samurai is one who does not cultivate, does not manufacture, and does not engage in trade, but it cannot be that he has no function at all as a samurai. . . .

If one deeply fixes his attention on what I have said and examines closely one's own function, it will become clear what the business of the samurai is. The business of the samurai consists in reflecting on his own station in life, in discharging loyal service to his master if he has one, in

deepening his fidelity in associations with friends, and, with due consideration of his own position, in devoting himself to duty above all. . . . The samurai dispenses with the business of the farmer, artisan, and merchant and confines himself to practicing this Way; should there be someone in the three classes of the common people who transgresses against these moral principles, the samurai summarily punishes him and thus upholds proper moral principles in the land. . . . Outwardly he stands in physical readiness for any call to service, and inwardly he strives to fulfill the Way of the lord and subject, friend and friend, father and son, older and younger brother, and husband and wife. Within his heart he keeps to the ways of peace, but without he keeps his weapons ready for use. The three classes of the common people make him their teacher and respect him. By following his teachings, they are enabled to understand what is fundamental and what is secondary.

Herein lies the Way of the samurai, the means by which he earns his clothing, food, and shelter; and by which his heart is put at ease, and he is enabled to pay back at length his obligation to his lord and the kindness of his parents. Were there no such duty, it would be as though one were to steal the kindness of one's parents, greedily devour the income of one's master, and make one's whole life a career of robbery and brigandage. This would be very grievous.

---

typhoon—a "divine wind" (*kamikaze*). Japan would not face a foreign invader again until American forces landed on the Japanese islands in the summer of 1945.

The resistance to the Mongols had put a heavy strain on the system, however, and in 1333, the Kamakura shogunate was overthrown by a coalition of powerful clans. A new shogun, supplied by the Ashikaga family, arose in Kyoto and attempted to continue the shogunate system. But the Ashikaga were unable to restore the centralized power of their predecessors. With the central government reduced to a shell, the power of the local landed aristocracy increased to an unprecedented degree. Heads of great noble families, now called *daimyo* ("great names"), controlled vast landed estates that owed no taxes to the government or to the court in Kyoto. As clan rivalries continued, the daimyo relied increasingly on the samurai for protection, and political power came into the hands of a loose coalition of noble families.

By the end of the fifteenth century, Japan was again close to anarchy. A disastrous civil conflict known as the Onin War (1467–1477) led to the virtual destruction of the capital city of Kyoto and the disintegration of the shogunate. With the disappearance of any central authority, powerful aristocrats in rural areas now seized total control over large territories and ruled as independent great

lords. Territorial rivalries and claims of precedence led to almost constant warfare in this period of "warring states," as it is called (in obvious parallel with a similar era during the Zhou dynasty in China). The trend back toward central authority did not begin until the last quarter of the sixteenth century.

Economic and Social Structures

From the time the Yayoi culture was first established on the Japanese islands, Japan was a predominantly agrarian society. Although Japan lacked the spacious valleys and deltas of the river valley societies, its inhabitants were able to take advantage of their limited amount of tillable land and plentiful rainfall to create a society based on the cultivation of wet rice.

As in China, commerce was slow to develop in Japan. During ancient times, each *uji* had a local artisan class, composed of weavers, carpenters, and ironworkers, but trade was essentially local and was regulated by the local clan leaders. With the rise of the Yamato state, a money economy gradually began to develop, although most trade was still conducted through barter until the twelfth century, when metal coins introduced from China became more popular.

LIFE IN THE LAND OF WA

Some of the earliest descriptions of Japan come from Chinese sources. The following passage from the History of the Wei Dynasty was written in the late third century C.E. The term Wa is a derogatory word meaning "dwarf" and was frequently used in China to refer to the Japanese people. The author of this passage, while remarking on the strange habits of the Japanese, writes without condescension.

HISTORY OF THE WEI DYNASTY

The people of Wa make their abode in the mountainous islands located in the middle of the ocean to the southeast of the Taifang prefecture. . . .

All men, old or young, are covered by tattoos. Japanese fishers revel in diving to catch fish and shell-fish. Tattoos are said to drive away large fish and water predators. They are considered an ornament. . . . Men allow their hair to cover both of their ears and wear head-bands. They wear loincloths wrapped around their bodies and seldom use stitches. Women gather their hair at the ends and tie it in a knot and then pin it to the top of their heads. They make their clothes in one piece, and cut an opening in the center for their heads. They plant wet-field rice, China-grass [a type of nettle], and mulberry trees. They raise cocoons and reel the silk off the cocoons. They produce clothing made of China-grass, of coarse silk, and of cotton. In their land, there are no cows, horses, tigers, leopards, sheep, or swan. They fight with halberds, shields, and wooden bows. . . . Their arrows are made of bamboo, and iron and bone points make up the arrowhead.

People . . . live long, some reaching one hundred years of age, and others to eighty or ninety years. Normally men of high echelon have four or five wives, and the plebeians may have two or three. When the law is violated, the light offender loses his wife and children by confiscation, and the grave offender has his household and kin exterminated. There are class distinctions within the nobility and the base, and some are vassals of others. There are mansions and granaries erected for the purpose of collecting taxes. . . .

When plebeians meet the high-echelon men on the road, they withdraw to the grassy area [side of the road] hesitantly. When they speak or are spoken to, they either crouch or kneel with both hands on the ground to show their respect. When responding they say "aye," which corresponds to our affirmative "yes."

Trade and manufacturing began to develop more rapidly during the Kamakura period, with the appearance of trimonthly markets in the larger towns and the emergence of such industries as paper, iron casting, and porcelain. Foreign trade, mainly with Korea and China, began during the eleventh century. Japan exported raw materials, paintings, swords, and other manufactured items in return for silk, porcelain, books, and copper cash. Some Japanese traders were so aggressive in pressing their interests that authorities in China and Korea attempted to limit the number of Japanese commercial missions that could visit each year. Such restrictions were often ignored, however, and encouraged some Japanese traders to turn to piracy.

Significantly, manufacturing and commerce developed rapidly during the more decentralized period of the Ashikaga shogunate and the era of the warring states, perhaps because of the rapid growth in the wealth and autonomy of local daimyo families. Market towns, now operating on a full money economy, began to appear, and local manufacturers formed guilds to protect their mutual interests. Sometimes local peasants would sell products made in their homes, such as clothing made of silk or hemp, household items, or food products, at the markets. In general, however, trade and manufacturing remained under the control of the local daimyo, who would often provide tax breaks to local guilds in return for other benefits. Although Japan remained a primarily agricultural society, it was on the verge of a major advance in manufacturing.

DAILY LIFE

One of the first descriptions of the life of the Japanese people comes from a Chinese dynastic history from the third century C.E. It describes lords and peasants living in an agricultural society that was based on the cultivation of wet rice. Laws had been enacted to punish offenders, local trade was conducted in markets, and government granaries stored the grain that was paid as taxes (see the box above).

Life for the common people probably changed very little over the next several hundred years. Most were peasants, who worked on land owned by their lord or, in some cases, by the state or by Buddhist monasteries. By no means, however, were all peasants equal either economically or socially. Although in ancient times all land was owned by the state and peasants working the land were taxed at an equal rate depending on the nature of the crop, after the Yamato era variations began to develop. At the top were local officials who were often well-to-do peasants. They were responsible for organizing collective labor services and collecting tax grain from the peasants and in turn were exempt from such obligations themselves.

The mass of the peasants were under the authority of these local officials. In general, peasants were free to

❖ **SCENE OF URBAN LIFE.** Although traditional Japan was largely an agricultural society, trade and manufacturing began to develop during the Kamakura period, sparked by the rapid growth of local daimyo families and market towns. Intraregional trade was transported by horse-drawn carts or by boats on rivers or along the coast. Portrayed here is a detail from a thirteenth-century scroll depicting the bustle and general confusion of the city of Edo (now Tokyo).

dispose of their harvest as they saw fit after paying their tax quota, but in practical terms their freedom was limited. Those who were unable to pay the tax sank to the level of *genin*, or landless laborers, who could be bought and sold by their proprietors like slaves along with the land on which they worked. Some fled to escape such a fate and attempted to survive by clearing plots of land in the mountains or by becoming bandits.

In addition to the *genin*, the bottom of the social scale was occupied by the *eta*, a class of hereditary slaves who were responsible for what were considered degrading occupations, such as curing leather and burying the dead. The origins of the *eta* are not entirely clear, but they probably were descendants of prisoners of war, criminals, or mountain dwellers who were not related to the dominant Yamato peoples. As we shall see, the *eta* are still a distinctive part of Japanese society, and although their full legal rights are guaranteed under the current constitution, discrimination against them is not uncommon.

Daily life for ordinary people in early Japan resembled that of their counterparts throughout much of Asia. The vast majority lived in small villages, several of which normally made up a single *shoen*. Housing was simple. Most lived in small two-room houses of timber, mud, or thatch, with dirt floors covered by straw or woven mats (the origin, perhaps, of the well-known *tatami*, or woven-mat

floor, of more modern times). Their diet consisted of rice (if some was left after the payment of the grain tax), wild grasses, millet, roots, and some fish and birds. Life must have been difficult at best; as one eighth-century poet lamented:

> *Here I lie on straw*
> *Spread on bare earth,*
> *With my parents at my pillow,*
> *My wife and children at my feet,*
> *All huddled in grief and tears.*
> *No fire sends up smoke*
> *At the cooking place,*
> *And in the cauldron*
> *A spider spins its web.*[2]

Evidence about the relations between men and women in early Japan presents a mixed picture. The Chinese dynastic history reports that "in their meetings and daily living, there is no distinction between . . . men and women." It notes that a woman "adept in the ways of shamanism" had briefly ruled Japan in the third century C.E. But it also remarks that polygyny was common, with nobles normally having four or five wives and commoners two or three.[3] An eighth-century law code guaranteed the inheritance rights of women, and wives abandoned by their husbands were permitted to obtain a divorce and remarry. A husband could divorce his wife if she did not

SEDUCTION OF
THE AKASHI LADY

*O*ut *of the Japanese tradition of female introspective prose appeared one of the world's truly great novels,* The Tale of Genji, *written around the year 1000 by the diarist and court author Murasaki Shikibu, known as Lady Murasaki. It is even today revered for its artistic refinement and sensitivity and has influenced Japanese writing for a millennium. A panoramic portrayal of court life in tenth-century Japan, it traces the life and loves of the courtier Genji as he strives to remain in favor with those in power while at the same time pursuing his cult of love and beauty. Truly remarkable is the character of Genji himself, revealed to the reader through myriad psychological observations. In this excerpt, Genji has just seduced a lady at court and now feels misgivings at having betrayed his child bride. A koto is a Japanese stringed instrument similar to a zither.*

LADY MURASAKI, *THE TALE OF GENJI*

A curtain string brushed against a koto, to tell him that she had been passing a quiet evening at her music.

"And will you not play for me on the koto of which I have heard so much?". . .

This lady had not been prepared for an incursion and could not cope with it. She fled to an inner room. How she could have contrived to bar it he could not tell, but it was very firmly barred indeed. Though he did not exactly force his way through, it is not to be imagined that he left matters as they were. Delicate, slender—she was almost too beautiful. Pleasure was mingled with pity at the thought that he was imposing himself upon her. She was even more pleasing than reports from afar had had her. The autumn night, usually so long, was over in a trice. Not wishing to be seen, he hurried out, leaving affectionate assurances behind.

Genji called in secret from time to time. The two houses being some distance apart, he feared being seen by fishers, who were known to relish a good rumor, and sometimes several days would elapse between his visits. . . .

Genji dreaded having Murasaki [his bride] learn of the affair. He still loved her more than anyone, and he did not want her to make even joking reference to it. She was a quiet, docile lady, but she had more than once been unhappy with him. Why, for the sake of brief pleasure, had he caused her pain? He wished it were all his to do over again. The sight of the Akashi lady only brought new longing for the other lady.

He got off a more earnest and affectionate letter than usual, at the end of which he said: "I am in anguish at the thought that, because of foolish occurrences for which I have been responsible but have had little heart, I might appear in a guise distasteful to you. There has been a strange, fleeting encounter. That I should volunteer this story will make you see, I hope, how little I wish to have secrets from you. Let the gods be my judges.

"It was but the fisherman's brush with the salty sea pine.
Followed by a tide of tears of longing."

Her reply was gentle and unreproachful, and at the end of it she said: "That you should have deigned to tell me a dreamlike story which you could not keep to yourself calls to mind numbers of earlier instances.

"Naive of me, perhaps; yet we did make our vows.
And now see the waves that wash the Mountain of
*   Waiting!"*

It was the one note of reproach in a quiet, undemanding letter. He found it hard to put down, and for some nights he stayed away from the house in the hills.

---

produce a male child, committed adultery, disobeyed her parents-in-law, talked too much, engaged in theft, was jealous, or had a serious illness.[4]

When Buddhism was introduced, women were initially relegated to a subordinate position in the new faith. Although they were permitted to take up monastic life— many widows entered a monastery at the death of their husbands—they were not permitted to visit Buddhist holy places, nor were they even (in the accepted wisdom) equal with men in the afterlife. One Buddhist commentary from the late thirteenth century said that a woman could not attain enlightenment because "her sin is grievous, and so she is not allowed to enter the lofty palace of the great Brahma, nor to look upon the clouds which hover over his ministers and people."[5] Other Buddhist scholars

were more egalitarian: "Learning the Law of Buddha and achieving release from illusion have nothing to do with whether one happens to be a man or a woman."[6] Such views ultimately prevailed, and women were eventually allowed to participate fully in Buddhist activities in medieval Japan.

Although women did not possess the full legal and social rights of their male counterparts, they played an active role at various levels of Japanese society. Aristocratic women were prominent at court, and some, such as the author Lady Murasaki, became renowned for their artistic or literary talents (see the box above). Though few commoners could aspire to such prominence, women often appear in the scroll paintings of the period along with men, doing the spring planting, threshing and hulling the rice, and acting as carriers, peddlers, salespersons, and entertainers.

In Search of the Pure Land: Religion in Early Japan

In Japan, as elsewhere, religious belief began with the worship of nature spirits. Early Japanese worshiped spirits, called *kami*, who resided in trees, rivers and streams, and mountains. They also believed in ancestral spirits present in the atmosphere. In Japan, these beliefs eventually evolved into a kind of state religion called Shinto (the Sacred Way or the Way of the Gods) that is still practiced today. Shinto still serves as an ideological and emotional force that knits the Japanese into a single people and nation.

Shinto does not have a complex metaphysical superstructure or an elaborate moral code. It does require certain ritual acts, usually undertaken at a shrine, and a process of purification, which may have originated in primitive concerns about death, childbirth, illness, and menstruation. This traditional concern about physical purity may help explain the strong Japanese concern for personal cleanliness and the practice of denying women entrance to the holy places.

Another feature of Shinto is its stress on the beauty of nature and the importance of nature itself in Japanese life. Shinto shrines are usually located in places of exceptional beauty and are often dedicated to a nearby physical feature. As time passed, such primitive beliefs contributed to the characteristic Japanese love of nature. In this sense, early Shinto beliefs have been incorporated into the lives of all Japanese.

In time, Shinto evolved into a state doctrine that was linked with belief in the divinity of the emperor and the sacredness of the Japanese nation. A national shrine was established at Ise, north of the early capital of Nara, where the emperor annually paid tribute to the sun goddess. But although Shinto had evolved well beyond its primitive origins, like its counterparts elsewhere it could not satisfy all the religious and emotional needs of the Japanese people. For those needs, the Japanese turned to Buddhism.

As we have seen, Buddhism was introduced into Japan from China during the sixth century C.E. and had begun to spread beyond the court to the general population by the eighth century. As in China, most Japanese saw no contradiction between worshiping both the Buddha and their local nature gods, many of whom were considered to be later manifestations of the Buddha. Most of the Buddhist sects that had achieved popularity in China were established in Japan, and many of them attracted powerful patrons at court. Great monasteries were established that competed in wealth and influence with the noble families that had traditionally ruled the country.

Perhaps the two most influential Buddhist sects were the Pure Land (Jodo) sect and Zen (in Chinese, Chan or Ch'an). The Pure Land sect, which taught that devotion alone could lead to enlightenment and release, was very popular among the common people, for whom monastic life was one of the few routes to upward mobility. Among the aristocracy, the most influential school was Zen, which exerted a significant impact on Japanese life and culture during the era of the warring states. In its emphasis on austerity, self-discipline, and communion with nature, Zen complemented many traditional beliefs in Japanese society and became an important component of the samurai warrior's code.

In Zen teachings, there were various ways to achieve enlightenment (*satori* in Japanese). Some stressed that it could be achieved suddenly. One monk, for example, reportedly achieved *satori* by listening to the sound of a bamboo striking against roof tiles, another by carefully watching the opening of peach blossoms in the spring. But other practitioners, sometimes called adepts, said that enlightenment could come only through studying the scriptures and arduous self-discipline (known as *zazen*, or "seated Zen"). Seated Zen involved a lengthy process of meditation that cleansed the mind of extraneous thoughts so that it could concentrate on the essential.

Sources of Traditional Japanese Culture

Nowhere is the Japanese genius for blending indigenous and imported elements into an effective whole better demonstrated than in culture. In such widely diverse fields as art, architecture, sculpture, and literature, the Japanese from early times showed an impressive capacity to borrow selectively from abroad without destroying essential native elements.

Growing contact with China during the period of the rise of the Yamato state stimulated Japanese artists. Missions sent to China and Korea during the seventh and eighth centuries returned with examples of Tang literature, sculpture, and painting, all of which influenced the Japanese.

LITERATURE

Borrowing from Chinese models was somewhat complicated, however, since the early Japanese had no writing system for recording their own spoken language and initially adopted the Chinese written language for writing. But resourceful Japanese soon began to adapt the Chinese written characters so that they could be used for recording the Japanese language. In some cases, Chinese characters were given Japanese pronunciations. But Chinese characters ordinarily could not be used to record Japanese words, which normally contain more than one syllable. Sometimes the Japanese simply used Chinese characters

A SAMPLE OF LINKED VERSE

*O*ne of the distinctive features of medieval Japanese literature was the technique of "linked verse." In a manner similar to haiku poetry today, such poems, known as renga, were written by groups of individuals who would join together to compose the poem, verse by verse. The following example, by three famous poets named Sogi, Shohaku, and Socho, is one of the most famous of the period.

THE THREE POETS AT MINASE

Snow clinging to slope,   Sogi
  On mist-enshrouded mountains
  At eveningtime.
In the distance flows   Shohaku
  Through plum-scented villages.

Willows cluster   Socho
  In the river breeze
  As spring appears.
The sound of a boat being poled   Sogi
  In the clearness at dawn
Still the moon lingers   Shohaku
As fog o'er-spreads
  The night.
A frost-covered meadow;   Socho
  Autumn has drawn to a close.
Against the wishes   Sogi
  Of droning insects
  The grasses wither.

as phonetic symbols that were combined to form Japanese words. Later they simplified the characters into phonetic symbols that were used alongside Chinese characters. This hybrid system continues to be used today.

At first, most educated Japanese preferred to write in Chinese, and a court literature—consisting of essays, poetry, and official histories—appeared in the classical Chinese language. But spoken Japanese never totally disappeared among the educated classes and eventually became the instrument of a unique literature. With the lessening of Chinese cultural influence in the tenth century, Japanese verse resurfaced. Between the tenth and fifteenth centuries, twenty imperial anthologies of poetry were compiled. Initially, they were written primarily by courtiers, but with the fall of the Heian court and the rise of the warrior and merchant classes, all literate segments of society began to produce poetry.

Japanese poetry is unique. It expresses its themes in a simple form, a characteristic stemming from traditional Japanese aesthetics, Zen religion, and the language itself. The aim of the Japanese poet was to create a mood, perhaps the melancholic effect of gently falling cherry blossoms or leaves. With a few specific references, the poet suggested a whole world, just as Zen Buddhism sought enlightenment from a sudden perception. Poets often alluded to earlier poems by repeating their images with small changes, a technique that was viewed not as plagiarism but as an elaboration on the meaning of the earlier poem.

By the fourteenth century, the technique of the "linked verse" had become the most popular form of Japanese poetry. Known as *haiku*, it is composed of seventeen syllables divided into lines of five, seven, and five syllables. The poems usually focused on images from nature and the mutability of life. Often the poetry was written by several individuals alternately composing verses and linking them together into long sequences of hundreds and even thousands of lines (see the box above).

Poetry served a unique function at the Heian court, where it was the initial means of communication between lovers. By custom, aristocratic women were isolated from all contact with men outside their immediate family and spent their days hidden behind screens. Some amused themselves by writing poetry. When courtship began, poetic exchanges were the only means a woman had to attract her prospective lover, who would be enticed solely by her poetic art.

During the Heian period, male courtiers wrote in Chinese, believing that Chinese civilization was superior and worthy of emulation. Like the Chinese, they viewed prose fiction as "vulgar gossip." Nevertheless, from the ninth century to the twelfth, Japanese women were prolific writers of prose fiction in Japanese. Excluded from school, they learned to read and write at home and wrote diaries and stories to pass the time. Some of the most talented women were invited to court as authors in residence.

In the increasingly pessimistic world of the warring states of Kamakura (1185–1333), Japanese novels typically focused on a solitary figure who is aloof from the refinements of the court and faces battle and possibly death. Another genre, that of the heroic war tale, came out of the new warrior class. These works described the military exploits of warriors, coupled with an overwhelming sense of sadness and loneliness.

The famous classical Japanese drama known as *No* also originated during this period. *No* developed out of a variety of entertainment forms, such as dancing and juggling, that were part of the native tradition or had been imported from China and other regions of Asia. The plots were normally based on stories from Japanese history or legend. Eventually, *No* evolved into a highly stylized drama in which the performers wore masks and danced to the accompaniment of instrumental music. Like much of Japanese culture, *No* was restrained, graceful, and refined.

ART AND ARCHITECTURE

In art and architecture, as in literature, the Japanese pursued their interest in beauty, simplicity, and nature. To some degree, Japanese artists and architects were influenced by Chinese forms. As they became familiar with Chinese architecture, Japanese rulers and aristocrats tried to emulate the splendor of Tang civilization and began constructing their palaces and temples in Chinese style.

During the Heian period (794–1185), the search for beauty was reflected in various art forms, such as narrative hand scrolls, screens, sliding door panels, fans, and lacquer decoration. As in the case of literature, nature themes dominated, such as seashore scenes, a spring rain, moon and mist, or flowering wisteria and cherry blossoms. All were intended to evoke an emotional response on the part of the viewer. Japanese painting suggested the frail beauty of nature by presenting it on a smaller scale. The majestic mountain in a Chinese painting became a more intimate Japanese landscape with rolling hills and a rice field. Faces were rarely shown, and human drama was indicated by a woman lying prostrate or hiding her face in her sleeve. Tension was shown by two people talking at a great distance or with their backs to one another.

During the Kamakura period (1185–1333), the hand scroll with its physical realism and action-packed paintings of the new warrior class achieved great popularity. Reflecting these chaotic times, the art of portraiture flourished, and a scroll would include a full gallery of warriors and holy men in starkly realistic detail, including such unflattering features as stubble, worry lines on a forehead, and crooked teeth. Japanese sculptors also produced naturalistic wooden statues of generals, nobles, and saints. By far the most distinctive, however, were the fierce heavenly "guardian kings," who still intimidate the viewer today.

Zen Buddhism, an import from China in the thirteenth century, also influenced Japanese aesthetics. With its emphasis on immediate enlightenment without recourse to intellectual analysis and elaborate ritual, Zen reinforced the Japanese predilection for simplicity and self-discipline. During this era, Zen philosophy found expression in the Japanese garden, the tea ceremony, the art of flower arranging, pottery and ceramics, and miniature plant display (the famous *bonsai*, literally "pot scenery").

Landscapes served as an important means of expression in both Japanese art and architecture. Japanese gardens were initially modeled on Chinese examples. Early court texts during the Heian period emphasized the importance

THE PROTECTIVE DRAGON. Viewing Heian culture as an era of decadent aristocratic excess, artists of the Kamakura period (1185–1333) strove to express spiritual purpose in their work. Illustrated narrative hand scrolls, for example, either dramatized the torments of hell or praised the lives of Buddhist saints. Here we see a colorful thirteenth-century painting that depicts a seventh-century Korean monk returning from his travels in China. At his departure from the dock, he rejected the love of a beautiful young woman because of his spiritual dedication. Brokenhearted, she plunges into the ocean, thus transforming herself into a dragon to guide him safely back to Korea. The woman was later recognized as a Buddhist saint whose sacrifice was deemed morally appropriate as a model for Japanese women of the era.

⟐ GUARDIAN KINGS.   Larger than life and intimidating in its presence, this thirteenth-century wooden statue departs from the refined atmosphere of the Heian court and pulsates with the masculine energy of the Kamakura period. Placed strategically at the entrance to Buddhist shrines, guardian kings such as this one protected the temple and the faithful. In contrast to the refined atmosphere of the Fujiwara court, the Kamakura era was a warrior's world.

⟐ A SEATED BUDDHA.   Buddhist statuary originated in India and China and evolved as a popular art form in Japan from the seventh century on. Characteristic of these statues are the *mudras*, or hand and body positions by which the Buddha communicated with his followers. Here his connected fingers indicate meditation. Whereas earlier Japanese sculptors worked in bronze, the depletion of metal reserves eventually necessitated the use of wood. This remarkable eleventh-century gilded wood carving, over 10 feet in height, is composed of fifty-three pieces of cypress and exudes a feeling of stability and calm, expressing the Buddha's deep spirituality. He is seated on a bed of lotus leaves, a Buddhist symbol for purity arising out of the mire.

of including a stream or pond when creating a garden. The landscape surrounding the fourteenth-century Golden Pavilion in Kyoto displays a harmony of garden, water, and architecture that makes it one of the treasures of the world. Because of the shortage of water in the city, later gardens concentrated on rock composition, using white pebbles to represent water.

Like the Japanese garden, the tea ceremony represents the fusion of Zen and aesthetics. Developed in the fifteenth century, it was practiced in a simple room devoid of external ornament except for a *tatami* floor, sliding doors, and an alcove with a writing desk and asymmetrical shelves. The participants could therefore focus completely on the activity of pouring and drinking tea. "Tea and Zen have the same flavor," goes the Japanese saying. Considered the ultimate symbol of spiritual deliverance, the tea ceremony had great aesthetic value and moral significance in traditional times as well as today.

Courtesy of William J. Duiker

Courtesy of Charles Gupton, Tony Stone Images

➤ RYOANJI TEMPLE GARDEN IN KYOTO.   As the result of a water shortage in the fifteenth century, Japanese landscape designers began to make increasing use of rocks and pebbles to represent water. In the Ryoanji Temple in the hills west of Kyoto, seventeen rocks surrounded by wavy raked pebbles are arranged in five groups to suggest mountains emerging from the sea. Here we experience the quintessential Japanese aesthetic expression of allusion, simplicity, restraint, and tranquillity.

➤ THE GOLDEN PAVILION IN KYOTO.   The landscape surrounding the Golden Pavilion displays a harmony of garden, water, and architecture that makes it one of the treasures of the world. Constructed in the fourteenth century as a retreat for the shoguns to withdraw from their administrative chores, the pavilion is named for the gold foil that covered its exterior. Completely destroyed by an arsonist in 1950 as a protest against the commercialism of modern Buddhism, it was rebuilt and reopened in 1987. The use of water as a backdrop is especially noteworthy in Chinese and Japanese landscapes, as well as in the Middle East.

Japan and the Chinese Model

Few societies in Asia have historically been as isolated as Japan. Cut off from the mainland by 120 miles of frequently turbulent ocean, the Japanese had only minimal contact with the outside world during most of their early development.

Whether this isolation was ultimately beneficial to Japanese society cannot be determined. On one hand, the lack of knowledge of developments taking place elsewhere probably delayed the process of change in Japan. On the other hand, the Japanese were spared the destructive invasions that afflicted other ancient civilizations. Certainly, once the Japanese became acquainted with Chinese cul-

ture at the height of the Tang era, they were quick to take advantage of the opportunity. In the space of a few decades, the young state adopted many aspects of Chinese society and culture and thereby introduced major changes into Japanese life.

Nevertheless, Japanese political institutions failed to follow all aspects of the Chinese pattern. Despite Prince Shotoku's effort to make effective use of the imperial traditions of Tang China, the decentralizing forces inside Japanese society remained dominant throughout the period under discussion in this chapter. Adoption of the Confucian civil service examination did not lead to a breakdown of Japanese social divisions; instead, the examination was administered in a manner that preserved and strengthened them. Although Buddhist and Daoist doctrines made a significant contribution to Japanese religious practices, Shinto beliefs continued to play a major role in shaping the Japanese worldview.

Why Japan did not follow the Chinese road to centralized authority has been the subject of some debate among historians. Some argue that the answer lies in differing cultural traditions, while others suggest that Chinese institutions and values were introduced too rapidly to be assimilated effectively by Japanese society. One factor may have been the absence of a foreign threat (except for the Mongols) in Japan. A recent view holds that diseases (such as smallpox and measles) imported inadvertently from China led to a marked decline in the population of the islands, reducing the food output and preventing the population from coalescing in more compact urban centers.

In any event, Japan was not the only society in Asia to assimilate ideas from abroad while at the same time preserving customs and institutions inherited from the past. Across the Sea of Japan to the west and several thousand miles to the south, other Asian peoples were embarked on a similar journey. We now turn to their experience.

KOREA: BRIDGE TO THE EAST

No society in East Asia was more strongly influenced by the Chinese model than Korea. Slightly larger than the state of Minnesota, the Korean peninsula was probably first settled by Altaic-speaking fishing and hunting peoples from neighboring Manchuria during the Neolithic Age. Because the area is relatively mountainous (only about one-fifth of the peninsula is adaptable to cultivation), farming was apparently not practiced until about 2000 B.C.E. The other aspect of Korea's geography that has profoundly affected its history is its proximity to both China and Japan.

In 109 B.C.E., the northern part of the peninsula came under direct Chinese rule. During the next several generations, the area was ruled by the Han dynasty, which divided the territory into provinces and introduced Chinese institutions. With the decline of the Han in the third century C.E., power gradually shifted to local tribal leaders, who drove out the Chinese administrators but continued to absorb Chinese cultural influence. Eventually, three separate kingdoms emerged on the peninsula: Koguryo in the north, Paekche in the southwest, and Silla in the southeast. The Japanese, who had recently established their own state on the Yamato plain, maintained a small colony on the southern coast.

Korea's Three Kingdoms

Ialu R.
Sea of Japan
Pyongyang
KOGURYO
Yellow Sea
PAEKCHE
SILLA
Kyongju
0   300 Kilometers
0   200 Miles

The Three Kingdoms

From the fourth to the seventh centuries, the three kingdoms were bitter rivals for influence and territory on the peninsula. At the same time, all began to absorb Chinese

political and cultural institutions. Chinese influence was most notable in Koguryo, where Buddhism was introduced in the late fourth century C.E. and the first Confucian academy on the peninsula was established in the capital at Pyongyang. All three kingdoms also appear to have accepted a tributary relationship with one or another of the squabbling states that emerged in China after the fall of the Han. The kingdom of Silla, less exposed than its two rivals to Chinese influence, was at first the weakest of the three, but eventually its greater internal cohesion—perhaps a consequence of the tenacity of its tribal traditions—enabled it to become the dominant power on the peninsula. Then the rulers of Silla forced the Chinese to withdraw from all but the area

KOREAN ROYAL CROWN. The Silla dynasty was renowned for the high quality of its gold, jewelry, crowns, and sword sheaths. Shown here is a jewel-inlaid royal crown of the fifth century C.E. that was excavated from a royal tomb in eastern Korea. Although much Silla artwork reflects Chinese influence, royal crowns located in Silla tombs often contain antlerlike motifs, reflecting the animistic traditions of Korea's pre-Chinese past. The comma-shaped jewels symbolize the King's Heaven-sanctioned authority on earth.

adjacent to the Yalu River. To pacify the haughty Chinese, Silla accepted tributary status under the Tang dynasty. The remaining Japanese colonies in the south were eliminated.

With the country unified for the first time, the rulers of Silla attempted to use Chinese political institutions and ideology to forge a centralized state. Buddhism, now rising in popularity, became the state religion, and Korean monks followed the paths of their Japanese counterparts on journeys to the Middle Kingdom. Chinese architecture and art became dominant in the capital at Kyongju and other urban centers, and the written Chinese language became the official means of communication at court. But powerful aristocratic families, long dominant in the southeastern part of the peninsula, were still influential at court. They were able to prevent the adoption of the Tang civil service examination system and resisted the distribution of manorial lands to the poor. The failure to adopt the Chinese model was fatal. Squabbling among noble families steadily increased, and after the assassination of the king of Silla in 780, the country sank into civil war.

Unification

In the early tenth century, a new dynasty called Koryo (the root of the modern word for Korea) arose in the north. The new kingdom adopted Chinese political institutions in an effort to strengthen its power and unify its territory. The civil service examination system was introduced in 958, but as in Japan, the bureaucracy continued to be dominated by influential aristocratic families.

The Koryo dynasty remained in power for four hundred years, protected from invasion by the absence of a strong dynasty in neighboring China. Under the Koryo, industry and commerce slowly began to develop, but as in China, agriculture was the prime source of wealth. In theory, all land was the property of the king, but in actuality, noble families controlled their holdings. The lands were worked by peasants who were subject to burdens similar to those of European serfs. At the bottom of society was a class of "base people" (*chonmin*), composed of slaves, artisans, and other specialized workers.

From a cultural point of view, the Koryo era was one of high achievement. Buddhist monasteries, run by sects

PULGUKSA BELL TOWER. Among the greatest architectural achievements on the Korean peninsula is the Pulguksa (Monastery of the Land of Buddha), built near Kyongju, the ancient capital of Silla, in the eighth century C.E. Shown here is the bell tower, located in the midst of beautiful parklands on the monastery grounds. Young Korean couples often come to this monastery after their weddings to be photographed in the stunning surroundings.

Courtesy of William J. Duiker

THE FLOWER GARDEN SCRIPTURE

By the eighth century, Buddhism had come to Korea from China, and like their counterparts in Christian Europe, Korean monks could accumulate merit toward salvation by copying the scriptures. In this passage, the eighth-century Master Yongi of Hwangyong monastery has volunteered to copy a scripture as a way of expressing gratitude for the love of his parents and assisting others in following the Buddhist Eightfold Way to wisdom. Note the careful attention to ritual as the process is brought to realization. This scripture, which was discovered in 1979, consisted of two scrolls of thirty white papers joined together, with characters in black ink. Each scroll was 45 feet long.

AN EIGHTH-CENTURY BUDDHIST SCRIPTURE

The scripture is made as follows: First scented water is sprinkled around the roots of a paperbark mulberry tree to quicken its growth; the bark is then peeled and pounded to make paper with a clean surface. The copyists, the artisans who make the centerpiece of the scroll, and the painters who draw the images of buddhas and bodhisattvas all receive the bodhisattva ordination and observe abstinence. After relieving themselves, sleeping, eating, or drinking, they take a bath in scented water before returning to the work. Copyists are adorned with new pure garments, loose trousers, a coarse crown, and a deva crown. Two azure-clad boys sprinkle water on their heads and . . . azure-clad boys and musicians perform music. The processions to the copying site are headed by one who sprinkles scented water on their path, another who scatters flowers, a dharma master who carries a censer, and another dharma master who chants Buddhist verses. Each of the copyists carries incense and flowers and invokes the name of the Buddha as he progresses.

Upon reaching the site, all take refuge in the Three Jewels (the Buddha, the Dharma, and the Order), make three bows, and offer the *Flower Garland Scripture* and others to buddhas and bodhisattvas. Then they sit down and copy the scripture, make the centerpiece of the scroll, and paint the buddhas and bodhisattvas. Thus, azure-clad boys and musicians cleanse everything before a piece of relic is placed in the center.

Now I make a vow that the copied scripture will not break till the end of the future—even when a major chilicosm is destroyed by the three calamities, this scripture shall be intact as the void. If all living beings rely on this scripture, they shall witness the Buddha, listen to his dharma, worship the relic, aspire to enlightenment without backsliding, cultivate the vows of the Universally Worthy Bodhisattva, and achieve Buddhahood.

---

introduced from China, including Pure Land and Zen (Chan), controlled vast territories, while their monks served as royal advisers at court. At first, Buddhist themes dominated in Korean art and sculpture, and the entire Tripitaka (the "three baskets" of the Buddhist canon) was printed using wooden blocks (see the box above). Eventually, however, with the appearance of landscape painting and porcelain, Confucian themes began to predominate.

Under the Mongols

Like its predecessor in Silla, the kingdom of Koryo was unable to overcome the power of the nobility and the absence of a reliable tax base. In the thirteenth century, the Mongols seized the northern part of the country and assimilated it into the Yuan empire. The weakened kingdom of Koryo became a tributary of the great khan in Khanbaliq (see Chapter 10).

The era of Mongol rule was one of profound suffering for the Korean people, especially the thousands of peasants and artisans who were compelled to perform corvée labor to help build the ships in preparation for Khubilai Khan's invasion of Japan. On the positive side, the Mongols introduced many new ideas and technology from China and farther afield. The Koryo dynasty had managed to survive, but only by accepting Mongol authority, and when the power of the Mongols declined, the kingdom declined with it. With the rise to power of the Ming in China, Koryo collapsed, and power was seized by the military commander Yi Song-gye, who declared the founding of the new Yi dynasty in 1392. Once again, the Korean people were in charge of their own destiny.

VIETNAM: THE SMALLER DRAGON

While the Korean people were attempting to establish their own identity in the shadow of the powerful Chinese empire, the peoples of Vietnam, on China's southern frontier, were trying to do the same. The Vietnamese began to practice irrigated agriculture in the flooded regions of the Red River delta at an early date and entered the Bronze Age sometime during the second millennium B.C.E. By about 200 B.C.E., a young state had begun to form in the area but immediately encountered the expanding power of the Qin empire (see Chapter 3). The Vietnamese were not easy to subdue, however, and the collapse of the Qin dynasty temporarily enabled them to preserve their independence. Nevertheless, a century later, they were absorbed into the Han empire.

A PLEA TO THE EMPEROR

*L*ike many other societies in premodern East and Southeast Asia, the kingdom of Vietnam regularly paid tribute to the imperial court in China. The arrangement was often beneficial to both sides, as the tributary states received a form of international recognition from the relationship, as well as trade privileges in the massive Chinese market. China, for its part, assured itself that neighboring areas would not harbor dissident elements hostile to its own security.

In this document, contained in a historical chronicle written by LeTac in the fourteenth century, a claimant to the Vietnamese throne seeks recognition from the Song emperor while offering tribute to the Son of Heaven in China. Note the way in which the claimant, Le Hoan, founder of the early Le dynasty (980–1009), demeans the character of the Vietnamese people in comparison with the sophisticated ways of imperial China.

LE HOAN, *ESSAY ON ANNAM*

My ancestors have received favors from the Imperial Court. Living in a faraway country at a corner of the sea [Annam], they have been granted the seals of investiture for that barbarian area and have always paid to the Imperial ministers the tribute and respect they owed. But recently our House has been little favored by Heaven; however, the death of our ancestors has not prevented us from promptly delivering the tribute. . . .

But now the leadership of the country is in dispute and investiture has not yet been conferred by China. My father, Pou-ling, and my eldest brother, Lienn, formerly enjoyed the favors of the [Chinese] Empire, which endowed them with the titles and functions of office. They zealously and humbly protected their country, neither daring to appear lazy or negligent. . . . [But then] the good fortune of our House began to crumble. The mandarins [officials], the army, the people, the court elders, and members of my family, all . . . entreated me to lead the army. . . . My people, who are wild mountain-dwellers, have unpleasant and violent customs; they are a people who live in caves and have disorderly and impetuous habits. I feared that trouble would arise if I did not yield to their wishes. From prudence I therefore assumed power temporarily. . . . I hope that His Majesty will place my country among His other tributary states by granting me the investiture. He will instill peace in the heart of His little servant by allowing me to govern the patrimony my parents left me. Then shall I administer my barbarian and remote people. . . . I shall send tributes of precious stones and ivory, and before the Golden Gate I shall express my loyalty.

At first, the Han were satisfied to rule the delta as an autonomous region under the administration of the local landed aristocracy. But Chinese taxes were oppressive, and in 39 C.E., a revolt led by the Trung Sisters (widows of local nobles who had been executed by the Chinese) briefly brought Han rule to an end. The Chinese soon suppressed the rebellion, however, and began to rule the area directly through officials dispatched from China. In time, however, these foreign officials began to intermarry with the local nobility and form a Sino-Vietnamese ruling class who, though trained in Chinese culture, began to identify with the cause of Vietnamese autonomy.

For nearly a thousand years, the Vietnamese were exposed to the art, architecture, literature, philosophy, and written language of China as the Chinese attempted to integrate the area culturally as well as politically and administratively into their empire. To all intents and purposes, the Red River delta, then known to the Chinese as the "pacified South" (Annam), became a part of China.

The Rise of Great Viet

Despite the Chinese efforts to assimilate Vietnam, the Vietnamese sense of ethnic and cultural identity proved inextinguishable, and in the tenth century, the Vietnamese took advantage of the collapse of the Tang dynasty in China to overthrow Chinese rule.

The new Vietnamese state, which called itself Dai Viet (Great Viet), became a dynamic new force on the Southeast Asian mainland. As the population of the Red River delta expanded, Dai Viet soon came into conflict with Champa, its neighbor to the south. Located along the central coast of modern Vietnam, Champa was a trading society based on Indian cultural traditions. Over the next several centuries, the two states fought on numerous occasions. By the end of the fifteenth century, Dai Viet had conquered Champa. The Vietnamese then resumed their march southward, establishing agricultural settlements in the newly conquered territory. By the seventeenth century, the Vietnamese had reached the Gulf of Siam.

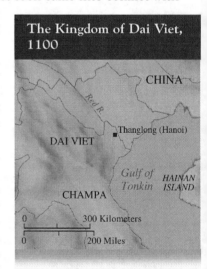

The Kingdom of Dai Viet, 1100

CHINA
Red R.
Thanglong (Hanoi)
DAI VIET
Gulf of Tonkin   HAINAN ISLAND
CHAMPA
0   300 Kilometers
0   200 Miles

The Vietnamese faced an even more serious challenge from the north. The Song dynasty in China, beset with its own problems on the northern frontier, eventually accepted the Dai Viet ruler's offer of tribute status (see the box above), but later dynasties attempted to

A LOST CIVILIZATION. Before the spread of Vietnamese settlers into the area early in the second millennium C.E., much of the coast along the South China Sea was occupied by the kingdom of Champa. A trading people who were directly engaged in the regional trade network between China and the Bay of Bengal, the Cham received their initial political and cultural influence from India. This shrine-tower, located on a hill in the modern city of Nha Trang, was constructed in the eleventh century and clearly displays the influence of Indian architecture. Champa finally succumbed to a Vietnamese invasion in the fifteenth century.

reintegrate the Red River delta into the Chinese empire. The first effort was made in the late thirteenth century by the Mongols, who attempted on two occasions to conquer the Vietnamese. After a series of bloody battles, during which the Vietnamese displayed an impressive capacity for guerrilla warfare, the invaders were driven out. A little over a century later, the Ming dynasty tried again, and for twenty years Vietnam was once more under Chinese rule. In 1428, the Vietnamese evicted the Chinese again, but the experience had contributed to the strong sense of Vietnamese identity.

THE CHINESE LEGACY

Despite their stubborn resistance to Chinese rule, after the restoration of independence in the tenth century, Vietnamese rulers quickly discovered the convenience of the Confucian model in administering a river valley society and therefore attempted to follow Chinese practice in forming their own state. The ruler styled himself an emperor like his counterpart to the north (although he prudently termed himself a king in his direct dealings with the Chinese court), adopted Chinese court rituals, claimed the Mandate of Heaven, and arrogated to himself the same authority and privileges in his dealings with his subjects. But unlike a Chinese emperor, who had no particular symbolic role as defender of the Chinese people or Chinese culture, a Vietnamese monarch was viewed, above all, as the symbol and defender of Vietnamese independence.

Like their Chinese counterparts, Vietnamese rulers fought to preserve their authority from the challenges of powerful aristocratic families and turned to the Chinese bureaucratic model, including civil service examinations, as a means of doing so. Under the pressure of strong monarchs, the concept of merit eventually took hold, and the power of the landed aristocracy was weakened if not entirely broken. The Vietnamese adopted much of the Chinese administrative structure, including the six ministries, the censorate, and the various levels of provincial and local administration.

Another aspect of the Chinese legacy was the spread of Buddhist, Daoist, and Confucian ideas, which supplemented the Viets' traditional belief in nature spirits. Buddhist precepts became popular among the local population, who integrated the new faith into their existing belief system by founding Buddhist temples dedicated to the local village deity in the hope of guaranteeing an abundant harvest. Upper-class Vietnamese educated in the Confucian classics tended to follow the more agnostic Confucian doctrine, but some joined Buddhist monasteries. Daoism also flourished at all levels of society and, as in China, provided a structure for animistic beliefs and practices that still predominated at the village level.

During the early period of independence, Vietnamese culture also borrowed liberally from its larger neighbor. Educated Vietnamese tried their hand at Chinese poetry, wrote dynastic histories in the Chinese style, and followed Chinese models in sculpture, architecture, and porcelain. Many

Courtesy of William J. Duiker

⇒ THE TEMPLE OF LITERATURE, HANOI. When the Vietnamese regained their independence from China in the tenth century C.E., they retained Chinese institutions that they deemed beneficial. A prime example was the establishment of the Temple of Literature, Vietnam's first university, in 1076. Here the sons of mandarins (officials) were educated in the Confucian classics in preparation for an official career. Beginning in the fifteenth century, those receiving doctorates had stelae erected to identify their achievements. Shown here is the central hall of the temple, where advanced students took the metropolitan examinations for the doctorate.

of the notable buildings of the medieval period, such as the Temple of Literature and the famous One-Pillar Pagoda in Hanoi, are classic examples of Chinese architecture.

But there were signs that Vietnamese creativity would eventually transcend the bounds of Chinese cultural norms. Although most classical writing was undertaken in literary Chinese, the only form of literary expression deemed suitable by Confucian conservatives, an adaptation of Chinese written characters, called *chu nom* ("southern characters"), was devised to provide a written system for spoken Vietnamese. In use by the early ninth century, it eventually began to be used for the composition of essays and poetry in the Vietnamese language. Such pioneering efforts would lead in later centuries to the emergence of a vigorous national literature totally independent of Chinese forms.

Society and Family Life

Vietnamese social institutions and customs were also strongly influenced by those of China. As in China, the introduction of a Confucian system and the adoption of civil service examinations undermined the role of the old landed aristocrats and led eventually to their replacement by the scholar-gentry class. Also as in China, the examinations

were open to most males, regardless of family background, which opened the door to a degree of social mobility unknown in most of the states elsewhere in the region. Candidates for the bureaucracy read many of the same Confucian classics and absorbed the same ethical principles as their counterparts in China. At the same time, they were also exposed to the classic works of Vietnamese history, which strengthened their sense that Vietnam was a distinct culture similar to, but separate from, that of China.

The vast majority of the Vietnamese people, however, were peasants. Most were small landholders or sharecroppers who rented their plots from wealthier farmers, but large estates were rare due to the systematic efforts of the central government to prevent the rise of a powerful local landed elite.

Family life in Vietnam was similar in many respects to that in China. The Confucian concept of family took hold during the period of Chinese rule, along with the related concepts of filial piety and gender inequality. Perhaps the most striking difference between family traditions in China and Vietnam was that Vietnamese women possessed more rights both in practice and by law. Since ancient times, wives had been permitted to own property and initiate divorce proceedings. One consequence of Chinese rule was a growing emphasis on male dominance, but the tradition of women's rights was never totally extinguished and was legally recognized in a law code promulgated in 1460.

Moreover, Vietnam had a strong historical tradition associating heroic women with the defense of the homeland. The Trung Sisters were the first but by no means the only example. In the following passage, a Vietnamese historian of the eighteenth century recounts their story:

The imperial court was far away; local officials were greedy and oppressive. At that time the country of one hundred sons was the country of the women of Lord To. The ladies [the Trung Sisters] used the female arts against their irreconcilable foe; skirts and hairpins sang of patriotic righteousness, uttered a solemn oath at the inner door of the ladies' quarters, expelled the governor, and seized the capital. . . . Were they not grand heroines? . . . Our two ladies brought forward an army of all the people, and, establishing a royal court that settled affairs in the territories of the sixty-five strongholds, shook their skirts over the Hundred Yueh [the Vietnamese people].[7]

 ## CONCLUSION

There are some tantalizing similarities among the three countries we have examined in this chapter. All borrowed liberally from the Chinese model. At the same time, all adapted Chinese institutions and values to the conditions prevailing in their own societies. Though all expressed admiration and respect for China's achievement, all sought to keep Chinese power at a distance.

As an island nation, Japan was the most successful of the three in protecting its political sovereignty and its cultural identity. Both Korea and Vietnam were compelled on various occasions to defend their independence by force of arms. That experience may have shaped their strong sense of national distinctiveness, which we shall discuss further in a later chapter.

The appeal of Chinese institutions can undoubtedly be explained by the fact that Japan, Korea, and Vietnam were all agrarian societies, much like their larger neighbor. But it is undoubtedly significant that the aspect of Chinese political culture that was least amenable to adoption abroad was the civil service examination system. The Confucian concept of meritocracy ran directly counter to the strong aristocratic tradition that flourished in all three societies during their early stage of development. Even when the system was adopted, it was put to quite different uses. Only in Vietnam did the concept of merit eventually triumph over that of birth, as strong rulers of Dai Viet attempted to initiate the Chinese model as a means of creating a centralized system of government.

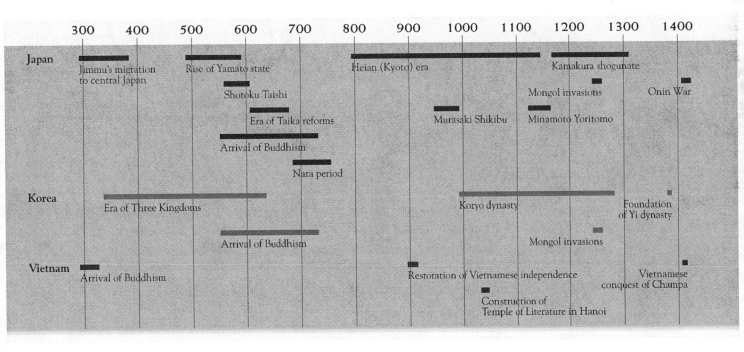

CHAPTER NOTES

1. Keith W. Taylor, *The Birth of Vietnam* (Berkeley, Calif., 1983), p. 75.
2. Quoted in David John Lu, *Sources of Japanese History*, vol. 1 (New York, 1974), p. 7.
3. From "The History of Wei," quoted in ibid., p. 10.
4. From "The Law of Households," quoted in ibid., p. 32.
5. From "On the Salvation of Women," quoted in ibid., p. 127.
6. Quoted in Barbara Ruch, "The Other Side of Culture in Medieval Japan," in Kozo Yamamura, ed., *The Cambridge History of Japan*, vol. 3, *Medieval Japan* (Cambridge, 1990), p. 506.
7. Quoted in Taylor, *The Birth of Vietnam*, pp. 336–337.

SUGGESTED READING

Some of the standard treatments of the rise of Japanese civilization appear in textbooks dealing with the early history of East Asia. Two of the best are J. K. Fairbank, E. O. Reischauer, and A. M. Craig, *East Asia: Tradition and Transformation* (Boston, 1973), and C. Schirokauer, *A Brief History of Chinese and Japanese Civilizations* (San Diego, Calif., 1989). A number of historical works deal specifically with early Japan. G. Sansom, *A History of Japan to 1334* (Stanford, Calif., 1958), is now somewhat out of date but is still informative and very well written. For the latest scholarship on the early period, see the first three volumes of *The Cambridge History of Japan*, ed. J. W. Hall, M. B. Jansen, M. Kanai, and D. Twitchett (Cambridge, 1988).

The best available collections of documents on the early history of Japan are D. J. Lu, ed., *Sources of Japanese History*, vol. 1 (New York, 1974), and Ryusaku Tsunoda et al., eds., *Sources of Japanese Tradition*, vol. 1 (New York, 1958).

For specialized books on the early historical period, see R. J. Pearson, ed., *Windows on the Japanese Past: Studies in Archaeology and Prehistory* (Ann Arbor, Mich., 1986). J. W. Hall, *Government and Local Power in Japan, 500–1700* (Princeton, N.J., 1966), provides a detailed analysis of the development of Japanese political institutions. The relationship between disease and state building is analyzed in W. W. Farris, *Population, Disease, and Land in Early Japan, 645–900* (Cambridge, 1985). The Kamakura period is covered in J. P. Mass, ed., *Court and Bakufu in Japan: Essays in Kamakura History* (New Haven, Conn., 1982). See also H. P. Varley, *The Onin War* (New York, 1977). For Japanese Buddhism, see W. T. de Bary, ed., *The Buddhist Tradition in India, China, and Japan* (New York, 1972).

A concise and provocative introduction to women's issues during this period in Japan, as well as in other parts of the world, can be found in S. S. Hughes and B. Hughes, *Women in World History* (Armonk, N.Y., 1995). For a tenth-century account of daily life for women at the Japanese court, see I. Morris, trans. and ed., *The Pillow Book of Sei Shonagon* (New York, 1991). For the changes that took place from matrilocal and matrilineal marriages to a patriar-

chal society, consult H. Tonomura, "Black Hair and Red Trousers: Gendering the Flesh in Medieval Japan," in *American Historical Review* 99 (1994).

The best introduction to Japanese literature for college students is still the concise and insightful D. Keene, *Japanese Literature: An Introduction for Western Readers* (London, 1953). The most comprehensive anthology is D. Keene, *Anthology of Japanese Literature* (New York, 1955), while the best history of Japanese literature, also by D. Keene, is *Seeds in the Heart: Japanese Literature from Earlier Times to the Late Sixteenth Century* (New York, 1993).

For the text of *The Tale of Genji*, see the translation by E. Seidensticker (New York, 1976). The most accessible edition for college students is the same author's abridged Vintage Classics edition of 1990, which captures the spirit of the original in 360 pages. Of the many works on the novel, a most stimulating presentation is I. Morris, *The World of the Shining Prince: Court Life in Ancient Japan* (New York, 1964).

For the most comprehensive introduction to Japanese art, consult P. Mason, *History of Japanese Art* (New York, 1993). Also see the concise J. Stanley-Baker, *Japanese Art* (London, 1984). For a stimulating text with magnificent illustrations, see D. Elisseeff and V. Elisseeff, *Art of Japan* (New York, 1985). See also J. E. Kidder Jr., *The Art of Japan* (London, 1985), for an insightful text accompanied by beautiful photographs.

For an informative and readable history of Korea, see Lee Ki-baik, *A New History of Korea* (Cambridge, 1984). P. H. Lee, ed., *Sourcebook of Korean Civilization*, vol. 1 (New York, 1993), is a rich collection of documents dating from the period prior to the sixteenth century.

Vietnam often receives little attention in general studies of Southeast Asia because it was part of the Chinese empire for much of the traditional period. For a detailed investigation of the origins of Vietnamese civilization, see K. W. Taylor, *The Birth of Vietnam* (Berkeley, Calif., 1983). T. Hodgkin, *Vietnam: The Revolutionary Path* (New York, 1981), provides an overall survey of Vietnamese history to modern times. See also J. Buttinger, *The Smaller Dragon: A Political History of Vietnam* (New York, 1966).

INFOTRAC COLLEGE EDITION

For additional reading, go to InfoTrac College Edition, your online research library at
http://web1.infotrac-college.com

Enter the search terms "Asia history" using Keywords.

Enter the search terms "Japan history" using Keywords.

Enter the search term "Shinto" using Keywords.

Enter the search terms "Korea history" using Keywords.

Enter the search terms "Zen Buddhism" using Keywords.

JAPANESE WRITINGS

1

......

An Introduction to Haiku

By Professor Ed Frame

Haiku is a Japanese form of writing that came from the 16th century. It is an extremely compressed form of composition and traditionally consists of seventeen syllables measuring 5-7-5 in three lines. The haiku poet attempts to give the reader an emotional insight into the subject matter. The images he or she presents are brief and an attempt is made to do so in a way that lets the reader 'see the image.' The reader of Haiku should use his or her bodily senses rather than intellect in attempting to appreciate the poem. In other words, the Haiku poet wishes to evoke mood and emotion, which can best be appreciated through intuitive thinking rather than logical thinking.

Two of the greatest Japanese writers of this form are Matsuo Basho (1644-1649) and Kobayashi Issa (1763-1827). Zen Buddhism and Chinese Taoism had a profound effect on almost all the writers and the best haiku seem to all reflect these influences. The poets are normally referred to by the last names in this tradition.

Basho was a writer of poetry in his early twenties and by his thirties was recognized as one of the best writers in Japan. At this point he also became a professional teacher of poetry writing. He then began to travel a lot and many of his Haiku relate to his experiences traveling. His ideas of nonattachment were essential to his writings.

Issa (his name means "a cup of tea") was, and still is, a much loved poet of the Japanese. He was a devote Buddhist and was born into the middle class. By the age of 25 he was publishing Haiku and then started his journeys, just like Basho. The experiences of life provided him with ample materials and subject matter for his poems.

I have composed the following Haiku using the very traditional 5-7-5 formula. These are based on my living and traveling in South East Asia for a period of years as a member of the Peace Corps and later as a teacher at a university in Malaysia.

Impressions of South East Asia

By Edward M. Frame

Calm Tropical Nights:
Even the stars and the sea
Sigh to each other.

The placid Sea shines;
Luminance from the ship's wake,
My heart is content.

Tropical forests;
Below the low morning clouds
Trees shine in the mist.

Houses raised on stilts:
Naked children run below,
Contentment abounds.

Tropical rainstorms:
Frogs jumping, lightning flashing,
Tonight I can't sleep.

Beyond the rice fields
Appears a clear Mountain peak,
It must be morning.

Orchids bloom, birds' sing,
Beneath the jungle awning,
The sun never shines.

At the Poring springs;
Birdwing butterflies floating,
Warm wine flows, time slows.

Islands in the sun;
White sand, warm breezes, cool drink,
I must be dreaming.

The summit above;
Just one step more says my mind.
No! Roars my body.

Alone in silence;
The mountain speaks of oneness,
Those that hear are rare.

A small bamboo cage;
Freedom! Freedom! Sing the birds,
It must be springtime.

Friends of adventure,
Danger and peril abide.
Take all or take none.

Longing to be one,
Lover's hearts play a game of
'You make the first move.'

2

......

JAPAN 1500-1750

BASHO (B. 1644): HAIKU

It is impossible to convey in translation the complexity and subtlety of Japanese haiku (consisting of seventeen syllables divided into two phrases followed by a third which makes a subtle connection between the first two), with its complex word-play, allusions to other poems both Japanese and Chinese, and the fact that what is left unsaid must often be inferred from a wide background knowledge of other works. However, Basho, the most famous of all writers of haiku, strove radically to simplify the haiku, striving for the utmost in understatement. His love of simplicity has been seen as reflecting the influence of Zen Buddhism. His love of nature is reflected even in his name; born Iga-ueno, he was renamed "Basho" after the banana tree he kept in his yard, and about which he wrote several poems. The influence of haiku on modern Western poetry would be difficult to overstate. Many poets, including especially the early 20th-Century writers known as "Imagists," have been drawn to its esthetic. The African American novelist Richard Wright devoted the last part of his career to writing thousands of haiku. All haiku are translated by Lucien Stryk.

On a bare branch
A crow is perched—
Autumn evening.

The fragrant orchid:
Into a butterfly's wings
It breathes the incense.

The sea darkens
And a wild duck's call
Is faintly white.

Quietly, quietly,
Yellow mountain roses fall—
Sound of the rapids.

Above a wintry garden
The moon thins to a thread:
Insects singing.

After the chimes fade
Cherry fragrance continues:
Evening dusk.

A monk sipping
His morning tea, and it is quiet—
Chrysanthemum flowers.

3
......

JAPAN 1750–1900

KAIBARA EKKEN OR KAIBARA TOKEN:
GREATER LEARNING FOR WOMEN (1762)

This treatise on proper roles for women was widely influential in the later Edo Period (1600–1868), and denounced as retrograde during the progressive period that followed the Meiji Restoration of 1868. It is commonly attributed to the Confucian scholar Kaibara Ekken (1630–1714), based on its similarities to one of his works; but it has also been suggested that it may be an adaptation of his ideas by his wife, Kaibara Token (1652-1713), also a scholar.

What qualities are considered undesirable in women in this passage?

Seeing that it is a girl's destiny, on reaching womanhood, to go to a new home, and live in submission to her father-in-law and mother-in-law, it is even more incumbent upon her than it is on a boy to receive with all reverence her parents' instructions. Should her parents, through excess of tenderness, allow her to grow up self-willed, she will infallibly show herself capricious in her husband's house, and thus alienate his affection, while, if her father-in-law be a man of correct principles, the girl will find the yoke of these principles intolerable. . . .

More precious in a woman is a virtuous heart than a face of beauty. The vicious woman's heart is ever excited; she glares wildly around her, she vents her anger on others, her words are harsh and her accent vulgar. When she speaks it is to set herself above others, to upbraid others, to envy others, to be puffed up with individual pride, to jeer at others, to outdo others,—all things at variance with the "way" in which a woman should walk. The only qualities that befit a woman are gentle obedience, chastity, mercy, and quietness.

From her earliest youth, a girl should observe the line of demarcation separating women from men; and never, even for an instant, should she be allowed to see or hear the slightest impropriety. The customs of antiquity did not allow men and women to sit in the same apartment, to keep their wearing-apparel in the same place, to bathe in the same place or to transmit to each other anything directly from hand to hand. . . .

Let her never even dream of jealousy. If her husband be dissolute, she must expostulate with him, but never either nurse or vent her anger. If her jealousy be extreme, it will render her countenance frightful and her accents repulsive, and can only result in completely alienating her husband from her, and making her intolerable in his eyes. Should her husband act ill[1] and unreasonably, she must compose her countenance and soften her voice to remonstrate with him; and if he be angry and listen not to the remonstrance, she must wait over a season, and then expostulate with him again when his heart is softened. Never set thyself up against thy husband with harsh features and a boisterous voice! . . .

---

1 Badly.

The five worst maladies that afflict the female mind are: indocility,[2] discontent, slander, jealousy, and silliness. Without any doubt, these five maladies infest seven or eight out of every ten women, and it is from these that arises the inferiority of women to men. A woman should cure them by self-inspection and self-reproach. The worst of them all, and the parent of the other four, is silliness.

---

2 Lacking submissiveness.

4
......

KATSU KOKICHI: MUSUI'S STORY

THE AUTOBIOGRAPHY OF A TOKUGAWA SAMURAI (1844)

Katsu Kokichi was born into the Samurai class, but began life in extreme poverty and experienced many ups and downs in fortune during a tumultuous career marked by his short temper and sometimes unscrupulous schemes for making money. His autobiography unabashedly and entertainingly recounts the catastrophes he encountered as well as the triumphs. The first part of the following passage is a good example of his candor in revealing his own shortcomings. Suicide was often used as a threat of last resort, since it was a great disgrace to have caused someone else to commit suicide. Katsu prided himself on his swordsmanship, even conducting a school for samurai at one point. The wild and violent impoverished samurai plays much the same role in the lore of japan as the lawless western gunfighter does in U.S. culture; and Katsu embodies that figure well.

How is Katsu convinced that he should devote himself his wife rather than to the woman he has become infatuated with?

It was when I was still living on Yamaguchi's property. I became hopelessly smitten with a certain woman. In desperation I told my wife about it.

"Leave everything to me," she said. "I'll get her for you."

"Oh, would you—"

"But first you must give me some time off."

"What ever for?"

"I intend to go to the woman's house and persuade her family one way or another to give her to you. You say they're samurai, too, so they could very well try to put me off. Don't worry, I'll get her for you even if I have to kill myself."

I handed my wife a dagger.

She said, "I'll go tonight and bring her back without fail."

I took off for the day looking for something to do and ran into Tonomura Nanpei. As we stood chatting, he said to me, "Katsu-san, I'll bet you're prone to woman trouble—I can tell by the features on your face. Can you think of any particular problem of that nature?"

I told him about the conversation I'd had with my wife earlier on.

"How very commendable of her," he said and went on his way.

I decided to drop by to see my friend Sekikawa Sanuki, a fortune teller. He took one look at me and said, "Something dreadful's about to happen. Come in and we'll talk about it." Inside, Sanuki went on to say that he could see right away that I was having woman trouble. "And this very night I foresee trouble over a sword. A lot of people may be hurt. Tell me, can you think of anything along these lines?" I told him about my infatuation with a woman and my wife's determination to get her for me. He was speechless at first but then started to give me counsel, saying how fortunate I was to have such a devoted wife and how I should take better care of her in the future. I thought about it for a moment. He was right. I was clearly in the wrong. I flew home.

My wife was just about to leave—she had sent her grandmother with our baby daughter to Hikoshiro's in Kamezawa-cho and had finished writing me a note. It took a lot of talking to convince her to give up the idea, but the incident ended without mishap. It wasn't the first time she got me out of trouble.

Woman's nature is passive. This passiveness, being of the nature of the night, is dark. Hence, as viewed from the standard of man's nature, the foolishness of woman fails to understand the duties that lie before her very eyes, perceives not the actions that will bring down blame upon her own head, and comprehends not even the things that will bring down calamities on the heads of her husband and children. Neither when she blames and accuses and curses innocent persons, nor when, in her jealousy of others, she thinks to set up herself alone, does she see that she is her own enemy. . . . Again, in the education of her children, her blind affection induces an erroneous system. Such is the stupidity of her character that it is incumbent on her, in every particular, to distrust herself and to obey her husband.

Translated by Basil Hall Chamberlain

5
......

Japanese Creation Myth (712 CE)

From Genji Shibukawa: *Tales from the Kojiki*

The following is a modern retelling of the creation story from the Kojiki, Japan's oldest chronicle, compiled in 712 CE by O No Yasumaro. The quest for Izanami in the underworld is reminiscent of the Greek demigod Orpheus' quest in Hades for his wife, Eurydice, and even more of the Sumerian myth of the descent of Innana to the underworld.

How does this story reflect the sense of its creators that Japan is the most important place in the world? Choose another creation story in this volume and compare it with this one.

The Beginning of the World

Before the heavens and the earth came into existence, all was a chaos, unimaginably limitless and without definite shape or form. Eon followed eon: then, lo! out of this boundless, shapeless mass something light and transparent rose up and formed the heaven. This was the Plain of High Heaven, in which materialized a deity called Ame-no-Minaka-Nushino-Mikoto (the Deity-of-the-August-Center-of-Heaven). Next the heavens gave birth to a deity named Takami-Musubi-no-Mikoto (the High-August-Producing-Wondrous-Deity), followed by a third called Kammi-Musubi-no-Mikoto (the Divine-Producing-Wondrous-Deity). These three divine beings are called the Three Creating Deities.

In the meantime what was heavy and opaque in the void gradually precipitated and became the earth, but it had taken an immeasurably long time before it condensed sufficiently to form solid ground. In its earliest stages, for millions and millions of years, the earth may be said to have resembled oil floating, medusa-like, upon the face of the waters. Suddenly like the sprouting up of a reed, a pair of immortals were born from its bosom. . . .

Many gods were thus born in succession, and so they increased in number, but as long as the world remained in a chaotic state, there was nothing for them to do. Whereupon, all the heavenly deities summoned the two divine beings, Izanagi and Izanami, and bade them descend to the nebulous place, and by helping each other, to consolidate it into terra firma. "We bestow on you," they said, "this precious treasure, with which to rule the land, the creation of which we command you to perform." So saying they handed them a spear called Ama-no-Nuboko, embellished with costly gems. The divine couple received respectfully and ceremoniously the sacred weapon and then withdrew from the presence of the Deities, ready to perform their august commission. Proceeding forthwith to the Floating Bridge of Heaven, which lay between the heaven and the earth, they stood awhile to gaze on that which lay below. What they beheld was a world not yet condensed, but looking like a sea of filmy fog, floating to and fro in the air, exhaling the while an inexpressibly fragrant odor. They were, at first, perplexed just how and where to start, but at length Izanagi suggested to his companion that they should try the effect of stirring up the brine with their spear. So saying he pushed down the jeweled shaft and found that it touched something. Then drawing it up, he examined it and observed that the great drops which fell from it almost immediately coagulated into an island, which is, to this day, the Island of Onokoro. Delighted at the result, the two deities descended forthwith from the Floating Bridge to reach the miraculously created island. In this island they thenceforth dwelt and made it the basis of their subsequent task of creating a country. Then wishing to become espoused, they erected in the center of the island a pillar, the Heavenly August Pillar, and built around it a great palace called the Hall of Eight Fathoms. Thereupon the male Deity turning to the left and the female Deity to the right, each went round the pillar in opposite directions. When they again met each other on the further side of the pillar, Izanami, the female Deity, speaking first, exclaimed: "How delightful it is to meet so hand some a youth!" To which Izanagi, the male Deity, replied: "How delighted I am to have fallen in with such a lovely maiden!" After having, spoken thus, the male Deity said that it was not in order that woman should anticipate man in a greeting. Nevertheless, they fell into connubial relationship, having been instructed by two wagtails which flew to the spot. Presently the Goddess bore her divine consort a son, but the baby was weak and boneless as a leech. Disgusted with it, they abandoned it on the waters, putting it in a boat made of reeds. Their second offspring was as disappointing as the first. The two Deities, now sorely disappointed at their failure and full of misgivings, ascended to Heaven to inquire of the Heavenly Deities the causes of their misfortunes. The latter performed the ceremony of divining and said to them: "It is the woman's fault. In turning round the Pillar, it was not right and proper that the female Deity should in speaking have taken precedence of the male. That is the reason." The two Deities saw the truth of this divine suggestion, and made up their minds to rectify the error. So, returning to the earth again, they went once more around the Heavenly Pillar. This time Izanagi spoke first saying: "How delightful to meet so beautiful a maiden!" "How happy I am," responded Izanami, "that I should meet such a handsome youth!" This process was more appropriate and in accordance with the law of nature. After this, all the children born to them left nothing to be desired. First, the island of Awaji was born, next, Shikoku, then, the island of Oki, followed by Kyushu; after that, the island Tsushima came into being, and lastly, Honshu, the main island of Japan. The name of Oyashi-ma-kuni (the Country of the Eight Great Islands) was given to these eight islands. After this, the two Deities became the parents of numerous, smaller islands destined to surround the larger ones.

THE BIRTH OF THE DEITIES

Having, thus, made a country from what had formerly been no more than a mere floating mass, the two Deities, Izanagi and Izanami, set about begetting those deities destined to preside over the land, sea, mountains, rivers, trees, and herbs. Their first-born proved to be the sea-god, Owatsumi-no-Kami. Next they gave birth to the patron gods of harbors, the male deity Kamihaya-akitsu-hiko having control of the land and the goddess Hay-aakitsu-hime having control of the sea. These two latter deities subsequently gave birth to eight other gods.

Next Izanagi and Izanami gave birth to the wind-deity, Kami-Shinatsuhiko-no-Miko-to. At the moment of his birth, his breath was so potent that the clouds and mists, which had hung over the earth from the beginning of time, were immediately dispersed. In consequence, every corner of the world was filled with brightness. Kukunochi-no-Kami, the deity of trees, was the next to be born, followed by Oyamatsumi-no-Kami, the deity of mountains, and Kayanuhime-no-Kami, the goddess of the plains. ... .

The process of procreation had, so far, gone on happily, but at the birth of Kaguts-uchino-Kami, the deity of fire, an unseen misfortune befell the divine mother, Izanami. During the course of her confinement, the goddess was so severely burned by the flaming child that she swooned away. Her divine consort, deeply alarmed, did all in his power to resuscitate her, but although he succeeded in restoring her to consciousness, her appetite had completely gone. Izanagi, thereupon and with the utmost loving care, prepared for her delectation various tasty dishes, but all to no avail, because whatever she swallowed was almost immediately rejected. It was in this wise that occurred the greatest miracle of all. From her mouth sprang Kanayama-biko and Kanayama-hime, respectively the god and goddess of metals, whilst from other parts of her body issued forth Haniyasu-hiko and Haniyasu-hime, respectively the god and goddess of earth. Before making her "divine retirement," which marks the end of her earthly career, in a manner almost unspeakably miraculous she gave birth to her last-born, the goddess Mizuhame-no-Mikoto. Her demise marks the intrusion of death into the world. Similarly the corruption of her body and the grief occasioned by her death were each the first of their kind.

By the death of his faithful spouse Izanagi, was now quite alone in the world. In tionr with her, and in accordance with the instructions of the Heavenly Gods, he had

created and consolidated the Island. Empire of Japan. In the fulfillment of their divine mission, he and his heavenly spouse had lived an ideal life of mutual love and cooperation. It is only natural, therefore, that her death should have dealt him a truly mortal blow.

He threw himself upon her prostrate form, crying: "Oh, my dearest wife, why art thou gone, to leave me thus alone? How could I ever exchange thee for even one child? Come back for the sake of the world, in which there still remains so much for both us twain to do." In a fit of uncontrollable grief, he stood sobbing at the head of the bier. His hot tears fell like hailstones, and lo! out of the tear-drops was born a beauteous babe, the goddess Nakisawame-no-Mikoto. In, deep astonishment he stayed his tears, and gazed in wonder at the new-born child, but soon his tears returned only to fall faster than before. It was thus that a sudden change came over his state of mind. With bitter wrath, his eyes fell upon the infant god of fire, whose birth had proved so fatal to his mother. He drew his sword, Totsuka-no-tsurugi, and crying in his wrath, "Thou hateful matricide," decapitated his fiery offspring. Up shot a crimson spout of blood. Out of the sword and blood together arose eight strong and gallant deities. "What! more children?" cried Izanagi, much astounded at their sudden appearance, but the very next moment, what should he *see* but eight more deities born from the lifeless body of the infant firegod! They came out from the various parts of the body—head, breast, stomach, hands, feet, and navel—and, to add to his astonishment, all of them were glaring fiercely at him. Altogether stupefied he surveyed the new arrivals one after another.

Meanwhile Izanami, for whom her divine husband pined so bitterly, had quitted, this world, for good and all and gone to the Land of Hades.

Izanagi's Visit to the Land of Hades

As for the Deity Izanagi, who had now become a widower, the presence of so many offspring might have, to some, extent, beguiled and solaced him, and yet when he remembered how faithful his departed spouse had been to him, he would yearn for her again, his heart swollen with, sorrow and his eyes filled with tears. In this mood, sitting up alone at midnight, he would call her name aloud again and again, regardless of the fact that he could hope for no response. His own piteous cries merely echoed back from the walls of his chamber.

Unable any longer to bear his grief, he resolved to go down to the Nether Regions in order to seek for Izanami and bring her back, at all costs, to the world. He started on his long and dubious journey. Many millions of miles separated the earth from the Lower Regions and there were countless steep and dangerous places to be negotiated, but Izanagi's indomitable determination to recover his wife enabled him finally to overcome all these difficulties. At length he succeeded in arriving at his destination. Far ahead of him, he espied a large castle. "That, no doubt," he mused in delight, "may be where she resides."

Summoning up all his courage, he approached the main entrance of the castle. Here he saw a number of gigantic demons, some red, some black, guarding the gates with watchful eyes. He retraced his steps in alarm, and stole round to a gate at the rear of the castle. He found, to his great joy, that it was apparently left unwatched. He crept warily through the gate and peered into the interior of the castle, when he immediately caught sight of his wife standing at the gate at an inner court. The delighted Deity loudly called her name. "Why! There is some one calling me," sighed Izanami-no-Mikoto, and raising her beautiful head, she looked around her. What was her amazement but to see her beloved husband standing by the gate and gazing at her intently! He had, in fact, been in her thoughts no less constantly than she in his. With a heart leaping with joy, she approached him. He grasped her hands tenderly and murmured in deep and earnest tones: "My darling, .I have come to take thee back to the world. Come back, I pray thee, and let us complete our work of creation in accordance with the will of the Heavenly Gods—our work which was left only half accomplished by thy departure. How can I do this work without thee? Thy loss means to me the loss of all." This appeal came from the depth of his heart. The goddess sympathized with him most deeply, but answered with tender grief: "Alas! Thou hast come too late. I have already eaten of the furnace of Hades. Having once eaten the things of this land, it is impossible for me to come back to the world." So saying, she lowered her head in deep despair.

"Nay, I must entreat thee to come back. Canst not thou find some means by which this can be accomplished?" exclaimed her husband, drawing nearer for hen After some reflection, she replied: "Thou hast come a very, very long way for my sake. How much I appreciate thy devotion! I wish, with all my heart, to go back with thee, but before I can do so, I must first obtain the permission of the deities of Hades. Wait here till my return, but remember that thou must not on any account look inside the castle in the meantime." " I swear I will do as thou biddest," quoth Izanagi, "but tarry not in thy quest." With implicit confidence in her husband's pledge, the goddess disappeared into the castle.

Izanagi observed strictly her injunction. He remained where he stood, and waited impatiently for his wife's return. Probably, to his impatient mind, a single heart-beat may have seemed an age. He waited and waited, but no shadow of his wife appeared. The day gradually wore on and waned away, darkness was about to fall, and a strange unearthly wind began to strike his face. Brave as he was, he was seized with an uncanny feeling of apprehension. Forgetting the vow he had made to the goddess, he broke off one of the teeth of the comb which he was wearing in the left bunch of his hair, and having lighted it, he crept in softly and glanced around him. To his horror he found Izanagi lying dead in a room: and lo! a ghastly change had come over her. She, who had been so dazzlingly beautiful, was now become naught but a rotting corpse, in an advanced stage of decomposition. Now, an even more horrible sight met his gaze; the Fire Thunder dwelt in her head, the Black Thunder in her belly, the Rending-Thunder in her abdomen, the Young Thunder in her left hand, the Earth-Thunder in her right hand, the Rumbling-Thunder in her left foot, and the Couchant Thunder in her right foot:—altogether eight Thunder-Deities had been born and were dwelling there, attached to her remains and belching forth flames from their mouths. Izanagi-no-Mikoto was so thoroughly alarmed at the sight, that he dropped the light and took to his heels. The sound he made awakened Izanami from her death-like slumber. "Forsooth!" she cried: "he must have seen me in this revolting state. He has put me to shame and has broken his solemn vow. Unfaithful wretch! I'll make him suffer, for his perfidy."

Then turning to the Hags of Hades, who attended her, she commanded them to give chase to him. At her word, an army of female demons ran after the Deity.

Translated by Yaichiro Isobe

VIETNAMESE LITERATURE

1
......

THE TALE OF KIEU[1]

NGUYEN DU

The country of Vietnam was ruled by China for some nine hundred years, gaining its independence in 939. During this period, Chinese influence in the region was sufficient to draw Vietnam permanently into the tradition of classical Chinese civilization. Much as British and Americans find their aesthetic models and intellectual roots in the classical world of Greco-Roman civilization, so the Vietnamese regard the traditions of Han China as their cultural heritage. Even after gaining independence, the proximity of its powerful northern neighbor ensured that Chinese institutions and attitudes would continue to exert a great influence on Vietnamese development. The Le dynasty gained control in 1427 and, from their base of power in the North, maintained their rule until 1788. The Le rulers quickly became tributaries of the Chinese emperors and were guaranteed protection by them from both external and internal threats. It is not surprising, therefore, to observe that the political administration of eighteenth-century Vietnam was in many ways an imitation of that of the Ch'ing dynasty of China (1644-1911). The administration of the country was entrusted to men who had proven their worth by mastering Confucian philosophy and the Chinese literary classics. Vietnam did not possess sufficient resources to support as complete a system as Ch'ing China, but its administrators rivalled those of China in their adherence to the scholarly tradition and loyalty to the ruling dynasty.

Nguyen Du (1765-1820) was born to a Northern family that had produced generations of scholar-administrators, and he was trained to follow that career. It was his misfortune, however, to be born during the waning years of the Le dynasty. In 1771, the popular uprising known as the Tay-son revolution broke out in the southern part of the country. Under the leadership of the charismatic Nguyen Hue and espousing ideals of social justice, the movement swept over Vietnam. The Chinese sent a large army in 1788 to defend the interests of the Le ruler, but were decisively defeated, and the Le dynasty was overthrown. No sooner had Nguyen Du and his fellow scholar-officials adapted to the necessity of transferring their loyalty to a new monarch than the Tay-son movement was defeated. The victorious Nguyen emperor Gia-long (1802–1820) established a new capital, Hue, in central Vietnam, and the scholar-officials faced the task of transferring their loyalty once again. The task was made harder because the new dynasty was from the South and was for this reason held in some contempt by the Northerners.

Nguyen Da served the Nguyen emperor for the rest of his life in a series of minor posts and poorly-endowed sinecures. He continued to cultivate the Chinese classics and wrote a verse novel entitled *The Tale of Kieu* (Kim Van Kieu Tan Truyen). The novel was

---

1   From Nguyen Du, *The Tale of Kieu*, trans. Huynh Sanh Thong (bilingual edition: New Haven, CF: Yale University Press, 1987), pp. 141, 143, 145, 147, 149, 151, 153, 155, 157, 159, 161, 163, 165, and 167.

circulated among his friends and published only shortly after his death. It was immediately recognized as the greatest work of Vietnamese literature ever produced and has continued to be so regarded.

As is only to be expected from a scholar steeped in the Chinese classics, the work is based on a Chinese model, a novel of the Ming dynasty (13681644), and is rich with literary allusions. It is not a pedantic work, however, but a very human tale that raises basic moral issues of universal significance. The tangled plot revolves around a beautiful, talented, and virtuous girl named Thuy Kieu. Kieu and Kim Trong, a young scholar, fall in love at first sight, but he is called away by the death of his father. Kieu finds her family arrested on some vague charge, and sells herself into prostitution to get money to save them. She is rescued from the brothel by a young man who marries her. He has another wife, however, a member of a powerful family, who has Kieu kidnapped and made a slave in her household. Kieu flees her constant humiliation and is taken up by the warrior Tu Hail. After fives years as his wife, Kieu is again forced to flee when Tu Hai is treacherously murdered. Kieu seeks refuse in a Buddhist convent. In the excerpt presented here, the action shifts to Kieu's first love, Kim. He returns to her home to find her gone and is persuaded to marry her sister, but cannot forget Kieu. He achieves the highest grade in the imperial civil service examinations and enters the imperial service. As time passes, he hears of Kieu's continuing misfortunes and degradations. Finally, by accident, he and Kieu's family discover Kieu in her convent. Kim marries her, thus restoring her honor, but Kieu cannot make love to him. Because of her past, she says, she would feel only shame. He replies that true lovers need not share a bed. As friends and companions, they contrive to make a full and prosperous life based on mutual respect and the deepest friendship.

The key concepts in the story are personal degradation and undeserved punishment. Kieu has done nothing to deserve what happens to her, and her only sin is to submit to what she cannot avoid. Those about her use her body, but she retains control of her inner self. She will not give Kim her body, because this has been sullied, but she does share with him her untarnished spirit. This distinction between the inner and outer self is a critical one, and explains much about the character of the Vietnamese people. It is not surprising that *The Tale of Kieu* is a treasured part of their national heritage.

Questions

1. How does Kieu's family convince her to abandon the life of a Buddhist nun?
2. What objections does Kieu raise to marrying Kim? How does Kim reply to them?
3. Why does Kieu refuse to share Kim's bed?
4. What does their eventual agreement to live with separate beds disclose about their love?

THE TALE OF KIEU

As Kieu shook off the filth of all past woes, how could her erstwhile love
    know she lived here?

If Kieu had shouldered her full load of griefs, young Kim himself had suffered much the while.

For mourning rites he'd made that far-flung trip and from Liao-yang came
      back in half a year. He hurried toward his dear Kingfisher's nest and
      took one startled look—the scene had changed.

The garden was a patch of weeds and reeds.

Hushed, moon-lit windows, weather-beaten walls.

Not one lone soul—peach blossoms of last year were smiling, flirting yet
      with their east wind. [2]

Swallows were rustling through the vacant house.

Grass clad the ground, moss hid all marks of shoes.

At the wall's end, a clump of thorns and briers: this pathway both had
      walked a year ago.

A silent chill was brooding over all—who could relieve the anguish of his
      heart? A neighbor happened by—approaching him,

Kim asked some questions he discreetly phrased.

Old Vuong? He'd somehow tangled with the law.

And Kieu? She'd sold herself to ransom him.

The family? All had moved a long way off.

And what about young Vuong and young Thuy Van?

The two had fallen on hard days of need:

he scribed, she sewed—both lived from hand to mouth. It was a firebolt
      striking from mid-sky:

Kim heard the news, was staggered by it all.

He asked and reamed where all those folks had moved—he slowly found
      his way to their new home.

A tattered hut, a roof of thatch, mud walls; reed blinds in rags, bamboo
      screens punched with holes; a rain. soaked yard where nothing grew
      but weeds: the sight distressed and shocked him all the more. Still,
      making bold, he called outside the wall.

Young Vuong, on hearing him, rushed out at once—he took him by the
      hand, led him inside.

From their back room the parents soon appeared. They wept and wailed as
      they retold their woes:

"Young man, you know what happened to us all?

Our daughter Kieu is cursed by evil fate: she failed her word to you, her
      solemn troth.

Disaster struck our family, forcing her to sell herself and save her father's
      life.

How torn and wrenched she was when she left home!

Grief-bowed, she told us time and time again: since she had sworn to you a
      sacred oath, she begged her sister Van to take her place and in some
      way redeem her pledge to you.

But her own sorrow will forever last.

In this existence she broke faith with you—she'll make it up to you when
      she's reborn.

---

2 The east wind blows in the spring and therefore favors love.

These were the words she said and said again: we graved them in our souls
      before she left.
O daughter Kieu, why does fate hurt you so?
Your Kim is back with us, but where are you?" The more they spoke of
      Kieu, the more they grieved—the more Kim heard them speak, the
      more he ached.
He writhed in agony, he sorely wept, his face tear-drowned and sorrow-
      crazed his mind.
It hurt him so he fainted many times and, coming to, he shed more bitter
      tears. When he saw Kim so desolate, old Vuong curbed his own grief
      and sought to comfort him:
"The plank's now nailed and fastened to the boat.[3]
Ill-starred and doomed, she can't requite your love.
Although you care so much for her you've lost, must you throw off a life as
      good as gold?" To soothe his pain, they tried a hundred ways—grief,
      smothered, flared and burned more fiercely yet.
They showed him those gold bracelets from the past and other keepsakes:
      incense, that old lute.
The sight of them rekindled his despair—it roused his sorrow, rent his
      heart again.
"Because I had to go away," he cried,
"I let the fern, the flower float downstream.
We two did take and swear our vows of troth, vows firm as bronze or stone,
      not idle words.
Though we have shared no bed, we're man and wife: how could I ever cast
      her from my heart?
Whatever it may cost in gold, in time,
I shall not quit until I see her face." He suffered more than all the words
      could say— stifling his sobs, he bade goodbye and left.
He hurried home, arranged a garden lodge, then he went back to fetch
      Kieu's parents there.
He saw to their well-being day and night like their own son, in their lost
      daughter's stead. With ink and tears he wrote away for news—
      agents he sent and missives he dispatched.
Who knows how much he spent on things, on men, and several times he
      trekked to far Lin-ch'ing.
He would search here while she was staying there.
Where should he look between the sky and sea?
He yearned and pined—he seemed to have his soul inside a kiln, his heart
      beneath a plow.
The silkworm, spinning, wasted day by day; the gaunt cicada, bit by frost,
      shrank more.

---

3 This proverb expresses resigned acceptance of an irreversible situation.

He languished, half alive, half dead—he'd weep real tears of blood, but lose his soul to dreams. His parents took alarm because they feared what, gone too far, his grief might lead him to.

In haste they readied things and chose a date: an early marriage tied young Kim and Van.

A graceful girl, a brilliant scholar wed, uniting charms and gifts in their full flush.

Though he found joy in matrimonial life, how could this happiness outweigh that grief?

They lived together—as he came to care for his new union, surged his love of old.

Whenever he remembered Kieu's ordeal, he wept and felt a tightened knot inside. At times, in his hushed study, he would light the incense burner, play the lute of yore.

Silk strings would sigh sweet moans while scentwood smoke spread fragrant wisps and breezes stirred the blinds.

[4]Examinations for the chin-shih or highest degree, the equivalent of a doctorate.

Then, from the steps beneath the roof, he'd hear a girl's faint voice—he'd glimpse what seemed a skirt.

Because he'd etched his love in stone and bronze, he'd dream of her and think she had come back.

His days and nights were steeped in dismal gloom while spring and autumn wheeled and wheeled about.

Heaven's broad gate swung open—flowers hailed them in His Majesty's park, fame reached their heaths. Young Vuong still kept in mind those days long past: he called on Chung to settle his great debt.

He paid it off in full, then took to wife Chung's daughter, thus allying their two clans. As Kim stepped briskly on amidst blue clouds,[5] he thought of Kieu and sorrowed all the more.

With whom had he exchanged those vows of troth?

With whom was he now sharing jade and gold?

Poor fern afloat down in the troughs of waves—with honors blessed, he mourned her wandering life. Then he was sent to serve in far Lin-tzu: with loved ones he trekked over hill and dale.

Now, in his yamen,[6] he lived leisured days amidst the lute's sweet sounds, the crane's soft cries.[7] On a spring night, in her peach-curtained room, asleep Van dreamed and saw her sister Kieu.

When she awoke, she told her spouse at once.

He wondered, torn between mistrust and hope:

---

4   For reamed men a contest now took place: young Vuong and Kim attained the honor roll.

5   An official career for chin shih graduates.

6   Official residence.

7   Under the Sung dynasty, Chao Pien (Trieu Bien) was an honest official with a simple way of life. When he was sent as governor to Shu (modern Szechwan) he took nothing with him but a lute and a crane.

"Lin-ch'ing, Lin-tzu—they differ by one word:[8] they may have been mis-
taken each for each.

Two sisters, kindred souls, met in a dream—perchance, we shall receive
good tidings here." Now, working in his office, he inquired.

Old Do, one of his clerks, gave this report:

"It all began more than ten years ago—

I knew them all quite well, each name, each face.

Dame Tu and Scholar Ma went to Peking—they purchased Kieu and
brought her back with them.

In looks and gifts she stood without a peer.

She played the lute and wrote both prose and verse.

She wished to save her virtue, fiercely fought, and tried to kill herself, so
they used tricks.

She had to live in mud till she turned numb, then marriage ties attached
her to young Thuc.

But his first wife laid cruel hands on her and held her in Wu-hsi to nip the
flower.

When she betook herself from there and fled, bad luck would have her fall
among the Bacs.

No sooner caught than she was sold once more: a cloud, a fern, she drifted
here and there.

She happened on a man: he beat the world in wit and grit, shook heaven by
sheer might.

Leading a hundred thousand seasoned troops, he came and stationed them
throughout Lin-tzu.

Here Kieu cleared off all scores from her sad past: she rendered good for
good or ill for ill. She proved her loyal heart, her kindly soul—she
paid all debts, won praise from near and far.

I did not get to know the hero's name—for this detail please query Scholar
Thuc." After he heard old Do's clear-drawn account,

Kim sent his card and bade Thuc visit him.

He asked his guest to settle dubious points:

"Where is Kieu's husband now? And what's his name?" Thuc answered:
"Caught in those wild times of strife,

I probed and asked some questions while at camp.

The chieftain's name was Hai, his surname Tu—he won all battles, overwhelmed all foes.

He chanced to meet her while he was in T'ai—genius and beauty wed, a
natural course.

For many years he stormed about this world: his thunder made earth quake
and heaven quail!

---

8   Kim had heard reports that Kieu was in Lin-ch'ing. He now begins to suspect that the reports were confused and
that Kieu is in Lin-tzu, where Kim is now stationed.

He garrisoned his army in the East—since then, all signs and clues of him
    are lost." Kim heard and knew the story root and branch— anguish
    and dread played havoc with his heart:
"Alas for my poor leaf, a toy of winds!
When could she ever shake the world's foul dust?
As flows the stream, the flower's swept along—
I grieve her wave-tossed life, detached from mine.
From all our broken pledges I still keep a bit of incense there, and here this
    lute.
Its soul has fled the strings—will incense there give us its fire and fragrance
    in this life?
While she's now wandering, rootless, far from home, how can I wallow in
    soft ease and wealth?"
His seal of office he'd as soon resign—then he could cross all streams and
    scale all heights, then he would venture onto fields of war and risk
    his life to look for his lost love.
But heaven showed no track, the sea no trail—where could he seek the bird
    or find the fish?
While he was pausing, waiting for some news, who knows how often cycled
    sun and rain?
Now from the throne, on rainbow-tinted sheets, arrived decrees that clearly
    ordered thus:
Kim should assume new office in Nan-ping,
Vuong was transferred to functions at Fu-yang.
In haste they purchased horse and carriage, then both families left together
    for their posts.
The news broke out: The rebels had been crushed—waves stilled, fires
    quenched in Fukien and Chekiang.
Informed, Kim thereupon requested Vuong to help him look for Kieu
    along the way.
When they both reached Hang-chow, they could obtain precise and proven
    facts about her fate.
This they were told: "One day, the fight was joined.
Tu, ambushed, fell a martyr on the field.
Kieu's signal service earned her no reward: by force they made her wed a
    tribal chief.
She drowned that body fine as jade, as pearl: the Ch'ien-t'ang river has
    become her grave." Ah, torn asunder not to meet again!
They all were thriving—she had died foul death. To rest her soul, they set
    her tablet up, installed an altar on the riverbank.
The tide cast wave on silver-crested wave: gazing, all pictured how the bird
    had dropped.[9]
Deep love, a sea of griefs—so strange a fate!

---

9 The fall of a wild goose is used as a metaphor for a quick, often heroic, death.

Where had it strayed, the bird's disconsolate soul?[10] How queerly fortune's
    wheel will turn and spin!
Giac Duyen now somehow happened by the spot.
She saw the tablet, read the written name.
She cried, astonished: "Who are you, my friends?
Are you perchance some kith or kin of hers?
But she's alive! Why all these mourning rites?" They heard the news and
    nearly fell with shock.
All mobbed her, talked away, asked this and that:
"Her husband here, her parents over there, and there her sister, brother,
    and his wife.
From truthful sources we heard of her death, but now you tell us this
    amazing news!"
    "Karma drew us together," said the nun, "first at Lin-tzu, and next by
    the Ch'ien-t'ang.
When she would drown her beauteous body there,
I stood at hand and brought her safe to shore.
She's made her home within the Bodhi gate—our grass-roofed cloister's
    not too far from here.
At Buddha's feet calm days go round and round, but her mind's eye still fas-
    tens on her home." At what was heard all faces glowed and beamed:
    could any bliss on earth exceed this joy?
The leaf had left its grove—since that dark day, they'd vainly searched all
    streams and scanned all clouds.
The rose had fallen, its sweet scent had failed: they might see her in after-
    worlds, not here.
She's gone the way of night, they dwelt with day—now, back from those
    Nine Springs,[11] she walked on earth! All knelt and bowed their
    thanks to old Giac Duyen, then in a group they followed on her
    heels.
They cut and cleared their way through reed and rush, their loving hearts
    half doubting yet her word.
By twists and turns they edged along the shore, pushed past that jungle,
    reached the Buddha's shrine.
In a loud voice, the nun Giac Duyen called Kieu, and from an inner room
    she hurried out. She glanced and saw her folks—they all were here:
    Father looked still quite strong, and Mother spry; both sister Van
    and brother Quan grown up; and over there was Kim, her love of
    yore.
Could she believe this moment, what it seemed?
Was she now dreaming open-eyed, awake?

---

10 According to Chinese mythology, after the daughter of Emperor Yen drowned at sea, her unhappy soul fumed into
a little bird that has tried ever since to fill up the deep with twigs and pebbles.

11 The nether world or the world of the dead.

Tear-pearls dropped one by one and damped her smock— she felt such
       joy and grief, such grief and joy. She cast herself upon her mother's
       knees and, weeping, told of all she had endured:
"Since I set out to wander through strange lands, a wave-tossed fern, some
       fifteen years have passed.
I sought to end it in the river's mud—who could have hoped to see you all
       on earth?" The parents held her hands, admired her face: that face
       had not much changed since she left home.
The moon, the flower, lashed by wind and rain for all that time, had lost
       some of its glow.
What scale could ever weigh their happiness?
Present and past, so much they talked about!
The two young ones kept asking this or that while Kim looked on, his sor-
       row fumed to joy.
Before the Buddha's altar all knelt down and for Kieu's resurrection of-
       fered thanks. At once they ordered sedans decked with flowers— old
       Vuong bade Kieu be carried home with them.
"I'm nothing but a fallen flower," she said.
"I drank of gall and wormwood half my life.
I thought to die on waves beneath the clouds—how could my heart nurse
       hopes to see this day?
Yet I've survived and met you all again, and slaked the thirst that long has
       parched my soul.
This cloister's now my refuge in the wilds—to live with grass and trees
       befits my age.
I'm used to salt and greens in Dhyana fare;
I've grown to love the drab of Dhyana garb.
Within my heart the fire of lust is quenched—why should I roll again in
       worldly dust?
What good is that, a purpose half achieved?
To nunhood vowed, I'll stay here till the end.
I owe to her who saved me sea-deep debts—how can I cut my bonds with
       her and leave?" Old Vuong exclaimed: "Other times, other tides!"[12]
Even a saint must bow to circumstance.
You worship gods and Buddhas—who'll discharge a daughter's duties, keep
       a lover's vows?
High Heaven saved your life—we'll build a shrine and have our Reverend
       come, live there near us."
Heeding her father's word, Kieu had to yield: she took her leave of cloister
       and old nun. The group resumed to Kim's own yamen where, for
       their reunion, they all held a feast.
After mum wine instilled a mellow mood,
Van rose and begged to air a thought or two;

---

12 Now is now, and then was then.

"It's Heaven's own design that lovers meet, so Kim and Kieu did meet and
    swear their troth.
Then, over peaceful earth wild billows swept, and in my sister's place I wed-
    ded him.
Amber and mustard seed, lodestone and pin!¹³
Besides, 'when blood is spilt, the gut turns soft.'¹⁴
Day after day, we hoped and prayed for Kieu with so much love and grief
    these fifteen years.
But now the mirror cracked is whole again.
Wise Heaven's put her back where she belongs.
She still loves him and, luckily, still has him—still shines the same old
    moon both once swore by.
The tree still bears some three or seven plums,¹⁵ the peach stays fresh¹⁶—
    it's time to tie the knot!" Kieu brushed her sister's speech aside and
    said:
"Why now retell a tale of long ago?
We once did pledge our troth, but since those days, my life has been ex-
    posed to wind and rain.
I'd die of shame discussing what's now past—let those things flow down-
    stream and out to sea!" "A curious way to put it!" Kim cut in.
"Whatever you may feel, your oath remains.
A vow of troth is witnessed by the world, by earth below and heaven far
    above.
Though things may change and stars may shift their course, sworn pledges
    must be kept in life or death.
Does fate, which brought you back, oppose our love?
Predestined, people are drawn together in love and marriage just as a
    mustard seed is attracted by amber and an iron pin or needle by
    lodestone.
We two are one—why split us in two halves?" "A home where love and con-
    cord reign" Kieu said, "whose heart won't yearn for it? But I believe
    that to her man a bride should bring the scent of a close bud, the
    shape of a full moon.
It's priceless, chastity—by nuptial torch, am I to blush for what I'll offer
    you?
Misfortune struck me—since that day the flower fell prey to bees and but-
    terflies, ate shame.
For so long lashed by rain and swept by wind, a flower's bound to fade, a
    moon to wane.

---

13 Predestined, people are drawn together in love and marriage just as a mustard seed is attracted by amber and an
iron pin or needle by lodestone.

14 A proverb about family solidarity: When a relative gets hurt, the other members of the family cannot remain un-
concerned about his or her troubles.

15 Van implies that Kieu is not yet too old for marriage by alluding to a courtship song.

16 The young, fresh peach tree is the image of a beautiful bride according to a wedding song.

My cheeks were once two roses—what's now left?

My life is done—how can it be remade?

How dare I, boldfaced, soil with worldly filth the homespun costume of a
  virtuous wife?[17]

You bear a constant love for me, I know—but where to hide my shame by
  bridal light?

From this day on I'll shut my chamber door: though I will take no vows, I'll
  live a nun.

If you still care for what we both once felt, let's turn it into friendship—let's
  be friends.

Why speak of marriage with its red silk thread?[18]

It pains my heart and further stains my life.""How skilled you are in spinning words!" Kim said.

"You have your reasons—others have their own.

Among those duties falling to her lot, a woman's chastity means many
  things.

For there are times of ease and times of stress: in crisis, must one rigid rule
  apply?

True daughter, you upheld a woman's role: what dust or dirt could ever
  sully you?

Heaven grants us this hour: now from our gate all mists have cleared; on
  high, clouds roll away.

The faded flower's blooming forth afresh, the waning moon shines more
  than at its full.

What is there left to doubt? Why treat me like another Hsiao, a passerby
  ignored?"[19] He argued, pleaded, begged—she heard him through.

Her parents also settled on his plans.

Outtalked, she could no longer disagree: she hung her head and yielded,
  stifling sighs. They held a wedding-feast—bright candles lit all flowers, set aglow the red silk rug.

Before their elders groom and bride bowed low—all rites observed, they
  now were man and wife. In their own room they traded toasts, still
  shy of their new bond, yet moved by their old love.

Since he, a lotus sprout,[20] first met with her, a fresh peach bud, fifteen full
  years had fled.

To fall in love, to part, to reunite—both felt mixed grief and joy as rose the
  moon. The hour was late—the curtain dropped its fringe: under the
  light gleamed her peach-blossom cheeks.

---

17 The phrase "a skirt of coarse cloth and a thorn for a hairpin" stands for virtuous wifehood according to Confucian
ethics.

18 A crimson or red silk thread spun by the Marriage God bound a man and a woman together in wedlock.

19 Under the T'ang dynasty, young Hsiao had a beautiful wife named Lu-chu. She was abducted and offered as a
concubine to the powerful general Kuo Tzu i. After that time, she no longer recognized her former husband and looked
away when she saw him in the street.

20 The lotus is long associated with love.

Two lovers met again—out of the past, a bee, a flower constant in their
      love. "I've made my peace with my own fate," she said.
"What can this cast-off body be good for?
I thought of your devotion to our past—to please you, I went through
      those wedding rites.
But how ashamed I felt in my own heart, lending a brazen front to all that
      show!
Don't go beyond the outward marks of love—perhaps, I might then look
      you in the face.
But if you want to get what they all want, glean scent from dirt, or pluck a
      wilting flower, then we'll flaunt filth, put on a foul display, and only
      hate, not love, will then remain.
When you make love and I feel only shame, then rank betrayal's better than
      such love.
If you must give your clan a rightful heir, you have my sister—there's no
      need for me.
What little chastity I may have saved, am I to fling it under trampling feet?
More tender feelings pour from both our hearts—why toy and crumple up
      a faded flower?" "An oath bound us together," he replied.
"We split, like fish to sea and bird to sky.
Through your long exile how I grieved for you!
Breaking your troth, you must have suffered so.
We loved each other, risked our lives, braved death—now we two meet
      again, still deep in love.
The willow in mid-spring still has green leaves—I thought you still at-
      tached to human love.
But no more dust stains your clear mirror now: your vow can't but increase
      my high regard.
If I long searched the sea for my lost pin,[21] it was true love, not lust, that
      urged me on.
We're back together now, beneath one roof: to live in concord, need two
      share one bed?" Kieu pinned her hair and straightened up her gown,
      then knelt to touch her head in gratitude:
"If ever my soiled body's cleansed of stains,
I'll thank a gentleman, a noble soul.
The words you spoke came from a kindred heart: no truer empathy be-
      tween two souls.
A home, a refuge—what won't you give me?
My honor lives again as of tonight." Their hands unclasped, then clasped
      and clasped again—now he esteemed her, loved her all the more.
They lit another candle up, refilled the incense urn, then drank to their new
      joy.
His old desire for her came flooding back—he softly asked about her luting
      skill.

---

21 "To grope for a pin on the bottom of the sea" is the Vietnamese equivalent of "to look for a needle in a haystack."

"Those strings of silk entangled me," she said, "in sundry woes which haven't
    ceased till now.

Alas, what's done regrets cannot undo—but I'll obey your wish just one
    more time." Her elfin fingers danced and swept the strings—sweet
    strains made waves with curls of scentwood smoke.

Who sang this hymn to life and peace on earth?

Was it a butterfly or Master Chuang?[22]

And who poured forth this rhapsody of love?

The king of Shu or just a cuckoo-bird?[23]

Clear notes like pearls dropped in a moon-lit bay.

Warm notes like crystals of new Lan-t'ien jade.[24] His ears drank in all five
    tones of the scale—all sounds which stirred his heart and thrilled his
    soul.

"Whose hand is playing that old tune?" he asked.

"What sounded once so sad now sounds so gay!

It's from within that joy or sorrow comes—have bitter days now set and
    sweet ones dawned?"

"This pleasant little pastime," answered she, "once earned me grief and woe
    for many years.

For you my lute just sang its one last song—henceforth, I'll roll its strings
    and play no more." The secrets of their hearts were flowing still when
    cocks crowed up the morning in the east.

Kim spoke, told all about their private pact.

All marveled at her wish and lauded her—a woman of high mind, not some
    coquette who'd with her favors skip from man to man. Of love and
    friendship they fulfilled both claims— they shared no bed but joys of
    lute and verse.

Now they sipped wine, now played a game of chess, admiring flowers, wait-
    ing for the moon.

Their wishes all came true since fate so willed, and of two lovers marriage
    made two friends. As pledged, they built a temple on the hill, then
    sent a trusted man to fetch the nun.

When he got there, he found the doors shut and barred— he saw a weed-
    grown rooftop, moss-filled cracks.

She'd gone to gather simples,[25] he was told:

---

22 A well-known passage in the Chuang-tzu, a Taoist classic, reads: "Chuang Chou once dreamed that he was a butterfly, fluttering to and fro and enjoying itself. Suddenly he woke up and was Chuang Chou again. But he did not know
whether he was Chuang Chou who had dreamed that he was a butterfly, or whether he was a butterfly dreaming that
it was Chuang Chou."

23 Emperor Wang ruled Shu (in modern Szechwan) as an exemplary sovereign until he fell in love with his minister's
wife and had an affair with her. Discovered, he yielded the throne to the offended husband and fled into shamed seclu-
sion in the mountains. He died there and fumed into the cuckoo (or nightjar), whose mournful cry bemoans the double
loss of his realm and his love.

24 A mountain in Shensi renowned for its jade.

25 Medicinal plants.

the cloud had flown, the crane had fled—but where?

For old times' sake, Kieu kept the temple lit, its incense candles burning night
    and day. The twice-blessed home enjoyed both weal and wealth.

Kim climbed the office ladder year by year

Van gave him many heirs: a stooping tree,[26] a yardful of sophoras and cassia
    shrubs.[27]

In rank or riches who could rival them?

Their garden throve, won glory for all times. This we have reamed: with
    Heaven rest all things.

Heaven appoints each human to a place.

If doomed to roll in dust, we'll roll in dust; we'll sit on high when destined
    for high seats.

Does Heaven ever favor anyone, bestowing both rare talent and good luck?

In talent take no overweening pride, for talent and disaster form a pair.

Our karma we must carry as our lot—let's stop decrying Heaven's whims
    and quirks.

Inside ourselves there lies the root of good: the heart outweighs all talents
    on this earth.

FURTHER READINGS

Studies in English of Vietnam before the Vietnam Conflict are relatively sparse. Joseph
Buttinger, *A Dragon Defiant: A Short History of Vietnam* (New York: Frederick Praeger,
1972), is a short survey concentrating on the twentieth century. The foundation of an
independent Vietnam is the subject of Keith W. Taylor, *The Birth of Vietnam* (Berkeley: University of California Press, 1983). Chinese influences on Vietnamese institutional
development are considered in Alexander B. Woodside, *Vietnam and the Chinese Model*
(Cambridge, MA: Harvard University Press, 1911), and *Historical Interaction of China
and Vietnam: Institutional and Cultural Themes*, compiled by Edgar Wickberg (Lawrence,
KS: Center for East Asian Studies, University of Kansas, 1969). Nguyen Khac Vien, ed.,
Traditional Vietnam: Some Historical Stages (Hanoi: Xunhasaba, 1965), is an interesting
survey of Vietnamese history, with good coverage of the end of the Le dynasty and the
Tay-son movement, written from a Marxist and patriotic point of view.

Maurice Durand and Nguyen Tran Huan, *A History of Vietnamese Literature*, trans.
D. M. Hawke (New York: Columbia University Press, 1985), is an excellent French study
newly translated into English. Some excellent examples of Vietnamese poetry are found

---

26   A tree with down-curving branches around which cling many vines. Originally, it must have referred to a lord, who
shelters and supports many dependents and retainers. In Vietnamese literary tradition, it has mainly stood for a first-
rank wife as the protector of her husband's concubines. In this line, while the "stooping tree" clearly designates Van as
Kim's chief spouse, it can also be broadly interpreted to mean a mother who takes good care of her numerous brood of
children, a tree that casts its shadow over "a yardful of sophoras and cassia shrubs."

27   Under the Sung dynasty, Tou Yu-chun was blessed with five brilliant sons: they all took the highest honors at literary examinations. The poet Feng Tao celebrated them in a poem as the Five Cassias. Again, under the Sung Dynasty,
Wang Hu who had three sons, planted in his front yard three sophora trees in symbolic hope that they all would grow
up to become ministers of state. Therefore, a yardful of sophoras means one's children, especially one's sons, for whom
one entertains great expectations.